KV-407-692

Contents

CHAPTER 1
What is this book about?   1

CHAPTER 2
What is plain language?   12

CHAPTER 3
Why plain language?   27

CHAPTER 4
Plain language around the world   64

CHAPTER 5
Fundamentals   90

CHAPTER 6
Structure   104

CHAPTER 7
Words   129

CHAPTER 8
Grammatical structures to avoid   149

CHAPTER 9
Legal affectations and other nasty habits   176

CHAPTER 10
Overused words and formulas   194

CHAPTER 11
Little words: big problems   199

CHAPTER 12
What about the principles of legal interpretation?   219

CONTENTS

CHAPTER 13
A plain language vocabulary   232

CHAPTER 14
Email and the internet   241

CHAPTER 15
Document design basics   258

CHAPTER 16
Designing documents for the computer screen   288

CHAPTER 17
Testing your writing   311

CHAPTER 18
Any questions?   331

Thank you   337

Index   338

Chapter 1
What is this book about?

I know that you believe you understand what you think I said, but I'm not sure you realise that what you heard is not what I meant.

Richard M Nixon, 1973[1]

There are things we know that we know. There are known unknowns. That is to say there are things that we now know we don't know. But there are also unknown unknowns. There are things we don't know we don't know.

Donald Rumsfeld, 2002[2]

Yes we can.

Barack Obama, 2008

You might have noticed that this book doesn't have a foreword. It doesn't have a preface or a prologue or an introduction either. Or a conclusion. At least, the conclusion isn't at the end. It's at the beginning. That's so you'll read my conclusions when your interest is at its peak. Now.

You might have noticed these things were missing, but it is likely you didn't miss them, because you would have skipped the foreword and the preface and the prologue. There is a good chance that you would have skipped the introduction too, because if you looked at the table of contents and saw that there was a chapter entitled "What is this book about?", you would have started there. At the logical beginning. Where the first thing you want to know is explained.

If you get the answers you want about plain language in this chapter, you might not read any further. That puts an obligation on

---

1   Attributed to President Nixon by *Australian Business*, 5 Sept 1990, p 89. Also attributed to American author Robert McCloskey.

2   Former US Secretary of Defense, Press Conference at NATO Headquarters, Brussels, 6 June 2002.

me, as a writer, to tell you right here what you want to know. That is why I've put my introduction and conclusions in Chapter 1. They are the most important parts of this book. They are what I want you to remember: anything else you can look up later. So even if you stop reading after Chapter 1, at least you'll know what plain language is about, why it is important for lawyers, and what you have to do now.

This book isn't a book on legal drafting in the usual sense of those words. It does deal with what we might call "drafting problems" and it does offer some drafting "solutions" or at least ideas to help you solve some drafting problems. The book does analyse text and deal briefly with some of the rules of interpretation. But it is not a book that will teach you everything there is to know about legal drafting, or give you step by step instructions in grammar and its role in clear drafting. What I want to do with this book is explain the basic principles of plain language drafting, and show how we as lawyers can make them work for us. For many of us, this means a significant change in the way we work, and it is this change that I am writing about.

So this book is about taking a different approach to drafting. About thinking of legal drafting as another aspect of all the communication we do every day. About doing more in our legal drafting than just recording a transaction or an event. About *really* communicating with our readers.

Drafting as communication

If what I have just said is true, then when we draft legal documents we should be able to use some of the same techniques that we use for other forms of communication: the techniques we use in everyday speech, for example, or ordinary letter writing. My task is first to convince you that that proposition is true.

I must show you that we should not treat legal drafting as if it has been elevated to some higher plane than other forms of communication, and that it *is* possible to write any legal document in the sort of language we use every day. That it will be just as "valid" and just as appropriate as a document written in what I might euphemistically call a "traditional legal style", but what the public calls "legalese".[3]

---

3   In Australia, the expressions "legal writing" and "legal drafting" tend to be used interchangeably, and I do the same in this book. Australians do not usually draw the same distinctions between them as US lawyers do, possibly

When I convince you of that, then I must get you started on the process of writing in plain language.

Can we change?

William Zinsser, in his excellent book *On Writing Well*,[4] ends his first chapter, on the need to achieve strength in writing without clutter, by saying: "Can such principles be taught? Maybe not. But most of them can be learned". I agree with Mr Zinsser.

The good news is that it is not at all difficult to learn the principles of plain language writing, even if we are talking about plain language drafting by lawyers. Those principles are simple, as I hope you'll see.

The hard part is "unlearning" all the bad habits we tend to pick up and cling to. And the really challenging part is putting what we have learned into practice when we are under pressure. That is the time when we cling most desperately to the magic formulas we've used for so long. Most of the time we've forgotten why we use the old formulas, if indeed we ever knew. Sometimes we just want the warm glow of security that they give us – and it is not easy to give that up.

Even if we know *why* we use a particular formula of words, we generally forget to ask ourselves why another, simpler form will not do as well. If we haven't asked that question, it is probably not because we don't care, but because we don't have time to think about it. And anyway, those words seemed to work last time (didn't they?) so why fix something that's not "broken"? Think of the professional indemnity position if we tamper with a tried-and-true formula …

Why should we change?

That's just my point. We can no longer be content to rely on the old words, the old clauses, the old precedents. Things have changed. The public perception of lawyers has changed. We are no longer seen as the learned custodians of unknowable secrets. We are no longer immune to challenge on our own ground. Our clients are asking

---

because we do not have the same tradition of written advocacy as they do. But this could change as our courts move to limit the time allowed for oral addresses and require written submissions.

4   2006, 7th (30th anniversary) edition, HarperCollins Publishers, New York, p 5.

questions. They demand the right to understand the advice we give and they want to be able to read the documents we draft for them. If they don't like the service we offer, they will go elsewhere. If they ask questions, they expect intelligible answers. If they don't get them, and in a reasonable time, they can complain to various officials and *demand* the answers.

Governments, too, have taken notice of the language of the law.

In 1993, the Australian Parliament issued *two* reports that looked critically at lawyers' language and its effect on public access to justice. The first was the report by the Senate Standing Committee on Legal and Constitutional Affairs into the cost of justice. It was called *The Costs of Justice: Foundations for Reform*, and was published in February 1993. On the issue of "lucidity", the Committee wrote:

> The law which people must obey should be readily understood by them ... Law, whether made by legislators or developed by judges, should be as comprehensible to members of the public as possible.[5]

The second report was a report by the House of Representatives Standing Committee on Legal and Constitutional Affairs. The Committee was specifically inquiring into legislative drafting by the Commonwealth of Australia. The report was published in September 1993, and was called *Clearer Commonwealth Law*. The conclusions and recommendations of the report begin like this:

> This report is about making laws, particularly Commonwealth laws, easier to understand.
>
> At present too many of our laws are difficult to understand.[6]

The Committee recommended 46 ways to make legislation easier to understand and use. The government accepted the vast majority of the recommendations late in 1995.

Nowadays many of our laws look different. Jurisdictions in Australia and elsewhere have accepted the need to draft in plain language, and are experimenting with new drafting techniques and trying to produce legislation in new, easier-to-read formats.

Our courts, too, are looking critically at lawyers' language. They have for a long time been willing to set aside contracts on the basis that people did not understand what it was they were signing. The doctrine

5   1993, Commonwealth of Australia, Canberra, p 27.
6   1993, Commonwealth of Australia, p xiii.

of "non est factum" (literally, "it is not my deed") is an old common law defence that enables a person who has executed a document in ignorance of its character to say that even though they executed it, it was not their act. In other words, the document they signed was different from what they thought they were signing.[7]

However, for at least the past 25 years, the courts have looked closer into whether the parties understand more than just the "character" of the document or what sort of a document it is. There are more claims by borrowers of unconscionable conduct by banks. In these cases, the courts are asking whether the parties *really* and *independently* understood the effect of the document. They are looking at the circumstances of each case to see if the parties are under any special disadvantages and whether or not they received any advice or assistance with the document. They are more willing to hold that documents are unenforceable because the parties cannot understand them. They are no longer prepared to assume that a party who can read, has signed a document, and knows what kind of a document it is, must be held to it.[8]

Many of our laws now specify that particular documents must be written so that they can be understood. For example, in Australia there are laws that require documents to be written (and in some cases, explained) in language that is "easy to understand", "easily [be] understood", "readily understood", "readily understandable", "intelligible", "comprehensible" or "expressed plainly". And some specifically require "plain language" or "plain English". Under the Consumer Credit Code that applies in all Australian jurisdictions, credit contracts, mortgages, guarantees and notices given under the Code by "credit providers" must be "clearly expressed".[9]

The time has long passed for arguments against this trend. Lawyers can't wait until we are forced by law to write to be understood. We must take the initiative.

---

7   See, for example, *Saunders (Executrix in the Estate of Rose Maude Gallie) v Anglia Building Society* [1971] AC 1039; *Petelin v Cullen* (1975) 132 CLR 355; or, more recently, *Lloyd's Bank plc v Waterhouse* [1993] FLR 97.

8   See p 53 and following.

9   Section 162(1) and (1A). There is a list of some of the other laws in Chapter 3, pages 47-49.

Showing our skill

To change our ways does not involve going back to kindergarten and writing only in words of one syllable. We will still be able to show our skill. In fact, we show our skill more keenly, more sharply, when we write in plain words. The frills, the frippery, the bells and the whistles are stripped away and what remains is pure and clear. No misunderstandings. Just the facts. A professional document that is accessible by its users. One that shows our skills and focuses its readers on the issues, rather than the periphery of unnecessary detail and unfamiliar style.

Plain speaking in Laramie

Let me illustrate what I mean with an example that shows how refreshing plain language can be. It is an extract from a letter written by a lawyer in Laramie, Wyoming, in the United States of America to another lawyer in California.

Ms Becky Klemt was a partner in the law firm Pence and MacMillan, which in 1988 was a four-lawyer firm. She had won a child support judgment of $4240 for one of her clients and she needed to find another lawyer to collect the money from her client's husband in California.

Ms Klemt wrote to lawyer after lawyer in California, trying to find one who would be willing to collect such a relatively small amount for her client. She said that it was entirely possible that a single letter would be all that was needed. But she could not find anyone that was interested. Finally, she received a letter from a lawyer in California who had a most extraordinary practice.

"Without sounding pretentious", the California lawyer wrote, "my current retainer for cases is a flat $100,000". On top of that, he said, he charged $1000 per hour. He specialised in international trade and geopolitical relations between the Middle East and Europe. His client base, he said, was "very unique and limited". He declined the offer to collect the judgment.

Ms Klemt's letter in reply is worth quoting in full.

> Steve, I've got news – you can't say you charge a $100,000.00 retainer fee and an additional $1000.00 an hour without sounding pretentious. It just can't be done. Especially when you're writing to someone in Laramie, Wyoming where you're considered pretentious if you wear socks to court or drive anything fancier than a

Ford Bronco. Hell, Steve, all the lawyers in Laramie, put together, don't charge $1000.00 an hour.

Anyway, we were sitting around the office discussing your letter and decided that you had a good thing going. We doubt we could get away with charging $1000.00 an hour in Laramie (where people are more inclined to barter with livestock than pay in cash), but we *do* believe we could join you in California, where evidently people can get away with just about anything. Therefore the four lawyers in our firm intend to join you in the practice of international trade and geopolitical relations between the Middle East and Europe.

Now Steve, you're probably thinking that we don't know anything about the Middle East and Europe, but I think you'll be pleasantly surprised that this is not the case. Paul Schierer is actually from the Middle East – he was raised outside of Chicago, Illinois, and although those national newsmen insist on calling Illinois the Midwest, to us if it's between New York and the Missouri River, it's the Middle East.

Additionally, although I have never personally been to Europe myself, my sister just returned from a vacation there and told me lots about it, so I believe I would be of some help to you on that end of the negotiations. Hoke MacMillan has actually been there, although it was 15 years ago, so you might have to update him on recent geopolitical developments. Also, Hoke has applied to the Rotary Foreign Exchange Student Program for a 16 year old Swedish girl and believes she will be helpful in preparing him for trips abroad.

Another thing you should know, Steve, is that the firm has an extensive foreign language background, which I believe would be useful to you. Hoke took Latin in high school, although he hasn't used it inasmuch as he did not become a pharmacist or a priest. Vonnie Nagel took high school German, while Paul has mastered Spanish, by ordering food at numerous local Mexican restaurants. I, myself, majored in French in college, until I realized that probably wasn't the smartest career move in the world. I've forgotten words such as "international" and "geopolitical" (which I'm not *too* familiar with in English), but I can still hail a taxi or find a restroom, which might come in handy.

Steve, let us know when we should join you in California so that we can begin doing whatever it is you do. In anticipation of our move, we've all begun practising trying to say we charge $1000.00 an hour with a straight face, but so far, we haven't been able to do it. I suspect it'll be easier once we get to California where I understand they charge $500,000 for one-bedroom condos and everybody (even poor people) drive Mercedes. Anyway, because I'll be new to the area of international trade and geopolitical relations, I'm thinking of only charging $500-$600 an hour to begin with. Will that be enough to meet our overhead?

Becky added this postscript:

> Incidentally, we have advised our client of your hourly rate. She is willing to pay you $1000 per hour to collect this judgment provided it doesn't take you more than four seconds.

Becky Klemt's letter[10] created quite a storm. It appeared in the *Wall Street Journal* and she became something of a folk-hero. Her letter was described as a "masterpiece" by judges in the USA. The public perception was that lawyers needed to be brought back to reality and that Ms Klemt did just that *in plain words*. That made her not only news, but also a nationwide celebrity and a hero. A lawyer who writes plainly becomes a hero. It is worth investing a little time and thought, don't you agree?

So that's my introduction and conclusion. Lawyers need to take a different approach to legal writing. We have an obligation to communicate clearly and efficiently: with our clients, with our colleagues, with our opponents and with the general public. We cannot continue to pretend that legal writing is meant to be read and used only by lawyers. And we can no longer ignore the fact that legal writing *can* be simplified. If we do not take the time and effort to make a change in our bad writing habits, we will sooner or later pay the penalty. Society is demanding this change, the courts and the legislators require it, and our own professional integrity depends on it.

In the next chapter I explain what plain language is. In doing so I try to allay some of the fears and correct the misapprehensions some lawyers have about plain language. I examine some of the strange ideas we have had in the past about what legal language does, and look at some "magic" words to illustrate why I believe we lawyers have little to fear if we give up some of our "time-honoured" language. Then in Chapters 3 and 4, I look in more detail at the forces that are urging us to adopt plain language.

By the end of Chapter 4, I hope you are convinced that lawyers need to use plain language and are not in danger if they do. The following chapters go through the basic principles of plain language

---

10   Dated 17 Aug 1988.

writing, with the aim of giving you guidelines you can follow in your daily work, so that you can recognise the areas in your writing that might need attention. I use examples that should be familiar to you and suggest a few new ways of looking at and attacking both familiar and unfamiliar language. Chapter 14 focuses on a relatively new area of lawyers' writing: email and the internet. Then we'll consider the *look* of the documents we produce, both on paper (in Chapter 15) and on a computer screen (Chapter 16). And in Chapter 17 we look at ways of testing whether what we've written works for our readers.

If you are already convinced of the need for plain language in law, you could probably skip to Chapter 5 now. But you might find the material in the next three chapters useful. It could give you confidence in using plain language as a lawyer, and help you justify yourself in the face of scepticism.

If throughout this book I am critical of legal writing, I hope you will realise that I write as a lawyer who understands the difficulties that lawyers have to cope with when they write. There are so many critics of legal writing, but so few who take seriously the problems that lawyers encounter in their writing, and so few with anything practical and constructive to offer.

I am critical of convoluted legal writing, but I also know that many lawyers do not write in "legalese" and never have.

I do not believe that lawyers are intentionally obscure, and I think that the vast majority of those lawyers who remain unconvinced would embrace plain language in a moment if they knew what it involved and could be sure it was safe to do so. I have worked with many lawyers who have done just that. They have taken to plain language drafting with great enthusiasm, energy and creativity.

And we must not forget that "legalese" causes problems for lawyers as well as lay people. It weighs us down as a profession. It deadens our writing and drains us of creativity. Some of us have been tied up in the complexities of legal language for so long that we find it difficult even to contemplate change.

Legalese is often as difficult for lawyers to read as it is for lay people. How many times do we find ourselves reading and re-reading a document, a law, a judgment, without understanding a word that is written? Sometimes we blame our skills as a reader, when it is really the writer who is at fault. Young or inexperienced lawyers reading traditional legal writing can find themselves seriously doubting their powers of comprehension. They despair that they will ever be able to read legal writing without experiencing pain.

Why put up with the pain? The sense of liberation that using plain language can bring to us is tremendous. I hope that this book helps to liberate you.

There are other benefits as well. In the past 30 years or so, as the plain language message has begun to reach more and more of the legal world, lawyers are realising that their writing was a real barrier to communication with their clients. They have found that plain language can actually help them strengthen their relationships with clients. They have found that the documents they write and the advice they give both become more *usable* by clients, and more effective. But it took a fundamental change in attitude for those lawyers to reach that point. Now, after 30 years of movement towards plain language in the law, a whole generation of lawyers has grown up seeing legalese as the enemy, and aiming always to write in plain language.

By the end of this book I hope to have you looking at your writing from a new angle. You might not feel you need to change a thing about your writing. You might realise that you are already writing in plain language. But whether you need to make a radical change in your writing, just a few adjustments, or no change at all, I hope that two things happen to you:

1. you see how important it is for lawyers to write so that they can be easily understood; and

2. you drop the defensive guard that most writers (and not just lawyers) have about their writing – "there's nothing wrong with the way I write; anyone could understand it" – and learn to see your writing as others see it.

If those things happen, you will be well on the way to writing in plain language.

May I add one personal suggestion about how you might read this book? Over the four editions my footnotes have grown in size and number. This is because I have written this book for an audience that ranges from the reader with a casual interest in plain language, right through to law students and lawyers who are interested in the fine print. For the latter, I want to provide precise detail.

But footnotes create a problem for plain language writers. American philosopher, psychologist and pragmatist William James called them "the little dogs yapping at the heels of the text". They can distract the reader. So here, please treat them as reference points only. You can read the text without them. It is easier if you do. But if you want case references, book and article details, or extra tit-bits of information, look down. If not, just read on …

Chapter 2
What is plain language?

What it is and what it isn't

The first thing to say about the term "plain language" is that it is the same thing as "plain English", except that because "plain language" includes languages other than English, it is a more useful expression. I prefer the term "plain language" for that reason, so that is the term I use throughout this book.

The second thing to say about plain language is that it has a problem. It has a bad name among some lawyers. This is usually because they don't understand enough about it to judge it properly.

There is also a problem with the word "plain". It sounds drab. Plain language isn't drab.

Next, people think that plain language is some new kind of language, with a separate vocabulary from normal language. That's not right either. Plain language writing is just the practice of writing English (or French or German or whatever else) in a clear and simple style. That's all.

Some people think that because plain language is simple, it must be simplistic – a kind of baby-talk. That is also wrong. Simple in this sense doesn't mean simplistic. It means straightforward, clear, precise. It can be elegant and dramatic. It can even be beautiful. It does not mean that we may only write in words of one syllable – although we may choose words of one syllable if they are better than the alternative. And they may well be. As William Zinsser points out,[1] of the 701 words in Abraham Lincoln's Second Inaugural Address, 505 are words of one syllable and 122 are words of two syllables.

Another criticism of plain language is that it is not "dignified enough" for lawyers to use in legal documents. They would prefer to use language that is more remote and less personal than ordinary everyday language. But if this is so then the judgments of Lord

---

1   2006, *On Writing Well*, 7th (30th anniversary) edition, HarperCollins Publishing, New York, p 68.

Denning, the opinions of Oliver Wendell Holmes and the will-drafting advice of Justice Hutley of the Supreme Court of New South Wales are also not dignified enough.

Obviously, our tone must be appropriate for a formal document or letter, and we should not use the same tone as we would use for a note to a friend about our plans for the next weekend. But adopting an appropriate tone is different from adopting a remote, pompous or inflated drafting style in an effort to give more import to what we are saying.

As Mellinkoff puts it in his book *The Language of the Law*:

> There are those who believe that ordinary English is beneath a professional's dignity; as it should be when ordinary English is bad English or when law language is better. But ordinary English is not always bad English, and law language does not always say it better, or more precisely.[2]

Some people think that if you write in plain language you must use particular mannerisms – for example, always using "you" and "your" instead of giving the parties particular names like "Borrower" and "Lender". That is not a requirement of plain language writing. It might be helpful, but it is not essential. It is not compulsory. Plain language is not as rigid as that. In fact, one of its advantages is its flexibility.

There are many forms of plain language: not just one. As we will see in Chapter 5, what is appropriate in one context may be inappropriate in another. And it takes time to develop the necessary sensitivity to the problems of your readers. Those who try to write in plain language find that their skills develop with practice, and a natural style gradually emerges. If they look back over documents they have drafted in the past they can see the changes as they emerge. It is not possible to become a proficient plain language writer overnight, and there is no benchmark that tells you when you have become proficient. Improvement can continue for as long as you continue to write.

Writing in plain language is just writing in clear, straightforward language, with the needs of the reader foremost in mind. There are no hard-and-fast rules. There are no international standards or infallible tests. The main thing to remember is that if what you have written could be unclear or confusing for your reader, or difficult to read or use, you should rewrite it so that it becomes clear, unambiguous and easy to read and use. The trick is to recognise those qualities in your own writing.

---

2   1963, Little Brown, Boston, p 345.

Unfortunately, because so many people have had these misconceptions about plain language, and have even grown to mistrust it, others who are keen to promote simple, clear communication have shied away from using the labels "plain language" or "plain English". Some people have adopted other terms, such as "clear English" or even "user-friendly English". In the US, there's a trend in recent legislation, and within the Federal Reserve System and the Federal Trade Commission, to use the phrase "clear and conspicuous".[3] These terms make it look as though we now have a multitude of different dialects to choose from when trying to write. That is a pity. The plain language movement, whatever label is used to describe it, is not about learning a new language, or even a new dialect. It is about simplifying our writing, and making it easier to read, understand and act on.

One of the more recent criticisms of plain language is that it looks only at the words on the page, and ignores the other things that make documents difficult to read, use and understand. Again, this misunderstands the aims of the plain language movement.

When we draft in plain language we look at more than just the meaning of the words we are using and how they will be perceived by our readers. We also look at how the information is organised and presented. We look at the *organisation* of the words in a sentence, and of the sentences in a document, and the *design and layout* of the document itself. All these things can have an effect on whether the document can be read, understood and used by its intended readers – at a level of understanding or ease of use that suits them. We will look at the issue of organisation in more detail in Chapter 6, and the question of document design in Chapters 15 and 16. Then in Chapter 17 we will consider how we can test whether our readers can actually understand what we write. All these things are integral parts of plain language writing. The more we explore these areas, the more we learn about what we can do to make our writing easier to read, understand and use. And we have much to learn from the experts in these areas, because the concepts of document design and testing are new to many lawyers. Many of us have not concerned ourselves with them until recently.

---

3   For example, in the Credit Card Accountability, Responsibility and Disclosure Act of 2009, by the Board of Governors of The Federal Reserve System in the consumer financial services and fair lending laws administered by them, and by the FTC in disclosures required for consumer protection, such as those required in online advertising.

One thing lawyers pride themselves on is precision, and plain language lawyers agree. A plain language document needs not only to be clear and straightforward but also precise and complete. We never sacrifice completeness or precision for simplicity. We aim to achieve all of these things together. Sometimes there are trade-offs, because drafting can rarely be perfect in every respect – but we always aim high. Sometimes a plain language document can be longer than a document written in "legalese". This often happens when we have some extra explaining to do, perhaps to deal with a complex or technical concept. But whenever we can leave something unnecessary out, we do.

Paradoxically, plain language can be used to express highly technical or otherwise complex concepts far more effectively than convoluted drafting. And plain language does not ban all technical terms. But when plain language writers decide to use an uncommon or technical word in their writing, they usually do it for one of three reasons:

1. they know the readers will be specialists, who are familiar with the word; or
2. there is no accurate substitute for the word; or
3. the word will be a useful shorthand for a complicated subject matter that crops up more than just once or twice.

If the reader is not a specialist, the plain language writer will often give an explanation of the technical word – in plain language of course – and then continue to use the technical word as a convenient and accurate shorthand for a complex idea, perhaps even reminding the reader where to find the explanation each time the technical term is used.

Plain language writers also avoid using words that are no longer used in everyday speech – even if they are not "difficult". Of course, how far they take this idea depends on who their readers are and what the purpose of the document is. But as a general rule, plain language writers try to choose words that are most easily understood.

In summary, lawyers who write in plain language try to put themselves in the reader's shoes. They think about what they are writing and what it will mean to the reader – how the reader will react and how they can help the reader to understand, and act on, what they have written.

In order to anticipate the problems a reader might have with a piece of writing, it helps to have some idea of the process that is taking place when the words we write are taken in by someone else.

Ways to communicate

I said in Chapter 1 that legal drafting is another facet of all the communication we do every day. We communicate with each other using various means: there are the obvious methods of speaking and writing. There are other means, such as traffic signals and other common signs. There are less obvious ones, such as gestures and facial expressions. And then there are more subtle means of communication involving time and space: for example, how long you are kept waiting at a reception desk, or for a telephone call or letter, or where you are placed at a table in relation to the guest of honour. All these things can send messages, whether they are intended or not.

Being precise communicators: are lawyers different?

We who work in law must be precise in most of the messages we send in our work. We cannot be ambiguous or vague. We must express ideas in such a way as they cannot be misunderstood. We have a great responsibility. Terrible things can happen if we get it wrong, leave something out or leave open a loophole. We are always worried about whether or not we've "covered all the bases" – not to mention our backs.

We do so much writing in such a precise and detailed way that we tend to think our difficulties with language are unique, and that therefore it is necessary, or even desirable, to use a special way of writing that is appropriate only for lawyers. We claim that legal drafting is special, important, different from all other forms of language. We deal with rights and obligations: the contracts between people that govern their activities, the laws that govern society. When we describe an obligation, we describe it in appropriate, precise, "legal" language. We believe we can't be casual or informal, because that would not be precise or appropriate. So when some lawyers write about obligations and rights, they write things like:

> No person shall enter the Premises without prior written authorisation from the Lessee.

It is clear, isn't it? Crystal clear. And precise. And short, too. There are no "hard" words, really. Anyone signing a lease should be able to understand it. And if they don't, it's time they learnt.

Let's look at it more closely.

- *No person shall.* Well, *No person* means nobody – that's clear, isn't it? And *shall* – *shall* is a time-honoured word of obligation. We need to use *shall*. And anyway, people still use it for the future tense, so they should be able to understand it.

- *The Premises.* That's always used in leases. We didn't put *Demised Premises* because we knew you'd catch us out with that one! But surely *Premises* is OK. I mean, it's in the dictionary. It isn't really an uncommon word anyway. *And* we've defined it – see, there's a capital letter that shows it is defined – so they can look it up in the definition section and we even give the address of the premises there. That makes it really clear.

- *Prior written authorisation.* Well that's a common legal formula. And all those words are pretty ordinary – even plain, wouldn't you say? No need to change that.

- *Lessee.* Well, yes, some people might confuse *lessee* and *lessor* occasionally. Matter of fact, sometimes I do myself. But, look, it *is* defined, and it is a lease we're talking about here. Anyone with half a brain – who is about to sign a lease – will be able to work it out.

As a whole it really is quite a simple sentence. The words aren't too technical, it is short, straightforward and simple. No unnecessary legalese there. No need to change it at all, really. And it is a standard legal formula. Time-honoured. We all know what it means. No arguments over that sentence. It's the best way to put it. Right?

Wrong.

We're looking at it only from *our* point of view. A lawyer looks at that sentence and sees it in the context of someone protecting property. The lawyer doesn't ask why that person wants to impose the obligation. We lawyers just write the obligation into the contract. We either specify the consequences of disobeying it (or "breaching the contract", as lawyers prefer to describe it), or we leave the consequences unspecified and rely on the common law to punish those who disobey.

But let's take a different perspective. Imagine that the reason for the prohibition is that the property is in quarantine because the people

PLAIN LANGUAGE FOR LAWYERS

who live there have been contaminated by radiation. Imagine that the "written authorisation" is a card that says you are protected from the radiation and can enter without endangering yourself and others. How effective would our drafting be in stopping people from entering? Sure, it is accurate, precise, complete and *relatively* comprehensible. But is it an effective warning? Would it stop anyone?

How would you rephrase that sentence if you knew it was for a sign on the door of a quarantined property? How would you tell someone about it if you saw them about to open the door? Would you use different words? Why? If you used different words, does that mean that you have changed the message? Is it less accurate? Is it more effective? Which way is better? Is one way right and the other way wrong?

Right and wrong

What I am getting at here is that there is no magic in the words themselves. Any idea can be expressed in many different ways. Each of them may be as valid as the next. Each may mean the same thing, but we are free to select the one we prefer. There may be many reasons for our selection. We may consider one form more appropriate, perhaps because it has a different emphasis, or sounds more or less formal. We may like the sound of one more than the other. We may want to sound serious, learned, stern or polite. We may want to show off our facility with language. There may be different shades of meaning in the words we choose, or no difference at all (if the words are true synonyms). One form of words might achieve a particular result and the other may not. But none of the words we use is of itself "right" or "wrong".

For example, if we are talking about handing over important documents and we are looking for a verb to describe that action, we may choose between the words *furnish* and *give*. We may decide on *furnish* because we like the way it sounds, but we should not delude ourselves that the word *furnish* is "right" and the word *give* is "wrong".

If we make that mistake then we fall into the trap of thinking that words are inseparable from what they refer to. That real distinctions exist when the distinctions are only in the symbols chosen to represent the ideas. In the example I just gave, both the words *furnish* and *give* would do the job. There might be a slightly different emphasis, and one word might be easier for some people to understand, but (leaving aside the issue of accessibility for the moment) both words do the job. Neither is the "right" word.

Magic words

The phenomenon of the "rightness" of particular words is described at some length by Glanville L Williams in his essay titled "Language and the Law".[4] He shows how the English law gradually moved away from what he calls "word fetichism",[5] when the need to use a particular formula of words was paramount, but says that we still tend to confuse the form of words with their function. We still think that by choosing different words – even if they mean the same thing – we will alter the result. We still think that something in the words themselves is what achieves the different result. That, in short, the words are magic.

We all know that judges have often said that "there is no magic in words", but Glanville Williams shows that the courts have often considered two different sets of words that describe the same thing, drawn fine distinctions between them, and stipulated quite different legal consequences.

Williams uses the example of the "penalty" to explain this point. Here's how it works.

If A lends money to B on mortgage and states that the interest payable is 5%, but that if the repayments of the loan are not made promptly, interest is 6%, then the last part of the provision is void because it is a "penalty". The law does not allow you to impose a penalty for late payment. Yet if A had said that interest was 6%, but if repayments are made promptly it is reduced to 5%, the whole provision is valid, because there is no penalty – merely a reduction in interest for prompt payment.

Glanville Williams says that although this has been described often enough as a "fine distinction" being drawn between two sets of words, in fact it is not a distinction at all.[6] The reality is that the interest rates paid in either case, whichever form of words used, would be *exactly the same.* It is pure fiction to describe one provision as a

---

4   (1945) 61 *LQR* 71 at 74-81.
5   His spelling.
6   "Language and the Law" (1945) 61 *LQR* 71 at 79.

"penalty" and the other as "fair". If there is a different legal result, it is for policy reasons – not because the language requires it.

There are plenty of other examples in the same vein. Williams gives us the example of a covenant to pay an amount of £1000 "free of income tax", which was void under the United Kingdom Income Tax Act 1918. But a covenant to pay an amount which, after deducting income tax, would leave £1000, was considered valid because it did not offend against the section of the Tax Act that said that annuities made without allowing for a deduction for tax are void.

Or what about an agreement by A to give the whole of A's time to serve B? It clearly means that A will not be able to serve anyone but B, and Glanville Williams tells us it was held to be unenforceable. Yet an agreement by A not to serve anyone but B *would* have been enforceable, because it did not create a contract to provide "exclusive service", which was void.

The meaning of the alternatives in each set of words in these three examples is *the same*, but the legal result is different.

In each of these examples, there were two ways of saying the same thing. It was *exactly* the same thing, but expressed differently. And because it was expressed differently, the courts seized upon it and created a legal "fiction" that leads us to believe that there is a real distinction between the two sets of words. We all know that paying £1000 free of tax is the same thing as paying an amount which, after deducting tax, would leave £1000. But the court told us that it was quite different. There were reasons that the court chose to make that distinction and I'm certainly not saying that we should ignore the distinction, or draft as if it did not exist. What I *am* saying is that we should see that the distinction is a matter of *law*, and not of language.

There is nothing in the *words themselves* that makes that distinction. It is the policy that our courts or legislators impose on the words, which produces a different legal analysis and a different result. Those words are only "magic" because the court has decided to see them in a different way. And as long as we understand the reasoning of the court, we could no doubt select other words that would achieve the same result.

So what has all this word "magic" got to do with plain language drafting and the question that I asked earlier in this chapter – are lawyers different?

The point is this: we lawyers worry about the need to follow formulas of words that produce certain results. We think that because of the peculiar requirements of the laws of "penalties" or laws prohibiting contracts of exclusive service or making payments made free of taxes void, we are stuck with the old formulas of words and the strange and complex sentence structures that are not found in any other kind of writing.

But it is not so.

It is not the words or the complex sentence structures that the judges have prescribed – it is the concepts. It is the way the law reads what we write. And so, as long as we have a good understanding of the result we have to achieve, we can adopt whatever style we wish.

We might select plain words for our interest provisions, and a simple structure to express clearly the way that interest is paid so that it is not a penalty. Plain words and simple structures work just as well, even when they are only there to avoid some unwanted legal consequence. As long as we draft to achieve the desired result, we can choose simple or familiar words. We are not required to use archaic language or complex sentence structures.

In fact, using plain words to deal with unusual or technical legal points often helps. It can draw attention to peculiar provisions in a contract, which might need explaining to a client. It might prompt the client to ask why such a strange provision is necessary.

The true meaning of words

Words might not be "wrong" or "right" in themselves, but choosing the right words does present a real problem for lawyers. We have to write words that will mean what we want them to mean not only now, when our clients are signing the contract we've just drafted for their new business enterprise, but also tomorrow when they open for business, next week when the first orders come in, next year when they have their first major disagreement, and perhaps even into the future when the business collapses and they sue each other.

But words aren't static. Their meanings can change. Mr Justice Holmes, of the United States Supreme Court, understood this. Over 90 years ago, he said:

> A word is not a crystal, transparent and unchanged; it is the skin of a living thought and may vary greatly in colour and content according to the circumstances and the time in which it is used.[7]

The meanings of words can change because our courts or legislators impose a meaning on them or interpret them in an unusual way, which imposes a different legal result. They can change in the way language as a whole changes: with usage, as the years go by. Or the meaning of the words can seem to change because circumstances put a different light on them.

For example, two people might regulate their mutual business under a contract that deals with all the usual things that might happen in business. What if something happens that no-one thought of when the contract was written? For example, what if a new technology was invented that radically changed the way the business was conducted? And what if the words in the contract can be read as if the parties actually foresaw these unforeseen circumstances? What if the words coincidentally seem to be quite clear on the subject, but produce an unintended result? Of course this only causes a problem if one party intends to take advantage of the windfall in its favour. But either way the words of the contract have not changed: the circumstances have, and the contract can be read in a way that the parties did not intend.

Lawyers have to write today to cover tomorrow and they can't be sure what will happen tomorrow. So they try to do the best they can. They look for the "right" word. The word that "truly" means what they're trying to say. But unfortunately there are no "true", "proper", "actual" or "natural" meanings of words. There is more to communication than the words themselves. The communication takes place not only in the writing but also in the reading, not only in the telling but also in the hearing. What we think we're writing or saying might not be what the reader or listener is understanding.

I can best explain this as a linguistic principle, by using some examples used by Randolph Quirk in *The Use of English*.[8]

If I say something that sounds like *meel*, you may hear it as *meal* and think I am asking for food. If I said the same thing in France, the listener will hear it as *mille* and think I was counting. Similarly, the

---

7   *Towne v Eisner* 245 US 418 at 425 (1918).

8   1968, Quirk, R, *The Use of English*, 2nd edition, Longman, London, p 47.

sounds that make up the English word *cry* mean *edge* in Russian and would mean something like *circle* to a German.

As Quirk says, "We must not expect the signs of language to be direct symbols of what they mean, in the way that an 'x' symbolises a crossroads or blue on a map symbolises the sea". It is only because we all agree on a convention – that the sound *meal* refers to food – that it actually does so. But if the listener does not operate under the same convention, the meaning I intend will not be conveyed to that listener. So which of us has the "true" or "natural" meaning then?

Of course, you might think my example is a bit extreme. Surely words have "true" or "natural" meanings when we all speak the same language. But even when we all speak and understand the same language, it does not make sense to say that words have a meaning within themselves. The effect of those words depends on how the reader or listener understands them.

Another example might explain what I mean. Over the years, the word *decimate* came into vogue. But the meaning of the word is changing. This is reflected in the different dictionary definitions one can find. According to the Australian Concise Oxford Dictionary,[9] *decimate* has two meanings. The first is "destroy a large proportion of". The second meaning, prefaced by the word "originally", is "kill or remove one in every ten of". A usage note then says:

> The earliest sense of decimate, "kill one in every ten of" has been more or less totally superseded by the more general sense "kill or destroy (a large proportion of)". Some traditionalists argue that this sense is incorrect, but it is clear that this is now part of standard English.

There has been a steady shift from 18 years ago,[10] when the same dictionary gave the word three meanings. The first two were "put to death one in ten of" and "destroy tenth or large proportion". The third, "disputed" meaning was "destroy ... *nine*-tenths of". That third meaning has now disappeared, the "original" meaning is "more or less totally superseded" and the second part of the second meaning has just about taken the place of all the other meanings.

So when a television newsreader described[11] an attack by armed forces as "decimating" their opponents, which meaning of the

---

9   4th edition, 2004.
10   When the 1st edition of this book was published.
11   ABC Sydney television 7pm news, 31 Jan 1991.

word *decimate* did the newsreader mean to convey? And which was understood? If we take the view that the "correct" meaning of *decimate* is the one in "the dictionary", then first we must choose the dictionary we prefer. If we prefer, say, the Australian Concise Oxford Dictionary, then we must select from several listed meanings. If we have an out-of-date dictionary, or we select the "original" meaning of the word, we would say that the newsreader must have meant "one-tenth" and that is what the viewers should have understood. But if we did that in this case we'd be wrong. The news that night was written on the basis that *decimate* meant destroying a large proportion of the enemy forces, not one-tenth. The news had adopted the newer meaning of decimate. The other, earlier meaning was neither intended by the newsreader nor understood, I suspect, by the majority of viewers. Only those who clung to the older meaning of *decimate* would have misunderstood the news item. So which meaning of *decimate* was the "true" or "correct" meaning?[12]

Glanville Williams[13] goes into this issue in great depth. In summary, he says there are no "true" or "proper" meanings of words. There is only:

1. their "ordinary" or "commonly acceptable" meaning – which might be their meaning to the world at large or perhaps another meaning that operates within a small group of people, such as scientists or even lawyers, depending on the context the word is used in; and

2. a special meaning that is "assigned" by a particular person using it – like a definition given to a word by a lawyer (which I'll deal with in Chapter 7).

So if there is no "assigned" meaning – no definition – for a particular word, we are left with the "ordinary" or "commonly acceptable" meaning. Where do we find it?

---

12   There may yet be a fight-back. The daily newspaper for Brisbane had a p 1 story on 13 April 2009 with the headline: "DECIMATED. Jobs crisis hits one in 10 Queensland homes".

13   "Language and the Law" (1945) 61 *LQR* 71.

Looking at the past

As lawyers, when we are unsure of the meaning of a word we want to use, we go straight to the specialist legal dictionaries and "words and phrases" books to see if we can find any cases that will tell us "what it means" at law. But what do those books actually tell us? They tell us what the word was held to mean *in the past*, last time someone else argued over it. Unless we are lucky enough to be considering the meaning of the same word very shortly after it was last considered, the legal dictionaries and phrase books cannot help us with its *present* meaning. Those books give us more of a historical record of past meanings than a guide to likely present (or future) meanings. The past is an unreliable guide to the present meaning of a word, because meanings can change.

And then there is the different *context*. The words in the legal dictionaries are there either because others have argued about them, or because they were given a special meaning in a statute or a document. When we look up a word in the legal dictionaries, we are very lucky indeed if we find that it has been judicially considered in exactly the same context as ours. The odds are even worse against it having been considered recently.

As Dr Robinson has pointed out,[14] this difficulty of context was recognised by the English courts in the 1960s. In *Tophams Ltd v Earl of Sefton*, where the court had to consider the meaning of the word *permit*, Lord Wilberforce said:

> the use of precedents to attribute to plain English words a meaning derived from the use of those words in other documents is always of doubtful value and the inutility of this procedure is exemplified here. The cases in fact give no more than illustrations of the use of the word "permit" in certain isolated fact situations, and illustration is something less than we need.[15]

So how comfortable should we feel when we say that a word has years of case law behind it, telling us what it means? Surely what we are actually saying is that people have been arguing over its meaning in various contexts for years. How can that represent an "ordinary" or "commonly acceptable" meaning?

---

14 1973, *Drafting*, Butterworths, Sydney, p 84.
15 [1967] 1 AC 50 at 84.

It seems to me that what we should aim for in our writing is that it can be understood by all those likely to be affected by it. So we should do our best to make sure that the words we use are used in the way that the reader would use and understand them. As I've said, we can't be sure that anything we write will stand the test of time, but it seems sensible to start with our likely readers understanding what we write today, rather than relying on what the words might have meant to others in the past, or in another context.

Much has been said over many years about the need for lawyers to simplify and clarify their writing. In the next chapter I look at who has been saying these things and what incentives there are to spur us into action. But in focusing on the difficulties that "traditional" legal language presents, both for the reader and the writer, we should not lose sight of all the difficulties that lawyers face when they try to write documents that are not only clear and precise but also will stand the tests of time and close scrutiny.

I have not said all I want to say on that subject. For example, we need to consider how the courts, and others, may interpret our writing. In Chapter 12 I look at the principles of legal interpretation, and consider whether they are an impediment to plain language writing. But for the time being, let's focus on the past, in the hope that it will convince us we need to change.

Chapter 3
Why plain language?

Who says there's a problem?

The idea of trying to simplify our writing is not new. Nor is criticism of verbosity and confused, foggy writing. Over the years there have been plenty of people ready with advice about writing. Here is a brief rundown. Some of it, but thankfully not all, is criticism of law, lawyers and legalese.

Writing and language in general

Long before they began to focus on the way lawyers communicate, people valued plain language. Even in the 4th century BC, plain words were admired. Roger Ascham (1515-1568) records that Aristotle had some advice for writers:

> He that will write well in any tongue must follow this counsel of Aristotle, to speak as the common people do, to think as wise men do; so should every man understand him, and the judgment of wise men allow him.[1]

Sir Ernest Gowers, himself a barrister, advised writers:

> Be short, be simple, be human.[2]

And Albert Einstein said:

> Everything should be made as simple as possible but not simpler.[3]

Politicians, scientists, officials and others

Arthur Wellesley, first Duke of Wellington (1769-1852), counselled a new Member of Parliament:

---

1   *Toxophilus* (1545) "To all gentlemen and yeomen of England".
2   Gowers (Greenbaum and Whitcut eds), 1987, *The Complete Plain Words*, 3rd edition, Penguin Books, London, p 19.
3   Attributed to Albert Einstein by *The Bloomsbury Treasury of Quotations*, 1994, Bloomsbury Publishing plc, London, p 629.

Don't quote Latin; say what you have to say, and then sit down.[4]

George Orwell, in his seminal 1946 essay "Politics and the English Language", singled out political writing for criticism. He wrote:

> In our time it is broadly true that all political writing is bad writing.[5]

Scientists have recognised they have a problem writing clearly. Robert Schoenfeld, a chemist, identified a separate subspecies of English, which he called "Chemist's English".[6] One of its chief characteristics is a high proportion of passive verbs, and another is its lack of first person pronouns.

Scientists complain that impenetrable scientific writing can cause difficulty, even for their colleagues. George Gopen and Judith Swan argue that it is possible to be clear in scientific writing, without oversimplifying scientific issues. They conclude:

> The results are substantive, not merely cosmetic: improving the quality of writing actually improves the quality of thought.[7]

A breakthrough occurred in 2007, when one of the world's top science journals, *Science*, began to require its authors to write in plain language. Editor-in-chief Donald Kennedy issued the instruction, noting that as science writing becomes more technical and specialised, fewer scientists can read and understand any given scientific article.[8]

Recently, even police departments have experienced a similar problem caused by specialised jargon. In August 2008, police officers and dispatchers from Mesa, Arizona began phasing out the use of numerical police codes (such as a *913*, which means *send emergency backup and lights and sirens*, or a *998*, which means *an officer has been shot*). Instead, they will simply speak in plain language. The problem was that different police departments and agencies used different codes. Sometimes those departments and agencies had to work closely

---

4   Quoted in Muir, F, 1976, *The Frank Muir Book*, Corgi Books, London, p 90.

5   In *The Penguin Essays of George Orwell*, 1985, Penguin Books, London, p 361.

6   Schoenfeld, R, 1989, *The Chemist's English*, 3rd revised edition (reprinted 2001), Wiley-VCH Verlag GmbH, Weinheim, Germany, p 3.

7   Gopen, G & Swan, J, 1990, "The Science of Scientific Writing", *American Scientist*, Nov-Dec 1990 issue <http://www.americanscientist.org/issues/num2/the-science-of-scientific-writing/1>.

8   Spears, T, "Scientists told to cut the gobbledegook", *CanWest News Service*, 2 Nov 2007 <http://www.accountability.wa.gov/plaintalk/news/Scientists.pdf>.

together, under extreme stress, such as during Hurricane Katrina in 2005. It is easy to imagine how the discrepancy between the codes could cause great communication problems.[9]

William Zinsser believes that weakness in writing style actually *increases* in proportion to education and rank. He gives us a lovely example of officialese. This is a government memo describing a black-out order in 1942:

> Such preparations shall be made as will completely obscure all Federal buildings and non-Federal buildings occupied by the Federal government during an air raid for any period of time from visibility by reason of internal or external illumination.[10]

Zinsser tells us that when Franklin D Roosevelt saw this he took executive action. "Tell them", he said, "that in buildings where they have to keep the work going to put something across the windows".

Laws, lawyers and legal writing

Even as long ago as the 16th century, people were complaining about the proliferation of laws and the difficulties of legal language. King Edward VI (who reigned from 1547-1553) is said to have complained:

> I would wish that the superfluous and tedious statutes were brought into one sum together and made more plain and short so that men might better understand them.[11]

Jonathan Swift was a savage critic of legal language. In 1726 he wrote:

> there is a Society of Men among us, bred up from their youth in the Art of proving by Words multiplied for the purpose, that White is Black and Black is White, according as they are paid. To this society all the rest of the people are slaves.[12]

He was, of course, referring to lawyers.

---

9   Scarborough, S, "Mesa police ditching police codes for plain English", *The Arizona Republic*, 15 Aug 2008 <http://www.azcentral.com/news/articles/2008/08/15/20080815mr-policecodes0816.html>.

10   2006, *On Writing Well*, 7th (30th anniversary) edition, HarperCollins Publishing, New York, p 7.

11   Quoted by Kennan, the Hon J, QC MLA, in "The Importance of Plain English in Drafting" in Kelly, D StL (ed), 1988, *Essays in Legislative Drafting*, Adelaide Law Review Association, Federation Press, Sydney.

12   Swift, J, *Gulliver's Travels* (Crown ed, 1947), pages 295-296.

Across the Atlantic and a little later, Thomas Jefferson was complaining about wordy statutes. He was head of a committee whose task was to revise the laws of Virginia after the Declaration of Independence in 1770. His committee pledged itself "not to insert an unnecessary word, nor to omit a useful one".[13] He criticised statutes that:

> from verbosity, their endless tautologies, their involutions of case within case, and parenthesis within parenthesis, and their multi-plied efforts at certainty, by saids and aforesaids, by ors and by ands, to make them more plain, are really rendered more perplexed and incomprehensible, not only to common readers, but to the lawyers themselves.[14]

At around the same time, back on the other side of the Atlantic, Jeremy Bentham was railing against lawyers and their wordy jargon. He said the law was "spun out of cobwebs"[15] and "wrought up to the highest possible pitch of voluminousness, indistinctness and unintelligibility".[16]

As might be expected, Will Rogers (1879-1935) was even more blunt. He said:

> The minute you read something that you can't understand, you can almost be sure it was drawn up by a lawyer.[17]

In 1853, Charles Dickens had his say about the prolixity and foggi-ness of lawyers. In *Bleak House* (Chapter 1), he described Chancery practice, where the barristers were:

> mistily engaged in one of the ten thousand stages of an endless cause, tripping one another up on slippery precedents, groping knee deep in technicalities, running their goat hair and horse hair

---

13   1950, 2 Jefferson, *Papers* (Boyd ed) 325, quoted in Mellinkoff, D, 1963, *The Language of the Law*, Little Brown, Boston, pages 252-53.

14   1905, *The Writings of Thomas Jefferson* (Lipscom ed), p 65, quoted in Mellinkoff, *The Language of the Law*, pages 252-53 (cited at note 13).

15   1843 5 Bentham, *Works* (Bowring ed), p 485, quoted in Mellinkoff, D, 1963, *The Language of the Law*, p 261 (cited at note 13).

16   1843 6 Bentham, *Works* (Bowring ed), p 332, quoted in Mellinkoff, D, 1963, *The Language of the Law*, p 261 (cited at note 13).

17   See the "Official site of Will Rogers" <http://cmgww.com/historic/rogers/quotes5.htm>. Also quoted (with minor differences) in the information kit issued by the Canadian Law Information Council's Plain Language Centre, 1989.

warded heads against walls of words, and making a pretence of equity with serious faces, as players might.

Professor Carl Felsenfeld of Fordham Law School, New York City was one of the masterminds behind one of the first consumer documents to be "translated" into plain language – the First National City Bank (now Citibank) consumer loan note. He tells us:

> Lawyers have two common failings. One is that they do not write well and the other is that they think they do.[18]

In 1987 the members of the Victorian Law Reform Commission reported:

> The measure of success for legal writing is not how well drafters manage to *sound like lawyers* but how well they achieve accuracy of content combined with plainness of expression.[19]

In 1993, the former Chief Justice of the High Court of Australia, Sir Anthony Mason, criticised his fellow judges, saying:

> Unfortunately, judgments do not speak in a language or style that people readily understand. That is why academic lawyers tell me that students are much more interested in reading speeches and papers presented by particular judges than the judgments they write, even though they may cover the same ground. The judgment is so encrusted with discussion of precedent that it tends to be forbidding.[20]

Former Chief Justice Corbett of South Africa wrote in 1998 on the reasons society doesn't trust lawyers:

> There is no reason why the law should be, and remain, an occult science understood only by lawyers. In fact society's distrust of lawyers and the law is mainly due to the tendency of lawyers in the past to keep the law to themselves.[21]

And finally, Judge Mark P Painter, formerly of the Ohio First District Court of Appeals, and from 2009 a Judge of the United Nations Appeals Tribunal, has summed it all up:

---

18 "The Plain English Movement in the United States" (1981-82) 6 *Canadian Business Law Journal* 408 at 413.

19 30 June 1987, Law Reform Commission of Victoria Report No 9, *Plain English and the Law*, Appendix 1, p 1 – Drafting Manual.

20 Opening address to the NSW Supreme Court Judges' Conference, 30 April 1993, (1993) 1(3) *The Judicial Review* 185-190.

21 "Writing a Judgment" (1998) 115 *South African Law Journal* 116 at 122.

Most legal writing is atrocious.[22]

I hope after that list we can agree that there has been sufficient criticism for lawyers to recognise that there is a serious problem with much of our writing.

How did it get so bad?

Mellinkoff examines the origins of the problem in great detail in his book *The Language of the Law*.[23] During the early 15th century in England, law and legal procedures had gradually moved from the oral to the written. This meant that written pleadings had to be prepared outside the courtroom and could no longer be altered by the lawyer in court, depending on which way the evidence was shaping up and the way the court seemed to be leaning. It became more attractive to work from what had worked before.

Then in the mid-15th century, the printing press hit Europe. The market was ready, and the technique of printing spread rapidly. It reached London in 1480. Nearly every aspect of Western society felt its effects, and, according to James Burke, it almost completely destroyed the oral traditions of Western society.[24]

Printing is an invention that many commentators on legal history have pinpointed as a major contributing factor to the deluge of words. Mellinkoff tells us[25] that by the 17th century it was already being viewed with alarm by commentators such as John Locke (1669), and, in 1671, the Lord Chief Justice Sir Matthew Hale, who referred to it as "the rolling of a snow-ball".[26]

It seemed nothing could stop the printing presses from spewing out the growing mass of law. Almost two centuries later Benjamin Disraeli (1804-1881) echoed that view when he said:

> The greatest misfortune that ever befell man was the invention of printing.[27]

---

22 "Legal Writing 201" (March 2002), *Plain Language International Network*, p 4 <http://www.plainlanguagenetwork.org/Legal/legalwriting.pdf>.

23 Cited at note 13.

24 See Burke, J, 1985, *The Day the Universe Changed*, British Broadcasting Corporation, London, p 112.

25 Mellinkoff, D, 1963, *The Language of the Law*, p 140 (cited at note 13).

26 1 Hargrave (ed), 1787, *A Collection of Tracts*, 270 (quoted in Mellinkoff, D, p 141, cited at note 13).

27 Quoted in *The Frank Muir Book*, p 125 (cited at note 4).

The problems in the legal world were exacerbated by the discovery in the 16th century of the concept of the filing fee. The courts of those days were not completely supported by public funds. To generate income, they devised a system of fees for preparing and filing documents that was based on the number of pages; the longer the document, the higher the fees.

To compound matters, lawyers and clerks were also paid by the length of the documents they prepared. They filled out documents with unnecessary words. This was the heyday of the recital and the preamble. Drafters found they could lengthen their documents and repeat material by "reciting" it. But there were some attempts made to curtail this practice, and we have evidence that the judges were not afraid to act – and act creatively – to discourage overlong documents.

A dramatic attempt occurred, it seems, in 1596 (although Tothill gives the date as 1565) when Chancellor Egerton sentenced an offender – whose pleading was 120 pages long – to have his head put through a hole cut in his document, and to be led "bare headed and bare faced round about Westminster Hall".[28] Strangely enough, the offending document in that case was not drafted by a lawyer, but by the son of the person bringing the case to court, and happily the Chancellor was wise enough to punish the son rather than the father! We are left to wonder whether the offender would have received the same punishment had he been a lawyer.

In fact, although Chancellor Egerton was quick to punish non-lawyers whose pleadings were inflated or full of irrelevant or defamatory material, there is some evidence that lawyers did not completely escape punishment. During the reign of Elizabeth I, Lord Bacon ordered that if any pleadings were found to be of "immoderate length", *both* the litigant *and* the counsel who signed them should be fined.[29]

---

28 *Milward v Welden* (1565) Toth 102; 21 ER 136 – described in more detail (as *Mylward v Weldon* (8 & 10 Feb 1596)) by Spence, G, 1846, in *The Equitable Jurisdiction of the Court of Chancery*, Vol 1, V and R Stevens and GS Norton, London, p 376, note (e). Spence quotes as his reference Reg Lib A 1596, fol 667 and fol 672. He states that the reference in Tothill's reports (Toth) is "as usual, erroneous". The incident is also described, without noting a year, in Holdsworth, Sir W, 1945, *A History of English Law*, Sweet & Maxwell, London, 3rd edition, Vol 5, p 233, quoting Monro, *Acta Cancellaria* 692-693. The case is also available online (with yet another date: 15 Feb 1595) at <http://www.bailii.org/ew/cases/EWHC/Ch/1595/1.html>.

29 Spence, G, 1846, *The Equitable Jurisdiction of the Court of Chancery*, p 377 (cited at note 28).

In the centuries that followed, the amount of law and legal text increased dramatically. Court reports became available in print, and we begin to see the inexorable rise of the precedent: both in the sense of the book of forms and in the sense of prior decisions of the courts. Laws multiplied prodigiously as society and commerce became more complex. "Forms and precedents" books (of varying standards) became more readily available to lawyers, who took to them with enthusiasm. Some made wildly extravagant claims about their accuracy and efficacy, and sought legitimacy by invoking the mystical blessing of "precedent".

And so here we are today, weighed down by centuries of legal precedents, hog-tied by the precedent and form books, chained to our own drawers and folders full of "tried and true" precedents, trying to communicate with our clients clearly and efficiently in the 21st century. It is not easy to change the habits of a career, much less of a whole profession. Why bother? What's in it for me?

What's in it for me?

Does it save money? As we'll see in Chapter 4, the United States introduced various "plain language" laws beginning in 1975. But companies like Citibank (now part of Citigroup Inc) moved to a plain language policy *before* the laws were introduced. In 1973 Citibank began the process of rewriting a consumer promissory note in plain language. It was finished in 1975. That promissory note became an icon of the plain language movement.

The moving force was the feeling among the senior managers that rewriting an important consumer document in plain language was a valuable service they could provide to consumers. Citibank said that it has achieved better communication with its consumers, improved its image and saved costs on consumer litigation by simplifying documents.[30] Citibank went on to revise all its consumer forms. Teams of lawyers worked with Citibank managers to simplify the documents.

Imagine the position in 1973 when the decision was made to do the rewrite. A massive loan portfolio was to be "put at risk" by adopting what was thought to be "new" and "untested" language.

---

30   US Department of Commerce Office of Consumer Affairs, 1984, *How Plain English Works for Business*, US Government Printing Office, Washington, pages 3-10.

Today, Citigroup Inc is still committed to the policy of simplifying its documents. And they have said they can show that the simplified documents actually result in *fewer* suits against consumers.

In the US in recent years, financial institutions have been under pressure from Federal regulators and legislators to improve communication with their customers, at each point in the banker-customer relationship. Federal regulators first required credit card disclosure statements back in 1968, as a way of helping consumers make better informed decisions about their cards.

But research by the Government Accountability Office in 2006[31] showed that customers were still struggling to understand the increasingly complicated terms of their cards, particularly those imposing fees and penalties. The US Federal Reserve began to look again at how to improve disclosures, and how to better inform consumers about these fees and penalties.

In 2006 Citi Cards (the relevant Citigroup subsidiary) consulted with its customers through focus groups. It then rewrote and redesigned its disclosure statements, solicitation documents and billing statements, improving readability to an eighth grade level. And it introduced a new "Use Credit Wisely" booklet[32] written in plain language, especially for college students, and "new to credit" customers. Citigroup has received positive feedback from its customers about the new disclosures. And when it sent its "change in terms" customer notice to selected consumer advocacy organisations, they responded that the notices were "by far the most customer-friendly" they had seen.[33]

In Australia, in 2009, Citibank Australia won an award in the Canstar Cannex Bank Customer Service Awards, for "making their [online banking] system user-friendly and largely devoid of frustration for customers".[34]

These efforts make economic sense for banks: a 2009 survey in Ireland showed that 89% of the people surveyed would prefer banks

---

31   Government Accountability Office, "Credit Cards: Increased Complexity in Rates and Fees Heightens Need for More Effective Disclosures to Consumers", GAO-06-929, 12 Sept 2006. Summary at <http://www.gao. gov/products/GAO-06-929>.

32   Available on the Citi Card website.

33   Source: email from Citibank Australia to M Asprey 23 Sept 2009.

34   The words quoted are from the Award report.

to use plain English, and that 20% say they would switch financial institutions if they provided their information in a more user-friendly manner.[35]

Bank of America recently recognised this sentiment when they introduced their "Clarity Commitment" on 27 April 2009. From that date, all Bank of America mortgages come with a one-page summary of the terms of the loan – in "simple English". Unfortunately, though, the Clarity Commitment is said not to be a "legal document". So the borrower still needs to read the full mortgage. The Clarity Commitment has recently been extended to home equity loans and lines of credit, and to credit cards.

Over the years, many US corporations, such as Sentry Insurance, St Paul Fire and Marine Insurance Company, Aetna Life & Casualty, Home Owners Warranty Corporation, JC Penney Company Inc, Shell Oil Company, Pfizer Inc, Hoffman La Roche Inc and Target Stores, have publicly stated that adopting plain language increased their efficiency and improved their profiles in the market. None has complained of increased litigation about the meaning of the words in their documents, and some say there has actually been a decrease in litigation since they adopted plain language.[36]

The question "Does Quality in Document Design Pay?" was asked by a US commentator in an article published in the US journal *Technical Communication*.[37] She presented 16 examples of organisations that had saved time and money or won customers by rewriting and redesigning documents and forms. Here are some of them:

- The Motorola Corporate Finance Department estimated that rewriting the directions on its forms and computer screens helped it save US$20,000,000 per year.
- The Southern California Gas Company estimated a saving of US$252,000 a year because it simplified *one* billing statement form.

35 Research commissioned by the National Adult Literacy Agency and the EBS Building Society. See Walshe, J, "Jargon Buster debunks bank-speak", *Independent-ie* <http://www.independent.ie/national-news/jargon-buster-debunks-bankspeak-1646886.html>.

36 US Department of Commerce Office of Consumer Affairs, 1984, *How Plain English Works for Business* (cited at note 30).

37 Schriver, KA, "Quality in Document Design: Issues and Controversies", (1994) 40 *Technical Comm* 239 at 250-251.

- The Federal Communications Commission rewrote its regulations for citizens band radios and was able to reassign five employees who had done nothing but answer questions.[38]

In Canada, in 1977, Royal Insurance Company introduced a new Select Homeshield Policy for home insurance, written in "simple English". In one year, sales of the policy increased 38%, from $58 million to $79 million.[39]

Communication consultants Siegel & Gale helped the Cleveland Clinic to simplify their hospital bills in 2005. They were able to quantify the cost benefits: $1 million additional revenue per month due to an 80% increase in payments by patients, and a reduction in the length of bills from four pages to two or three.[40]

In 2006, Merrill Lynch, with the help of plain language consultants, reduced 196,000 pages of documents they sent out each year, to one concise brochure. The Merrill Lynch "Relationship Statement" won an industry award, and customer surveys have shown how well it has been received.[41]

In Australia, NRMA Insurance Limited (as it then was[42]) was so happy with its decision in 1976 to move to "Plain English" car and home insurance policies that it has undertaken several further reviews of its policies: reviewing language, format and layout to make the policies even more "user-friendly". NRMA Insurance took the view that insurance is a difficult enough concept for the average person to understand: there is no need to make things more difficult by using complicated traditional language.

---

38 Professor Joseph Kimble has collected more evidence about the money (and time) saved by using plain language, in his article "Writing for Dollars, Writing to Please" 6 *Scribes J Legal Writing* 1 (1996-1997). He lists 11 case studies of time and money saving from the US, Canada, UK and Australia. The article also deals with the ability of plain language to please and persuade readers.

39 <http://www.plainlanguagenetwork.org/literacy/CostSavings.html>.

40 Etzkorn, I, *Amazingly Simple Stuff*, Presentation to Center for Plain Language 2008 Symposium, 7 Nov 2008 <http://www.centerforplainlanguage.org/events/symposium_2008.html>.

41 Mercer, M, "Plain Language Symposium: a Success by Any Measure", *Simply Plain*, Vol 2, Issue 2, Oct-Dec 2007, p 1 <http://www.centerforplainlanguage.org/downloads/Simply_Plain_No6_Winter_Vol2_Iss2.pdf>; "Merrill Lynch Unveils New Financial Tool", *Business Wire*, 17 Jan, 2006 <http://findarticles.com/p/articles/mi_m0EIN/is_2006_Jan_17/ai_n16004280/>.

42 Now called Insurance Australia Group, trading as NRMA Insurance.

Far from experiencing difficulties with the language of the plain English policies, NRMA Insurance said in 1991 that the new language had caused no significant problems at all. I interviewed one of NRMA Insurance's legal advisors, Peter Mann,[43] who handled NRMA Insurance's insurance contract litigation from 1984. He said that in that time there had been "precious few" disputes over the meaning of words in the plain English policies. He could only recall "one or two" cases when judges had criticised any aspect of the policies' drafting style. Given the huge volume of insurance that is underwritten by NRMA Insurance, that is quite remarkable. "You could say", he said, "that the relative absence of any litigation involving an interpretation of the NRMA Insurance policies would tend to support the assertion that the move from traditional insurance language to plain language is beneficial".

NRMA Insurance continues to use plain language in its insurance policies. This not only keeps the focus on the customers' needs – a key objective for NRMA Insurance – but it also helps the company meets its obligations as a financial products issuer under the Corporations Act 2001 (Cth).[44]

The Bank of Nova Scotia (Canada) has a similar approach. They began rewriting and redesigning their loan forms in 1979. Over the years they have continued in their commitment to plain language in consumer documents. They are on record saying that they have never had any litigation over plain language.[45]

In fact, a case decided in 1994 in Canada shows that using plain language in legal documents may even result in more wins for insurers. In *Munro v Shackleton*, a decision of the Saskatchewan Queen's Bench, a judge was construing an insurance contract. The plaintiffs claimed that the insurance agent had arranged the wrong policy for them – they needed a policy that would cover commercial business premises. But the judge was not prepared to let the plaintiffs win on

---

43   Partner, Abbott Tout Russell Kennedy (as it then was), interviewed on 5 March 1991.

44   Section 1013C(3) requires Product Disclosure Statements to be "clear, concise and effective". Telephone interview with Ms Melinda Mulroney, General Counsel Australia – Direct Insurance, 20 Oct 2009.

45   Quoted on the Plain Language Association International website: <http://www.plainlanguagenetwork.org/literacy/CostSavings.html>; See also Watkinson, J, "Canadian Bank Takes Plain-Language Approach with VISA Cards", *Michigan Bar Journal*, June 1996 <http://www.michbar.org/generalinfo/plainenglish/columns/canadianbank.html>.

the basis of the agent's negligence. The judge found that the policy the agent arranged was written in plain English and the plaintiffs should have read it. They were literate adults capable of reading such a contract. Justice Larry A Kyle said:

> I am not prepared to hold that insured persons are under no obligation to read the contracts which they make. There was a time when insurance policies were so poorly drawn that no-one could reasonably be expected to understand them without special training. Efforts made by insurance companies to relieve this problem have resulted in documents such as those filed in evidence in this case. It is not appropriate to place the entire burden upon the insurance agent to meet the needs of the applicant unless the facts demonstrate a complete reliance ...[46]

How can we measure the benefits? Several Australian companies, including NRMA Insurance, have tried to measure their savings from documents that were redesigned and rewritten in plain language. In 1991, NRMA Insurance estimated its savings at $500,000 a year and in 1989 Capita Finance Group estimated $530,000 of savings a year, on the basis of reduced staff time and fewer customer errors.[47] Another insurance group, the Norwich Group, estimated that 30% of its staff's time was wasted on tasks that had to be performed because a written communication was inadequate. They believed that rewriting documents in plain English cut that waste dramatically.[48]

The public sector has also experienced the efficiencies of plain language drafting. The Victorian Attorney-General's Department said it had saved over $400,000 a year in staff time after rewriting and redesigning just one court form.[49]

After the United Kingdom government adopted a plain English policy for government forms in 1982, various government departments rewrote, redesigned and eliminated many thousands of forms.

---

46 *Munro v Shackleton* (1993) 115 Sask R 104 at [9].
47 Duckworth, M and Mills, G, 1994, *The Costs of Obscurity: a discussion paper on the costs and benefits of plain legal language*, Centre for Plain Legal Language, Centre for Microeconomic Analysis, Law Foundation of New South Wales, Sydney, p 3.
48 Balmford, C, "Plain English Policy Making" (1993) 8(10) *Australian Insurance Law Bulletin* 79.
49 *Reader Friendly Campaign Materials*, 1990, published by the International Literacy Year Secretariat, Department of Employment, Education and Training, Canberra.

They estimated that they saved millions of pounds as a direct result, and that in 1984-85 alone they saved £4 million. The sorts of costs that were saved related to reduced errors in completing forms – leading to less staff time, fewer telephone calls and visits being devoted to correcting those errors and answering questions, and reduced delay in clients receiving service and benefits to which they were entitled.[50]

But so many of these figures are just estimates. Is there any hard evidence? One of the most systematic attempts so far to collect hard evidence was made by the Centre for Plain Legal Language and the Centre for Microeconomic Policy Analysis (both then operating within the University of Sydney). First, they established the analytical framework needed to evaluate the costs and benefits of using documents written in plain language, and tried to work out a way to identify and measure them. In 1994 they published a discussion paper outlining the existing anecdotal evidence, and previous attempts to quantify the benefits of plain language. They also looked at some of the problems and the methodology involved in such a study.[51]

The results of their research study were published early in 1996. Unfortunately, for reasons beyond the control of the researchers, there was not enough data for a complete cost-benefit analysis. But they reported important statistical information and useful qualitative information.

Based on three case studies, together with their knowledge of other plain language projects, the researchers found statistical evidence of the following benefits of plain language writing projects:

- time saved in completing forms
- reduced need to amend forms later
- less effort to understand forms
- fewer questions from form processors
- fewer applications rejected because of form problems.

In the case studies, the researchers also found that a plain language project often revealed legal and policy problems with old documents.[52]

---

50   1987, Law Reform Commission of Victoria Report, No 9, *Plain English and the Law*, p 60.

51   Duckworth, M and Mills, G, 1994, *The Costs of Obscurity: a discussion paper on the costs and benefits of plain legal language* (cited at note 47).

52   Mills, G, & Duckworth, M, 1996, *The Gains from Clarity: A research report on the effects of plain-language documents*, Centre for Microeconomic Analysis, Centre for Plain Legal Language, Law Foundation of New South Wales, Sydney.

In Canada, the project co-ordinator for the Alberta Agriculture, Food and Rural Development took the trouble to take measurements before and after their plain language forms review project. By April 1996, 92 of 646 forms had been revised. Using surveys, focus groups and participant descriptions, the co-ordinator was able to prove to Alberta Agriculture that improving the forms had saved them a minimum of C$3,472,014 in salaries. And the amount of staff time saved on just six of the forms was 62.1 workdays or C$9077.[53]

Another project in which the organisers took the trouble to measure the results of their efforts was the Veterans Benefits Administration (VBA), a section of the US Department of Veteran's Affairs. Because they were concerned at the potential cost of training staff in a wide variety of geographic locations in their "Reader-Focused Writing Tools" course, they undertook a careful cost-benefit analysis.

The formal results found by the independent evaluators were:

- Significant increase in performance. The participants' writing improved markedly when measured by two separate scales of evaluation.
- Sustained and retained learning and application. Evaluation that took place over a year after the course showed that participants remembered what they'd learned and continued to apply it: they took lasting benefits from the course.[54]

In 2008, the US Securities and Exchange Commission started a project to measure the effects of their efforts to improve disclosures to investors (including the use of plain language). The SEC intends surveying investors periodically, hoping that this information will give them a foundation for further improving these documents.[55]

Does it save time? Most of the available figures on the savings and benefits of plain language relate to commerce or government. It is more difficult to estimate in concrete terms the savings that lawyers in

---

53   For more information, see Mowat, C, "Alberta Agriculture saves money with plain language", *Clarity* No 38, Jan 1997, p 6.

54   Summarised from Kleimann, Dr S and Mercer, M, "Changing Bureaucracy – One paragraph at a time", *Clarity* No 43, May 1999, p 26.

55   Abt SRBI, 30 July 2008, *Mandatory Disclosure Documents Telephone Survey*, <http://www.sec.gov/pdf/disclosuredocs.pdf>; Cox, C, *Plain Language and Good Business*, Keynote address by SEC Chair to the Center for Plain Language, 12 Oct 2007 <http://www.sec.gov/news/speech/2007/spch101207cc.htm>.

private practice might expect to make by adopting a policy of writing in plain language. The Victorian Law Reform Commission attempted to do so. It ordered a study aimed at comparing the time it took to read, understand and apply law written in the traditional manner with law written in plain English. They used traditional and plain English versions of the Companies (Acquisition of Shares) Act 1980 and the Futures Industry Act 1986.[56] The psychologist who conducted the study asked groups of lawyers to read extracts from those laws and apply the law to hypothetical facts. They found that the standard of accuracy of the answers did not vary significantly between the groups of lawyers, but that the lawyers who were working from the plain language versions took *one-half* to *one-third the time* to get the answer that the lawyers working from the traditional version took.[57]

A study done in 1980 by the Document Design Center (later the Information Design Center) of the American Institutes for Research in Washington DC showed that a plain language version of an administrative rule was quicker to work with than the original rule. Those who had used the plain language version of the rule to answer a set of questions did 102% better on the test than those using the original rule, and they finished the test in *just over half the time* that the others took.[58]

A 1983 US study presented medical consent forms to readers in the original form and in a revised form. Readers of the revised form were able to respond to questions in less than two-thirds of the time that those using the original form took.[59] And in Chapter 17, I mention the testing involved in the project to rewrite New Zealand tax laws. Researchers showed that even tax professionals found the plain language versions of tax laws quicker to comprehend than the original versions.[60]

Faced with the results of this objective kind of test and all the other efficiency-related benefits that flow from plain language, it seems pointless to argue about whether or not it takes more or less time

---

56   Both now repealed.

57   1987, Law Reform Commission of Victoria Report, No 9, *Plain English and the Law*, p 61.

58   Redish, JC, 1991, *How to Write Regulations and Other Legal Documents in Clear English*, Document Design Center, Washington, p 43.

59   Kaufer, DS et al, "Revising Medical Consent Forms: An Empirical Model and Test" (1983) 11 *Law Medicine & Health Care* 155 at 161.

60   See p 315.

to write in plain language. Blaise Pascal (1623-1662), the theologian, mathematician and incidentally the inventor (at the age of 18) of the calculator, seems to have thought that it takes longer to write less. He wrote in 1656:

> I have made this letter longer than usual, only because I did not have the time to make it shorter.[61]

George Orwell also thought it takes longer to write less. He wrote:

> It is easier – even quicker, once you have the habit – to say "In my opinion it is a not unjustifiable assumption that" than to say "I think".[62]

But it is not just a matter of measuring how long it takes us to write. If we want to work out whether writing in plain language makes us more efficient, we must count not only the time it takes us to produce the first draft, but also the extra time involved in improving the first draft so that it meets a proper professional standard. And this does take time if you are at all interested in the quality of your writing, because you are involved in a "write", and then one or more "rewrites". Remember what Orwell said: "It is easier – even quicker, *once you have the habit*" – to write badly. It is the *habit* – the habit of picking up the dictaphone and speaking off the top of our heads with no thought for the reader and no attempt to plan how we will arrange our information – that makes it *seem* quicker to write in legalese and with no planning. But the result is often poor writing, which needs rewriting. It is much more efficient to put in extra time at the planning stage, so that the time is invested, not wasted, and the quality of the end-product is high.

Whether we can say that speed is one of the advantages of plain language drafting depends on whether we measure it with a stop-watch: starting when the writer takes up a pen or a dictaphone and stopping when the document goes off to be typed, or whether we look at the process as a whole, right through any edits by the writer, to the moment when the client or colleague has read the letter and says "I understand. Now I know what to do". On the latter scale, plain language wins every time.

---

61   Lettres Provincales, XVI (1657).
62   "Politics and the English Language", in 1985, *The Penguin Essays of George Orwell*, Penguin Books, London, p 360.

Is it more effective? This question of whether a reader understands what you have written and can act on it, is an important and difficult one. But there is hard evidence that plain language improves comprehension. Much of this evidence has been cited by Professor Joseph Kimble in his article "Answering the Critics of Plain Language".[63] He lists about 20 studies (including a few of his own). For example, there have been several studies involving oral instructions given to juries. Each showed that plain language instructions improved jurors' comprehension by significant margins – in one study there was 100% improvement.[64]

I have already mentioned the US study of medical consent forms that showed that readers could respond *faster* to questions about the forms if the forms were in plain language.[65] Readers of the plain language forms also answered *more questions correctly* – they did 91% better, in fact.[66] And I have mentioned the Victorian Law Reform Commission study using traditional and plain English versions of the Companies (Acquisition of Shares) Act 1980 and the Futures Industry Act 1986, in which lawyers got to the correct answer much more quickly.[67] I'll mention more studies in the context of document testing in Chapter 17.

There have been many other studies using legal documents, forms and legislation written in plain language, in which readers are asked questions about the documents. In each study, readers are more accurate in their answers if they are using the plain language version. In some cases the improvement is only slight. In others it is massive. The evidence is there, even if it is difficult to pin down exactly what it was that improved the readers' comprehension.

The fact is that we don't yet know exactly what it is that best helps readers to understand a document or the words in it. There are so many variables involved in the studies done so far, and so many different factors like individual reader capacities and requirements. That is one reason why "testing" documents has become such an important

---

63   5 *Scribes J Legal Writing* 51 (1994-95).

64   Steele, WW Jnr and Thornburg, EG, "Jury Instructions: A Persistent Failure to Communicate" (1991) 74 *Judicature* 249 at 250.

65   See p 42.

66   Kaufer, DS et al, 1983, "Revising Medical Consent Forms: An Empirical Model and Test", pages 155, 161 (cited at note 59).

67   See p 42.

aspect of plain language writing. There is more about "testing" in Chapter 17.

Will it give me a competitive edge? This is another benefit that is difficult to measure. I've already mentioned that various United States corporations have gone on record as saying that adopting plain language increased their efficiency and improved their profiles in the market. There are many Australian corporations and firms who have experienced similar benefits from writing in plain language. I've already mentioned the benefits experienced by corporations such as NRMA Insurance and Citibank Australia. And I've already referred to the possibility of cost and time savings. These can all contribute to the competitive edge. But there is another, less tangible factor for lawyers: the expectations of their clients.

It used to be thought that clients expect their lawyers to write in legalese and would be disappointed if they didn't. Those days are receding fast; public attitudes are changing. In fact, my experience is that clients respond very well to plain language documents. I've actually had the experience of delighted clients writing and calling to say things like "Your documents were a joy to read" and "I could understand every word".

Law firms that have adopted a plain language policy can testify that they have actually picked up new clients because of the policy. New clients can *become* new clients because they are impressed by the plain language documents they see when they participate in other transactions. Next time, they may well instruct lawyers who have experience in drafting in plain language.

Australian firms with an eye on Asian, and other non-English-speaking markets are also seeing the advantages of plain language drafting in legal documents. They understand that these markets have special needs, and one of those needs is for clear and straightforward communication to minimise the problems caused by language and cultural differences. The benefits of plain language writing are clear in that context. Why export legalese?

Not only is it possible to pick up new clients who like their documents in plain language, it is also possible to pick up an entirely new type of work: the business of drafting special purpose plain language documents. In Australia, this has been driven by law reform, the negative attitude of the courts to poorly written documents, and the increasing number of laws that require documents to be written so that they can be understood.

For example, in 1992, the Australian Trade Practices Commission (as it then was) issued a comprehensive discussion paper on the home building industry, and recommended that home building contracts should be written in plain language. Soon afterwards, the first plain English building contracts emerged.

Also in 1992, the Trade Practices Commission issued a comprehensive report on the insurance industry. One of the criticisms made in the report was that superannuation and life insurance proposals and policies were difficult for people to understand. At about the same time, the Life Insurance Federation of Australia was briefing lawyers to prepare model plain language documents that were intended as industry standards. NRMA Insurance and several other insurance companies had pioneered plain language in home and car insurance policies in the 1970s. Since then they have tackled other types of insurance as well.

When the Australian government announced plain language reviews of both company law and the tax laws in the 1990s,[68] the government looked to private lawyers and language experts for help. In the case of the Corporations Law Taskforce, two of the Australian law firms that had established plain language policies won the right to help with the redrafts.

Then there are the banks. Since at least the 1980s, they have run into trouble in Australian courts because their documents can be hard for customers to understand. A 1988 government inquiry into banking, the Martin Inquiry, called on the banks to adopt plain language, especially in security documents. The Australian Bankers' Association responded by issuing a Code of Banking Practice in November 1993, most recently revised in May 2004.[69] The Code states (under the heading "Our key commitments and general obligations") that banks will "provide information to you in plain language".[70]

Some banks have realised the advantages of plain language documents. Several Australian banks have produced security documents, such as residential property mortgages, in plain language. And banks

---

68   See pages 74-75.

69   Another review was completed in Dec 2008, but at the time of writing the Code had not yet been revised and republished.

70   Paragraph 2.1 (d).

across Australia have rewritten their credit contracts, guarantees and notices to comply with the Consumer Credit Code requirement that those documents be "clearly expressed".[71]

It is about 30 years since the idea of law firms marketing legal services in plain language was a novel one in Australia. Now it is seen as mainstream by the larger firms. Smaller firms, too, have also seen its advantages.[72] Some of these firms specifically advertise their special plain language services and issue brochures describing what they can do. They have set up plain language units. They've realised that plain language drafting is here to stay, and they're making it work for them.[73]

Are there laws that are relevant to legal language or drafting? I mentioned in Chapter 1 that there are now many laws that require us to write certain documents, or otherwise communicate, in simpler language: language that is "easy to understand", "easily [be] understood", "readily understood", "readily understandable", "intelligible", "comprehensible" or "expressed plainly", or requiring us to use "plain language" or "plain English". They include the following Commonwealth laws:

- Fair Work Act 2009[74]
- Crimes Act 1914[75]
- Family Law Act 1975[76]
- Therapeutic Goods Regulations 1990[77]
- Telecommunications (Interception and Access) Act 1979.[78]

---

71 Section 162(1) & (1A). This Code is set to be replaced on 1 July 2010 by the National Credit Code. The corresponding provisions are section 184(1) and (2).
72 See Kabos, J, 1995, "The Small Firm Perspective: Kabos Elder", *Clarity* No 33, July 1995, pages 44-45 and Miles, T (Precedents Manager of Australian Law Firm Spark Helmore), "How Dolly Cruickshank Changed the Writing Culture of a Law Firm", *Plain Language Association International (PLAIN) Fourth Biennial Conference Proceedings* Toronto, Canada, 26-29 Sept 2002 <http://www.plainlanguagenetwork.org/conferences/2002/dolly/dolly.pdf>.
73 Accountants, too, have seen the benefits of plain language drafting and find that their clients notice and appreciate it: see McKerihan, S "Plain English in a Big 5 Accounting Firm", *Clarity* No 43, May 1999, p 34.
74 Sections 134(1)(g) and 601(3).
75 Sections 16F(1), 19B(2) and 20(2).
76 Sections 63DA(2)(g), 112AF(5) and 112AG(4).
77 Schedule 12 (regulation 9A(1)) and Schedule 13 (regulation 9A(1A)).
78 Section 103A(2).

Those requirements are also in the following New South Wales laws:

- Fair Trading Act 1987[79]
- Legal Profession Act 2004[80]
- Subordinate Legislation Act 1989[81]
- Children (Community Service Orders) Act 1987[82]
- Workplace Injury Management and Workers Compensation Act 1998[83]
- Gas Supply (Natural Gas Retail Competition) Regulation 2001[84]
- Electricity Supply (General) Regulation 2001.[85]

In Victoria, they are in:

- Legal Profession Act 2004[86]
- Local Government Act 1989[87]
- Fair Trading Act 1999[88]
- Sentencing Act 1991[89]
- Adoption Regulations 2008,[90]

in Queensland:

- Industrial Relations Act 1999[91]
- Legal Profession Act 2004[92]
- Fair Trading Act 1989,[93]

in South Australia:

- Local Government Act 1999[94]

---

79   Section 60F(2).
80   Sections 315(1) and 323(3)(c).
81   Schedule 1 clause 4 (section 4).
82   Section 6.
83   Section 74(2B) refers to "plain language" but sections 62(1) and 255(1) refer to "ordinary language".
84   Schedule 1 Part 1 clause 1(1).
85   Schedule 1 clause 1(1).
86   Sections 3.4.15(1) and 3.4.27(3).
87   Schedule 8 clause 1(f).
88   Sections 83(1) and 163(3).
89   Section 95.
90   Regulation 17(1).
91   Sections 126 and 333.
92   Sections 314(1) and 323(3).
93   Section 58(2).
94   Section 247(g).

- Fair Work Act 1994[95]
- Fair Work (General) Regulations 2009[96]
- Retirement Villages Regulations 2006,[97]

in Western Australia:

- Young Offenders Act 1994[98]
- Legal Profession Act 2008[99]
- Fair Trading (Retirement Villages Code) Regulations 2006[100]
- Poisons Regulations 1965[101]
- Industrial Relations (Superannuation) Regulations 1997,[102]

in Tasmania:

- Legal Profession Act 2007[103]
- Subordinate Legislation Act 1992,[104]

in the Australian Capital Territory:

- Legal Profession Act 2006[105]
- Dangerous Substances (Explosives) Regulation 2004,[106]

and in the Northern Territory:

- Retirement Villages Act[107]
- Legal Profession Act[108]
- Local Court Rules[109]
- Work Health Court Rules.[110]

---

95   Section 93(1).
96   Regulations 6(3)(a) and 7(3)(a).
97   Regulation 5(b).
98   Sections 44(2)(a), 52(1) and 137(1).
99   Sections 266(1) and 283(3)(c).
100 Schedule 1 Division 4 para 4.1(1).
101 Regulation 52(3)(g).
102 Regulation 4(1)(b).
103 Sections 298(1) and 307(3).
104 Schedule 1 clause 4 (section 19).
105 Sections 275(1) and 283(3).
106 Regulation 282(2).
107 Section 48(2)(b).
108 Sections 309(1) and 318(3).
109 Rule 5.09(1)(a).
110 Rule 8.01(a) and Forms 9A and 9B in the Schedule.

Soon, amendments to the Trade Practices Act 1974 (Cth) will mean that all businesses using standard from contracts in their dealings with consumers run the risk that provisions will be found to be "unfair terms" if, among other things, they are not "expressed in reasonably plain language".[111]

Then there is the Consumer Credit Code, which applies in all Australian jurisdictions. Section 162(1) requires that all credit contracts, guarantees and notices given under the Code by credit providers:

(a) must be easily legible; and
(b) to the extent that it is printed or typed must conform with the provisions of the regulations as to print or type; and
(c) must be clearly expressed.[112]

Section 70 also allows the court to reopen transactions that gave rise to contracts, mortgages or guarantees that are "unjust".[113] When doing so, the court is to have regard to (among other things) "the form of the contract, mortgage or guarantee and the intelligibility of the language in which it is expressed".[114]

The Queensland Residential Tenancies Act 1994 requires residential tenancy agreements to be "written in a clear and precise way".[115]

The Corporations Act 2001 (Cth) includes a requirement that the information in a notice of a members' meeting "must be worded and presented in a clear, concise and effective manner".[116] And we have seen that the same Act requires Product Disclosure Statements to meet the same standard.[117]

The old Rules of the Supreme Court of Queensland used to have an admirable penalty for long-winded lawyers. Order 22 rule 1(5) said that a court or judge could:

---

111 See clause 3(3)(a), Trade Practices Amendment (Australian Consumer Law) Bill 2009. In the Bill's second reading speech, the Minister proposed that the Act commence as early as 1 Jan 2010.
112 There's a similar requirement in section 162(1A). This Code is set to be replaced on 1 July 2010 by the National Credit Code. The corresponding provisions are section 184(1) and (2).
113 Section 70(1). Section 70 will be replaced by section 76 in the new National Credit Code.
114 Section 70(2)(g).
115 Section 39(5).
116 Section 249L(3).
117 Section 1013C(3). See p 38.

inquire into any unnecessary prolixity, and may order the costs occasioned by such prolixity to be borne by the party responsible for the same.

Sadly, it is no longer on the books. But the good news is that all the rules were superseded by a streamlined, simplified and uniform set of rules for the Supreme, District and Magistrates Courts of Queensland. The Uniform Civil Procedure Rules 1999 have been drafted in a plain language style. And, to replace Order 22 rule 1(5), there are rules requiring pleadings to be "as brief as the nature of the case permits"[118] and allowing the court to strike out pleadings and order indemnity costs against a party whose pleadings are considered to be "an abuse of the process of the court", for being "unnecessary" or "frivolous", among other things.[119]

Requirements for fairness and justice In addition to these specific laws, there are other laws that deal in wider terms with the fairness of a contact, or whether a party was fully informed before entering the contract, or misled or deceived in some way.

With that in mind, we need to consider seriously whether it might be foolish – even negligent – to ignore plain language techniques in our drafting.

The Contracts Review Act 1980 is a New South Wales law that describes itself in its long title as "an Act with respect to the judicial review of certain contracts and the grant of relief in respect of harsh, oppressive, unconscionable or unjust contracts". Section 9 allows the court to look at all the circumstances of a case when it considers whether a contract or a provision of a contract is "unjust". One of the things the court can look at is:

> where the contract is wholly or partly in writing, the physical form of the contract, and the intelligibility of the language in which it is expressed.[120]

We also have, in Australia, laws that protect people in a more general way from misunderstandings about contracts and their terms. The Trade Practices Act 1974 is another federal law, which prohibits corporations from being involved in certain "unfair practices".

---

118   Rule 149(1)(a). In NSW see Uniform Civil Procedure Rules 2005, rule 14.8.
119   Rule 171.
120   Section 9(2)(g).

Three sections are particularly relevant for our purposes. First, section 52 prohibits a corporation in trade or commerce, from engaging in conduct that is "misleading or deceptive or likely to mislead or deceive". Next, section 51AA(1) prohibits a corporation, in trade or commerce, from engaging in "conduct that is unconscionable within the meaning of the unwritten law, from time to time, of the States and Territories". We know from the Explanatory Memorandum to the Bill, which contained the new section 51AA, that these words were not intended to cover conduct that is merely unfair or unreasonable. Rather, the section is aimed at the concept of "unconscionable conduct" as recognised by the High Court of Australia in cases like *Blomley v Ryan*[121] and *Commercial Bank of Australia v Amadio*.[122] In *Blomley v Ryan*, Justice Kitto explained the concept this way:

> This is a well-known head of equity. It applies whenever one party to a transaction is at a special disadvantage in dealing with the other party because illness, ignorance, inexperience, impaired faculties, financial need or other circumstances affect his ability to conserve his own interests, and the other party unconscientiously takes advantage of the opportunity thus placed in his hands.[123]

Even with the twin requirements of "special disadvantage" and "taking advantage", it is still easy to see how that equitable principle could apply to a person who has had difficulty reading a document written in complex legalese. And that was exactly what happened in *Amadio's* case.[124]

Similarly, section 51AB prohibits a corporation in trade or commerce, in connection with the supply or possible supply of goods or services to a person, from engaging in conduct that is "unconscionable" in all the circumstances. In deciding whether conduct is "unconscionable", the court may look at, among other things:

> whether the consumer was able to understand any documents relating to the supply or possible supply of the goods or services.[125]

Sections 51AB and 52 of the Trade Practices Act 1974 are mirrored in the Fair Trading Acts of New South Wales, Victoria, Queensland,

---

121   (1956) 99 CLR 362.
122   (1983) 151 CLR 447 (discussed on pages 53-54).
123   (1956) 99 CLR 362 at 415.
124   (1983) 151 CLR 447 (discussed on pages 53-54).
125   Section 51AB(2)(c).

South Australia, West Australia, Tasmania and the Australian Capital Territory.

Other laws take different approaches to matters of fairness and intelligibility in more specific circumstances. At this stage there is no indication that any one standard of readability, objective or subjective, will be applied to Australian legislation.

But regardless of what might or might not be on the horizon, lawyers who take the plain language initiative will be seen by their clients and potential clients as modern, progressive, efficient and responsive to their clients' needs and the needs of the public in general. And what better way to counter all the criticism of legal language?

What are the courts doing? As we saw earlier in this chapter, throughout history judges have criticised legal writing for being wordy, pompous and so on. I quoted a few examples, and I could have quoted dozens more. But what are the courts doing about the problem?

As I said in Chapter 1, the courts are beginning to focus more closely on whether people understand the effect of their contractual obligations.

Look, for example, at what the High Court of Australia did in *Commercial Bank of Australia v Amadio*.[126] It set aside a mortgage and guarantee given by Mr and Mrs Amadio to a bank as security for their son's debt to the bank. It did so on the basis that the transaction was unconscionable, and that it would be unfair to allow the bank to rely on the guarantee. In coming to that conclusion, the court looked at all the circumstances, including the fact the Mr and Mrs Amadio were elderly and did not have a good command of English, especially written English, and that the bank manager knew this. There were other factors that added up to a finding of unconscionable conduct, including the fact that Mr and Mrs Amadio were accustomed to rely on their son's judgment in business matters. But the court paid particular attention to the capacity of Mr and Mrs Amadio to *understand* the document they were signing and the obligations they were undertaking. Justice Deane said:

> there was no proper basis at all for any assumption that Mr and Mrs Amadio had received adequate advice from Vincenzo [their son] as to the effect of the document which Mr Virgo [the bank

---

126   (1983) 151 CLR 447.

manager] presented to them for their signature. Even if that were not the case, it would be difficult to accept as reasonable a belief that Vincenzo had successfully explained to his parents the content and effect of a document which embodied eighteen separate covenants of meticulous and complicated legal wording ...

In several cases since then, including *National Australia Bank Ltd v Nobile*[127] (a decision of the Full Court of the Federal Court of Australia), Australian courts have looked at the capacity of the parties to read and understand the documents they sign. Sometimes, as in *Amadio's* case and the *Nobile* case just mentioned, someone was at a disadvantage because English was not their first language. Other times, such as in *Goldsbrough v Ford Credit Aust Ltd* (a decision of the Supreme Court of New South Wales, Equity division[128]) the parties have not had difficulties with English, but there have been difficulties with the document itself. In that case, Justice Young singled out a lease agreement for special criticism. He mentioned during his judgment the "rather disorderly fashion" in which the lease appeared to have been prepared. He mentioned the "relatively small print". He mentioned the difficulty that he had trying to work out what two of the clauses meant. Of one clause, he said:

> The default interest rate which they were also guaranteeing is, as I have said, hidden away in cl 5(m) among matters as venial as reporting a deficient odometer. The lease transaction was written in such legalese that not even the New South Wales office manager of the defendant realised what it meant.

Justice Young was critical of the structure of the document, which, he said, "made it impossible to work out the commencement value of the goods in the document itself" and he said that the complicated rebate formula "made it impossible to work out with any accuracy the rebate". He said these were "matters which cry out for relief". He held that the lease was unenforceable.

In 1992 another difficult-to-read document caused problems for the parties to it. In the Supreme Court of the Australian Capital Territory, in *Houlahan v Australian & New Zealand Banking Group Ltd*,[129] Justice Higgins held that a bank could not rely on a guarantee to cover advances it made above the overdraft limit that it had originally

---

127 (1988) 100 ALR 227.
128 (1989) ASC ¶55-946.
129 (1992) 110 FLR 259.

agreed with the Houlahans. The reason was that there had been a mutual mistake about what each side thought was in the agreement. In fact, no one involved in the transaction, including senior bank staff, really knew what was in the document. Even the barrister for the bank was unable to explain the first clause of the guarantee when the judge asked him. Justice Higgins pointed out that the first clause was:

> a single sentence of 57 lines in length couched in the most incomprehensible legal gobbledy-gook. That is, it must be conceded, the most extreme example. However, many of the other clauses would be understood only by a commercial lawyer with the time and patience to read them carefully.[130]

Another interesting aspect of *Houlahan's* case is that at the end of the guarantee, the Houlahans had signed a statement, which read in part:

> I HEREBY ACKNOWLEDGE that I have carefully read and understand the purport of the within Guarantee ...

That statement did not save the bank. As Justice Higgins dryly observed, it was obvious that the statement was false.

In 1998 the High Court of Australia handed down a landmark decision on the need for banks to ensure that their guarantee documents are properly understood. In *Garcia v National Australia Bank Limited*,[131] a married woman signed a guarantee for the debts of her husband's business. She did not fully understand the obligations she was assuming under the document. The Bank had left it to the husband to explain the guarantee. The court ruled that in the circumstances the onus was on the Bank to ensure that she properly understood the effect of the guarantee. The court set aside the guarantee. *Garcia's case* is influential: it has been applied or considered in over 130 reported and unreported cases in Australia up to September 2009.[132]

In 2003, the Supreme Court of the Australian Capital Territory[133] had yet another bank guarantee to consider. In that case parents had mortgaged the family home to help out their son-in-law and daughter's business. The court found that the parents did in fact understand at least the general nature of the obligations under the guarantee. But

---

130   (1992) 110 FLR 259 at 263.
131   (1998) 194 CLR 395.
132   LexisNexis Casebase online service as at 28 Sept 2009.
133   *Watt v State Bank of New South Wales Ltd* [2003] ACTCA 7.

Justice Madgwick, noting how common this sort of case was becoming, suggested a legislative solution requiring lenders to take steps to advise personal guarantors – in plain language – about this potential liability.[134]

So the courts are quite willing to hold that documents are unenforceable because they cannot be understood. This directly implicates the lawyers who drafted them.

In 1983 in the United Kingdom, a finding of negligence for unintelligible drafting came close to happening. On 7 October that year *The Times* reported that a firm of London solicitors had been ordered to pay £95,000 damages for giving "disastrous" advice to a client, written in "very obscure" English.[135] In fact, the problem was not so much the *way* the letter was written, but the fact that the advice, if you could decipher it, was just plain wrong. Nevertheless, the judge chose to blame the obscure language for at least part of the problem, and so the result for cautious lawyers is the same. Badly written advice, right or wrong, may constitute negligence.

A recent case in the English High Court reinforces this. In *Levicom International Holdings BV and Levicom Investments Curacao NV v Linklaters*, Justice Smith said:

> I conclude that [the solicitors'] letter was negligent, not because they failed to express proper skill, care or competence in reaching the opinions they were seeking to express in it, but because the letter did not properly convey their advice ...[136]

And:

> In order to discharge his duties, a solicitor in [that] position must exercise proper skill and care to ensure that his advice is sufficiently clear. In the end the question is whether any reasonably competent solicitor of [that] standing and in [that] position could have given the advice they gave in the terms they gave it.[137]

What about our image? Surveys in the United States over at least the past 15 years have consistently shown that people have a poor opinion of lawyers. Among the most recent was a survey in 2009,

---

134 [2003] ACTCA 7 at [38].

135 *Socpen Trustees v Wood Nash & Winters*, The Times, 7 Oct 1983, p 5.

136 [2009] EWHC 812 (Comm) at [299]. Only nominal damages were awarded, and an appeal is pending.

137 Same case at [279].

which asked 1000 American adults whether they had a "favourable" or "unfavourable" opinion of nine major professions. Lawyers were rated third from the bottom, with 54% of people surveyed having an unfavourable opinion of them (and 20% specified "very unfavourable"). Only stockbrokers, financial analysts and CEOs rated below lawyers.[138]

The position in Australia is not much better – going right back to the 1980s. The annual Roy Morgan Image of Professions survey for 2009 rated 29 professions for ethics and honesty. Lawyers were ranked 14th out of 29. But the basis of that ranking was that only 30% of Australians thought lawyers had "high" or "very high" standards of ethics and honesty. (Nurses have ranked first in the survey for 15 years in a row. Car salesmen always rank last.)[139]

And how about our writing skills? How are they perceived? In a Canadian survey done in 1991 by the Plain Language Institute of British Columbia, respondents rated lawyers and politicians as the most difficult to understand out of eight vocations. Out of 10 kinds of publications, respondents rated legal documents as the most difficult by far: 57% said legal documents were hard to understand. This was almost 40% higher than instruction manuals rated, and they were rated second-hardest to understand. 64% said they always or sometimes feel frustrated or angry when they read legal documents.[140]

What do clients want? Strangely, when I first began preaching the plain language word, some lawyers were astounded to think their clients might have a negative opinion of them because of the peculiar way they used language. These lawyers used to say that their clients *wanted* them to write in legalese. Ninety-nine times out of 100 they were wrong.

A survey done in Australia in April 1994 by a large advertising agency then called George Patterson, supports what I've been telling lawyers for years – that clients really do want their legal advice in plain language.

---

138   *Rasmussen Report*, 21 Sept 2009: National telephone survey for 17-18 Sept 2009 <http://www.rasmussenreports.com/public_content/business/general_business/september_2009/americans_now_view_congress_as_least_respected_job>.

139   <http://www.roymorgan.com/news/polls/2009/4387/>.

140   Plain Language Institute Report, 1993, *Critical Opinions: the Public's View of Lawyers' Documents*, Vol 11, pages 5-6.

The agency assembled focus groups of corporate executives – executives who were responsible for making legal decisions for their companies. Only major corporations were included in the groups. The psychologist conducting the study asked these corporate decision-makers to talk about law firms, and monitored their responses.

When the discussion came around to the image of law firms, the overall impression was that they were arrogant. And one of the key areas of arrogance was seen to be in "Legal speak". One of the most common requests made in the focus groups was: "Give me plain English advice".

These people said they wanted their lawyers to give them practical, commercial advice that they could actually use to solve their problems – and they wanted it in plain language. They wanted to feel confident and empowered in their dealings with lawyers. They wanted to have a true business partnership with a law firm that understood their business. Is that so very surprising? As plain language consultant Christopher Balmford has said: "I have never yet met a client who has said: 'Please write me a letter I don't understand because then I will think that you are smarter'."[141]

Interviews of US jurors conducted after trials have shown that one of the behaviours that jurors say enhances the credibility of a witness is using understandable language.[142] It's not much of a stretch to suggest that jurors might look for the same quality in trial lawyers.

This gels with recent research in cognitive psychology from Princeton University, New Jersey. That study showed that writers who needlessly use long words – and, interestingly, choose complicated font styles – are seen as less intelligent than people who write simply and plainly, using plain typefaces.[143]

A 1994 analysis of complaints made against solicitors in New South Wales revealed that by far the largest proportion of complaints

141 Quoted in Toomey, S, "Simple writing works", *Business Smarts, News.com.au*, 20 Nov 2007 <http://www.news.com.au/business/story/0,23636,22789724-5012424,00.html>.

142 Trial Behavior Consulting, *Presenting Insurance Company Witnesses*, <http://www.trialbehavior.com/articles/Presenting%20Insurance%20Company%20Witnesses.htm> (no date: last accessed 21 Oct 2009).

143 Oppenheimer, DM, "Consequences of Erudite Vernacular Utilized Irrespective of Necessity: Problems with Using Long Words Needlessly", *Journal of Applied Cognitive Psychology*, 2005, DOI: 10.1002/acp.1178.

related to problems caused by poor communication.[144] The Law Society of New South Wales recognised that this was a major problem for the profession, and identified communication as one of the most important duties of lawyers. The Society's Statement of Ethics for solicitors in New South Wales, as proclaimed in 1994, listed the duty to "communicate clearly with their clients" second in a list of 12 duties. Interestingly, in the revised Statement of Ethics proclaimed by the Council of the Law Society of New South Wales on 28 May 2009, the issue of communication does not specifically appear at all. But it should, because communication is still a problem.

In 2002, issues of negligence, poor communication and over-charging dominated clients' concerns about their lawyers: those categories made up 45.2% of complaints to the Office of the Legal Services Commissioner in New South Wales in the years 2001-02.[145] The Office's 2007-08 Annual Report shows the problem is still with us. Of the complaints received by the Office on the phone inquiry line, communication was the most common problem (21.2% of complaints). Of the written complaints, 14.5% related to communication (third, after complaints of negligence and ethical matters). The Commissioner wrote:

> It is of great concern to the OLSC that failure to communicate with clients forms such a significant proportion of complaints received.[146]

And later:

> Underlying these issues, as always, is the repeated failure of lawyers to find the time and the skill to communicate regularly, clearly and openly with their clients.[147]

By contrast, Australian law firm Phillips Fox conducted a survey to find out what clients and potential clients thought of the firm. They found that the survey participants recognised – and valued highly – the clarity of the firm's advice and documents, and its plain language rewriting services. Even survey participants who were not Phillips Fox clients knew of the firm's expertise in plain language writing.[148] That's

---

144 Source: Ian S Bowden, Lawcover, 1994.

145 Office of the Legal Services Commissioner, *Annual Report 2001-2002*, p 5.

146 Office of the Legal Services Commissioner, *Annual Report 2007-08*, p 9.

147 *Annual Report 2007-08*, p 13.

148 See Balmford, C, "Plain Language: beyond a 'movement'", *Plain Language Association International (PLAIN) Fourth Biennial Conference Proceedings*

more clear evidence that plain language is what today's clients want from their lawyers, and they are prepared to pay for it.

Between the devil and the deep blue sea?

So are we now confident enough to make the jump and embrace plain language? Or would we prefer to stay with traditional legalese? At least we know and understand legalese, don't we? We feel comfortable with it, perhaps, but do we *really* know and understand it?

When was the last time we looked at all those familiar clauses in our forms and precedents and remembered why each clause was there? Has there ever been a time when a client asked us what a particular provision meant and we couldn't answer?

Let's be specific: in a security document, what does the provision that payments are to treated as *payments in gross* do? In indemnities why do we often see the words *and keep indemnified*? Do they do anything more than the word *indemnify* on its own? What about the words *and save harmless*? What do they add?

If we can't answer straight away, how can it be that we think using traditional language is safer than using plain language? Imagine yourself in a witness box explaining on oath *why* you chose those words. Surely it is a minimum requirement of a being a lawyer that we understand what we ourselves have written.

But what of the alternative? How is plain language different from legalese? Is it dangerous? What are we likely to lose by updating our language?

It is easy for lawyers to say that using plain language in legal documents is dangerous, but where is the evidence? Certainly not in cases like the controversy over the prospectus issued by the NRMA, which has been quoted by some as a warning against the "dangers" of plain language.

In that case,[149] an Australian motorists' association (the NRMA) and its related insurance company decided to change their structures. They wanted to change from being mutual organisations, without share capital, and instead operate through a company with shares

---

Toronto, Canada, 26-29 Sept 2002, p 6 <http://www.plainlanguagenetwork. org/conferences/2002/movement/1.htm>.

149   *Fraser v NRMA Holdings Ltd* (1995) 55 FCR 452.

listed on the stock exchange. The proposal had to be approved by the members, but in return they would get shares in the new company.

The NRMA issued a prospectus booklet to its members. In keeping with the NRMA's reputation as a supporter of plain language, the prospectus was well designed and tried to explain the proposal in simple language. But it frequently mentioned that members would get "free shares" if they approved the plan.

NRMA officials who were not in favour of the proposal tried to get court orders to stop it. One of their grounds was that the booklet breached section 52 of the Trade Practices Act 1974, which prohibits misleading or deceptive conduct in trade or commerce. They said that the shares were not "free" at all: members had to give up their mutual ownership of the organisations and the benefits of membership.

The Federal Court of Australia agreed. It held that the prospectus booklet was misleading.

The decision in the *NRMA* case was claimed by some to vindicate using technical language. They said it justified the need for long and complex documents for important and complex legal procedures. That is not so. And the court said as much. It said:

> The need to make a full and fair disclosure must be tempered by the need to present a document that is intelligible to reasonable members of the class to whom it is directed, and is likely to assist rather than confuse … In complex cases it may be necessary to be selective in the information provided, confining it to that which is really useful. Clearly the present case was one of this kind.[150]

Others claimed that the case showed that people should be particularly cautious about documents written in plain language. But this is misguided. The main problem with the prospectus was not that it was written in plain or simple language, or that it left out complex explanations. It just left out something that the court decided had to be said: that when the members received their "free" shares, they would be giving up something in return.

At the turn of the 21st century, Professor Joseph Kimble wrote an influential essay entitled "The Great Myth that Plain Language is Not Precise".[151] In it he went through the redrafting into plain language

---

150   (1995) 55 FCR 452 at 468.
151   7 *Scribes J Legal Writing* 109 (1998-2000). Now revised and collected with other essays in Kimble, J, 2006, *Lifting the Fog of Legalese,* Carolina Academic Press, Durham, North Carolina.

of a very complex "mutual-indemnification" clause, and the various criticisms that were subsequently levelled at the redrafted clause by critics of plain language. He concluded:

> The choice is not between precision and plain language. Plain language can be at least as precise – or as appropriately vague – as traditional legal writing. The choice is between perpetuating the vices of four centuries and finally breaking free, between inertia and advancement, between defending the indefensible and opening our minds.[152]

Summary

So that's the case in favour of plain language:

- Traditional legal language has been complained about and even ridiculed for centuries.
- Plain language is efficient – it saves time, effort and money, and we can measure those efficiencies.
- Plain language is effective – readers generally comprehend plain language documents better and quicker than documents written in traditional legal language, and we can measure those benefits.
- Plain language can give you a competitive edge.
- Many laws already require plain language, or similar standards of readability or comprehensibility.
- Our courts are quite willing to hold that documents are unenforceable because they cannot be understood.
- Plain language can improve the image of lawyers – surveys confirm this.
- Clients want good communication with their lawyers. They know plain language when they see it, and value it highly.
- Traditional legal language may not be as "safe" as we think it is.
- Using plain language does not mean giving up legal precision. Plain language can be at least as precise as traditional legal language.

There's still more persuasive evidence in favour of plain language. There's a history of over 35 years of the plain language movement

---

152   Same (latter) work, at p 45.

around the world. Plain language is truly international now, with a refreshing degree of cross-pollination and shared learning. To find out more, we can review the major developments in plain language around the world, which we'll do in Chapter 4. But if you're already convinced, or you are keen to get down to the practicalities of plain language writing, then skip to Chapter 5, which is where the writing process begins.

Chapter 4
Plain language around the world

A consumer-driven movement spreads worldwide

We saw in Chapter 3 that plain language has always been a valued commodity, even in ancient times. But over the past 35 years or so there has been a significant move to plain language in business, government and the law – all around the world.

In the first edition of this book I included information about developments in the United States, Canada, the United Kingdom, New Zealand and Australia. By 1996 and the second edition, the plain language movement had spread further and gained in stature and maturity. I added information about plain language developments in the European Community, Sweden, Denmark, South Africa and India. By the third edition in 2003, there was so much information that we could not include it all here. Since then, an expanded version of this chapter has been available on the internet.[1]

In this Chapter 4 I highlight just some of the major developments in plain language worldwide. I have arranged them by category or interest-group, to show how the phenomenon spread throughout the world. My aim is to show that plain language cannot be seen as a passing fad, or as something radical, foolhardy or dangerous. We have over 35 years of experience to draw on.

Plain language began in the 1970s as a part of the consumer movement, when various corporations were prompted to explore the benefits of plain language in their consumer documents. Its growth coincided with an era of demystification of (and disenchantment with) the professions. It was a time of increasing interest by linguists and others in the *process* of communication. But even so, plain language soon entered the mainstream of business and the law, quickly gaining legitimacy as lawyers and clients began to understand its advantages.

---

1   Go to <http://www.federationpress.com.au> and click on Book Supplements and then *Plain Language for Lawyers*.

Beginnings – banking, insurance and the 1970s

United States The document that marks the coming-of-age of plain language in the United States is the plain language consumer loan note launched on 1 January 1975 by First National City Bank (now Citibank). In 1973 Citibank made the decision to move to plain language because it had become worried by the large number of suits against consumers it had to run to collect its debts.[2]

Not only was their plain language initiative praised by clients, consumer advocates, politicians and judges, but Citibank also noticed a substantial reduction in the number of suits the bank brought against consumers.[3] Citibank acted voluntarily to rewrite its loan note, but legislation to require certain documents to be written in plain language was not far off.

In 1975, the Magnuson-Moss Consumer Product Warranty Act was passed by Congress. It stated that warranties must be written in "simple and readily understood language". Soon, US insurance companies, such as Sentry Insurance, St Paul Fire and Marine Insurance Company and Aetna Life & Casualty, started thinking about simplifying a wide range of insurance policies, even though the Magnuson-Moss Act did not specifically apply to insurance policies. Other plain language laws would soon follow.[4]

Australia Here, too, insurance companies were among the first corporations to move to plain language. NRMA Insurance introduced its "Plain English" car insurance policy in September 1976, and "Plain English" versions of all the other NRMA insurance policies were introduced over the next five years. Other insurance companies, such as NZI and AMP soon followed NRMA Insurance.

Canada The insurance and banking industries were at the fore-front of the move to plain language in Canada as well. In 1979 the Bank of Nova Scotia worked with lawyer Robert Dick to redesign and rewrite its loan forms. At the same time, Royal Insurance of Canada had produced a plain language insurance policy.

But even before this, in 1976, the Canadian Legislative Drafting Conventions had been produced and sanctioned by the Uniform

---

2 See p 34.

3 US Department of Commerce Office of Consumer Affairs, 1984, *How Plain English Works for Business*, US Government Printing Office, Washington, pages 3-7.

4 See p 67.

Law Conference of Canada. These conventions adopted many of the principles of plain language drafting.

United Kingdom In 1979, Chrissie Maher and Martin Cutts founded the Plain English Campaign.[5] It had its origins in a consumer advice centre Maher and Cutts had set up three years earlier in Salford, near Manchester.

During the 1980s, the Plain English Campaign worked with the National Consumer Council to review thousands of government forms that were badly worded and poorly designed. The National Consumer Council published several booklets on plain language writing, including *Gobbledegook* (1980), *Plain Words for Consumers* (1984), *Plain English for Lawyers* (1984), *Making Good Solicitors* (1989) and *Plain Language – Plain Law* (1990).

Sweden In 1976 the Swedish government appointed a linguist to the Cabinet Office. His task was to modernise legal language in laws and ordinances. Since 1980 there has been a team of language experts who revise written material before it reaches the parliament, prepare writing guidelines and run training courses.

In fact, Sweden was way ahead of the rest of the world in plain language. It was as early as 1713 that King Charles XII dictated this ordinance:

> His Majesty the King requires that the Royal Chancellery in all written documents endeavour to write in clear, plain Swedish and not to use, as far as possible, foreign words.

The US plain language laws

In 1969, President Nixon had ordered that the daily government journal, the *Federal Register*, be written in "language which is readily understandable by the layman".[6] Almost a decade later, in 1978, President Carter issued an order that "regulations should be as simple and clear as possible".[7] He followed this up in 1979 with an order that government forms "should be as short as possible and should elicit information in a simple straightforward fashion".[8]

---

5   Since 1994, Martin Cutts has operated his own plain language and document design consultancy, the Plain Language Commission. His website is <www.clearest.co.uk>. The Plain English Campaign's website is <www.plainenglish.co.uk>.

6   Special message to the Congress on Consumer Protection, 30 Oct 1969.

7   US Executive Order 12044, 23 March 1978.

8   US Executive Order 12174, 30 Nov 1979.

In 1978 the State of New York introduced its plain language law (often called the "Sullivan Law" after the politician who introduced it) which required that all residential leases and consumer contracts be written in understandable language. The exact requirement is that they have to be "written in a clear and coherent manner using words with common and everyday meanings". It applies to agreements involving amounts of $50,000 or less "primarily for personal, family or household purposes".[9]

Since then, 10 other US states[10] have passed laws that require either plain, clear, conspicuous, accurate or understandable language to be used in certain consumer transactions. Many other state and federal laws and regulations govern the language to be used in a variety of documents, including life insurance policies, ballots and utility bills. Some use the Flesch Reading Ease Test[11] to measure readability.

In 2009 there were two Plain Language Bills in Congress: one in the Senate and one in the House of Representatives. At the time of writing, neither had passed both Houses, but the legislative process was still alive, and a vote was possible early in 2010.

The Law Commission and Committee Reports

Several Law Commission and Committee reports proved to be catalysts for much of the progress made in plain language.

United Kingdom In the early 1970s, the Renton Committee was appointed to investigate and report to Parliament on the process of formulating statutes. On 7 May 1975 the *Renton Report*[12] was published. It highlighted examples of convoluted drafting in British statutes and recommended improving the explanatory materials that accompany statutes. This Report provoked discussion, but it would not begin to bear fruit until the late 1990s, when two major projects began in

---

9   NY Gen Obl Law 5-702.
10 The 11 states with plain language laws are: Connecticut, Hawaii, Maine, Minnesota, Montana, New Jersey, New York, Oregon, Pennsylvania, Texas, and West Virginia.
11 Named for the person who devised the test, Rudolph Flesch: see Flesch, R, 1974 *The Art of Readable Writing*, revised 25th anniversary edition, Harper & Row, New York. See p 322 and following for more information about, and criticism of, readability formulas.
12 *The Preparation of Legislation* 1975, Cmnd 6053, Chapter VI, Appendix B, HMSO, London.

the UK. One was the project to rewrite UK tax laws.[13] The other was the review of the format of UK legislation, with the introduction of explanatory notes in 1998, and the new legislative format in 2001.

In addition, the Report of Lord Justice Woolf, called *Access to Justice*, was commissioned in 1994, published in 1996, and led to the reform of the Civil Procedure Rules,[14] which came into effect in 1999.

New Zealand The New Zealand Law Commission (established in 1985) has a brief to "propose ways of making legislation as understandable and accessible as practicable and of ensuring that it is kept under review in a systematic way". It must also "ascertain what changes, if any, are necessary or desirable in the law relating to the interpretation of legislation".[15]

In its Report No 17, issued in December 1990, the Commission made suggestions for improving the form and style of laws, and prepared a draft Interpretation Act. The Act's subtitle was its purpose: "to avoid 'Prolixity and Tautology'". In 1993 the Commission published Report No 27, called *The Format of Legislation*,[16] in which it recommended changes to the design and typography of legislation. Report No 35, from 1996, is called *Legislation Manual, Structure and Style*. It gives guidelines for drafting legislation, and recommends plain language principles. These Reports paved the way for the now-completed simplification of New Zealand's tax laws.[17]

The Law Commission continues to work in this area, producing two more reports on statute law, in 2008 and 2009.

Australia One of the major catalysts for plain language in the law in Australia was the Victorian Law Reform Commission's report, called *Plain English and the Law*, published in June 1987. That report made 15 recommendations and included a drafting manual, which it recommended be adopted as the official drafting guide for government departments and agencies for Acts, regulations, forms and explanatory material. The report and manual remain influential over 20 years later, and have led to many reforms in the language of the law.

---

13   See pages 69-70.
14   See pages 79-80.
15   Law Commission Report No 17, Dec 1990, *A New Interpretation Act to Avoid "Prolixity and Tautology"*, Law Commission, Wellington, p ix.
16   Law Commission Report No 27, Dec 1993, Law Commission, Wellington.
17   See pages 73-74.

Canada In 1988, the Justice Reform Committee of British Columbia issued a report called *Access to Justice*. It recommended establishing a plain language committee to develop a strategy for introducing plain language into the justice system. Then in 1990, the Canadian Bar Association and the Canadian Bankers' Association issued a report called *The Decline and Fall of Gobbledygook: Report on Plain Language Documentation*. It recommended ways to promote the use of plain language in the legal profession and in banking. The Canadian Bar Association adopted these recommendations by resolution in 1991, urging banks (and governments and other organisations) to draft their documents in plain language. Ironically the first word of the resolution was "Whereas". The report and the resolution continue to have effect in Canada, with the banks resolving in 2000 to move towards plain language in mortgage documents.[18]

Ireland The Irish Law Reform Commission called for plain language in legislation in its report *Statutory Drafting and Interpretation: Plain Language and the Law*, published in December 2000. The Commission recommended:

> a comprehensive programme of plain language reform in Irish statute law. In this regard we support the initiatives currently being undertaken by the Office of the Parliamentary Counsel to the Government and the Statute Law Revision Unit.[19]

One of the initiatives of the Office of Parliamentary Counsel was the legislative Drafting Manual prepared for drafters in that Office. It was published in November 2001, and advocates plain language principles "in so far as that is possible without giving rise to ambiguity".[20]

Government departments and agencies

United Kingdom The UK government adopted a plain English policy for government forms in 1982. Many thousands of forms were reviewed, redesigned or abandoned altogether. In 1994 the Secretary of State for Wales announced a program to simplify, and reduce the

---

18   See p 85.

19   Report LRC 61-2000. Recommendation at para 6.23.

20   The description is that of Brian Hunt, a research officer in the Office of Parliamentary Counsel, in "Plain Language Developments in Ireland: An Overview", *Plain Language Association International (PLAIN) Fourth Biennial Conference Proceedings Toronto, Canada, 26-29 Sept 2002* <http://www.plain-languagenetwork.org/conferences/2002/ip_panel/ireland/1.htm>.

number of, government forms and circulars. Since then, simplification has occurred in local government, small business, the arts, the Ombudsman's service and other areas. Probably the major effort, though, has been the UK tax law rewrite, undertaken by HM Revenue & Customs.[21]

United States I've already mentioned the orders of Presidents Nixon and Carter, which were early signs of a move to plain language in US government. Another encouraging development in plain language came on 1 June 1998 when President Clinton issued his Executive Memorandum on plain language. This was sent to the heads of executive departments and agencies, directing them to:

- By October 1, 1998, use plain language in all new documents, other than regulations, that explain how to obtain a benefit or service or how to comply with a requirement you administer or enforce. For example, these documents may include letters, forms, notices, and instructions. By January 1, 2002, all such documents created prior to October 1, 1998, must also be in plain language.
- By January 1, 1999, use plain language in all proposed and final rulemaking documents published in the *Federal Register*, unless you proposed the rule before that date. You should also consider rewriting existing regulations in plain language when you have the opportunity and resources to do so.

Long after the end of the Clinton administration, there is still US government support for this initiative. A volunteer group of federal government employees began meeting in the mid-1990s and formed what became "PLAIN" – the Plain Language Action & Information Network. PLAIN works to improve communications from the federal government to the public. PLAIN has an informative website <www.plainlanguage.gov>, still holds monthly meetings, and also presents workshops and seminars. Membership of PLAIN is open to non-federal government employees as well.

US Securities and Exchange Commission A great leap forward for plain language came in January 1998 when the US Securities and Exchange Commission (SEC) announced new rules calling for plain language in prospectuses.[22] These rules applied to the prospectus that

---

21   See p 74.
22   SEC Release 33-7497 (and 34-39593 and IC-23011), <www.sec.gov/rules/final/33-7497.txt>.

a public company or mutual fund must give to prospective investors in their securities. Help for companies trying to comply with these rules is in the SEC's *Plain English Handbook,* which is available in print and online.[23] In recent years the SEC has continued its plain language efforts in the areas of mutual fund disclosure and executive fund disclosure, and it has ambitious plans to overhaul its forms-based disclosure system, replacing it with an online system.

Other US government departments and agencies using and working in plain language include the Federal Aviation Administration, the Office of the Federal Register, the Food and Drug Administration, Health and Human Sciences, the National Institutes of Health, the Social Security Administration and the Veteran's Benefits Administration.[24]

Canada The Communications Policy of the Government of Canada has always had a plain language component. It says, in part:

> To ensure clarity and consistency of information, plain language and proper grammar must be used in all communication with the public. This principle also applies to internal communication as well as to information prepared for Parliament or any other official body, whether delivered in writing or in speech.[25]

Various provincial and federal government offices and agencies, including the Office of the Auditor-General of Alberta,[26] Alberta Agriculture, Food and Rural Development[27] and the Canada Customs and Revenue Agency have redesigned and rewritten various forms and other documents in plain language. And the Canadian Public Health Association established a Plain Language Service in 1997. It offers assessment, revision, editing, design and translation services for the public, private and voluntary sectors.

Australia Federal and state government departments have been working towards plain language since at least 1983, when the

---

23   <www.sec.gov/news/extra/handbook.htm>.

24   See Cheek, A, 2006, "Plain language in the United States Government", *Clarity* No 55, May 2006, pages 30-31, and Locke, J, 2004, "A History of Plain Language in the US Government" <http://plainlanguage.gov/whatisPL/history/Locke.cfm>.

25   Last updated 1 Aug 2006 <http://www.tbs-sct.gc.ca/pol/doc-eng.aspx?id=12316>.

26   For more information, see Saher, M, "The plaining of writers", *Clarity* No 49, May 2002, p 27.

27   See p 41.

Australian government launched its "Plain English and Simpler Forms" program. Much work was done by the Department of Administrative Services to produce model documents and guides to better, simpler writing.

One case study in plain language is the Independent Commission Against Corruption (ICAC). ICAC was established in 1988 to expose and minimise corruption in the New South Wales public sector. ICAC realised early on that to communicate effectively with the public, they had to do so in plain language. They brought in plain language consultants, organised training programs and developed a plain language style guide. Then they wrote a document called *Practical Guide to Corruption Prevention*, in plain language. And they reviewed their website and their archive of publications to ensure they were written in plain language. This plain language policy is now reflected in the advice ICAC gives, for example, to organisations that want to establish codes of conduct.[28]

Most government departments and agencies in Australia either have a plain language policy, or say that they do. For example, the Australian Taxation Office's *Taxpayers' Charter* says, in section 3:

> To make it as easy as possible for you to comply with your tax obligation we ... try to use plain and clear language in our publications and when speaking or writing to you ...[29]

But the results are variable. The Plain English Foundation (established in Sydney in 2003) analysed the readability of more than 600 documents from dozens of government agencies from 2001-06 and found they came in at grade 16,[30] with about 40% of the writing in the passive voice. They found poor language, and an overly formal tone.[31]

But improvement may be in sight for NSW government departments and agencies. At the 2009 PLAIN conference in Sydney,[32] the then NSW Premier Nathan Rees gave the opening address, announcing that he would publish a memorandum requiring plain English to be used by all NSW government agencies. This will be followed up

28   ICAC, 2002, *Codes of Conduct: The Next Stage* <http://www.icac.nsw.gov.au/files/pdf/pub2_55cp1.pdf>.

29   <http://www.ato.gov.au/corporate/content.asp?doc=content/33928.htm>.

30   See Readability Formulas, Chapter 17, p 322.

31   James, N, 2006, "Plain language developments in Australia", *Clarity* No 55, May 2006, p 20.

32   See p 84.

by random audit, and by using focus groups to test the effectiveness of government documents. There will also be a new category – best use of plain English – in the Premier's annual Public Sector Awards.

Tax law rewrite projects

In the 1990s, three major projects were launched in three different countries, all with the aim of improving existing tax laws.

Australia The Tax Law Improvement Project (TLIP) was established in 1993 to restructure, renumber and rewrite the existing Income Tax Assessment Act 1936. The TLIP team produced three substantial instalments of rewritten law, dealing with the core provisions of tax law and some specific areas such as capital gains tax. These were enacted in the Income Tax Assessment Act 1997. But after a change of government, priority shifted to tax *policy* reform and the introduction of, among other things, the Goods and Services Tax. So by 1999 the resources and expertise of the TLIP had been reallocated to the new tax reform effort. It is not correct to assert, as Rt Hon Sir Geoffrey Palmer did (perhaps humorously) in a speech to the New Zealand Law Commission, that the project was "so difficult that Australia gave up on it".[33]

Since then some further sections of the old Act (dealing with thin capitalisation and dividend imputation) have been rewritten and placed in the 1997 Act. Those rewrites, and other "stand-alone" tax legislation resulting from the continuing tax reform process, continue to use the new style, and many of the features, developed by the TLIP.[34] However, as we will see in Chapter 15,[35] very few pieces of later tax legislation use the new numbering system developed by TLIP.

New Zealand In 1994, New Zealand undertook what was to be a five-year project to review and simplify its tax laws. The first part of the rewrite process involved reorganising the structure of the Income

---

33   Palmer, Rt Hon Sir G, 2006, *Innovation in New Zealand Statute Law*, paper delivered on 20th anniversary of the Law Commission, 25 Aug 2006, para 75, p 31 <http://www.lawcom.govt.nz/SpeechPaper.aspx>.

34   There is a list of these features in Attachment C to the Australian Parliamentary Counsel's *Drafting Direction no 1.8: Special Rules for Tax Code Drafting*, released 1 May 2006, p 37 <http://www.opc.gov.au/about/drafting_series/DD%20 1.8.pdf>.

35   Page 278.

Tax Act 1976, so that it is more logical and accessible. That resulted in the Income Tax Act 1994. The next stage involved rewriting "core provisions" of the old Tax Act. That became law in 1996, with effect from the 1997-98 tax year.

The huge Income Tax Act 2007 (at around 3000 pages) was passed into law in October 2007, completing the historic rewrite. The NZ Inland Revenue described the rewrite as designed to produce "income tax law that is clear, written in plain language and is structurally consistent".[36]

United Kingdom On 28 November 1995, the Chancellor of the Exchequer announced a five-year project to rewrite the existing direct tax legislation. The stated aim for the project was "to rewrite the United Kingdom's primary direct tax legislation to make it clearer and easier to use, without changing the law".[37] The five-year project is now in its 13th year, but will close down in 2010.

At the time of writing, the project had produced the following rewritten law:

- Capital Allowances Act 2001
- Income Tax (Earnings and Pensions) Act 2003
- Income Tax (Pay as You Earn) Regulations 2003
- Income Tax (Trading and Other Income) Act 2005
- Income Tax Act 2007
- Corporation Tax Act 2009.

Other developments in legislation

Tax law is not the only area of legislation to be written or rewritten in plain language.

Australian corporations law In 1993 the Australian government announced another major project to simplify law: the Corporations Law Simplification Program.[38] The First Corporate Law Simplification Act commenced on 9 December 1995. A key feature of this Act was to

---

36   Inland Revenue, *Annual Report 2008*, Part 1, About Us, p 1 <http://www.ird.govt.nz/aboutir/reports/annual-report/annual-report-2008/part-1/ar-2008-part1-advising-policy.html>.

37   Inland Revenue Annual Report, *Tax Law Rewrite: Plans for 2003/2004*, or see <http://www.hmrc.gov.uk/rewrite/>.

38   Announced in April 1993.

make company law more accessible through improved layout.[39] This was achieved by navigation aids such as including running headers with chapter, part, division and section, and using tables and diagrams. The drafting approach also adopted shorter sentences, careful use of definitions, and explanatory notes. The project team conducted document testing of the proposed structure of the changes and of the text, using focus groups.[40] The team considered that it received "generally good press" for the project.[41]

The Second Corporate Law Simplification Bill was introduced into Parliament on 3 December 1997 and enacted as part of the Company Law Review Act 1998. By this time, the federal government had established the Corporate Law Economic Reform Program (CLERP) to take corporate law reform beyond simplification into the area of policy reform and economic development.[42] But corporate law continues to be rewritten to simplify procedures.

Other Australian laws Australian Commonwealth Acts, beginning with the Social Security Act 1991, have been rewritten in a "reader-friendly" form. That Act pioneered a number of drafting and design innovations that would later become standard legislative drafting techniques. It has a better structure than the old law, and uses shorter sentences. It has a "Reader's Guide", notes, "method statements" and examples to help readers find information and use it.

In the years from 1992 to 1999 the Australian Office of Parliamentary Counsel rewrote legislation in the following areas:

- sales tax (1992)
- offshore mining (1994)
- corporations (1995-2000)[43]

---

39 See *Designing the Law Drafting Issues*, Corporations Law Simplification Program Task Force information paper, June 1995 <http://www.takeovers. gov.au/content/Resources/corporations_law_simplification_program/ downloads/Designing_the_Law_June_1995.pdf>.

40 See p 312.

41 Robinson, V, 2001, *Rewriting Legislation – Australian Federal Experience*, paper presented to a conference in Ottawa, Canada in March 2001, Appendix A, Corporations Law Rewrite team report, p 21 <www.opc.gov.au/plain/docs. htm>.

42 Company Law Advisory Committee Second Interim Report, Parliamentary Paper No 43, p 6.

43 Described on pages 74-75.

- income tax (1995-2000)[44]
- aged care (1997)
- incentives for export market development (1997)
- public service (1999).

The Office continues to rewrite major parts of Acts, or whole Acts. Some are simply to improve the drafting, and others involve policy changes. The office says rewrites that are intended only to improve drafting often turn out to raise difficult policy issues that have to be solved before drafting can continue.[45]

Canadian projects In 1995 the Canadian government chose a portion of the Explosives Regulations (the Consumer Fireworks Regulations) for a pilot project to rewrite government regulations in plain language.

Then in 1997 the Canadian government decided to rewrite the Employment Insurance Act in plain language, and test it on potential users.[46] The rewriting was completed in 2003, with the model Bill ready to pass into law. Unfortunately, for a variety of reasons both legal and political, the Bill has not yet been passed. But it stands as a model for new and different drafting techniques, as used in a complex and sensitive area of the law.[47]

European Union In 1993, the European Council of Ministers passed a resolution on the quality of drafting of European Community legislation,[48] which began by stating:

> 1. the wording of the act should be clear, simple, concise and unambiguous; unnecessary abbreviations, 'Community jargon' and excessively long sentences should be avoided;

and went on to specify other ways of helping make legislation more accessible. Unfortunately, the spirit of the resolution is not always reflected in the material the Eurocrats publish.

---

44 Described on p 73.
45 Office of Parliamentary Counsel, "Working with the Office of Parliamentary Counsel – A Guide for Clients", 3rd ed, March 2008, paras 106-108 <http://www.opc.gov.au/about/docs/WorkingWithOPC.pdf>.
46 See p 315.
47 More information on the drafting of the model Bill is at <http://142.236.54.112/eng/ei/legislation/readability.shtml>.
48 93/C 166/01.

In 2004 the EU got its first ever Communications Commissioner, Sweden's Margot Wallstrom. Her tenure ended in 2009. She listed improved communication, easier-to-read citizens' summaries of proposed legislation, and brokering a deal between the EU institutions on communication priorities, as her major achievements over those five years.[49]

From 2008, all "strategic and priority initiatives" in the European Commission's annual work program are accompanied by a Citizens' Summary. It is a maximum of two pages long, and is meant to explain clearly and simply the basics of the particular report, recommendation or proposal for a change in European law.[50]

South Africa In 1995, as the South African government began to dismantle the legal legacy of Apartheid, it decided to reflect the transformation to a democratic state in the language of its legislation. It also wanted to improve the people's access to justice, encourage participation in the new democratic system, and demystify government.

The government faces two major problems in communicating with its citizens. The new South Africa has 11 official languages, and more than that number are spoken there. And nearly half the population is functionally illiterate.[51]

The government called on international plain language experts[52] to help it kick-start its plain language work. Plain language experts helped to draft the Labour Relations Act 1995 and the Constitution of 1996. Since then, plain language principles have been applied in a variety of Bills, though drafters have not always been as successful as they may have wished.[53] Another developing area is that of the several

---

49   Mahony, M, "Wallstrom: EU needs a commissioner for citizens", *Eurobserver. com*, 1 Sept 2009 <http://euobserver.com/18/28598>.

50   Wallstrom, M (V-P of EC), "Transparency and Clear Language in the EU", Speech 09/378, 9 Sept 2009 <http://europa.eu/rapid/pressReleasesAction. do?reference=SPEECH/09/378&format=HTML&aged=0&language=EN& guiLanguage=en>.

51   Viljoen, F, "Baring the nation's soul through plain language", *Clarity* No 46, July 2001, p 15.

52   The Plain English Campaign (UK), Christopher Balmford (Australia), Philip Knight (Canada) and Professor Joseph Kimble (US). See *Clarity* No 33, July 1995, pages 8-10.

53   See the critique of the Promotion of Equality and Prevention of Unfair Discrimination Act 2000 in Nienaber, A, "A search for clarity in South Africa's new equality legislation", *Clarity* No 46, July 2001, p 11.

new laws that impose plain language obligations on businesses in South Africa.[54]

United Kingdom In June 2006 the UK Government announced with much fanfare "the first Bill to be Written in Plain English",[55] the Coroner Reform Bill. It was said to be published in plain English "so that anyone can read it and know what changes it is making". In fact this was simply the first in a series of "Draft Bills", published in a new format to enable public discussion and comment. The Bill itself was drafted in the usual parliamentary language. The "plain English" of the Bill was made up of explanatory notes, and explanatory notes have been published with Bills since November 1998.

If this experiment is not exactly a giant leap for plain language, there is better news from the Office of the Parliamentary Counsel for the United Kingdom. Since at least July 2008, its drafting policy – as described on its website – is "clarity". This includes "the use of plain language, but also includes other things also associated with plain language drafting, like layout, structure, and typography". [56]

Parliamentary Counsel also adopted a gender-neutral drafting policy in 2008 "so far as is practicable, at no more than a reasonable cost to brevity or intelligibility".[57] From the 2008-09 session of Parliament, all Government bills were being drafted in gender-neutral form. Secondary legislation changed from October 2008.[58]

Plain language in the courts

United States federal court rules A major achievement in the US is the effort to "restyle" all the rules of procedure in the federal courts. In 1991 the formidably named Judicial Conference of the United States' Style Subcommittee of the Standing Committee on Rules of Practice and Procedure began a monumental job: reviewing and rewriting the Federal Court rules for clarity, simplicity and consistency. So far the

---

54   See pages 87-88.

55   Press Notice, Department of Constitutional Affairs, 12 June 2006.

56   Office of the Parliamentary Counsel, *Clarity in Drafting: Principles and Techniques*, para 3, p 1 <http://www.cabinetoffice.gov.uk/media/190016/clarity%20paper%20with%20hyperlinks.pdf>.

57   See Chapter 8, p 173.

58   *Draft Legislative Programme – 2008/09*, Improving Legislation, para 22 <http://www.commonsleader.gov.uk/output/Page2448.asp>.

Federal Rules of Appellate Procedure, of Criminal Procedure, and of Civil Procedure have been restyled. There is only one *shall* left in any of these restyled rules. Now work continues on the Federal Rules of Evidence, with no *shalls* left so far.

Two leading lights of the plain language world are key figures in this work: Bryan Garner was the initial drafting consultant to the project, and Professor Joseph Kimble was the drafting consultant for the restyling of the first three sets of rules and main drafter for the work on the Federal Rules of Evidence. In 2007, the Advisory Committee, the Standing Committee and Professor Kimble all received Burton Awards for Legal Achievement for their work on this project.[59]

UK Civil Procedure Rules 1998 I mentioned earlier[60] the reform of the Civil Procedure Rules of England and Wales, based on the recommendations of Lord Chief Justice Woolf. The Civil Procedure Rules 1998 came into force on 26 April 1999.

The new Rules combined the rules for most county courts, the High Court and the Court of Appeal in a single set of rules. They are written in plain language and were intended to streamline civil litigation. They also introduced certain changes in terminology: for example, "pleadings" became "statement of case", "writ" became "claim form", "plaintiff" became "claimant", "subpoena" became "witness summons" and "discovery" became "disclosure". Latin is out and more familiar, everyday words are in.

Ten years on from the introduction of these Rules, a number of surveys show that the changes have been a "qualified success".[61] Swifter timetables, more mandated settlements, and less "interlocutory skirmishing" are some of the positives. But the negatives include disclosure getting out of control, and costs. The Civil Justice Council

---

59 For more information, see Garner, BA, "The Substance of Style in Federal Rules", *Clarity* No 42, Sept 1998, p 15, Garner, BA, 2002, *Guidelines for Drafting and Editing Court Rules*, Administrative Office of the US Courts, Washington DC, "Restyled Civil Rules Win Burton Awards", *The Third Branch* (Newsletter of the Federal Courts), Vol 39, No 6, June 2007 <http://www.uscourts.gov/ttb/2007-06/restyled/index.html> and the series of articles by Prof Kimble in the *Michigan Bar Journal* Aug-Dec 2007 and Aug-Dec 2009: see index at <http://www.michbar.org/generalinfo/plainenglish/columns.cfm>.

60 See p 68.

61 Rose, N, "Civil Procedure Rules: 10 years of change", *The Law Gazette*, 28 May 2009 <http://www.lawgazette.co.uk/features/civil-procedure-rules-10-years-of-change>.

has begun a three-year project, called "A vision for civil justice", to update research and test certain aspects of civil procedure for usefulness and social relevance.

Australia: judgment-writing programs The courts of Australia are becoming more conscious of the need to communicate clearly and plainly.

The Judicial Commission of New South Wales organises and supervises continuing professional development for judicial officers in New South Wales. It conducts a half-day session on judgment writing in its orientation programs for judges and magistrates. It also conducts judgment-writing workshops, which give judges and magistrates the opportunity to develop their judgment-writing skills so as to write clearer, more concise and well-structured judgments. As Ruth Windeler, the Commission's Education Director, told me: "No one would dare to suggest that judges should be writing in anything other than plain English".[62]

The Family Court of Australia and the Judicial Commission of New South Wales began a major effort around 10 years ago to improve judicial communication. The Family Court of Australia had a Judicial Development Program, with two-and-a-half days of seminars and lectures on judgment writing. Writing in plain language was an integral part of that course. The course is now conducted by the National Judicial College of Australia.

Not one, but two judicial colleges were set up in Australia in 2002: the National Judicial College of Australia and the Judicial College of Victoria. The role of these Colleges is to provide professional development and continuing education and training for judicial officers in their respective jurisdictions. Both Colleges intend to work together – and with the Judicial Commission of New South Wales – to integrate judicial education in Australia.

Since 2005, the National Judicial College has offered an annual course on judgment writing, running over three days. This course is modelled on the program that the Family Court had pioneered – which itself had borrowed from a similar course offered in new Zealand, and which in turn was based on a Canadian course. A range of international and local experts present the course. The course is run

62   Telephone interview with M Asprey, 2 Sept 2002. Confirmed by email from Ms Windeler, 22 Sept 2009.

in different cities for different participants such as magistrates, local courts and superior courts. There is also a special program for appeal courts.

With help from the Australian Institute of Judicial Administration and the Judicial College of Victoria, the National Judicial College organises an annual National Orientation Program for new judicial appointees from Australia and neighbouring countries. A day is devoted to judgment writing.

The Judicial College of Victoria runs its own courses in judgment writing (two-and-a-half days), and in delivering oral decisions (two days). Again, international and local experts present the courses.

Lawyers and others promoting plain language in law

United States Many organisations and committees in the US are devoted to reviewing legal practice and procedure to simplify legal language. The Plain English Subcommittee of the State Bar of Michigan's Publications Committee was formed in 1979. Every month since 1984 it has published the influential and informative "Plain Language" column in the *Michigan Bar Journal*. Committee Chair, Professor Joseph Kimble, claims that this is the longest-running column about legal writing anywhere.[63]

Another long-standing organisation was the Information Design Center of Washington DC (formed in 1979 as the Document Design Center, but closed in the late 1990s). This organisation did much to increase our knowledge of how lawyers can use plain language techniques (including improved document design) in their daily work.

At its 1992 conference, the Legal Writing Institute (a non-profit organisation dedicated to improving legal writing) adopted a landmark resolution. Among other things, it declared that legalese was "unnecessary and no more precise than plain language", and that "plain language is an important part of good legal writing". This resolution was significant, because most of the members of the Legal Writing Institute teach legal writing at law schools, and so influence the writing styles of future lawyers in America.

Canada From 1988-92, the Canadian Law Information Council ran a Plain Language Centre in Toronto. It provided resources to those

---

63   Index of columns at <http://www.michbar.org/generalinfo/plainenglish/columns.cfm>.

interested in plain language, and designed and ran training courses in plain language drafting. There was a Plain Language Institute in Vancouver, which played a similar role there from 1990-93. A Plain Language Society was formed in British Columbia in 1993, and then the BC Plain Language Section of the Canadian Bar Association was formed in 1994.

The Alberta Law Reform Institute organised a demonstration project to draft several model plain language documents, including a guarantee. They were published in 1992 as part of its Plain Language Initiative.[64] In 2008, the Institute released its recommendations for new rules of court for Alberta. This is the culmination of a seven-year project for the Institute. The proposed rules are in plain language, shorter, clearer and have better organisation and layout.[65]

For over 25 years the Canadian Institute for the Administration of Justice has held courses on legal drafting and judgment writing. Those courses incorporate plain language principles.

Australia From 1990-97, the Centre for Plain Legal Language operated within the University of Sydney. It began by developing and running successful training programs for lawyers and others in plain legal writing. It formed a library of plain language resources, it did valuable research into various aspects of plain language drafting, and provided consultancy services. In 1995 it was involved in a major research project with the Centre for Microeconomic Policy Analysis at the University of Sydney.[66]

The Law Societies of New South Wales and Queensland both established plain language committees in the 1990s. The Law Society of Western Australia has had a Clear Writing Committee since 1996. Each year for more than a decade it has conducted a plain English drafting competition for students. The Queensland Committee published a book on plain language that is now used in law schools.[67] Unfortunately, the New South Wales Committee was subsumed

---

64   The suite of documents included a will, a guarantee, an enduring power of attorney, minutes of settlement, a restraining order and a parental consent form.

65   The Institute's final report, *Rules of Court Project*, dated Oct 2008, is at <http://www.law.ualberta.ca/alri/docs/4.%20Final%20Report%2095.pdf>.

66   See p 40.

67   Clark-Dickson, D and Macdonald, R, 2005, *Clear and Precise*, 2nd edition, Thomson Custom Publishing, Sydney.

into another committee after a few years of doing interesting work, including running plain language seminars and doing a survey of the attitudes of New South Wales solicitors to plain language in the law.[68]

In 2003 the Plain English Foundation was formed in Sydney. It works to improve public communication by helping organisations, including lawyers, use plain language in their writing.

One of the greatest success stories of plain language in Australia is that of Australian law firms.[69] They were early adopters of plain language. From the late 1980s, many firms began to revise and rewrite their forms and precedents in plain language, and train their staff in plain language techniques. Some have even established plain language units that provide plain language writing services.

With Australian lawyers enthusiastically embracing plain language, we can now see it reflected in documents in the marketplace. And as that continues, plain language will become the norm – or at least the benchmark – for legal drafting. As plain language expert Christopher Balmford put it in 2002:

> [T]oday, commercial clients of Australian law firms are prepared to pay for legal services that are plain. One day, clients everywhere will refuse to pay for legal services unless they are plain.[70]

The Law Society (of England and Wales) The Law Society published in 2005 its *Better Law-Making Charter*, which set out 10 proposals to improve the way legislation is made at Westminster. Proposal no 8, titled "Use Plain Language and Good Design" says:

> Legislative texts should be produced using plain language and modern, accessible structure, layout and design, whether on the internet or paper.[71]

---

68 See Asprey, M, "Trend Overwhelmingly in Favour of Plain Language, Survey Shows" (1994) 32(9) *NSW Law Society Journal* 70 and "Lawyers Prefer Plain Language, Survey Finds" (1994) 32(10) *NSW Law Society Journal* 76.

69 Including Mallesons Stephen Jaques, DLA Phillips Fox, Freehills, Minter Ellison, Allens Arthur Robinson, Deacons, Corrs Chambers Westgarth, and many others.

70 See Balmford, C, "Plain Language: beyond a 'movement'", *Plain Language Association International (PLAIN) Fourth Biennial Conference Proceedings Toronto, Canada, 26-29 Sept 2002*, p 6 <http://www.plainlanguagenetwork.org/conferences/2002/movement/1.htm>.

71 Plouvier, A, 2006, "Plain language, the 'Better Law-Making Charter' and some UK developments", *Clarity* No 56, Nov 2006, p 14.

The Solicitors Regulation Authority was set up in 2007 to set and regulate the standards of behaviour and professional performance of solicitors in England and Wales. It did a baseline study in 2008, and one of the conclusions of this research was that one of the main areas of dissatisfaction with solicitors' service was:

> A key failure on the part of solicitors to communicate effectively and in plain language with the consumer.[72]

The Solicitors' Code of Conduct 2007 (administered by the Solicitors Regulation Authority) does not refer specifically to a duty to communicate with clients in "plain language", but it does refer in Rule 2 – Client relations, to:

- a duty to "give the client a clear explanation of the issues involved and the options available to the client" (Rule 2.02(1)(b)), and
- a requirement that "Any information about the cost must be clear and confirmed in writing" (Rule 2.03(4)).

Clarity In 1983 in the United Kingdom, an enthusiastic group of lawyers and others formed "Clarity", an international association to promote plain legal language.[73] Clarity's journal, also called *Clarity*, is a mine of information both on plain language in the law, and on drafting techniques. It is published twice a year. Clarity has a website,[74] holds regular meetings in London, has an international conference every second year, and gives occasional awards – the Clarity Awards.

PLAIN Two Canadians, Cheryl Stephens and Kate Harrison, were the founders of what is now called PLAIN (the Plain Language Association InterNational).[75] PLAIN is a "growing volunteer nonprofit organization of plain-language advocates, professionals, and organizations committed to plain language".[76] PLAIN has a website,[77] a lively

---

72   May 2008, "Consumer views and their experiences on using solicitor services and their awareness of the Solicitors Regulation Authority", p 28 <http://www.sra.org.uk/documents/consumer-reports/consumer-research-2007.pdf>.

73   Clarity's President to the end of 2010 is Australian Christopher Balmford.

74   <www.clarity-international.net>.

75   This is a different PLAIN from the organisation mentioned on p 70.

76   Quoted from PLAIN's website: <http://www.plainlanguagenetwork.org/networkindex.html>.

77   <http://www.plainlanguagenetwork.org>.

internet discussion group,[78] and it holds an international conference every other year. In 2008, PLAIN was incorporated in Canada.

Developments in the business sector

Canada In March 2000 the Canadian Bankers Association followed up on the *Decline and Fall of Gobbledygook* report and subsequent resolution. It announced that its members were "committed to providing customers with banking information which they can easily understand and use". And it promised to begin the process of "translating" existing mortgage documents into plain language, and to apply plain language principles when revising or developing new mortgage documents.[79] The voluntary *Plain Language Mortgage Documents CBA Commitment* dated 7 March 2000 is still in force. It includes a model plain language Mortgage Disclosure Statement.

The CBA has also published the *Small Business Code of Conduct*, which states:

> Banks will provide the customers with documents, including contracts that are written in clear and understandable language.[80]

But as these codes are voluntary, it is up to the individual financial institutions to decide how they adapt their mortgages and other documents to reflect these commitments.

Since 2001 there has been federal law (the Cost of Borrowing (Banks) Regulations), requiring the language of disclosure statements and related consents given to borrowers under the regulations to be:

> in plain language that is clear and concise. It must be presented in a manner that is logical and likely to bring to the borrower's attention the information required by these Regulations to be disclosed.[81]

In 2009, anticipating amendments to these regulations, the Financial Consumer Agency of Canada issued guidelines to help financial

---

78   <plainlanguage@yahoogroups.com>.
79   See <http://www.cba.ca/contents/files/misc/vol_20040929_plainlan-guagemortgagedocument_en.pdf> .
80   Note the missing comma, after "contracts" <http://www.cba.ca/index.php?options=com_content&view=article&id=71%3Asmall-business-banking-code-of-conduct&catid=45%3Asmall-business-services&lang=en&itemid=55>.
81   Regulation 6(4). Very similar regulations apply to certain foreign banks, trust and loan companies, and insurance companies.

institutions comply with their obligations, and generally to use "clear language and presentation" in communicating with customers.[82]

Also in the financial services sector, the insurance company Clarica embarked on a major plain language program in 1999. From that date its policy is to write all new documents in plain language. At the same time it began to rewrite its existing insurance policies and related documents in plain language.[83] Now there are legislative incentives for other financial services sector companies to do the same.[84]

Ireland The private sector has taken the lead in moving towards plain language in Ireland. The largest telephone company, Eircom plc, has a policy of using plain language. So has a major life assurance company, Irish Life, which began working with plain language consultants in 1998. Irish Life's "Plain English Programme" was chosen as one of the best 10 examples of innovative best practice in corporate social responsibility from almost 200 case studies collated from 2003-08 by the non-profit organisation "Business in the Community Ireland".[85] The Bank of Ireland and the Allied Irish Bank also use plain language, and they and other Irish banks have worked in recent years with plain language consultants.

South Africa A landmark was reached on 1 April 2000 when all the major banks of South Africa adopted a Code of Banking Practice. Under the Code, all banking contracts were to be revised in plain language before October 2000. This timetable proved to be overly ambitious, but most major retail banks had complied at least to some extent by the deadline. The Office of the Banking Adjudicator, which enforces the Code, announced on 11 November 2000 that, to avoid

---

82   FCAC *Clear Language and Presentation Principles and Guidelines for the Industry* <http://www.fcac-acfc.gc.ca/eng/industry/RefDocs/ClearLanguage/CLPI-eng.asp>. The proposed amendments would delete the word "plain" from the expression "plain language", but would retain a requirement that the language of the disclosure be "clear, simple and not misleading". This change of wording is said to be "to ensure consistency with other regulations which apply to federally-regulated financial institutions", according to an email I received from the Department of Finance, Canada, dated 7 Nov 2009.

83   For more information, see Milne, S, "Plain language at Clarica", *Clarity* No 45, Dec 2000, p 19.

84   For more detail see the expanded Chapter 4 at <http://www.federationpress.com.au> (Book Supplements, Plain Language for Lawyers).

85   Watch the You Tube video clip at <http://www.youtube.comwatch?v=hqqf6cvMWts>.

injustice, "unfair terms" and "legal and technical language" would be "disregarded unless the bank could show it was explained to the client".[86]

The Code of Banking Practice was finally introduced on 1 October 2004. Several of its provisions promise to provide services and products, rights and responsibilities,[87] in plain language, and the banks undertake that they will:

> Use legal and technical language only where necessary. Where legal and technical language is used, we will explain what we mean.[88]

Unfortunately, none of the provisions of the Code is legally binding, and they cannot be used to "influence the interpretation of the legal relationship" between the customer and the bank, nor to "give rise to a trade custom or tacit contract or otherwise" between the customer and the bank.

The National Credit Act 2005 imposed new obligations on financial institutions and other creditors to use "plain language" in documents that the Act requires a lender to give to a borrower. Interestingly, it does not set out an objective test of "plain language" (such as a Flesch Reading Ease Test[89]). Instead, it imposes a test that looks at whether the

> ordinary consumer of the class of persons for whom the document is intended, with average literacy skills and minimal credit experience, could be expected to understand the content, significance and import of the document without undue effort ...

having regard to certain listed characteristics.[90] This is a novel approach for South Africa, but one that is repeated (with minor differences) in two other new laws.

Businesses in South Africa will soon be required to use plain language in consumer transactions. The Consumer Protection Act 2008 became law on 24 April 2009. Its aim is to make plain language a basic consumer right, and an obligation of business. The Act establishes the

---

86   Lane, W, "South African banks must use plain language", *Clarity* No 46, July 2001, p 6.

87   Paragraphs 2.4 & 2.5 respectively.

88   Paragraph 3.1. See <http://www.banking.org.za/consumer_info/code_of_banking/code_of_banking.aspx>.

89   See p 322.

90   Section 64(2). For an analysis of the requirements of section 64, see Knight, P, 2006, "Clarity for South Africa's credit consumers", *Clarity* No 56, Nov 2006, p 19.

National Consumer Commission by April 2010, and the associated regulations also take effect then. The rest of the Act takes effect six months later.

The definition of "plain language" in the Consumer Protection Act[91] is very similar to the one in the National Credit Act 2005, and to the one in the Companies Act 2008.[92] There are also plain language requirements in the Long-term Insurance Act 1998 and the Short-term Insurance Act 1998, which apply to representations and disclosures. South African lawyers and businesses are on the alert to see how these laws will be interpreted and applied.

New Zealand There are definite moves towards consumer-oriented reform in the banking, real estate and insurance industries.[93]

The New Zealand Bankers' Association's Code of Banking Practice promises plain language in two places, but with a little equivocation. Under the heading "governing principles and objectives of the code", paragraph 1.2 says:

> In order to achieve these objectives we will:- …
>> (ii) provide you with timely information, using plain language where we can, to help you understand how your accounts and products or services operate, so that you can decide whether they are appropriate to your needs …

Paragraph 2.2, in the section titled "communication with you", says:

> We will provide information to you from time to time using plain language where we can.[94]

Since 2006, the organisation called WriteMark has held a plain English conference and given Plain English Awards. From 2009, the week leading up to the conference has been dubbed "Plain English Week".

In July 2009, the Real Estate Institute of New Zealand (REINZ) published a new plain English Agreement for Buying and Selling Real

---

91   Section 22.
92   Section 6(5).
93   State Insurance, Tower Corporation and Sun Insurance have all moved towards plain language insurance documents: Campbell, N, 1999, "How New Zealand Consumers Respond to Plain English", *Journal of Business Communication*, Oct 1999 <http://www.entrepreneur.com/tradejournals/article/58082898.html >.
94   New Zealand Bankers' Association, July 2007, *Code of Banking Practice*, 4th edition, revised 1 July 2008.

Estate in New Zealand, and it caused quite some controversy. At the time of writing, this debate was in its early days. Advocates of plain language will be following it closely.

Back in 1994, the Rugby rulebook was rewritten in plain language so that the rules would be easier to understand for referees, players and spectators.[95] Surely there could be no stronger evidence that plain language had really begun to take hold in New Zealand.

They are just a few of the more significant plain language developments throughout the world. You can explore them further in my internet supplement.[96]

Yet despite over 35 years of experience in many jurisdictions around the world, some lawyers are still cautious about or suspicious of plain language. There is no way to address those fears by using generalisations or speaking in the abstract. Even all this evidence of what is happening around the world is not enough. The only way to understand the effect of plain language on legal writing is to begin to write in plain language. So let's learn what to do, and see what happens. That is what the rest of this book is about.

---

95   "Rugby in plain English", *New Zealand Herald*, 31 Aug 1994, Section 3, p 1.
96   See note 1.

Chapter 5
Fundamentals

Consider your reader

If I could give you only one guideline to follow it would be just that. Consider your reader. That's the secret of plain language drafting in three words.

And who is your reader? Your client? The lawyer acting on the other side of the transaction? The judge? Your barrister? A clerk working in the claims department of a corporation that you act for? That clerk's supervisor? That supervisor's manager? That corporation's board? Or all of these people? It is an important question.

When lawyers draft in the traditional style for clients, their main aim is to protect their client. They must accurately and completely document what the client wants to do. They must not leave anything out. They must anticipate what might happen and do their best to cover that too. If they do that well, they feel they have done their job. They always have in the back of their minds the possibility that a court might have to interpret the contract, and so if they get it technically right they believe they will be beyond criticism and their clients will be safe and secure.

In plain language drafting, that is not enough. There is more to it than getting it technically right. And there is more to it than just "translation" from legalese to "plain language". If we simply translated, then we would use a single definitive "dictionary", and we would always come up with the same solution to a particular problem. But we would not be taking the needs of our readers into account. All readers are different.

Play to your audience

Even the most accurate and elegantly drafted document can be completely ineffective if it misses its mark. Here is a proclamation issued by Sir George Arthur (1784-1854), when he was Lieutenant-Governor of Van Dieman's Land (Tasmania). It reads:

And I do hereby strictly command and order all Aborigines immediately to retire and depart from, and for no reason, and on no pretence, save as hereinafter provided, to re-enter such settled districts, or any portions of land cultivated and occupied by any person whomsoever, on pain of forcible expulsion therefrom, and such consequences as may be necessarily attendant on it.[1]

Unfortunately, this meant nothing to the Aboriginal people, who could not read it. They kept on returning to the "settled districts" and kept on suffering the "pain of forcible expulsion", which was probably considerable, as well as "such consequences as may be necessarily attendant", which no doubt included death.

The proclamation did not do anything but give the authorities an excuse to punish the Aboriginal people for breaking a law they couldn't possibly have understood.

If a client has instructed you to prepare a document, the client has a right to be able to read the document. The client is your primary audience and so the document should be drafted so it can be understood by that client. If it is something more "public" you are drafting, like a prospectus or a piece of legislation, then regardless of who instructed you to draft the document, your primary audience is the general public, and the general public should be able to understand it.

By saying that, I don't mean to imply that you have to explain *in the document* all its legal ramifications. A contract to sell goods should not be a textbook on the law of sale of goods.

What I am saying is that the client (or member of the public) should be able to read the document from cover to cover, if he or she wants to, and comprehend it as a document. The client may have questions and need to ask you to explain some things, or to give more details or examples, but the client should have been able to get through the document with a feeling that he or she understood all the words, if not all the concepts or the reasons why all the words were there.

More than one audience?

If the client is the primary audience, is there a secondary audience? There may well be. It depends what the document is and what happens in the future. Even if the contract you are drafting or the letter you are writing is for or to your closest friend, the secondary

---

1   Quoted in Hughes, R, 1987, *The Fatal Shore*, Collins Harvill, London, p 419.

audience is lurking in the background. It might be your friend's partner, that partner's lawyer, a judge, a jury, future business rivals, future shareholders, or even the executor of a will in 50 years time. All these people will need to be able to read and understand the document without having you around to explain what you really meant, or how the parties would have understood what you wrote.

How much should we be writing for them?

Earlier in this chapter I said that lawyers in the past have been content to write to get things technically correct: as if accuracy was their only goal. The audience that style of writing is aimed at is the secondary audience – the judges. But plain language says we must write for the primary audience as well. We need to be accurate, precise *and* able to be understood by all our likely readers.

How do we strike a good balance?

This is an important decision to make, because, for example, if your client is thoroughly experienced in the sort of matter you are advising about and documenting, you may not need to spell things out in the same way as you would for someone less experienced. You may be able to take short-cuts, use technical terms, and leave things unsaid.

What if we are not sure how sophisticated or knowledgeable our readers are? What do we do then? The experts recommend that in that case we write for the audience that is *least* likely to understand what we are writing,[2] or *least* familiar with the subject matter.[3] But then that brings with it the worry that it might, as Charrow and Erhardt put it, "damage your credibility with a more sophisticated audience",[4] or force you to leave out material that is too complex for some of your readers.

Charrow and Erhardt offer three useful suggestions to deal with this problem. Whether any or all of them are suitable depends on what your document is, what its purpose is and what its readership will be. The three suggestions are:

---

2   Charrow, VR and Erhardt, MK, 2007, *Clear & Effective Legal Writing*, 4th edition, Aspen Publishers, New York, p 110.

3   Redish, JC, 1991, *How to write Regulations (and Other Legal Documents) in Clear English*, American Institutes for Research, Document Design Center, Washington DC, p 8.

4   Charrow, VR and Erhardt, MK, 2007, *Clear & Effective Legal Writing*, p 110 (cited at note 2).

1. Consider dividing your document up into different sections addressed to different audiences. Or include a glossary explaining terms and concepts that some audiences might not understand.
2. Consider creating two or more versions of the document.
3. Consider carefully which is your most important audience, and write primarily for them.[5]

Plain language writer George Clark has offered his own suggestion – he calls it "multi-layering":

> Some plain language materials deal with huge topics for huge audiences [for example, UN system publications for global distribution]. These materials have to be multi-layered. On the surface they are simple and limited to the basic ideas but underneath they have to point to the complexity of the issues and to some of the more subtle points. In these situations you can think of the material having a 'core' with 'extensions'. The 'core' is aimed at the less sophisticated end of the audience and the 'extensions' at the more sophisticated end.[6]

He proposes two techniques for doing this: "cute phrasing" and text boxes. Cute phrasing involves using what seems like an ordinary phrase, but one that can stimulate a wide range of thoughts in someone who is already familiar with the topic.[7] Text boxes can be explanatory or can contain quotes, which themselves can be supportive, contrary, philosophical or in the voice of the ordinary person, for example.

The question of who is the audience for legislation is an interesting one. It was considered by the Victorian Law Reform Commission in its 1987 report *Plain English and the Law*. The report said:

> The plain English movement does not require that laws always be drafted in such a way as to make them intelligible to the average citizen. However, it does require that every effort be made to make them intelligible to the widest possible audience.[8]

---

5   Same work, p 110.
6   Clark, G, Feb 2003, *Multilayering in plain language texts* <http://www. hakikazi.org/papers/030205.pdf>.
7   His example, in the context of the UK government's Millennium Development Goals: "One of the central challenges for the future is to help poor people to work more efficiently and to be better paid for their work". This, he says, not only sets topics for discussion but also alludes to a more sophisticated idea: what the International Labour Organisation calls "Decent Work".
8   1987, Victorian Law Reform Commission Report No 9, *Plain English and the Law*, p 45.

The Australian House of Representatives Standing Committee on Legal and Constitutional Affairs Report, *Clearer Commonwealth Law*, also considered this question and concluded:

> The Committee accepts that there are often many different groups in the readership of legislation. Nevertheless, the Committee considers that it is essential that the drafter bear the readership in mind when drafting.
>
> The Committee believes that the problem of multiple audiences should be overcome as far as possible by placing primary importance on drafting for the people who may be affected by a particular piece of legislation.[9]

The Corporations Law Simplification Taskforce attempted to deal with the problem of multiple audiences for legislation with its "Small Business Guide", which is now Part 1.5 of Chapter 1 of the Corporations Act 2001 (Cth). Representatives of small business had told the Taskforce that they wanted a separate part of the law for small corporations. But there is a great deal of overlap in the provisions that apply to all corporations, no matter what size they are.

The Taskforce came up with a compromise: draft for all corporations in the usual way, but gather together the provisions that relate to small businesses and repeat them in a more convenient format in a separate part of the law, which doesn't have operative effect. That has two benefits:

- The operative sections of the Act can deal with *all* corporations, regardless of size, and none of this is repeated in other operative sections. That eliminates the possibility of having two conflicting laws on the same topic.
- The non-operative section – the "Small Business Guide" – can be published separately in a convenient format for those who need to read and use those sections and no others.

The Small Business Guide was originally part of the first Corporations Law Simplification Act, which commenced on 9 December 1995. Before the Act commenced, a member of the Taskforce said that the reaction of small business to the Guide had been overwhelmingly positive. But some lawyers have thought it inappropriate to include material in a law if it doesn't have legal effect. They were concerned that it might be "misleading" in some way. The contrary seems to be

---

9   1993, Commonwealth of Australia, p 95.

the case. Small business people told the Taskforce that reading the Guide was the first time they understood their obligations.[10]

One of the senior members of the Taskforce, First Assistant Parliamentary Counsel Vince Robinson, worked on several other projects to rewrite laws in plain language. He described the way his office views the audience for legislation:

> Our rewrites have been pragmatic rather than ideological. We have aimed, by and large, to make the legislation more readable and easier to use for its actual current users. We have not tried to make the legislation accessible to people who, from a practical point of view, we believed were highly unlikely ever to read the legislation. We have sometimes factored in people who did not currently read the legislation but were likely to do so if it were easier to read ...
>
> We have not aimed to make the legislation readable by the average citizen. It is unusual for the average citizen to encounter a scheme through the legislation itself. The average citizen is more likely to encounter the scheme through brochures, notices, forms or websites.
>
> The average citizen who does wish to look up the legislation for himself or herself has a number of difficulties to overcome quite apart from the readability of the text ...
>
> This suggests that, as well as it being unlikely that the average citizen will consult the legislation itself, it may also be inadvisable.[11]

This view is obviously a pragmatic one born of experience. But plain language has never held that the reader must be able to understand all of the law behind a law, or behind a document. And with more and more legal material becoming available on the internet, access to the law is getting easier. So the potential audience for law – even tax law – may well be getting larger.

In so much legal writing, both public and private, we can't be sure about where our writing will end up. So we will often need to *assume* that there will be a secondary, wider audience. But that does not mean that we must write *primarily* for the secondary audience. After all, the secondary audience knows that there was a primary audience, and it wasn't them. It just means that we should also keep the secondary

---

10   Unpublished interview of Taskforce member Claire Grose by M Asprey on 18 Aug 1995.

11   Robinson, V, *Rewriting legislation: Australian Federal Experience* (paper presented to a conference in Ottawa, Canada, March 2001), pages 8-9 <http://www.opc. gov.au/plain/docs.htm>.

audience in mind. We are not writing *to* them, but they might need to understand what we have written.

In short, our first duty is to satisfy the needs of our primary audience, but we must also make sure that what we write can be understood by our secondary audience. Fortunately, our secondary audience can take into account the fact that we were writing with our primary audience in mind.

The New South Wales Parliamentary Counsel's Office considers it has at least three audiences for its drafting:

- Parliament itself
- the public or the section of the public to whom the legislation is directed
- the courts and the legal system

and each has different requirements.[12]

If we always keep our likely audience (or audiences) in mind when we write, and adjust our writing style to be appropriate for those audiences, then there is no need to ask ourselves whether we should adopt a particular writing style for particular *types* of documents. We are writing for the people who read our documents, not for the documents themselves. If we bear the people's needs in mind, our documents will be exactly tailored to the circumstances for which they were written, no matter what "types" of documents they are.

Purpose

We have talked at length about our audiences, and who they might be. To a degree, this governs what they will want from the document we are writing for them, but it is also important to think more specifically about:

- what our readers want to do with the document, and
- what we, the writer, want them to do with the document.

In other words: what is the document's *purpose*?

There is no point in drafting the most beautifully written, plainly expressed, expertly designed document, if it is of no use to the reader.

---

12   NSW Parliamentary Counsel's Office *Policies relating to Plain Language and gender-neutral expression* <http://www.pco.nsw.gov.au/corporate/plainlanguagepol.pdf> (at p 3).

This happens more often than you might imagine. Lawyers who are asked to advise a client on a particular issue routinely write detailed and lengthy letters of advice that are of absolutely no practical use to their clients. Not all clients want to know the law in detail. Often the reason they want the advice is to help them decide whether or not (or how) to do something. That is the reason they have consulted a lawyer. That is the *purpose* of their question. Therefore, the written advice should address that purpose, and give them the advice they need in order to make their decisions. If this context is not crystal clear to you, it might be apt to ask questions like:

- *"Why* do you want to know this?", or
- *"What* do you actually want to do?", or
- *"How* do you want to be able to use this document?", or
- *"Who* will be using this document?"

The answers may well surprise you.

The other aspect of purpose I've mentioned is what *we* want the reader to do with the document:

- Do we really want them to read every word? Or is it better to give them the option of skimming and selecting the parts of the document that they need at particular times or for particular purposes?
- Do we want them to sign and date the document and return it to us? If so, we should make that very quick and easy to do, by making the signing and dating pages very obvious to the reader, and easy to complete. It seems a basic point, but often these pages are hidden in a document, and are hard to find unless flagged by sticky notes or the like. Sometimes it is not at all clear who signs where. And what date do you put where? To the reader, it might not be as clear as it is to us.
- Do we need the answers to a set of questions? If so, then make a list of questions that is obvious and complete – and in the one place. Don't scatter questions throughout your text, and expect the reader to pick up every one, no matter how deeply hidden.

These things are fundamental, but are often overlooked. They seem obvious, but they only become obvious if you have considered your reader, and thought carefully about the document's purpose.

Tone and formality

Without being conscious of it, most of the time when we speak we are pretty adept at adjusting our tone. If we speak to a child, we adjust more than just our vocabulary so that the child can understand us. We adopt a different tone.

When we write privately, we can also adjust our tone to the appropriate setting. When we accept an invitation from people we don't know very well, we write differently from the way we would write to a good friend. A letter to the editor of a newspaper would be different in tone from a love letter. But when we write letters in the course of our work, we tend to adopt only one tone. Where is all the subtlety we show when we write when we are not at work? Why don't we use it?

Perhaps it is because we think it is appropriate to adopt a "formal" tone in all our work. And so it may be. But there are different levels of formality. And, as Professor Joseph Kimble has pointed out, formality can be dangerous: it can degenerate into pomposity. Simple and straightforward writing need not be undignified or informal, he says, and to illustrate the point he has rewritten the orders on articles of impeachment for the US President.[13] Here's the order that ended President Clinton's impeachment trial in 1999:

> *Original order*
> The Senate, having tried William Jefferson Clinton, President of the United States, upon two articles of impeachment exhibited against him by the House of Representatives, and two-thirds of the Senators present not having found him guilty of the charges contained therein: it is, therefore, ordered and adjudged that the said William Jefferson Clinton be, and he is hereby, acquitted of the charges in this said article.[14]

And here's how Professor Kimble rewrote it:

> *Rewrite*
> After a trial on two articles of impeachment against the President, William Jefferson Clinton, fewer than two-thirds of the Senators present have found him guilty. Therefore, it is ordered that he be acquitted.

---

13   "How to Write an Impeachment Order", *Court Review*, Vol 36, Issue 2, Summer 1999, p 8 or *Clarity* No 44, Dec 1999, p 10.

14   145 Cong Rec S1459 (daily ed 12 Feb 1999).

The original order is a model of legalese: one long sentence, embedded clauses, archaic and inflated words, even a "doublet" (*ordered and adjudged*): all things that we will encounter later in this book. Professor Kimble describes his rewritten version as "whittled down". It might even be capable of more "whittling". But is it undignified or informal? Is it inappropriate for such a grave document? I say no. I say the clarity of the words actually emphasises the gravity of the order. We are faced with the stark reality of the alleged crime and the acquittal, and there is no padding to get in the way of that message.

But tone is not just about formality and dignity. There are also questions of the relationship you have with the person you are writing to, and what they need from you. They may need quick, sharp incisive legal advice on a difficult matter, or they may need hand-holding. You should adjust your tone to provide that. And what do *you* need to convey? Are you warning the client of dire consequences? Are you showing that you mean business, and have a lot more up your sleeve, or are you being conciliatory? Good writers adjust their tone to convey that.

Unfortunately (or perhaps fortunately), there are no rules to guide us about the levels of formality we should adopt in our writing. Each time we pick up the pen or the dictaphone, or sit at the keyboard, we need to decide what is the appropriate degree of formality for that piece of writing, remembering to base that decision on who our audience is, not what the document is. But even if we decide that less formality is required in a particular case, we should always take a professional approach to our legal writing, no matter how familiar we may be with our primary audience. Remember the secondary audience.

Once we realise that we don't have to adopt an unduly stiff or formal tone in legal writing, we can even begin to enjoy our writing. And we can use it to cement our relationships with our clients.

In Chapter 3, I mentioned a survey done by an Australian advertising agency in April 1994 of corporate executives, and their views about law firms.[15] One of the things the corporate executives said they wanted was a true business partnership with a law firm that understood their business. That has to involve good communication – as equals. A simple thing like adjusting the tone of your writing in letters to clients can really make a difference.

---

15   See pages 57-58.

After one plain language seminar I gave for a large law firm in Sydney, one of the partners told me that he had made an effort to write letters of advice to clients in a more natural tone, using their names, less formal language, and being more direct. He was delighted with the results: clients had been telephoning him to say they had noticed a change. They had begun, they said, to receive letters of advice from the person they knew and spoke to often!

Taking a professional approach: don't patronise

Taking a professional approach involves recognising the duty we have as lawyers to assist our readers to understand the law as it affects them. It involves being sensitive to the difficulties the reader may be experiencing; recognising the level of understanding the reader has and supplying whatever additional information the reader might need. But it does *not* mean patronising the reader.

For example, there is a formula of words that we often see in lawyers' letters of advice, which introduces an explanation. It is:

> As you are no doubt aware …

But *is* the client aware? How do clients react to being told they are "no doubt" aware, especially if they aren't aware? Could you blame the clients if they came storming into your office and said, "Of course we're not aware – that's what we pay *you* for".

Think about those little phrases. It could be that the ones we use all the time – the ones we don't even think about – could cause great offence. Even starting a sentence with the word "obviously" could be offensive. Think about it. Is it really that obvious?

If you need to explain something, explain it. But don't tell clients that it is "obvious". If you don't know what the client's level of understanding is, then ask, *before* you begin to write.

Remember, too, that you are writing a letter of advice to a client – not an essay for a university professor. Your client wants to know the answer to the question that he or she asked you. It is a letter of advice, not a thesis. So cut out all those formulas of words like those you see in undergraduate essays – things like:

> Before we can discuss the question you have asked, we need to examine the history of the legislation in this area …

The first (and probably the *only*) thing the client wants to read is the answer to the question. Anything else is detail. The client doesn't want to read an essay – no matter how clever. The client wants an answer – and as briefly as possible. Of course, if there are qualifications and exceptions that the client needs to understand, you must explain them, but first give the client your advice, and then explain the qualifications and exceptions. The client needs to know what you recommend, before the client can grasp the rest of the relevant material. And don't give the client a survey of all the relevant laws unless that's been asked of you. Give an answer to the question, and qualify it as you must. But make sure it *is* an answer.

The way you arrange the information you have to convey should be governed by the needs of your readers – not by the information itself or the way you stumbled on the answer. I'll be dealing with this issue in more detail in Chapter 6.

Courtesy

Taking a professional approach also involves courtesy. No matter how acrimonious the dispute is, our writing should always reflect the fact that we are professionals conveying our client's instructions. We should not identify ourselves *personally* with the client's position. We should never write anything in anger. Our client's opponent's lawyer is our colleague, not our enemy. We are our client's professional advisors, not an extension of our client. Again, remember that secondary audience who may scrutinise our writing outside the context in which it was written. We must do our best for our client, but we can do that and at the same time keep cool and maintain professional control.

Courtesy has always been a fundamental principle of good drafting, and is not unique to plain language drafting. But the reason I mention it is because I want to make it clear that using plain words does not mean rudeness. There is plenty of room in plain language for courtesy, and the struggle to be brief does not require that all signs of courtesy be deleted from our writing. But always remember the distinction between courtesy and pomposity. Formulas such as:

> We beg to remain, dear sirs, your faithful servants

add nothing and do not even sound sincere. They can be safely omitted and no one will miss them.

Courtesy also involves having sensitivity about the reader as an individual. As we have seen, plain language is all about considering the reader. Asking the question: "What are the reader's needs?" also implies the question "What are the reader's sensitivities?" Perhaps the reader has special needs. They might have a physical or mental handicap, a particular religious faith, culture or philosophy, an ethnic background, or some other feature, such as youth or old age, which might need to be taken into account in your writing. We'll look at an aspect of this question again in Chapter 15, in the context of colour in document design.[16]

Pomposity

Pomposity is an intangible quality, harder to describe than most of the other concepts in this book. Still, it is a quality that the general public strongly associates with legal writing.

On the other hand, one of the common criticisms lawyers make of plain language is that it is not "dignified enough". It seems to be this search for "dignity" that leads us away from simplicity and clarity and into pomposity. We choose language that is more remote and less personal than ordinary everyday language.

The interesting thing about pomposity is that, unlike most of the other characteristics of legal writing that I've described in this book, pomposity often appears in speech as well. Mellinkoff quotes a judge of a US federal court saying to a group of students at Harvard:

> I give it to you as my considered opinion, gentlemen, that this is a government of checks and balances.[17]

I have a favourite example of my own. Some years ago at a legal conference I attended, the delegates were given this instruction:

> I have to advise, ladies and gentlemen, that available outside the door to my immediate left are facilities for the making of coffee, and indeed, tea.

Pompous statements are usually wordy as well, and that contributes to their dullness. We all agree that important subjects demand serious treatment, but there is no need to clothe our writing with ponderous trappings and adopt a remote or inflated drafting style.

---

16   Page 284.
17   Mellinkoff, D, 1963, *The Language of the Law*, Little Brown, Boston, p 27.

Clarity and simplicity contribute much more to the dignity of our writing than a forced or artificial tone of respect.

So that is a brief rundown of some of the threshold issues in plain language drafting – things that you have to bear in mind long before you put pen to paper. Here they are again, in summary.

- Consider your reader. There is more to good legal writing than just getting it technically right.
- Remember that your writing will probably have both a primary and a secondary audience, so you need to keep the needs of both those audiences in mind.
- If unsure, write for the audience that is *least* likely to understand.
- Ask yourself (and your reader) about the purpose of the writing. What does *the reader* want to do with it, and what do *you* want them to do with it?
- Decide on your tone and the appropriate degree of formality. Don't be afraid to use your own voice in your writing. But always take a professional approach. Remember that secondary audience.
- Arrange your information with the reader's needs in mind, not yours. Give your client an answer, not an essay.
- Never write in anger. You are an advisor, not a party.
- Always be courteous. Plain words do not require rudeness. They may require sensitivity to the reader as an individual.
- Don't be pompous. Clear and simple writing can be dignified too.

In the next chapter, we actually begin the writing process. We examine how the structure you choose for your writing can affect its clarity and readability, and talk about how, and where, to begin writing.

Chapter 6
Structure

Planning

All good writing begins with a plan. But even before the plan there is the thinking stage. The stage when you begin to analyse the problem you have to deal with. This is the stage when you should ask yourself a series of questions. What am I trying to achieve? What does the client want? What information do I need before I start? Has the client given me all the information I need? Perhaps I didn't understand all the ramifications of the client's problem when the client first came to me. Should I now contact the client again and get the additional information I need or clarify anything that I don't understand?

Once you have assembled all the information you think you'll need – read it! You may read something that changes your mind about your approach, or tells you that you need still more information. Don't begin work on the document until you think you have a clear idea of all the issues. You might make notes as you are reading, but resist the temptation to start work on the document until you think you've covered all the research you need to do.

One question you might ask yourself is: do I really need a document at all? Mark Adler points out in his book, *Clarity for Lawyers*,[1] that putting something in writing is sometimes unnecessary and a waste of time and money.

Sometimes the best document for the job is not the one you think it is. Lawyers are so used to producing the same types of document over and over again – just cranking out the precedents – that they often miss the opportunity to give their client a document in a form that will do the job better that the more traditional form. We should ask ourselves: is there better a way to achieve the result the client wants? Is it a deed I need, or would a contract that looks more like a form or a checklist suit the client better? A document like that will do more than just record

---

1   Adler, M, 2007, *Clarity for Lawyers*, 2nd edition, The Law Society, London, p 40.

the transaction as a matter of law. It will also show your creativity and your interest in how client's business works. It will be a marketing tool.

The time to ask these questions is *before* you begin to write. Answer them first. *Then* take up the pen and paper or to sit at the keyboard. But it is not yet time to write "Dear Sirs", "Dear Ms Jones" or "This Deed". It is time to write a plan.

Even quite simple letters should follow a plan. The more complex the document, the more detailed the plan.

Your plan may be a diagram, a list, a flow chart, or a series of headings and points. Find whatever it is that suits you. I usually use the headings and points method, but that is just what suits me.

Put down every aspect of the research that you thought was important, and arrange them in the order that suits your purpose, your client. Don't leave them in the order they occurred to you, or the order that the textbooks had them, or the order the last person who drafted a similar document used. Arrange them in the best order for the purpose. For example, it might be best to put the most important points first, or the basic answer first, and all the exceptions and detail later.

As you write, your views about order may change. It doesn't matter: that's the beauty of a plan. You can easily shuffle things around later, because you aren't locked in to any particular structure. It is much more difficult to do this if you are working with a first draft of a document. There is something about the structure of a document – even a rough draft – that looks permanent, and we are tempted to stay with the existing structure and try to fit our own ideas in here and there.

When you use a plan you can set your own structure, tailored for the particular task at hand. Your ideas can set the structure; they shouldn't have to fit an existing structure if it isn't the best structure.

Again, this sort of approach is simply good drafting practice. It is not unique to plain language drafting, but it is essential for plain language drafting. I said earlier[2] that plain language drafting looks not only at the words being used and what they mean, but also at the organisation of the words in a sentence, the sentences in a document, and the design and layout of the document itself.

The combination of all these things governs how effective the document is at communicating information and helping readers

---

2   Page 14.

understand and use it. A document written in the simplest words and arranged in short sentences will still be difficult to understand if the information is poorly organised or presented. This is particularly so if the document is long or complex.

Organisation

So what is the best way to organise information? To a degree, it depends on what the document is, what its purpose is and what the reader requires from it. A letter of advice on a complex question might need to be arranged so that the reader is carefully taken, step by step, through a logical sequence that will help the reader to understand why you are giving the advice you are giving. A document such as a mortgage or lease is not susceptible to the same sort of logical arrangement as a letter of advice, but the provisions can still be arranged in the order that best draws the parties' attention to the clauses that are most important for them. Acts, and other laws, can be set out so that their main points aren't hidden among their procedural and mechanical aspects.

Important things first

In each of these cases, there is one common factor governing the best way to organise the information: the most important parts should be put first. And when we are deciding what is the most important part, we look at it from the reader's point of view – not ours. That is a very important distinction to make. Again we fall back on that fundamental of plain language drafting: consider the reader.

What is the most important part of a document for a reader?

It depends on what the reader is looking for in each particular case – but here are a few general guidelines.

Letters of advice: the most important part of a letter of advice is the answer to the client's question. Everything else is secondary.

Loan and security documents: in a document such as a mortgage, the most important parts are *the loan amount, the security, the interest rate* and *the repayment dates*. There are other very important aspects of a mortgage, but these four things are the very essence of the transaction. There are other matters, like events of default, that are extremely important for the parties to understand, but they are not as important as the four things I've listed. You could not have a mortgage without those four things.

Leases: in a lease, the most important things are *the property leased, the term of the lease, the rent amount* and *the rent payment dates.* Other things, like the obligations of the tenant, and even the termination provisions are less important. It stands to reason: the four things I've listed are what the bargain is all about. The landlord and tenant are interested in the parts of the lease that are peculiar to *their* agreement: names, addresses, amounts and dates. Other things might also be very important, but when the landlord and tenant are reading the documents for the first time, their main concerns are those four items, which form the essence of the lease.

Legislation: in a statute, the most important thing is what it is about – not when it commences, who administers it, what other legislation is affected by it, and so on. Of course, it does depend on who is reading the Act and what they are looking for. For example, a particular bureaucrat may only be interested in the provision dealing with the power to make regulations. But the main purpose of laws is to regulate behaviour, and so that is the point of view that we should take when assessing the relative importance of different parts of Acts and other laws.

Judgments: in a court case, the most important thing is the verdict. That is what the parties to the case are there to hear. The reasons for that verdict are next in importance, but the answer to the question being argued must come first.

To organise your material in this way means that you have to look at it from the reader's point of view. Once you have this knack, you will probably find that your legal drafting style is completely transformed. You will no longer organise material in the form that is most convenient for you, or most familiar to you. Let me illustrate this with a hypothetical letter of advice.

Here is a letter about whether a floating charge can be created simply by means of a minute of a meeting of directors recording a resolution passed to create the floating charge. It was written quite a few years ago, so pay no attention to the detail of the law and just focus on the structure. Why did the writer structure it this way? Think about it while you read.

Dear Sir,

1   We are asked to advise as to the sufficiency of the creation of a floating charge over the entire assets and undertaking of a company by use of a Minute of a Meeting of the Directors of such company recording the passing of a resolution to that effect.

5   We advise as follows:

1.   *Stamp Duty Liability*

In New South Wales, the relevant duty imposed is payable on a "loan security". A loan security is defined to mean a mortgage, bond, debenture or covenant (Section 83(1) of the Stamp Duties

10   Act). Mortgage is further defined to mean a security by way of mortgage or charge for the payment of a certain sum of money lent at the time or previously or repayment of money to be thereafter lent upon an account current (Section 3(1)). Mortgage is further defined in Section 83(1). For relevant purposes, the

15   extended definition includes:

- A Security by way of mortgage or charge given in consideration of the transfer of property;

- An agreement, contract or covenant for the making of a mortgage accompanied by or relating to documents of title;

20   - Any instrument of mortgage for the purpose of securing repayment of debentures.

Nothing in the above (except perhaps the definition incorporating the word "instrument") specifically excludes *oral* transactions creating a "loan security". Presumably, the classic

25   legal definition of "bond and covenant" would also exclude those from the definition as each would require instruments or agreements under seal. However, this is not necessarily the case as regards "mortgage" which security can be created orally.

The learned authors of *Stamp Duties Legislation* (Tolhurst &

30   Ors) state at paragraph 1.20 that in the absence of express reference to a memorandum, there is no general rule that a document which is evidence of an unwritten or oral transaction is dutiable as if it were a written document. The authors go on to refer to some exceptions to the rule and state that there is authority to

35   indicate that a document which is brought into existence as part of the transaction is dutiable as if it effected the transaction.

In the present case your "Minute" evidences a resolution by the company through a meeting of its directors to accept moneys and in return to give a floating charge (as security) upon certain

40   terms.

> We do not think that, on any view, a resolution to do
> something could be said to constitute the doing of that act.
> Further, as regards a Minute prepared exclusively for one party
> in relation to the prior entry into a transaction it has been said:

45   ...

Do we have the answer yet? The suspense is killing me! 45 lines and it looks like it will be a while yet. And so it was. The answer to the question took another 40 lines. Even then it was hidden in the middle of a paragraph. And the writer went on to say that in any case the risk was too great and they'd be better off to create the charge the usual way. This revelation came after 75 lines. After that there were four more pages of advice dealing with other problems associated with a charge evidenced by a minute, with the various pitfalls scattered throughout the paragraphs.

This letter is a good example of the point I'm making here. It is actually quite well written if you look only at the language. It uses reasonably simple words, quite short sentences and paragraphs, and follows a careful logical sequence. It explains a fairly technical area of the law with care, and it shows considerable respect for the intelligence of the reader.

But what is the *answer*?

That is what the client is asking while pacing up and down with the letter.

It is unlikely that the writer wanted to hold the client in suspense. It is just that the structure of the letter is a reflection of the thought processes the writer had to go through to get to the answer. The writer takes the reader through all those steps as well, whether they like it or not, before the writer yields up the answer.

See how the writer first repeats the question that the client asked (lines 1-4). This might be of some benefit to a client who has forgotten what they asked their solicitor, but it is really there for the writer's benefit: so the letter stands on its own as a record for the writer's file.

Next, the writer takes the reader through the legislation: the reader has to learn about "loan securities" (lines 6-10), the various definitions of "mortgage" (lines 10-28), what various commentators say about oral transactions (lines 29-36). It is not until line 37 that we even get a mention of "the present case". And no conclusion is drawn by the author until line 41. Even then it isn't the one the reader is looking for.

Is it fair to inflict that kind of torture on the reader? We may think it is important that the reader understands why we have come to the conclusion that we did, and be aware of the assumptions that we've had to make, and that the answer isn't cut and dried. Of course, those are all important, both for the client, and for the writer. But isn't the client entitled to the answer *first*? It's what they're paying for.

Then, by all means, take the reader step by step through all the nooks and crannies of the law. But do it *after* you've given the client what they have asked for.

Sometimes, it is better to put all the detailed explanation of a complex advice into a separate document or memorandum. Then you can make the main point in a short covering letter and tell the reader that the rest of the detail is attached. That way the reader can come to grips with the basic advice first and deal with the rest when it suits.

Once we have given the reader the most important part of the advice, we should continue to arrange the rest of our material in the order that we think will best suit the reader. As I said before, this might depend on the document, its purpose and what the reader requires of the document. There are no hard and fast rules, but your guide should always be the best interests of the reader.

Arranging things so that the reader gets the answer to the question or the most important material first has two other advantages:

- It gives the reader a context in which to read all the subsidiary information. That makes it easier on the reader. It is likely that the reader will understand the material better because they have a context – they know where it is all leading.
- It makes the information more useable by the reader. That in turn shows that you are sensitive to the reader's needs and – if the reader is your client – you are presenting material in a way that makes your client more efficient in his or her business. Again, your writing becomes a marketing tool.

Put related material together

The other guiding organising principle is to put related material together. If the reader can see a pattern in your logic, it will be easier for them to grasp. This might seem simple, but it requires discipline to identify and classify material in this way. It also requires you to be willing to rewrite and reclassify material if new relationships between parts of the material occur to you as you are writing, or as you collect new material.

This is where the plan we discussed at the beginning of the chapter comes into its own. If you have the skeleton of your document in a plan before you begin to write, then it is not much trouble to reorganise the bones. It is only when you begin to put flesh on the bones that it becomes more work to rethink, reorganise, reclassify and then reorder your document.

If the plan you are using has headings, you need to rethink those headings too as you rework the plan. In the final document, the headings will be for the reader – both to help them find the material they are looking for, and to help them grasp the structure of the document.[3] But at this stage the headings can be part of the organisation process.

And don't neglect the headings as the document evolves. Remember to look at them from time to time as you write – to make sure that they change if the text below them changes. Too many times I have seen headings that no longer relate to the text they are supposed to describe. Too many writers write their headings once, and never look at them again. A good example of this is in email, where a discussion between two or more people might begin on one topic, with an appropriate heading, but then range across other topics, without anyone thinking to change the heading. So later messages in the email string are completely mislabelled.

So now that we have slabs of related material, with good descriptive headings, how do we deal with them? We divide them again.

Paragraphs

As readers, we know instinctively that it is easier to cope with material that is divided into "bite-sized chunks". This enables our brains to process one "chunk" of information before moving on to the next one. After all, reading is a learning process, and cognitive psychologists tell us that we learn incrementally, by putting smaller chunks of information together to build a gradual understanding of the whole.

We also like to see lots of "white space" around what we're reading. It makes it look easier to read, and more inviting.[4]

---

3   See pages 271-273 for more on headings.
4   There is more about this in Chapter 15, on document design. See pages 268-270.

So why, when we come to write, do we write paragraphs that go on and on without a break? It looks as if we have adopted the "stream of consciousness" technique of writing.

When we write we usually start slowly, collecting our thoughts and sifting them. Then, if we're lucky, we start to pick up some momentum and it all begins to flow. This is particularly so when we write by dictating. We pick up on an idea and run with it and before we know it, it runs away with itself. A huge unbroken paragraph is the result.

What causes this run-on effect? The writer is dealing with too much information at once, and hasn't taken the time to organise like thought with like, or to separate different aspects of the same topic from each other. If your paragraphs are too long, it is probably because you are dealing with more than one idea in each paragraph.

Plain language consultant Elizabeth Murphy has said that a paragraph should be a unit of thought, not of length. She suggests having one main topic sentence and perhaps several supporting sentences, plus a final sentence leading the reader to the next paragraph.[5]

And one other thing. Don't be afraid of the one sentence paragraph. If you use it sparingly, and in the right place, it can be very effective as a device for emphasis.

It will catch the reader's eye.

See?

Sub-paragraphs

Sub-paragraphs help to divide the material up so that it is more easily digested, but they can also be used for emphasis, or to draw the reader's attention to a similarity in the subject-matter. For example:

> The trustees may invest in:
> (a) shares;
> (b) debentures;
> (c) bills of exchange; and
> (d) certificates of deposit.

makes a *list* for the reader. Next time they want to know what to invest in, the trustees can go back to the list and check off the items they are interested in. It is much easier to follow, even just visually, than:

---

5   "Plain English – Style of Choice" in the Australian Government Department of Finance and Administration publication *Stylewise* Vol 7, No 1, 2001, p 2.

> The trustees may invest in shares, debentures, bills of exchange and certificates of deposit.

This is particularly so when the list is long, or the individual items have to be described in more than a few words.

But a word of warning about sub-paragraphs: don't use them instead of paragraphs. Remember that a sub-paragraph works best as part of a paragraph. If you use sub-paragraphs instead of paragraphs then you'll force yourself to use sub-sub-paragraphs, and *they* should really be reserved for emergencies. Here is what I mean; it is an example from a traditional form sale of business agreement:

5.   *Assignment of Leases*

5.1 (a) The Vendor agrees to use its best endeavours to procure the assignment of the Leases to the Purchaser. The Purchaser agrees to accept such assignment and to keep the Vendor indemnified against any claims made under the Leases in respect of the period after the Completion Date and the Purchaser acknowledges that it has inspected copies of the Leases and is aware of their terms.

(b) Consent to assignment of the Lease to the Purchaser or its nominee on terms acceptable to both parties shall be a condition precedent to this sale and purchase of Business. If the terms of the landlord's consent to the assignment of the Leases are not acceptable to the parties then this Deed shall be at an end and all moneys paid by the Purchaser shall be refunded forthwith.

(c) In consideration of these presents the Covenantors jointly and severally agree:

(i) to indemnify and keep the Vendor indemnified against any and all claims made under the Leases assigned by or at the request of the Vendor to the Purchaser pursuant to this Deed in respect of the period on and from the Completion Date; and

(ii) to notify the Vendor of any such claims made or threatened as soon as they are notified to the Covenantors.

What has happened here? First, and most obviously, the text has moved right across to the right side of the page because of all the "tabs" the typist has had to insert to cope with the paragraph structure. Of course, there are layouts that minimise this problem, but it should not be necessary to resort to them. The real problem is that the writer went straight to the sub-paragraph (that is, 5.1(a)), to break up the material. The writer could simply have used a paragraph (that is, 5.1)).

Without even attempting to change the language – although it is very tempting, because there is so much to work with in that example – we can make the text more manageable by reorganising the paragraphs like this:

5. *Assignment of Leases*

5.1 The Vendor agrees to use its best endeavours to procure the assignment of the Leases to the Purchaser. The Purchaser agrees to accept such assignment and to keep the Vendor indemnified against any claims made under the Leases in respect of the period after the Completion Date and the Purchaser acknowledges that it has inspected copies of the Leases and is aware of their terms.

5.2 Consent to assignment of the Lease to the Purchaser or its nominee on terms acceptable to both parties shall be a condition precedent to this sale and purchase of Business. If the terms of the landlord's consent to the assignment of the Leases are not acceptable to the parties then this Deed shall be at an end and all moneys paid by the Purchaser shall be refunded forthwith.

5.3 In consideration of these presents the Covenantors jointly and severally agree:

(a) to indemnify and keep the Vendor indemnified against any and all claims made under the Leases assigned by or at the request of the Vendor to the Purchaser pursuant to this Deed in respect of the period on and from the Completion Date; and

(b) to notify the Vendor of any such claims made or threatened as soon as they are notified to the Covenantors.

See how much easier the text is to cope with. We've moved more type over to the left and we're left with the roman numerals up our sleeve in case we need them. We've saved a couple of lines, even though we haven't deleted a word, and we haven't lost *any* of the "white spaces".

One other difficulty to avoid with sub-paragraphs is what is sometimes called "shredding", or making "clause sandwiches". This is when writers over-enthusiastically divide up information into unnecessary or irritating sub-paragraphs, which sometimes return to the margin several times, as in:

1. If a person:
   (a) is aged over 75 years; and
   (b) is in good health,
   the person may apply for a discount card for travel on:
   (c) State government transport; and
   (d) private buses,
   unless they already hold a Gold Pass.

This kind of structure interrupts the sentence in order to force items into categories that don't really help the reader. When the sub-paragraphs are longer, the whole paragraph becomes even more difficult to handle. This is usually because there is more than one idea being dealt with in the paragraph. In this example, the material might be better divided into two groups, but using only one list, as in:

1. A person may apply for a discount card for travel on State government transport and private buses if that person:
   (a) is aged over 75 years;
   (b) is in good health; and
   (c) does not already hold a Gold Pass.

Our readers expect to see lists at the end of sentences, not at the beginning or in the middle. And giving readers what they expect to get nearly always helps their comprehension.

In addition to this, the structure and order you choose should also depend on the emphasis you want to give. Here again, the question to ask is: which parts of the information are more important than others? What do I want people to remember and act on? Don't hide the important parts in the middle of a list. In a list, the beginning is the best place for the most important pieces of information.

Document "Add-ons": schedules, appendixes, annexures

It is often convenient to be able to "hive off" material that does not need to appear in the main body of the document. If that material is not of primary importance, it can be put in schedules, appendixes or annexures.

Some people draw distinctions between these things, saying that they are all for different purposes. Some say that a schedule is for short details, like the parties' names and addresses, the address of the leased property, the rent payable and the termination date. Some say an appendix should be reserved for documents, and annexures might be for unwieldy things like maps and computer printouts. There is also the theory that schedules are part of an agreement itself, and therefore come after the "testimonium" (the "In witness whereof …") but before the execution clauses.

Whatever the validity of these views and the authority for them, there is little purpose in making those distinctions. There might be agreements that have all three – schedules, appendixes *and* annexures – and that would be very confusing for the reader who probably doesn't know all those theories.

It is better to pick *one* of these labels, put all your "hived off" secondary material into it, and use numbering (Schedule 1, 2, 3 etc) to separate the different items. It is also helpful to have another label: a heading that describes what is actually in each schedule or other attachment.

And what sort of material should be hived off? There are two types of material that I think are best separated from the main body of the document.

1. *Details that make up the essence of a document* – details that, if you read them apart from the rest of the document, give you a feel for the most important parts of the transaction. In an employment contract, for example, you might have a schedule that sets out:

   - the names of the employer and employee
   - their addresses
   - the job title and description
   - the period of employment
   - the starting date
   - the annual salary
   - other benefits.

   Anyone reading a schedule with this material in it would then know the essence of the contract. The same sort of thing can be done for any common sort of document or transaction: leases, loans, share and business sales and the like.

2. *Material that is secondary to the main body of the agreement*. Things that the reader can assume while reading the document, keep in the back of their mind and look at later. Things

like maps, computer printouts, lists, secondary documents and other matters of less important detail.

Where should the schedule (or annexure, or appendix) go?

Now that we are considering putting very important details in our schedule, we don't want anyone telling us it isn't really part of the rest of the document – even if we call it an appendix or an annexure. We want to ensure that the signatories acknowledge that too. So there are two possible places for the schedule: at the beginning of the document or at the end of the substantive clauses of the document.

If it is the type of schedule that summarises that transaction (as in the example I just set out), then it stands to reason that it should be the first page of the document. This material is of primary importance in the document. It can form a summary of the main points of the document, and so it should be the very first thing the reader encounters. This is a technique I like very much because it demonstrates efficiency, consideration of and respect for the reader, and a mastery of the detail of the document, all on p 1.

Schedules of this kind should have plenty of visual help for the reader – headings, bold type and so on, so that the reader can see what kind of information is being summarised.

If the schedule contains only secondary material, or if there is more than one schedule, the schedule or schedules should be at the end of the document, just before the testimonium and the execution clauses. There is no reason to use a schedule to separate the testimonium from the execution clauses. After all, the testimonium, when translated into plain language (as it can and should be), is the bit that tells us "I am signing here to show I agree with everything in the document". That should include the schedules. So the testimonium's logical place is just before the signatures, and after any schedules. And the testimonium could be words as simple as "Executed as a deed" or "Executed as an agreement".

Sentence structure

So far in this chapter I've concentrated on the more mechanical matters of the structure of a document. The framework, so to speak. Now we need to focus on the material we will use to fill in the framework: the sentences. In the next chapter we will focus in even closer – we'll look at the words that make up the sentences. But before we do that, a few words about the way we string words together in coherent units.

We need to look at sentence length, sentence structure, and the way we join sentences and the words in them: punctuation.

Sentence length

We all know that we should avoid writing long sentences. We know that we find them difficult to read. Unfortunately, the "stream of consciousness" that I mentioned earlier[6] can intervene and we end up with not only long paragraphs but also long sentences.

We have seen that the mind processes written information in "chunks" or short "bites". In a sentence, this is basically clause by clause. The brain can handle only a couple of clauses at a time, depending on their length. If we pile up the clauses in a sentence and embed them one in the other, we virtually ensure that what we write won't be understood on the first reading.

Out of consideration for our readers, and in the interest of efficiency, we should learn to write in relatively short sentences. As to how short – I think it is probably counterproductive to specify a length. Some authorities suggest 20-25 words is an appropriate average length.[7] A well known Australian journalist has said[8] that his editor's view was that 24 was the optimum number of words, but his personal aim was for a maximum of 17 words. The New South Wales Parliamentary Counsel's Office aims for sentences with a maximum length of five lines (in their B5 legislative format), expressing one central idea.[9] The Australian Office of Parliamentary Counsel also includes in its *Plain English Manual*[10] this "5 line rule" as a rough guide to avoiding "slabs of unbroken text". The US Federal Court's Committee on Rules of Practice and Procedure recommends aiming for fewer than 25 words, and 30 at most.[11]

---

6   Page 112.
7   Statistic quoted in 1987, Law Reform Commission of Victoria, Report No 9, *Plain English and the Law*, Appendix 1, p 33 – Drafting Manual.
8   Gareth Powell of the Sydney Morning Herald, speaking at a meeting of the Society of Business Communicators on 27 Nov 1990.
9   NSW Parliamentary Counsel's Office *Policies relating to Plain Language and gender-neutral expression*, p 2 <http://www.pco.nsw.gov.au/corporate/plainlanguagepol.pdf>.
10 <http://www.opc.gov.au/about/docs/PEM.pdf> p 25.
11 Garner, BA, 1996 (reprinted 2002), *Guidelines for Drafting and Editing Court Rules*, Administrative Office of the United States Courts, Washington DC, p 13.

Few of us have the time or inclination to count the number of words per sentence in our writing. And, of course, not *all* long sentences are difficult. Those constructed with care can be a joy to read. In 1931, the Fowler brothers put it this way:

> No sentence is to be condemned for mere length; a really skilful writer can fill a page with one and not tire his reader, though a succession of long sentences without the relief of short ones interspersed is almost sure to be forbidding. But the tiro,[12] and even the good writer who is not prepared to take the trouble of reading aloud what he has written, should confine himself to the easily manageable.[13]

However, by 1986 the commentators were harder on long sentences. Greenbaum and Whitcut said in their revision of Gowers's *The Complete Plain Words*:

> The two main things to be remembered about sentences by those who want to make their meaning plain is that they should be short and should have unity of thought.[14]

I think the point to be made is that short sentences are not an end in themselves, but that habitually using long sentences can be tiring for the reader. And they require extra time and care with punctuation and other aspects of structure.

There are plenty of examples of long sentences in legal writing and we are only too familiar with them. Long sentences appear both in laws and in private documents, especially, it seems, in leases, loan documents, security documents, trust deeds and insurance documents.

All that needs to be said about long sentences has probably already been said. No amount of punctuation and care can save a sentence of 368 words (which, at the time of writing, still existed in the Credit Act 1984 (New South Wales)).[15] The Credit Act is set to be replaced on 1 July 2010 as part of the National Consumer Credit Reform legislation. Unfortunately the proposed replacement provision, section 129(2), is actually six words *longer* – at 374 words!

---

12 Means *beginner*.

13 Fowler, HW and FG, 1931, *The King's English*, 3rd edition, Oxford University Press, Oxford, p 309.

14 1987, 3rd edition, Penguin Books, London, p 175.

15 Section 24(2): defences available to a "linked credit provider" against liability for misrepresentation.

PLAIN LANGUAGE FOR LAWYERS

It is sometimes said that sub-sections or sub-clauses should only be one sentence long. Some people even say this rule applies to sections and clauses. It seems to have been a rule of legislative drafting from the past, perhaps designed to stamp out long sub-sections and sub-clauses. Whether or not this ever was a valid principle of drafting, it is far too restrictive to follow as a general rule. The subject-matter will always have to govern the number of sentences, and no rules about numbers can guarantee good drafting.

Punctuation

The only thing that actually controls sentence length is the full stop. But for the long sentences we all have to use from time to time, punctuation can make them manageable.

This is not the place for a grammar lesson, and there are plenty of grammar and other texts that give guidelines on how to punctuate. The Australian government's *Style Manual*[16] gives all the conventions in detail. But remember to use punctuation to help readers. It can help avoid confusion and ambiguity. Use it as you would in non-legal writing – in a natural way.

The best advice I've seen about the full stop (or period) comes from William Zinsser. He said:

> There's not much to be said about the period except that most writers don't reach it soon enough.[17]

There is no rule of legal construction that says that punctuation is to be disregarded. There is a legal myth to that effect, which has persuaded some lawyers that documents must be written so they can be understood without punctuation, if it were to be deleted. This is nonsense. It harks back to the days when punctuation was the printers' responsibility. That was hundreds of years ago, and for many years now the courts have taken punctuation into account when construing legal writing.

It is true that over the years the courts have hedged their bets on punctuation. Adler points out[18] that the House of Lords came down

---

16   2002, *Style Manual for Authors, Editors and Printers*, 6th edition, John Wiley & Sons Australia Ltd, p 95 and following pages.

17   2006, *On Writing Well*, 7th (30th anniversary) edition, HarperCollins Publishing, New York, p 71.

18   Adler, M, 2007, *Clarity for Lawyers*, p 76 (cited at note 1).

clearly in favour of punctuation in 1918 – in *Houston v Burns*, when Lord Shaw said:

> Punctuation is a rational part of English composition, and is some-times quite significantly employed. I see no reason for depriving legal documents of such significance as attaches to punctuation in other writings.[19]

As recently as 2003, the New South Wales Supreme Court cited *Houston v Burns* as authority for the proposition that one can be guided by punctuation marks, or the lack of them, in interpreting a will.[20]

But the courts aren't always keen to be constrained by punc-tuation. Mellinkoff has been able to compile a long list of conflicting pronouncements on the significance of punctuation by different state and federal courts in the United States.[21] Richard Wydick made his own list in an article in *The Scribes Journal of Legal Writing*.[22] The courts' ambivalence about punctuation was repeated in a decision of High Court of Australia, when Justice Dawson said:

> Whilst punctuation may sometimes be helpful as an aid to construc-tion, in these circumstances it would be wrong, in my view, to allow the presence of a comma to control the meaning of the sub-section.[23]

Clearly the judges like to keep their options open. This is also true in Canada, where in a case decided in 2000, the Supreme Court refused to believe that the absence of a comma in a revised statute indicated that the legislature intended to give a different meaning to the section. The court construed the statute by looking at the purpose of the law instead.[24]

---

19   [1918] AC 337 at 348.

20   *Kay v South Eastern Sydney Area Health Service* {2003] NSWSC 292.

21   Mellinkoff, D, 1963, *The Language of the Law*, Little Brown, Boston, pages 368-371.

22   Wydick, R, 1990, "Should Lawyers Punctuate?" (1990) 1 *Scribes J Legal Writing* 7 at 21-22.

23   *Chew v The Queen* (1992) 173 CLR 626 at 639 (a casual observation only).

24   *Nanaimo (City) v Rascal Trucking Ltd* 2000 SC 13. Another Canadian case, dubbed "the $2.1m comma case", concerned the misplacement of a comma, but that was a decision (*Telecom Decision CRTC 2007-75*) of the Canadian Radio-television and Telecommunications Commission, whose decision was not in the end based on punctuation, but on the French version of the same section of the bilingual contract. An application in 2008 to review and vary part of this decision did not revisit the comma issue (*Telecom Decision CRTC 2008-62*).

Occasionally the law provides some specific guidance on punctuation. In the Interpretation of Legislation Act 1984 (Victoria), section 35(b) specifically says that in interpreting Acts or subordinate instruments, punctuation is one of the matters that can be taken into account. And section 36(3B) says that for Acts or subordinate instruments made or punctuated after 1 January 2001, punctuation forms part of that legislation. In Queensland, the position is more straightforward: punctuation in an Act is part of the Act.[25] In South Australia, punctuation forms part of an Act "subject to any express provision to the contrary".[26]

So should lawyers punctuate? Richard Wydick says "yes, but carefully". He gives three reasons:

1. Punctuated documents are less puzzling to other lawyers and judges.
2. They are easier for clients and other non-lawyers to understand.
3. They are easier to translate into other languages – an especially important consideration in Europe these days.[27]

All the leading commentators on legal writing agree: lawyers should punctuate. Everyone else does. Unfortunately, there is no guarantee that a court will always read every comma and dash the way we intend it. But that is a hazard of all drafting. Punctuation is not exempt.

Quirk[28] points out that when we write we don't have all the communicative advantages of the spoken language, like intonation and facial movements. So, he says, we have an obligation to give the reader all the help we can, by punctuating. We have to try to anticipate what might cause the reader difficulty.

Even so, we should try not to over-punctuate. Otherwise we can lose our reader along the way, because we have forced them to stop and pause too often. Perhaps the best advice is to try to punctuate only where a reader would naturally need to pause if the writing were read aloud.

---

25   Section 14(6), Acts Interpretation Act 1954 (Qld).
26   Acts Interpretation Act 1915 (SA), section 19(1).
27   Wydick, R, 1990, "Should Lawyers Punctuate?", pages 23-24 (cited at note 22).
28   1968, *The Use of English*, 2nd edition, Longman, London, p 239.

One particular area of punctuation has caused problems for lawyers in the past is punctuation in lists. Does a list of items have to be punctuated as one sentence, like this:

Here is my list:
    (a) a paragraph;
    (b) another paragraph; and
    (c) a final paragraph?

I don't believe it does. You may notice that throughout this book I am quite relaxed about the punctuation for lists. Sometimes I use a broken sentence to introduce a list of full sentences, like this:

A broken sentence, introducing full sentences, such as:
    (a) This complete sentence has a capital letter, a verb and a full stop.
    (b) This one does too.
    (c) And so does this. In fact it has two.

At other times, I don't use punctuation after each item in the list, especially if they are not full sentences. For example:

When I use bullet points to list short sharp items, such as:

- this item
- that item
- the other item.

The reasoning behind this relaxed attitude is that the *list itself* shows that one item is finished by beginning text on a new line. A letter or symbol indicates the start of the new item. So we don't need to fuss over punctuation to help our reader make sense of the list.

The second list has complete sentences that help the reader make sense of the material within the individual items in the list. But we are not necessarily helping the reader if we always try to pretend (as in the first list) that a list is one full sentence, and each item in a list has to be a series of clauses separated by semi-colons. We are forcing the reader to connect all the items in the list together, instead of allowing them to read them individually.

The third list has no punctuation at all between the individual items. But this does not hinder the reader. The bullet points and new lines give all the signals the reader needs.

There is more about lists in chapter 11, when we discuss *and* and *or*.

Building a sentence

I mentioned Gowers's view that we need unity of thought in our sentences. That is a principle that is easier for lawyers to bear in mind than a grammatical theory about clauses, sub-clauses and subordinate clauses and adverbial, adjectival and relative clauses.

Try to keep to one thought per sentence. If you do this, it is easy to keep control of your sentence length and complexity.

Commas are sometimes a good indicator of a sentence that is too complex. If you find yourself putting in commas after every few words in your sentence and never quite getting to a full stop, it is likely that your sentence is becoming entangled in a mess of clauses that are out of control. Stop: break the sentence up into the various different thoughts you are expressing, and separate them into separate sentences.[29]

Cases and conditions: Coode's rules

Many lawyers are hampered by some old rules of legal drafting called "Coode's rules".

George Coode was an English barrister who wrote a famous analysis of legal drafting in 1843. His work, *On Legislative Expression* was probably the first attempt ever made to analyse what happened in the legal drafting process. [30] He set down what he said were "natural" rules of drafting.

Coode's idea was that there are four basic elements in legislative drafting: the legal subject, the legal action, the case and the conditions. He said that they should appear in this order (my examples alongside):

1. *Case:* "Where a person owns more than one property ..."
2. *Condition:* "... and if application has been made for a dispensation ..."
3. *Legal Subject:* "... the Commissioner ..."
4. *Legal Action:* "... may exempt one property from liability to duty."

---

29   See also **Interrupting a sentence with phrases and clauses**, pages 159-161.
30   It was an extract from the introduction to the Appendix to the *Report of the Poor Law Commissioners on local taxation to Her Majesty's Principal Secretary of State for the Home Department*: House of Commons papers 1843, vol XX; set out in full in Robinson, Dr S, 1973, *Drafting*, Butterworths, Sydney, Appendix A, p 335.

Coode thought that confused drafting resulted from a neglect of these rules. That may well be true. But the problem is that clear drafting does not always result from following these rules.

Coode has been criticised by a number of commentators, among them Dr EA Driedger QC,[31] and Robert Dick QC,[32] both of whom are well respected Canadian authorities on drafting. Piesse notes that, today, Coode's structure may seen "overly rigid and formal",[33] and that "To force all sentences into the structure would be unduly formalistic … it should not be applied inflexibly".[34] Other commentators recommend adhering to Coode's rules.

I think it is a mistake to accept Coode's analysis as gospel, appropriate for all forms of drafting today. Following the sort of rigid structure that Coode recommended can create problems. For example, as the Law Reform Commission of Victoria pointed out,[35] putting a condition at the beginning of a sentence can create a problem for the reader, and if there is more than one condition, the reader has to keep them all in mind, while still in a state of suspense as to what the core of the provision is about.

All this difficulty is compounded when you add a "case" up-front as well, as Coode's Rules would require.

Here's what I mean. It is an example taken from the Conveyancing Act 1919 (NSW), section 81(1):

> Whenever, in any deed of mortgage which is expressed to be made in pursuance of this Act [case], or in any mortgage under the Real Property Act, 1900 [case], the mortgagor employs the form of words contained in the first column of Part I of the Fourth Schedule, and distinguished by a number therein [condition], such form of words [legal subject] shall imply a covenant by the mortgagor for himself or herself, his or her executors, administrators, and assigns, with the mortgagee, his or her executors, administrators and assigns, in

---

31   1976, *The Composition of Legislation, Legislative Forms and Precedents*, 2nd edition, Department of Justice, Canada and 1982, *A Manual of Instructions for Legislative and Legal Writing*, Department of Justice, Canada, pages 3-4.

32   1995, *Legal Drafting in Plain Language*, 3rd edition, Carswell, Toronto, p 60 and following pages.

33   Aitken, JK & Butt, P, 2004, *Piesse: The Elements of Drafting*, 10th edition, Lawbook Co, Sydney, p 32.

34   Same work, p 34.

35   1987, Law Reform Commission of Victoria, Report No 9, *Plain English and the Law*, Appendix – Drafting Manual, p 35.

the terms contained in the second column of the said schedule, and distinguished by the corresponding number [legal action].

The writer certainly followed Coode's Rules. But is it really clear? It is intelligible – if you read it slowly with the help of the words in brackets, and look over it a couple of times – but is it clear?

Lawyers are used to this sort of structure, because it follows step by step the thought processes that the drafter went through to get to the main point. But for general readers it is most unusual.

Normal people say things like: "You can come with me if you are on time". The action is stated up-front, and the condition comes later. Of course, putting the condition first really isn't confusing if there is only one condition. But even just two conditions (or cases) at the beginning of a sentence can make a sentence difficult.

Let's try redrafting section 81(1) of the Conveyancing Act with the conditions and cases at the end and see if it improves things:

> The form of words contained in the first column of Part I of the Fourth Schedule, and distinguished by a number therein, [legal subject] shall imply a covenant by the mortgagor for himself or herself, his or her executors, administrators, and assigns, with the mortgagee, his or her executors, administrators and assigns, in the terms contained in the second column of the said schedule, and distinguished by the corresponding number [legal action], whenever, in any deed of mortgage which is expressed to be made in pursuance of this Act [case], or in any mortgage under the Real Property Act, 1900 [case], the mortgagor employs the form of words contained in the first column of Part I of the Fourth Schedule, and distinguished by a number therein [condition].

The language is still difficult, but at least now we know what we are talking about before we have to run off at a tangent into cases and conditions.

Today, not too many lawyers know about Coode and his rules. They couldn't imagine themselves drafting in that fashion. But there is a common structure that has the same problem for the reader as Coode's structure. It is one we probably use every day, thinking it is quite logical and simple. It is the *If … then …* structure. For example:

> If a person who has no criminal record makes an application, pays the scheduled fee, and waits for the statutory cooling off period, the Commissioner may issue a gun licence.

It is nice and logical. It follows the format for mathematical formulae. But it keeps the reader waiting for far too long to get to the action. Our sentence is much better in this format:

> The Commissioner may issue a gun licence to a person who has no criminal record, makes an application, pays the scheduled fee, and waits for the statutory cooling off period.

In that form, it is easier to follow and it is much more positive and lively as well.

Not all *if ... then ...* sentences are difficult to follow. In the example I chose, there are several requirements that a person must satisfy to get a gun licence. If there is only one condition, then an *if ... then ...* structure can be quite straightforward. Like that one.

A sentence with only one condition does not tax the reader's short-term memory too much. It gives some context first, and then the action follows. So we have:

> If it is sunny tomorrow, we can go to the beach.
> (Context/condition)   (Action),

which is easy to follow.

One exception might be when the condition is unlikely or does not apply to most people – when it is more like an exception. In that case it is probably better to put the action first and the condition last, as in:

> At 65 you qualify for the age pension, unless you are a non-resident.
> (Action)   (Condition: unlikely)

The information that contains the action comes first – it is most important to the reader – and the unlikely or mostly inapplicable condition comes last, and can be disregarded by most people.

When we have more than one condition, the sentence starts to become more difficult for the reader. Two conditions *may* not be too much to handle, but three certainly will be. When our sentence becomes complicated enough to strain short-term memory, it is time to break the sentence into paragraphs.[36]

The Australian Office of Parliamentary Counsel treats it this way:

> In drafting, you often need to put the conditional clauses first because they spell out all the facts, and the main clause would be meaningless without them. However, if the main clause is very simple and the conditional clauses are long and/or numerous, put

---

36   See p 111.

the main clause first. This way, the reader knows what it's about before ploughing through the paragraphs.[37]

I would probably quibble with the word "often" there. Certainly it depends on the individual sentence. As is frequently the case in matters of plain language, it is a question of judgment for the writer. How much complication is too much for the reader to cope with before they get to the "action" of the sentence? How much context do they need to understand it?

So that's structure: the framework on which we hang our words, and the way we arrange the paragraphs, sentences, words and thoughts in our documents. In the next chapter, we leave behind the way we put words together, and focus on the words themselves.

37   *Plain English Manual*, para 54, p 14, online version dated 11 March 2003 <http://www.opc.gov.au/about/docs/PEM.pdf >.

Chapter 7

Words

Technical terms

I said in Chapter 2 that plain language can be used to express highly technical or otherwise complex concepts far more effectively than convoluted drafting. I said that plain language writers may choose to use an uncommon or technical word in their writing if they know the readers will be specialists, who are familiar with the word.

Technical terms can be really useful for lawyers. They can be a shorthand way of expressing a complicated idea: "expressio unius" for example. It is shorthand Latin for the legal maxim "Expressio unius est exclusio alterius" – which means "the expression of one is the exclusion of the other". It refers to the doctrine that to express or include one thing implies the exclusion of an unexpressed alternative.

It is helpful for lawyers to write "expressio unius" and know that other lawyers will know all the detail that goes with it. But it doesn't help general readers. It is precise, but unintelligible to the public at large.

Using technical terms in legal writing is acceptable if the writer either explains what they mean or is sure that *all* the likely readers will be able to understand.

In fact, it is not really the technical terms that cause problems for readers of legal documents. The main problems are more to do with long sentences and unfamiliar, complex sentence structures. Using the occasional technical term will not mar an otherwise well written document

But if you suspect the technical term might cause difficulty, explain it. Better still, unless it really works well as shorthand for a long explanation that you'd have to make over and over again, don't use it at all! Your client probably only wants the facts, not technical jargon. Especially if the client needs lessons in Latin to understand it.

For example, if the point you are explaining to your client is that to specify particular items in a will might be counter-productive if you want to give more than just the specified items (because a court might restrict the gift to *only* the items that have been listed) then *say so*. Explain that there is a legal doctrine that has that effect. Don't even mention "expressio unius". It is not necessary.

There are some technical terms, though, that really are useful labels. Things like *affidavit, withholding tax, hearsay, injunction, warranty* and *subpoena*[1] that don't really have a neat alternative. There is no problem in using these words, even when they are unfamiliar to your reader, as long as their meaning is explained. Depending on the document (and the intended readers), you might even consider putting the explanation in a box alongside the text.[2]

Terms of art

I've used a separate heading for this, because lawyers are inclined to say about a word: "Ah, but that is a term of art – I can't change that". And sometimes they are right. There are some special terms, such as the word *indemnify*, that are "loaded" with meaning and might be difficult, or even dangerous to do without. Very often, though, there are alternative words that are easier and more common, and it may not be necessary to use the term of art at all.

Another example is the word *estoppel*. Lawyers often say that it is a term of art, which must be used because it is loaded with meaning. And that might be so, *if* you are pleading estoppel as part of a cause of action or making a submission to a judge, referring to the doctrine of estoppel. But if you are just referring to the *effect* of estoppel, there is nothing to stop (or estop) you from using *stop* or *prevent* instead. So, you could say:

> Because of what Mr Smith said to you at the time, the law prevents him from denying it now.

In fact in the 5th Australian edition of one of the major Australian texts on contract law, *Cheshire & Fifoot's Law of Contract*, the word *estopping* was relegated to brackets in favour of the word *stopping*:

> *Waiver, estoppel.* Statements or other conduct which suggest that a party will not terminate the contract, though entitled to do so, may

---

1   See p 176
2   See pages 281-282.

be considered as waiving the right or as stopping ("estopping") the party from going back on his or her apparent intention.[3]

A similar point has been made about the word *waiver*. Far from being a precise term of art, it seems that waiver has *too many* meanings, which makes it something of a dangerous word. In a 2008 case in the High Court of Australia, the majority judges said:

> Leading scholars have long cautioned against, even condemned, its use. Roscoe Pound, in his Foreword to Ewart's work *Waiver Distributed*, described[4] waiver as one of a number of "solving words" which are "but substitutes for thought" and as one of a number of "pseudo-conceptions" or "soft spots in what appears a hard legal crust" ... And Corbin spoke[5] of waiver as a word of "indefinite connotation" which "like a cloak ... covers a multitude of sins.[6]

Be careful, too, when using terms of art that have a different meaning for the general public. We may completely overlook the fact that although the technical meaning is familiar to us, it might be unknown to our readers, or the word may mean something quite different to them. For most readers, words and phrases such as *execute, good faith, demise, instrument, satisfaction* and *dishonour* mean something different from the meaning lawyers give to them. They might be completely misunderstood.

Just because something is a term of art doesn't mean we have to use it. If there is an easier alternative, use that. But of course we should make sure the alternative is a true alternative. It is our responsibility as lawyers to know when we must use particular words. As Professor Mellinkoff says:

> Correct use of his terms of art marks a lawyer.[7]

We must know why we are using terms of art, and any other words for that matter. The classic excuse for continuing to use old formulas and old forms and precedents is that there is a reason every

---

3   1988, 5th Australian edition, Butterworths, Sydney, para 2114. In the latest edition, the concept of estoppel has its own chapter. Unfortunately there is no plain language translation of *estoppel*, although it is described (at p 63) as an "old-fashioned word": Seddon, NC & Ellinghaus, MP, 2008, 9th Australian edition, LexisNexis Butterworths, Australia, Chapter 2, p 61.

4   Ewart, *Waiver Distributed* ("*Ewart*"), (1917) at v.

5   "Conditions in the Law of Contract" (1919) 28 *Yale Law Journal* 739 at 754.

6   *Agricultural and Rural Finance Pty Limited v Gardiner* [2008] HCA 57.

7   Mellinkoff, D, 1963, *The Language of the Law*, Little Brown, Boston, p 391.

word is there and if we alter any we take too great a risk. But if we don't know why each word is there, how much greater the risk? And how can we consider ourselves professionals? It is our job to know. If we know why we use a term of art, or a particular formula of words, then we know if alternatives do the same work.

Legal buzzwords

There is another class of words that lawyers use that isn't technical, and isn't composed of terms of art – it is more like the secret language of a club. We seem to pick it up at law school, perhaps from reading cases, perhaps from talking to other lawyers. We pepper our conversations with these odd words and phrases: expressions such as *on all fours with, cover the field, at first blush, jointly and severally, a fortiori, otiose* and *nugatory*.

Many lawyers would say that they use these expressions as a kind of legal shorthand, and that it helps them to communicate efficiently. But when you really look at the words, you see that they do not involve complex legal descriptions and that they all have equivalents in everyday language. There are no valid technical reasons for using them, but we continue to use them almost as a badge of our legal status. Even though we may recognise that they are potentially confusing for non-lawyers, it is tempting to think that there is no real harm in lawyers continuing to use those sorts of expressions among themselves.

But I wonder about the wisdom of doing that. The expressions slip too easily into our conversations with and writings to people who have not been initiated into the legal club. We have to watch that they don't set up barriers in communication. Otherwise we may find ourselves asking our friends for "further and better particulars" of the restaurant they have "jointly and severally" chosen for tonight's dinner, accusing them of "negligent misstatement" when it turns out to be dreadful, and demanding "aggravated damages" for the "nervous shock" the meal induced.

Colourful language

Lawyers do use some wonderfully colourful phrases to describe particular legal concepts. I would not suggest that we should get rid of them. Things like the *eggshell skull*, the *fertile octogenarian* (and her friend, the *precocious toddler*), the *man on the Clapham omnibus* (or in

Australia, the *Bondi tram*, or in Hong Kong, the *Shau Ki Whan tram*). Then there is the *snail in the ginger beer bottle*, and the verb to *Mirandise*[8] (or should it be *Mirandize?*). And even though that latter one is really only used in the United States, Australians, Britons and others can still be *Marevaed*[9] or even, perhaps, *Anton Pilleried*.[10]

These colourful expression are not only fun, they also help to make legal principles easier to remember. They are descriptive and they enliven legal communication.

Word strings

How we lawyers love to use words. They are our tools of trade. But how difficult we find it to use only one word if we can use two. Or three. Or more.

It isn't that we're naturally long-winded, or that we like using paper. It is just that we are afraid to leave anything out. It is our job to imagine all the possibilities and make sure that they are covered. So we pile up words to cover each individual case.

But that can be dangerous.

I've already mentioned the "expressio unius" rule.[11] There is also the "ejusdem generis" rule. This operates when a document has specific words followed by more general words. The "ejusdem generis" rule restricts the meaning of the general words to the same class or category as the specific words. For example, "My toolbox, my tools, and my workbench and the other things in my garage" may not include my car, because the general words may be interpreted as referring only to things in the tool/workbench category.[12]

---

8   *Miranda v Arizona* 384 US 436 (1965).
9   *Mareva Compania Naviera SA v International Bulk Carriers SA* [1975] 2 Lloyd's Rep 509.
10 *Anton Piller KG v Manufacturing Processes Ltd* [1976] 1 Ch 55. However, under the Civil Procedure Rules introduced in England and Wales in 1998, Mareva injunctions became "freezing orders" and Anton Piller orders became "search orders". Australia has followed suit. See Federal Court Rules, Orders 25A & 25B and Uniform Civil Procedure Rules 2005 (NSW), Rules 25.11 & 25.19. But judges are still in the habit of using the terms "Mareva" and "Anton Piller".
11 Meaning explained on p 129.
12 The New South Wales Court of Appeal has held that using the *ejusdem generis* rule in statutory construction is rarely justified: *Deputy Commissioner of Taxation v Clark* [2003] NSWCA 91 at [127].

In both these cases, the writer would have been better off avoiding the specified items, and leaving the general description to stand on its own. "Everything in my garage" is quite clear on its own and doesn't attract any strange rules of construction – although the writer should probably also check everything that's in the garage, and maybe specify a time at which those items are to be counted.

The alternative, to get around both the "expressio unius" and the "ejusdem generis" rules is to use a phrase like "including, but not limited to", which shows that the list is not meant as a complete one. This works, but it is the word string that caused the problem and so it would be better to leave out the word string and rely on some suitable general words, as long as they are clear and precise. Lists of words can be trouble, unless you are absolutely certain that they are complete.

But is also important to bear in mind that both of these rules are merely canons of construction that courts use to help them interpret a document if it is ambiguous or unclear. If the intention of the parties or the legislature is clear from the document or law, it is not necessary to apply the rules of construction.[13] So there is no need use the phrase "including, but not limited to" as a magic incantation in every document that contains a list. Use it only if your list is (possibly, or intentionally) incomplete.

Synonyms

Even worse are strings of synonyms. If they really are synonyms, the string of words can be avoided altogether. One word should do. One of my favourite strings of synonyms is the magical phrase:

> release remise and forever quitclaim unto …

It is amazing how many times that ancient phrase crops up in modern release documents. Of course, *release* does exactly the same work in one word.

Often these synonym strings come in pairs ("doublets") or threes ("triplets"). Professor Mellinkoff has explained how this came about.[14] When French, which used to be the language of the law, declined and English took over, lawyers and others were reluctant to choose between two words, and sometimes kept both. So we have:

13 The High Court of Australia has confirmed that "expressio unius" is not automatically applied. See *PMT Partners Pty Ltd v Australian National Parks and Wildlife Service* (1995) 184 CLR 301 at 311 and 320. See also Chapter 12.

14 1963, *The Language of the Law*, p 121 and following pages (cited at note 7).

fit and proper
free and clear
goods and chattels
had and received
keep and maintain
save and except
will and testament.

Mellinkoff says that doubling became a habit and we now have doublets where both words came from Old English:

each and every
from and after
have and hold

to name just a few.

Sometimes Latin got into the act as well. And so, at the end of the 20th century, we still have the doublets – and the triplets:

give devise and bequeath
null void and of no effect
rest residue and remainder
remise release and quitclaim.

Robert Dick describes this as killing one bird with three stones.[15]

This problem is simply another example of what happens when writers do not select their words with care, but just follow the old formulas. They assume that there must be a reason for using two or three similar words.

As I said before in the context of terms of art, it is a lawyer's responsibility to know when to use particular words. If a word adds nothing, we shouldn't use it.

Rarely are two similar words needed, much less three. Rather than assuming that more than one word is needed, and straining to find reasons why one word is not enough, we should make sure we know the limits of the words we use. We should select additional words only if they really add to the meaning.

For a list of some of the doublets and triplets where the second and third words are probably unnecessary, see the lists set out in Dick's book *Legal Drafting in Plain Language*.[16]

---

15   1995, *Legal Drafting in Plain Language*, 3rd edition, Carswell, Toronto, p 128.
16   Same work, pages 127-129.

Word clusters

There is another way that lawyers (and others) pile up words. They usually do it at the beginning of a sentence, when they are circling around and winding themselves up to say what they have to say. It is the "word cluster" – a kind of throat clearing ritual. Here are some examples:

It is important to note that …
It should be remembered that …
We should point out that …
At this point in time …
Before we answer your question it is necessary to refer to …
You should take great care to ensure that …
We refer to previous correspondence and now advise as follows …
Having regard to (or notwithstanding) the foregoing …

All of these are meaningless and could be deleted. They are just a cascade of words that don't mean anything, or to the extent they do, are so insincere or such a familiar formula, as to be practically worthless. They are simply a waste of time and effort, both for the reader and the writer.

Archaic words

We all know what these are and we know we shouldn't be using them. If they aren't technical terms and they aren't terms of art, that is, if there is no reason to cling to the archaic language, then why do so? The only possible reason is habit. It isn't much of a reason, is it? Especially when it can interfere so drastically with our ability to communicate with non-lawyers.

All you need to do to make a list of archaic words is picture in your mind's eye the bare bones of a deed, and write down the words in the deed that you never use in everyday speech. Here are a few favourites:

hereinafter, witnesseth, these presents, the premises (in the sense of "the matters") hereby, herein, herewith, hereafter, heretofore, abovementioned, aforesaid, in witness whereof, the day and year first hereinbefore written, hereunto, unto and upon.

They really speak for themselves, don't they? Many of them, such as *heretofore, hereinafter, abovementioned* and *aforesaid* are imprecise. For instance, what precisely does *abovementioned* or *aforesaid* refer to?

Where is *above*? Where is *afore*? The "time" words, such as *heretofore* and *hereinafter* have a similar problem. I'll deal separately with that in Chapter 9.

There are perfectly good alternatives for all of them.

Then there are *whatsoever, wheresoever, whosoever* and *howsoever*. These words are archaic too. We rarely see them outside legal writing. Other writers use them – if they use them at all – only for emphasis. In or out of legal writing they rarely, if ever, add meaning.

Compare, for example, these two definitions of "Secured Property". The first is a shortened variation of the classic mortgage definition :

> "Secured Property" means all the assets and undertaking of the Mortgagor whatsoever and wheresoever situate

and

> "Secured Property" means all the assets and undertaking of the Mortgagor.

Is there a difference? If there is, what is it?

Unfortunately, in legal writing many words that might be useful have been overused and abused and have lost much of their impact. But if, like the archaic words I have listed, they have lost most of their impact *and* their meaning, we should not be using them.

Many legislative drafters have long since abandoned these archaic words. Unfortunately, they still seem to pop up in private documents. Perhaps this is due to our reliance on forms and precedents, which still contain archaic language. If so, even if there is no time for us to review all our old forms and precedents, we should at least make time now to search for and destroy all the archaic words.

Definitions

Words pose a particular problem for lawyers because their meanings can change. Lawyers are concerned with making their writing last, and making sure it reflects the intentions of those involved at the time of writing.

One of the ways that lawyers try to keep words under control is by using definitions. A good proportion of the documents that lawyers write (and even some letters) have definition sections. If there isn't a separate section for definitions, there'll probably be some definitions scattered about the text. Most Australian legislation has a definition section at or near the beginning.[17]

These definitions do several things.

1. They enable the writer to use a convenient shorthand label for complicated concepts, so that the writer doesn't have to repeat the long explanation each time the writer wants to use the concept. (For example, "'Tax Act' means the Income Tax Assessment Act 1936 (Commonwealth) as amended" or "'Land' means the land situated at 44 Northern Highway, North Beach, New South Wales, and described in certificate of title volume 4444 folio 555").

2. They can clear up ambiguity by allowing the writer to give details of what was meant by a particular word (for example, "'Stock' means all the stock in the factory at the close of business on 30 June 2009").

3. They can also clear up ambiguity by allowing the writer to specify one of several common meanings (for example, "'month' means calendar month").

4. They allow the writer to be intentionally flexible about what a word means (for example, "'Business Assets' *includes* the plant, fixtures, fittings and stock of the Business").

5. They allow the writer to stretch the word a little to include things that would not usually be encompassed in the normal meaning of the word (for example, "'sell' includes offer to sell").

The one purpose that lawyers rarely use a definition for is the dictionary-type definition. The one that tells us what an unfamiliar word means.

Rarely do we write in our documents that "'writ of execution' means a document issued by a court under its own seal, commanding a sheriff or bailiff to take the property of a debtor to satisfy what the debtor has been judged liable to pay". It would be most unusual to see a definition like "'scheme of arrangement' means an arrangement made between a company and its creditors or shareholders, which is

---

17 But not all – in Australia, older Acts had the definitions at the end, and the Income Tax Assessment Act 1997 has its "Dictionary" at the end of the Act. See p 144.

approved by the court under section 411 of the Corporations Act 2001, to enable the company to reorganise its affairs".

Now of course I'm not suggesting that we should use the definition section of the documents we write to explain to the lay person all the unfamiliar or technical terms we use in the document. As I said before,[18] there is no need to explain all the legal ramifications of a document *in the document itself.* I am just making the point that we lawyers use definitions in a different way from the way some of our readers might expect. That is why I do not favour the technique of using the word "Dictionary" for a definitions section. Generally the definitions are not the ones you would find in a dictionary.

We can see this in the long title of the Acts Interpretation Act 1901, an Australian Commonwealth law. It is: "An Act for the Interpretation of Acts of Parliament and for Shortening their Language".

What does that tell us about the way lawyers use definitions?

It tells us that lawyers use definitions more for their own convenience rather than for their readers'. Definitions can allow them to use a kind of shorthand in their documents. But what it means for readers is that they have to keep flicking back to the definition section to see what particular words might mean, and then try to keep all those meanings in their mind as they read the whole document.

This process is sometimes made even harder in the documents that don't use any kind of signal (like capital letters, for instance) to point out which words have a special meaning. Yet lawyers don't often see this as a defect in their writing style. Perhaps that is because they see that it is economical to use definitions – they can use fewer words but still be as precise.

Lawyers are often happy with a document that begins or ends with scores of definitions – especially if it means that the rest of the document is very short. A document like that is almost invariably unreadable. But the lawyers who draft like that don't see the unreadability as a problem, perhaps because they prize the brevity it gives them in the main clauses of a document.

But with definitions, we should remember that the longer way round is sometimes the shortest way out. Even though definitions are a useful way of shortening a document, they can often interfere with the flow of meaning in a sentence. The aim is not to use definitions to create a "code" that the reader must know by heart to read a document.

---

18   Page 91.

For example, a sentence like this:

> The Covenantor is liable for the Primary Obligations under any Secondary Security except the Excluded Obligations.[19]

conveys no concrete meaning on its own. We have to look up four definitions to understand it. But if those defined words are not often repeated in the document, it would have been better to forget about defining them altogether. Not defining them might mean we have to pay more attention to drafting the main clause, to make sure that the information is manageable and clear. But then the main clause will be meaningful on its own.

A few pointers

Means and includes

In the examples of definitions I gave, some used the word *means* and some used the word *includes*. Using the word *means* in a definition limits the meaning of your defined word to the meaning you give it. The defined word means *only* what you specify and nothing else. Look at the examples of definitions on page 138. Examples 1, 2 and 3 are quite definite. The defined word means only one thing.

Using the word *includes* in your definition leaves your definition open-ended. You have not closed off your definition. The defined word means what you've described, *and* anything else that the defined word would normally mean.

In the first example I gave of an "inclusive" definition (example 4), the plant, fixtures, fittings and stock of the Business are all "Business Assets", but other things might also be Business Assets as well. Maybe the books and records of the business, for example. The writer didn't want to close off the definition so it could include things that weren't specified.

Of course, this looseness can create difficulties as well: what if the writer didn't want the book debts of the business to be included. Would they be? What about the leased assets? Are they included? You need to be sure that your inclusive definition won't work against you.

Sometimes you see a definition that mixes both *means* and *includes*. For example:

---

19   Defined words indicated with a capital letter.

"Company" means ABC Limited and includes its employees.

The writer wanted to be definite, and then extend the definition a little. This method works well if you use it correctly (as in "*means* X and *includes* Y"), but it should never be used in the "*means and includes* ..." format (as in "'Company' *means and includes* ABC Limited"). As you can see, the word *includes* there did no extra work and was only confusing. It leaves the reader querying. Did the writer mean to say that Company only meant ABC Limited? Or could it mean something else? It is not clear.

Once only definitions

Never define a word or phrase if you only use it once. If you define a word or phrase and then use it only once, you don't need to use a definition at all. Put the full details in the text, where the reader needs it. Don't impose a definition on the reader unless it is going to be helpful.

Misleading definitions

Don't define so as to mislead the reader. Try to choose a label that is consistent with the full definition, so that the defined word can sensibly stand in the place of the full definition. There was a good example of a misleading definition in the New Zealand Poultry Act 1968,[20] which said in section 2:

> For the purposes of this Act "day old poultry" shall be deemed to be any poultry of an age of 72 hours or less.

Or take a definition like "'Furniture' includes computer equipment". You might find it in a business sale agreement. Most people would not automatically assume that the word "Furniture" would be used to include computer equipment, so when they see the word "Furniture" in the text, they probably won't even bother to check the definition. They will assume it means the things that people normally speak of when they use the word "furniture". The writer should have chosen a better label, like "Movable items", for instance, which at least is flexible enough to include both concepts. In fact in this case, it probably would be clearer to refer to the computer separately.

---

20   Repealed in 1993.

Useless definitions

Don't define things that are obvious. For example, "'Animal' includes dog". Was there ever any doubt? Or "'Agreement' means this agreement". That's a common one, and people persist in using that definition because they say there might be more than one agreement referred to in any document. They forget that whenever they refer to "this agreement", they *write* "this agreement"! And if they have to refer to a different agreement, they describe it, either by using its name and perhaps its date, or in terms of its function.

Elegant variation

This is an expression that is used to describe the way writers can vary the words they choose to avoid repeating themselves. This is most often done in fiction writing to make the writing interesting and lively. The writer selects many different words for similar concepts. The classic example is all the different ways of saying *said: replied, asked, cried, shouted, sighed* and so on.

There is no place for elegant variation in legal drafting. We are in the business of being precise and so if we choose to use a word to refer to a particular concept, we should continue to use it whenever we refer to that concept. Otherwise we deceive our readers.

We should make sure that if we refer to a person by their name – even if we haven't used a definition – we *always* refer to them by that name. For example, if we are talking about Mr Smith and the proceedings he is taking, we should not suddenly call him "the plaintiff" or "the appellant". The reader may not be used to that sort of terminology and might think that we are now referring to someone else. It is clear to lawyers, because we know that as soon as the proceedings (or the appeal) comes to court Mr Smith will "become" the plaintiff (or the appellant). But our client may not know that. To our client, his name is Mr Smith, we called him Mr Smith at the beginning of the document, and Mr Smith he should remain.

Confusing labels

When you are choosing your labels for the words you are defining, don't choose confusing ones. Even lawyers mix up similar words like *lessor* and *lessee, mortgagor* and *mortgagee* and *chargor* and *chargee*. Try to find something less confusing, like *landlord* and *tenant* or *borrower* and *lender*. Or better still, use the parties' names, in a shortened version if necessary. Remember that readers don't want to have to keep checking the front page to find out who's who. Give them some help so they can keep the parties' names in their minds. But be careful not to make the names themselves too cryptic. If you use abbreviations for company names, don't make them too similar. For example if ABC Limited sells land to ABC Holdings Limited with finance provided by AIBC Limited and leases it to ABCD Pty Limited, you begin to get an alphabet soup.

Have another look at some of the other labels you use. What about something like *vendor* and *purchaser*? They are very familiar words to lawyers, but some readers would say that *vendor* is an unfamiliar word: it has the ring of an icecream seller about it. The English Law Society has obviously recognised this problem: in the 1990 version of their *Standard Conditions of Sale of Land* they decided to start using the terms *buyer* and *seller* instead. This document is now in its fourth edition (2003), and retains those terms, despite some initial resistance. A British colleague[21] told me that more than once, early on, he had seen a special condition added to the Standard Conditions that read:

> In this contract, "Seller" shall mean "the Vendor",

but now he says the terms *buyer* and *seller* are entrenched.

Too many definitions

As I have mentioned, nothing is more tiresome in a document than being confronted with scores of definitions, all appearing in the first clause of a document. Not only are we forced to read all the definitions before we get to the main point of the document, so they make little sense until we get the gist of the document, but we are also forced to keep flipping back and forward to check the definitions to decode the message.

Of course, definitions can be extremely useful and without them documents would be much longer. But if we want to write in plain language, we must balance that advantage against the disadvantage that the reader suffers when faced with a very long list of definitions. Finding that balance is most difficult for a writer of a long and complex document, but here are a few suggestions to soften the blow.

---

21 Mark Adler, author of *Clarity for Lawyers*, 2007, 2nd edition, The Law Society, London.

- Put the definitions at the end of the document, but clearly mark the defined words, each time they appear, with a sign that shows they are defined (I'll mention this again shortly).

- Make sure you've used each defined term more than once. If not, don't use the defined word – put the concept directly in the text.

- Look at the defined words you've used only twice or three times. Would it be easier on the reader if you abandoned the defined term and put the concept in the text? Even if it makes the document slightly longer, it could end up being easier to read.

- Have you defined anything that is obvious? If so, cut the definition out.

- Make sure you have no definitions *within* definitions. That is beyond the pale!

Where should the definitions go?

In modern statutes, the definitions have usually (though not always) appeared at the beginning. In documents, some writers put the definitions at the beginning and some at the end. Where is best?

The prime rule of plain language – consider your reader – would tell us that they should go at the end, because the definitions are one of the "technical" parts of the document. They are detail. The detail is important for our full understanding of the document, but not vital to our first reading of the document when we want to find out the basics of the transaction. We need to use the definitions to understand the document properly, but we can't use them properly until we know what the transaction is all about.

If the definitions are at the end of the document, then we get to them when we've got through the document. Then we are ready for the detail.

That was the view of the Australian Tax Law Simplification Project team, working in the 1990s. It considered definitions to be "mechanical" provisions. The team gathered together those definitions that are used regularly throughout the Act and placed them in a Chapter called "Dictionary" at the end of the Act.[22]

---

22 Section 995-1 of the Income Tax Assessment Act 1997. See also Tax Law Improvement Project, 1995, Information Paper No 2: *Building the New Tax Law*, Australian Government Publishing Service, p 13.

The Corporations Law Simplification Project team, also working in the 1990s, suggested another possibility: publishing the definitions in a separate volume. That way, readers could look up a definition and at the same time keep the page of the relevant section open.[23] This seems a very practical benefit – but of course it is only feasible for reasonably long laws or documents, and it does not work in the same way if the Act is viewed on a computer screen.

It is important, though, that we warn our readers that some words have special meanings and they can find them in the definition section. Traditionally, this has been done in private documents by using a capital letter for each defined term. In statutes, though, this has not always been the case. Failing to warn people that a term is defined allows people to miss defined terms and so it is not a good drafting practice.

But are capital letters a good enough symbol? I think not. Capital letters are used for another purpose: for proper nouns. So we risk misleading people into thinking that the proper nouns are defined or that the defined words are proper nouns. And there is another problem: lawyers (and others) love to dignify words by giving them a capital letter. So we have Directors and Companies and Partners and Shareholders and even Shares and Loans and Mortgages. More confusion! Are they defined or aren't they?

Clearly we should be using another signal.

The Law Reform Commission of Victoria suggested that italics or bold type, combined with a footnote on each page referring the readers to the definition might do the trick.[24] When they came to their report on the structure and format of legislation[25] they actually adopted the practice of marking the defined term each time it appears with a "plus" symbol (+) to show it is defined, with a corresponding footnote pointing the way to the definition section. *And* the first time the defined word appears it is put in italics to alert readers to the special meaning, and footnoted with the whole definition at the foot of the page.

---

23   Corporations Law Simplification Task Force, 1995, *Drafting Issues: Organising the Law*, p 6. However, as enacted in the Corporations Act 2001, most definitions appear towards the beginning, in the "Dictionary" in section 9, and some appear at the beginning of the chapters, parts, divisions, subdivisions or sections to which they relate (see Corporations Act 2001, section 7).

24   1987, Law Reform Commission of Victoria Report No 9, *Plain English and the Law*, p 55.

25   1990, Law Reform Commission of Victoria Report No 33, *Access to the Law: the structure and format of legislation*.

The Tax Law Improvement Project used a similar system, with most defined words appearing with an asterisk and a footnote telling the reader that the word is defined in the "Dictionary" starting at section 995-1. However, there are other defined words that are not indicated by an asterisk, including those that are defined within the Division or Subdivision they are used in, and some other "basic" terms used often throughout the Income Tax Assessment Act 1997. So the system is something of a hybrid. The details of the system are explained in Subdivision 2-C of the Act. This system is now used for most Acts (apart from very short Acts) forming part of the Tax Code.

The Australian Office of Parliamentary Counsel's *Plain English Manual* has for several years specified that defined terms should be printed in bold type when they're first defined.[26]

As a direct result of the system of asterisks developed for the Australian Tax Code, from 1 May 2006 asterisks have begun to be used in other legislation. In new legislation, the legislative drafter can decided whether to use asterisks to identify defined terms. So far, this practice has been confined to quite large Acts. The drafter places asterisks in front of the first occurrence of each defined term: in each section, subsection, definition, row of a table, step in a method statement and clause in a non-amending Schedule. But, as in the Tax Code, some defined terms that are used very frequently in an Act are not asterisked, as it would be too distracting to have too many asterisks. These "non-asterisked" terms are listed in a table at the front of the Act, and they are kept to a minimum.[27]

The rewritten New Zealand tax legislation uses a different method. It alerts the reader to important definitions by putting lists of defined terms at the end of various segments of the Act.[28]

Martin Cutts considered these issues carefully in his review of the UK Timeshare Act.[29] He worried that using footnote symbols throughout the text might be "visually intrusive". So he proposed a three-part solution:

---

26   *Plain English Manual*, para 147, p 30, online version dated 11 March 2003 <www.opc.gov.au/plain/docs.htm>.

27   Australian OPC *Drafting Direction No 1.6* <http://www.opc.gov.au/about/drafting_series/DD%201.6.pdf>.

28   Income Tax Act 2007 (NZ).

29   See Cutts, M, 2000, *Lucid Law*, 2nd edition, Plain Language Commission, High Peak, England.

- The first time the defined word appears it is in italics.
- All defined words are listed in the margin of every page – and readers are directed to the definitions section.
- The definitions are grouped together and listed in one section at the end of the Act.

This system might not work too well for a long Act, with many definitions (although Martin Cutts says it would have been possible for him to include as many as 65 definitions in his margins if he'd needed to, and after that he'd consider listing only the definitions used in that particular section of the Act).[30] Even if this seems to be too elaborate a system for private documents, it should at least be possible to select one symbol that indicates that a term is defined. Whatever it is, it should be unique. So if we use capital letters for proper nouns and bold type instead of underlining, perhaps we should use something else to indicate that a term is defined.

I have tended to use an asterisk or a footnote reference because it is not a "style" applied to the word itself, and so it doesn't distract the reader too much, and doesn't make the text look too busy. I prefer to see one system applied consistently throughout the whole document, if possible. And I do like Martin Cutts' system of listing defined words in a margin. But that system may not always work. As with most plain language principles, there is no one "right" answer that applies to every document. We need to think about what works best in the particular context. Remember that the main thing is to alert the reader that they should be checking the definition.

When to draft the definitions

It is very tempting to begin drafting a document by drafting the definitions. I don't think it is good drafting practice at all.

I've already pointed out how important it is to begin with a plan. If you do that, you won't get to the definitions until you've mapped out the structure of the document and listed everything that will go in it. Then you will be better able to select and fine tune the words you will be using.

But you will be even better placed to think about the definitions when you are putting the text in place. That is the time to work on the

---

30   Private correspondence with M Asprey, 17 Nov 1995.

definitions. If you do that you will never waste time on defining words that you don't need. You also won't saddle yourself with unhelpful concepts that are hard to discard when you've been playing with them for a while. You'll only work on the concepts and words that you actually need. So working out the definitions at that later stage is much more efficient.

Now we have seen some of the problems there are with the words lawyers use. In the next chapter, we look at what we sometimes do to our words – by means of grammar – and see how it can make our writing turgid and tiring to read.

Chapter 8
Grammatical structures to avoid

About grammar and its place in legal drafting

Very few lawyers are also linguists. But they do use language all the time. That means they are using grammar all the time. Grammar deals with words, their inflexions (the variations on the root of a word that allow us to use it in different ways) and the arrangements of words.

In Chapter 2 I asked the question whether lawyers were different – whether they were stuck with having to use unusual words and strange and complex sentence structures because of the nature of the law and its practice. I answered *no* to that question. Lawyers can write as simply as other writers and still be accurate. But we all know that much legal drafting looks different from other writing. Why is that?

In the last chapter we dealt with the words that lawyers use, and there is no doubt that lawyers can use very strange words, but there is something else that can make legal writing look strange, and that is the grammatical structures that lawyers use.

Even if you don't know anything about grammar, you are using it all the time when you write. This chapter isn't intended as a grammar lesson, but I do need to explain some of the unusual grammatical structures that lawyers use, so that we can recognise and avoid them.

The future tense

Why do many lawyers slip into the future tense when they write? Why don't they write in the present tense? Why do they write:

> *Future*
> "Company" shall mean ABC Ltd.
> The Company shall sell and the Buyer shall buy ...
> This agreement shall be governed by the laws of ...
> If A shall learn that B shall have granted an easement ... (future tense followed by future perfect tense)

instead of:

Present

"Company" means ABC Ltd.

The Company sells and the Buyer buys ...

This agreement is governed by the laws of ...

If A learns that B has granted an easement ... (present tense followed by perfect tense)?

Maybe it is because they think that, as they are writing for the future, they should write about things as if they will occur in the future. But this only makes the document sound stilted. And of course, the document operates in the future, but by that time the future will be the present! So it is much more sensible to draft in the present tense.

Another concern some lawyers have is that the present tense might not cover things that happen "in the future" (after the document is drafted and signed). For example, in a provision like:

The Company indemnifies the Distributor against any loss it suffers because of claims by the Customers.

they worry that a court might allow only one claim, and only if it is a current claim at the date of the document.

That is not so.

There is a general principle of interpretation that says that the law can be regarded as "constantly speaking". This means that we can apply the relevant provision again and again to different circumstances as they arise.

This principle that the law speaks constantly was recognised long ago by Coode in the context of legislation.[1] Some jurisdictions have decided to spell it out as it applies to legislation. For example, section 8 of the Interpretation Act 1984 of Western Australia says:

A written law shall be considered as always speaking and whenever a matter or thing is expressed in the present tense, it shall be applied to the circumstances as they arise, so that effect may be given to every part of the law according to its true spirit, intent, and meaning.

The corresponding provision in the South Australian Acts Interpretation Act 1915 says:

Every Act will be considered as speaking at all times, and every enactment, whether expressed in the present or the future tense,

---

[1]   Coode, 1843, *On Legislative Expression*, set out in full in Robinson, Dr S, 1973, *Drafting*, Butterworths, Sydney, pages 392-396.

will be applied to the circumstances as they arise, so that effect may be given to each Act and every provision according to its spirit, true intent and meaning.[2]

There are similar provisions in the interpretation Acts of other countries, including Northern Ireland[3] and Canada.[4] New Zealand's Interpretation Act 1999 says:

An enactment applies to circumstances as they arise.[5]

These sections are strictly speaking unnecessary, but they do enunciate the "constantly speaking" principle quite clearly as it relates to legislation.

How does it apply to private documents?

The leading drafting commentators seem to agree that there is no doubt that the principle *does* apply to private documents: that we are safe to draft in the present tense in the knowledge that our documents can be read as "constantly speaking".

Piesse states that the trend towards using the present tense in statutes to express provisions that operate continuously, after the provisions come into force is not new, and continues:

The technique is now commonly found in both statutes and private legal documents. Both operate continuously while they remain in force. Any doubt whether a subordinate clause in the present tense would "speak constantly" throughout the operation of the instrument can be overcome by introducing the subordinate clause with *If at any time*. But this would rarely be necessary.[6]

Dick agrees. He refers to Piesse's analysis when he suggests that drafters of private documents might like to use the phrase *if at any time,* if they feel that the present tense doesn't express the time relationship that applies to the circumstances they are describing in their document. He says:

An equally effective method of ensuring correct interpretation would be to specifically insert an interpretation section at the beginning of the document. However, this is unnecessary. As an Australian authority has pointed out, the courts will hold that

2   Section 21.
3   Interpretation Act (Northern Ireland) 1954, section 31.
4   Interpretation Act, section 9.
5   Section 6.
6   Aitken, JK & Butt, P, 2004, *Piesse: The Elements of Drafting*, 10th edition, Lawbook Co, Sydney, p 67.

circumstances, conditions and stipulations expressed in the past or present and not in the future, will be interpreted as applying whenever the circumstances arose or the condition or stipulation has to be satisfied or performed.[7]

This point is also nodded to with approval by Dr Robinson, who says in a footnote to some comments he makes on the use of the present tense for conditions:

remember that documents are treated as if continually speaking.[8]

I have been unable to find any specific pronouncements by the courts that confirm that private documents are "constantly speaking", just like statutes. But perhaps that isn't surprising. It would be very difficult for a court to frame a blanket rule on that subject. After all, it does depend on the context of the document and the intention of the parties. For example, a provision such as: "I agree to sell my house to you" is intended to apply just once. But a provision like the example I gave a few paragraphs ago: "The Company indemnifies the Distributor against any loss it suffers because of claims by the Customers" must be intended to apply again and again, each time a customer makes a claim. It will always be a matter of looking at the words in their context. That is why both Piesse and Dick suggest the occasional use of words such as *if at any time*, in case things need clarifying.

Common sense, of course, and ordinary language use would say that something written in the present tense is intended to operate in the present, whenever that may be. That is certainly true for statutory interpretation.

Maxwell[9] points out that the present tense in the words of a statute will be read as indicating the present at the time the section is *applied*, not the time it was *enacted*. For example, Maxwell quotes, among others, a case in which a section enabled a minister to make an order if a school "is being administered" in contravention of the relevant law. The court held that the minister could only consider the *present* conduct of the school at the time the minister was making the order, and not the past.[10]

---

7   Dick QC, RC, 1995, *Legal Drafting in Plain Language*, 3rd edition, Carswell, Toronto, pages 88-89.

8   Robinson, Dr S, 1973, *Drafting*, p 42 (cited at note 1).

9   Langan, PStJ, 1969, *Maxwell on the Interpretation of Statutes*, 12th edition, Sweet & Maxwell, London, p 31.

10   *Maradana Mosque (Board of Trustees) v Mahmud* [1967] 1 AC 13.

Maxwell makes these points when he is discussing the "rule of literal interpretation". His point is that the literal meaning of the present tense is that it applies to the present – when the words are being interpreted. I discuss the principles of legal interpretation in Chapter 12. These days it comes down to this: if the context allows, and it is consistent with the objective intention of the parties, the present tense in a private document applies to the time it is read, and each time it is read.

All this demonstrates that there is no need to anticipate the future by drafting in the future tense. The present tense is not only adequate and appropriate, but also leads to simpler sentence structure and easier comprehension.

The principle that the law constantly speaks is also important to remember when we draft provisions that relate to time. I deal further with this in Chapter 9.

One other thing before we leave the topic of the future tense: lawyers like to use the word *shall* not only to express the future, but also in one of its special senses – to express an obligation. This is the "imperative" sense of *shall: shall* as a command. If lawyers want to use the imperative *shall* and also draft in the future tense, things can become very confused indeed. It is better to avoid those problems by drafting in the present tense.

It is also possible to avoid the imperative *shall* altogether, as we'll see in Chapter 11.

The passive voice

The difference between the next two sentences illustrates the difference between the active and passive voices:

> *Active:* The lawyer sat on a chair.
> *Passive:* A chair was sat on by the lawyer.

See how the active is more direct, more lively, less complicated (and shorter) than the passive? The structure is simple: subject, active verb, object, rather than object, complex verb, subject. The subject of the sentence is the "actor" – the person acting (which is the lawyer) and the object (which is being "acted on") is the chair. The structure is simplest if the actor-subject comes first. The vast majority of all writing[11] follows that formula: subject verb object. It is therefore the easiest word order for us to grasp when we read.

Yet lawyers seem to love the passive. Here are a couple of common examples of the passive voice from legal writing:

Shares may *be* issued *by* the Directors.

Application must *be* made *by* the Tenant to the Landlord in writing.

These two sentences can be rewritten in the active voice as:

The Directors may issue shares.

The Tenant must apply to the Landlord in writing.

The subjects, who do the action, come first, and the objects, who have something done to them, come later.

But this guideline is not an absolute rule against using the passive voice. Occasionally we might want to use the passive for a particular reason. For example:

- if we do not have a subject: we do not know (or do not wish to state) who is doing the action, as in:

    Trespassers will be prosecuted.

    The victim was robbed in the park.

In each case the only possible structure is the passive; or

- if it is more important to stress something other than the subject of the sentence, as in:

    Even though it was late, the notice was *served*.

    To acquit the accused, the jury must believe the accused's alibi. The *alibi* must be confirmed by the evidence.

One way to recognise the passive voice is by using the *be/by* test: look for some form of the verb *to be*, and then the preposition *by*, as in these examples:

You must *be* seen *by* the Dean.

The witness *was* called *by* the defence.

But this test does not work for sentences that do not have a subject, as in:

Trespassers will *be* prosecuted.

---

11   In English, and in many (but not all) other languages.

Subjunctive mood

This structure isn't much of a problem, simply because the subjunctive mood is not used very often, even by lawyers. But it still occasionally crops up in legal documents. Some of us use it without being aware that we are doing so, and without knowing what its function is.

The subjunctive mood is another form of the verb. It is used to express a wish, a command, a hypothetical circumstance or an anticipated event. Its use is rare now – and has been rare for many years, except for a few specific examples. Here are some. You can see the unusual verb inflections reflecting the fact of the subjunctive mood.

> God *save* the Queen!
> If I *were* you …
> *Come* Monday, I'll be gone.
> I suggest that he *leave*.
> I move that standing orders *be* suspended.
> If the court finds that the evidence of the witness *be* false …
> If it *should appear* to the court …

These uses still crop up in speech and writing, but there's no telling how long the subjunctive will last. Most grammarians seem to agree that the subjunctive is dying, even though a few examples live on in some parts of the world, but some suggest there is a last-minute revival coming from America.[12] Some of the examples I have given will probably stay around longer than others, but the last three, which are the sort we are most likely to encounter in legal drafting, could easily be rewritten in the indicative mood (which is the one we normally use in everyday speech and writing) as:

> I move that standing orders are suspended.
> If the court finds that the evidence of the witness is (or was) false …
> If it appears to the court …

It looks a little less formal that way, and is a more natural form for most readers.

---

12   See the comments of Greenbaum and Whitcut (eds), 1987, *Gowers's The Complete Plain Words*, 3rd edition, Penguin Books, London, pages 138-139. See also the (as yet) unpublished paper "International Trends in Style and Usage" presented by Professor Pam Peters at the PLAIN 2009 conference, 17 Oct 2009, Sydney, Australia <http//www.plainenglishfoundation.com>.

Negatives

It is easier to read something that is written in a positive way. In other words, it is not as easy to read something that is not written in a positive way.

Do you see the difference?

Of course, as lawyers we deal with negatives all the time: some things can only be expressed in the negative. For example, some of the ten commandments would be pretty strange if they were expressed as positives. Imagine the 6th and 8th commandments:

6. You must keep everything alive.
8. You may only keep what you have rightfully acquired.

The 7th, on the other hand, has a nice ring to it in the positive:

7. Always be faithful to your spouse.

A negative statement can often be rewritten as a positive statement and that usually makes it easier to comprehend. For example:

The Secretary may not register shares without the consent of the Directors.

could be rewritten as a positive statement:

The Secretary may only register shares with the consent of the Directors.

May not and *may only*

The sentence:

The shareholders may not transfer shares to persons who are not shareholders unless the Foreign Investment Review Board has approved the transfer.

is even more difficult, because it already has a negative in it that is difficult to make into a positive. But we can make the first negative into a positive, so that the sentence becomes:

The shareholders may only transfer shares to persons who are not shareholders if the Foreign Investment Review Board has approved the transfer.

It is often a matter of giving permission to those who follow the rules, rather than denying it to those who break them, as in the example:

Persons without a licence may not …

which could be rewritten as:

Only persons with a licence may …

The words *may only* were considered in 1995 by the High Court of Australia, in a case involving legislation that set a time limit for taking action. So we have authority from the High Court for the proposition that when the words *may only* are used in a statute, they mean exactly what they say. In *David Grant & Co Pty Limited (Rec Apptd) v Westpac Banking Corporation*,[13] the High Court was considering provisions of a statute (section 459G(1), (2) and (3)) which read:

(1) A company may apply to the Court for an order setting aside a statutory demand served on the company.

(2) An application *may only* be made within 21 days after the demand is so served.

(3) An application is made in accordance with this section *only if*, within those 21 days: …[14]

The court found that the word *only* in that context means what it says – that it excludes all other possibilities. Justice Gummow said:

The force of the term "may only" is to define the jurisdiction of the court by imposing a requirement as to time as an essential condition of the new right conferred by section 459G. An integer or element of the right created by s 459G is its exercise by application made within the time specified … it is a condition of the gift in subs (1) of s 459G that subs (2) be observed and, unless this is so, the gift can never take effect. The same is true of subs (3).

This consideration gives added force to the proposition which has been accepted in some of the authorities that it is impossible to identify the function or utility of the word "only" in s 459G(2) if it does not mean what it says, which is that the application is to be made within 21 days of service of the demand, and not at some time thereafter and that to treat s 1322 as authorising the court to extend the period of 21 days specified in s 459G would deprive the word "only" of effect.[15]

The words *may only* appear elsewhere in the corresponding statute – it is now the Corporations Act 2001 (Cth). Section 588FF(3) says:

13   (1995) 184 CLR 265.
14   Emphasis mine.
15   (1995) 184 CLR 265 at 277.

An application under subsection (1) may only be made:

(a) within 3 years after the relation-back day; or

(b) within such longer period as the Court orders on an application under this paragraph by the liquidator within those 3 years.

In each of *Greig v Stramit Corporation Pty Limited*,[16] *Star v National Australia Bank Limited*,[17] *BP Australia Ltd v Brown*,[18] and *Horne v Deputy Commissioner of Taxation*,[19] the courts of various Australian states have applied the reasoning of the High Court in *David Grant* to construe *may only* in section 588FF(3) in the same way: you can *only* apply in the relevant period. Other sections of the Act, giving the court a discretion to extend the time for doing things, do not apply.

Similarly, section 1317HD of the Corporations Law 1989 (Cth) (as it then was) used the words *may only*. In a 2008 case, *Newtronics Pty Limited (recs and mgrs apptd) v Gjergja*, the Victorian Court of Appeal also applied the reasoning of the High Court in *David Grant*, and held that when that section said "proceedings may only be begun within six years after the contravention", it excluded any right to extend the time.[20]

Double negatives

One negative is difficult enough, but two negatives are worse. The US Securities and Exchange Commission, normally praised for its efforts to introduce plain language to the securities industry, blotted its copybook with a double negative. It approved a rule that specified when lawyers who notice that their client companies are breaking securities laws have to report them to the authorities. The relevant part of the definition within the rule reads:

Evidence of a material violation means credible evidence, based upon which it would be unreasonable, under the circumstances, for a prudent and competent attorney not to conclude that it is

---

16   [2004] 2 Qd R 17.
17   (1999) 30 ACSR 583.
18   (2003) 58 NSWLR 322.
19   [2005] VSC 409.
20   (2008) 67 ASCR 468. Special leave to appeal to the High Court was refused on 11 Feb 2009.

reasonably likely that a material violation has occurred, is ongoing, or is about to occur.[21]

That sentence has many ideas going on in it. It is complicated enough already without the double negative *unreasonable ... not to conclude*. There was an earlier, simpler version that read:

Evidence of a material violation means information that would lead an attorney reasonably to believe that a material violation has occurred, is occurring, or is about to occur.

That version is not only simpler, but it is also a stricter obligation on the lawyer. But after much lobbying and discussion with lawyers and other interest groups, the SEC adopted the more complicated, more difficult to prove version.[22]

If more evidence is needed that double negatives confuse people, there is the unfortunate turn of phrase that former New Zealand Prime Minister Helen Clark used when giving the eulogy at the state funeral service for New Zealand hero and Mt Everest conqueror, Sir Edmund Hillary. She said:

Sir Ed's achievement on that day cannot be underestimated.[23]

I think it can. But it is hard to *over*estimate it. Double negatives require double thinking.

Interrupting a sentence with phrases and clauses

This sounds technical, too, but it is a really common problem for lawyers. We have so much to say and so many digressions to make that we often try to do it all too quickly in the one sentence.

Here is an example of a problem sentence:

The Tenant may, with the prior written consent of the Landlord, which consent shall not be unreasonably withheld, and which

---

21   SEC Release No 33-8185, 29 Jan 2003, *Implementation of Standards of Professional Conduct for Attorneys*, Release No 34-47276, IC-25919, File No S7-45-02, effective 5 Aug 2003. This definition is section 205.2(e) in Title 17, Chapter II, Code of Federal Regulations. See <http://www.sec.gov/rules/final/33-8185.htm>.

22   See Norris, F, "No Positives in this Double Negative", *The New York Times*, 24 Jan 2003.

23   22 Jan 2008. I heard Ms Clark say this live on television. The eulogy is reprinted at <http://www.nzherald.co.nz/nepal/news/article.cfm?l_id=509&objectid=10488154>.

consent, if it is to be given, must be given within 14 days of application, assign the Lease.

What has happened to the verb in this sentence? It has been split down the middle and several clauses have been stuck in between the auxiliary (may) and the main verb (assign). So we lose track of what it is the Tenant can or can't do until we get to the end of the sentence.

The best way to keep up the interest of the reader through all the conditions and requirements that surround the main idea of the sentence is to give the reader the verb up-front. Then they know what the sentence is about before they have to deal with the detail. So, one rewrite of the sentence would be:

> The Tenant *may assign* the Lease with the prior written consent of the Landlord, which consent shall not be unreasonably withheld, and which consent, if it is to be given, must be given within 14 days of application.

But still the sentence is not perfect, because the writer has tried to pack three ideas into the one sentence. The ideas are:

1. The Tenant may assign the Lease with the prior written consent of the Landlord.
2. The Landlord may not unreasonably withhold consent.
3. If the Landlord gives consent, he or she must give it within 14 days of application by the Tenant.

Arranged as three separate sentences, they are simpler to grasp. Depending on what else is in the document, we might need to refine this draft further. But the new arrangement makes the logic much more apparent than before.

Incidentally, there was another way we could have put the auxiliary and the verb back together in this example. We could have written:

> The Tenant, with the prior written consent of the Landlord, which consent shall not be unreasonably withheld, and which consent, if it is to be given, must be given within 14 days of application, *may assign* the Lease.

This way isn't as effective because it keeps the reader in suspense. The auxiliary and verb are together, but at the end, rather than at the beginning, of the sentence. The problem here is that the subject and the verb are still separated by too large a gap. The reader needs to know not only what is happening, but also who is doing it. These are the things that keep a reader reading. The rest are details that the reader can deal with better once the reader has the primary information needed to make sense of the sentence.

Making verbs into nouns

I like this concept because the word that describes it is an example of the very phenomenon it describes: *nominalisation*.

Lawyers, and many other writers, seem to want to make their writing sound more important by multiplying the number of words they use to say exactly the same thing. So they make verbs into nouns. They never *state*, they always *make a statement*. They never *apply*, they always *make an application*. They never *consider*, they always *give consideration to*. They never *provide*, they always *make provision*. They never *pay*, they always *make payment*.

You can see how much weaker the noun-based phrase sounds. It sounds removed, indifferent, uninvolved. The single verb sounds more active and positive. It makes the sentence more readable.

Provisos

Most lawyers know that they shouldn't use provisos. But many still do. A proviso is nearly always an afterthought. A clause is drafted, and then later the writer remembers something else and tacks it on as a proviso. Even if the proviso is not an afterthought, it *looks* like an afterthought because it is tacked on after the main statement, instead of being integrated with it.

The problem with a proviso is its tendency to put information in the wrong place: most provisos are exceptions or modifications of a statement that has just been made, and often they contradict the preceding statement. So drafting by using provisos can often mislead the reader.

The proviso-user must recognise this – at least sub-consciously – because the hallmark of a proviso is that its introductory words are often in capitals:

> PROVIDED THAT …
> AND PROVIDED THAT …
> AND PROVIDED FURTHER THAT …

The writer seems to feel the need to draw attention to the provisos, in case they are missed.

Today's computer-using lawyer has no excuse for using provisos to cope with afterthoughts. It is easy to amend the text to insert the extra material in the right place.

How can we rewrite provisos? It depends on what is in them and how long and complex they are. Here are a few hints.

- If the material in the proviso is a short statement of an exception to a preceding statement, the exception can be linked to the statement by the word *but*. For example:

  > The Lender may demand payment of the loan PROVIDED THAT it may not do so unless the Borrower has failed to make an interest payment.

  can be rewritten as:

  > The Lender may demand payment of the loan, *but* it may not do so unless the Borrower has failed to make an interest payment ...

- If the material in the proviso is really a condition, rather than an exception, the link word should be *if*. For example:

  > The Purchaser may pay the lower price PROVIDED THAT it pays on or before 1 January 2010.

  can be rewritten as:

  > The Purchaser may pay the lower price *if* it pays on or before 1 January 2010.

- If there is a series of exceptions or conditions, they are better divided up into a series of separate paragraphs, all linked with *and* or *or*, depending on whether they are alternatives or all operate together. For example:

  > The Trustee may distribute funds PROVIDED THAT it has a surplus of funds AND PROVIDED THAT the beneficiaries are over 21 AND FURTHER PROVIDED THAT no loans to beneficiaries are outstanding.

  can be rewritten as:

  > The Trustee may distribute funds *if*:
  > 1. it has a surplus of funds; *and*
  > 2. the beneficiaries are over 21; *and*
  > 3. no loans to beneficiaries are outstanding.

because all three conditions operate together. If they had been alternatives – that is, if the fulfilment of only one condition is enough to allow the Trustee to distribute, the clause would have been rewritten like this:

> The Trustee may distribute funds *if*:
> 1. it has a surplus of funds; *or*
> 2. the beneficiaries are over 21; *or*
> 3. no loans to beneficiaries are outstanding.

To be more restrictive, the examples in the last two bullet-points can be written using *may only* in place of *may*.[24]

Other rules of grammar

There are many other rules of grammar that we know, or used to know. Many people fuss about things like the problem of whether it is acceptable to split an infinitive, or end a sentence with a preposition, or whether we should say "It is I" or "It is me" and so on. How important are they?

The first thing to bear in mind about these rules is that they can't be said to come naturally any more. Many of us were taught them and told that to break them was "bad English". Yet how often do we hear people breaking the rules and how much of this "bad English" has been written – even by our most admired writers?

It is not just a matter of being "correct". Many of these rules are slipping out of general language use. It is reaching the point where staying with the "correct" version can sound stilted, or even wrong.

The second thing to bear in mind is that many commentators on language take a flexible approach to the bending or breaking of these rules. And it is not a new flexibility. For example, in 1962, Randolph Quirk wrote:

> On points like these, where there is divided usage, we find a good deal of controversy, and much energy is fruitlessly expended in attempting to prove that one or other is "correct". Two issues which are particularly notorious in this way are illustrated in the sentences "I am sure we will succeed" and "It is me", some people being strongly of the opinion that "It is I" is the only acceptable form and that only "we shall succeed" is correct when we want to indicate the future ... it should be made clear that disputed points of this kind are small in number and that their importance has been exaggerated beyond all measure by the distorted judgment of

---

24   See pages 156-158 on *may only*.

those whose feelings run high on the subject. It is surely time we rid ourselves of the idea that *they* are what grammar is all about. The very fact that usage is divided, that we are all aware that some say one thing and some another in these disputed areas, should itself make it obvious that it is impossible to say one is "correct" and the other "incorrect". One might as well argue about whether *begin to work* is more correct than *start to work* or whether a plain tie is more correct than a striped one ...[25]

Samuel Johnson, too, recognised the power of spoken language usage. He said:

The pen must at length comply with the tongue.[26]

Respected writers have lampooned the inflexible adherence to these rules. Winston Churchill said that the rule against ending a sentence with a preposition was "the type of arrant pedantry, up with which I shall not put".[27] And James Thurber had fun with *who* and *whom:*

The number of people who use "whom" and "who" wrongly is appalling. Take the common expression "Whom are you, anyways?" That is of course, strictly speaking, correct – and yet how formal, how stilted! The usage to be preferred in ordinary speech and writing is "Who are you, anyways?" "Whom" should be used in the nominative case only when a note of dignity or austerity is desired. For example, if a writer is dealing with a meeting of, say, the British Cabinet, it would be better to have the Premier greet a new arrival, such as an under-secretary, with a "Whom are you, anyways?" rather than a "Who are you, anyways?" – always granted that the Premier is sincerely unaware of the man's identity. To address a person one knows by a "Whom are you?" is a mark either of incredible lapse of memory or inexcusable arrogance.[28]

George Orwell was generous in recognising the need to be flexible in our approach to writing – even to the point of breaking his own rules. His essay "Politics and the English Language" begins with the proposition that the English language is in a bad way. At the end, he

25   1968, *The Use of English*, 2nd edition, Longman, London, pages 113-114.
26   Quoted in Zinsser, W, 2006, *On Writing Well*, 7th (30th anniversary) edition, HarperCollins Publishing, New York, p 41.
27   Quoted in Flesch, R, 1974, *The Art of Readable Writing*, revised 25th anniversary edition, Harper & Row, New York, p 163.
28   Thurber, J, 1931, *The Owl in the Attic and Other Perplexities*, Harper & Bros.

gives us six rules to follow "when instinct fails", and we are in doubt about whether to use a particular word or phrase. The last rule is:

> Break any of these rules sooner than say anything outright barbarous.[29]

In summary, we should respect the rules of grammar, but never become their slaves. And the same is true for these plain language guidelines as well.[30]

The gender problem

The gender problem in writing is this: our language doesn't cope very well with the fact that both men and women participate in society. Most of our older laws are written on the basis that laws only apply to men. Unfortunately, this is not the case.

Our private documents have traditionally followed the drafting style of our older laws, and so *she* and *her* are not often mentioned.

It is not always a simple matter to fix this problem, for two reasons:

1. our language doesn't make it easy to refer to both male and female genders together (or to neither); and
2. some people don't see this as an issue in the first place. They either consider it unimportant, or they think that attempting to deal with the problem does "violence" to the language.

I think that those who hold the second view are being overtaken by the rest of us who recognise the need for our language to adapt to fit a changing society. Language has always done this: it is hardly a radical view to suggest that it should continue to do so.

Years ago, when the word *Ms* as a form of address was new, some people said it was "stupid" and "unnecessary": that no self-respecting woman would use it because it would be a sign that she was ashamed of her marital status. The word *Ms* was often said with a sneer. These days it is the rule, not the exception, to address a woman as *Ms* if you don't know her preferred form of address.

In the future, Mrs and Miss might be considered "stupid" or "quaint" or "unnecessary".

---

29   Orwell, G, "Politics and the English Language", in 1985, *The Penguin Essays of George Orwell*, Penguin Books, London, p 365.
30   See pages 174-175.

It seems pointless to try to resist the trend to gender-neutral language. Who can tell whether their readers will be male or female? Why should we write assuming that the world is male when we risk offence by doing so? It is not always *easy* to make your writing gender-neutral, but it is always *possible*.

I have come up against the problem a few times in writing this book. I wonder if you noticed. It might help to illustrate a few of the "tricks" of gender-neutral writing if I point out those parts of the book to you.

Here are nine ways to be gender-neutral in your writing. Choose whichever achieves the most harmonious result in your context.

- *Use "he or she" instead of "he"*

  The common criticism of this technique is that it is tiresome. So is anything, if it is overused. I have been writing in this book about *lawyers* and *writers* and *clients* and *readers* who can be male or female and I have used *he or she* several times – twice in this paragraph from p 91:

  > What I am saying is that the client (or member of the public) should be able to read the document from cover to cover, if *he or she* wants to, and comprehend it as a document. The client may have questions and need to ask you to explain some things, or to give more details or examples, but the client should have been able to get through the document with a feeling that *he or she* understood all the words, if not all the concepts or the reasons why all the words were there.

  and once in a paragraph on p 100:

  > Remember, too, that you are writing a letter of advice to a client – not an essay for a university professor. Your client wants to know the answer to the question that *he or she* asked you.

  If this seems tiresome, don't forget how tiresome it is for some of us to read writing that refuses to deal with the gender problem!

- *Repeat the noun*

  For example, on p 125 I wrote:

  > putting a condition at the beginning of a sentence can create a problem for *the reader*, and if there is more than one condition, *the reader* has to keep them all in mind, while still in

> a state of suspense as to what the core of the provision is about,

rather than:

> putting a condition at the beginning of a sentence can create a problem for *the reader*, and if there is more than one condition, *he* has to keep them all in mind, while still in a state of suspense as to what the core of the provision is about.

* *Drop the pronoun*

For example, on p 131 I quoted Professor Mellinkoff, who said:

> Correct use of his terms of art marks a lawyer.[31]

Because I was quoting, I couldn't make the language gender-neutral. But if I had written that sentence, I would have dropped the pronoun and expressed it like this:

> Correct use of terms of art marks a lawyer.

Or in a case like:

> The President may, if *he* is of the opinion that …

we could rewrite it as:

> The President may, if of the opinion that …,

which avoids the problem by dropping both *he*, and the verb *is*.

* *Use something other than a pronoun*

In the example before the last one, I could have written:

> Correct use of legal terms of art marks a lawyer,

which uses an adjective to tie the *terms of art* to the lawyer.
Or we could replace the pronoun with *a, an* or *the*. For example, in a case like:

> A trustee who abuses the authority of *his* position may be replaced.

we could replace the *his* with *the*, so that it reads:

> A trustee who abuses the authority of *the* position may be replaced.

We could also replace a noun with a verb, like this:

> A lawyer who gives *his* undertaking to provide a document.

---

31   Mellinkoff, D, 1963, *The Language of the Law*, Little Brown, Boston, p 391.

becomes:

> A lawyer who *undertakes* to provide a document.

- *Write in the plural*

For example, on p 15 I wrote:

> In summary, lawyers who write in plain language try to put themselves in the reader's shoes. They think about what they are writing and what it will mean to the reader – how the reader will react and how they can help the reader to understand, and act on, what they have written.

My first thought had been to write: "in summary, the lawyer who writes in plain language tries to put himself in the reader's shoes. He thinks about …". I caught myself so quickly that that version never reached the paper. I simply converted the same words to the plural. It is not always appropriate to use the plural, but it is one of a range of options to consider.

- *Use "you" or "one"*

For example, see p 172:

> The particular solution you pick is less important than the fact that you have addressed the problem.

This could be also be written with *one* instead of *you*.

- *Change the phrasing*

If … then clauses that are gender-specific can be changed to avoid the pronoun. For example:

> If a member applies for a dispensation, *he* must do it in writing.

becomes:

> A member *who* applies for a dispensation must do it in writing.

Similarly,

> If a director decides to vote on a resolution, he must disclose all relevant interests.

might become:

> On deciding to vote on a resolution, a director must disclose all relevant interests.

- *Select neutral words*

  This book is about *writers, drafters* and *authors* – not *draftsmen* or *authoresses*. The negative implication of a word like "poetess", for example, is that she is not a *real* poet. And using the suffix *-man* can imply that women are excluded or invisible. As the Australian government *Style Manual* points out:

  > With women now routinely undertaking roles once performed exclusively by men, the use of 'man' in such titles seems out of step.

  and:

  > The principle of avoiding gender-specific occupational terms means that those that specify women should also be set aside. Thus 'actress', 'manageress' and 'waitress' are better replaced by 'actor', 'manager' and 'waiter'. The use of gender-specific modifiers, as in 'woman doctor' or 'male nurse' should only be used where the information is essential to the context.[32]

  There is almost always a perfectly acceptable alternative word. Etymological arguments about whether the suffix *-man* is a generic term for both sexes don't address the real problem, which is the question of how the reader perceives the word.

- *Use "they" with a singular noun*

  Did you notice on p 109 when I wrote:

  > The writer takes the reader through all those steps as well, whether *they* like it or not, before the writer yields up the answer?

  I used the plural pronoun *they* with the singular subject *the reader*. This is a fairly common usage in spoken English, and it is a structure that has been approved by the United States Council of Teachers of English for written usage. Before it is too quickly dismissed as "ungrammatical", we should remember that at some point in our language's past we switched our second person singular pronoun from the "grammatical" *thou* to the "ungrammatical" *you*. I wonder if there was as much justification for that "error".

---

32   2002, *Style Manual for Authors, Editors and Printers*, 6th edition, John Wiley & Sons Australia Ltd, pages 59-60.

Most people don't realise that they are already using *they* as singular pronoun, in speech and perhaps in writing. When we don't know the gender of the subject we are referring to, we might say, "If anybody wants me, tell them I'm out" or "No one can tell what lies in store for them". This usage has been recognised by the three great unabridged dictionaries of the English language: the Oxford English Dictionary,[33] Webster's Third New International Dictionary,[34] and the Dictionary of the English Language.[35] Their entries for *they* all quote this usage as far back as the 14th century. Many other dictionaries also refer to this singular use of *they*.

More than 15 years ago the Australian Corporations Law Simplification Program adopted this technique for its rewrite of the Corporations Law, and has published compelling evidence, including the dictionaries I've just mentioned, to support the move.[36] The paper supports the technique with references to dictionaries, literature, HW Fowler, research done at Sydney University and Macquarie University, legal documents and forms, and legislation already in force in Australia and elsewhere.

One of the other jurisdictions that has adopted the singular use of *they* as part of a gender-neutral drafting policy is the province of Ontario in Canada. The reasoning behind this decision has been outlined by Ontario's Chief Legislative Counsel, Donald Revell, in a paper called "'Themself' and nonsexist style in Canadian legislative drafting".[37] The article notes that they have had no negative comments from the Parliament, the press or the public about the "nonsexist" drafting policy. In fact, they say, there have been almost no comments at all. The authors of the article believe this confirms that the issue is taken for granted, even in legislation.[38]

33   (1989) 2nd edition, Clarendon Press, Oxford.
34   (2002) Merriam-Webster Inc.
35   (1987) Random House.
36   Corporations Law Simplification Task Force, 1995, *Drafting Issues: A singular use of THEY*, Commonwealth Attorney-General's Department, (1994-95) 5 *Scribes Journal of Legal Writing* 87. See also extracts reprinted in *Clarity* No 34, Jan 1996, p 29.
37   Article by Revell, D, Schuh, C and Moisan, M, originally published in *English Today* 37, Vol 10, Jan 1994 and reprinted in *Clarity* No 31, Oct 1994, p 27.
38   Same article, *Clarity* No 31, p 41.

South Africa has also adopted the technique: in the South African Constitution, section 10 reads:

> Everyone has inherent dignity and the right to have their dignity respected and protected.

Still, it takes some confidence for lawyers to "break" a grammatical "rule" like this. Some worry that their clients will think less of them for using "bad grammar". But lawyers are hardly at the cutting edge of our language's development. This technique of using the singular *they* has been standard policy for some book publishers for around 20 years. The spoken language has already moved in that direction. Written language is following. Lawyers should not lag too far behind, just because they fear being seen as ill-educated by those who believe that language cannot change.

Salutations

One of the most obvious formulas in legal and business writing that does not allow for women as participants in law and business, is the common salutation of a letter: *Dear Sirs*.

In these days when women often outnumber men in law schools it seems absurd for firms of lawyers to continue to refer to each other in this way. Several possible solutions have been tried. Some are:

- Find out exactly who you are writing to and address the letter to that person by name (for example, *Dear Ms Smith*).
- If that is not possible write to the organisation using its name (for example, *Dear Smith, Smith & Smith*).
- If that doesn't appeal, write *Dear Sir or Madam*.
- One salutation I have seen occasionally from law firm to law firm is *Dear Partners*.
- A more radical alternative adopted by one New Zealand firm some years ago is to abandon the salutation altogether and start the letter with the heading. After all, in a letter, the address appears in full immediately above where the salutation normally goes, so there is no question of confusion about the intended recipient. Now that much communication is by email (with the header also setting out the name and address of the recipient) perhaps leaving out the salutation will become the norm, especially for less formal messages.

The particular solution you pick is less important than the fact that you have addressed the problem.

In case there is anyone who still thinks this exercise in gender-neutral drafting is pointless, or merely an unnecessary cosmetic exercise, consider that the Australian government *Style Manual* devotes a whole chapter to "Effective and inclusive language",[39] and gender-neutral drafting is part of the policy of many governments, including the Australian, Victorian and New South Wales governments.

Australians were early adopters of gender-neutral drafting. In New South Wales, the Parliamentary Counsel's Office officially adopted a policy of gender-neutral drafting on 16 August 1983, making New South Wales the first Australian jurisdiction to do so. In 1994 the Office began a specific program to get rid of gender-specific language in the existing statutes. Various Statute Law (Miscellaneous Provisions) Acts have been passed to remove gender-specific language from New South Wales Acts and replace it with gender-neutral language. Gender specific language is being removed from subordinate legislation by staged repeal under the Subordinate Legislation Act 1989.

The Australian Office of Parliamentary Counsel (OPC) began a gender-neutral policy soon after, issuing its first Drafting Directions on the topic in 1984. This policy is enshrined in, among other places, the Acts Interpretation Act 1901, which no longer says that a reference to the male gender includes the female. It was amended in 1984 to say:

> In any Act, unless the contrary intention appears:
>
> (a)   words importing a gender include every other gender.[40]

There is also a section dealing with the way to refer to a *Chair* (or *Deputy Chair*) of a body. It says:

> (1) Where an Act establishes an office of Chair of a body, the Chair may be referred to as Chair, Chairperson, Chairman, Chairwoman or by any other such term as the person occupying the office so chooses.
>
> (2) If a person occupying an office mentioned in subsection (1) does not make known his or her choice of term, the person may be referred to by whichever of the following terms that a person addressing that person considers appropriate:
>
> (a)   Chair;
>
> (b)   Chairperson;

---

39   Chapter 4, which also deals with the need for writers to be ethnically and culturally sensitive (book cited at note 32).

40   Section 23.

(c)   Chairman;

(d)   Chairwoman.

The provisions are repeated for Deputy Chairs.[41] (When amending an Act that establishes an office of *Chairman*, the Commonwealth OPC has a policy of replacing that title with *Chair*.)[42]

The corresponding section in the New South Wales Interpretation Act[43] has a subsection that allows a person whose statutory title is "chairperson", "chairman" or "chairwoman" to use "whichever of those words is appropriate" for the office-holder. Again, there is room for personal preference.[44]

Drafting in gender-neutral language has been the practice of the New Zealand Parliamentary Counsel Office since the mid-1980s. Most governments in Canada had a gender-neutral drafting policy by the early 1990s. The United Kingdom Office of Parliamentary Counsel adopted a gender-neutral drafting policy in 2008 "so far as it is practicable, at no more than a reasonable cost to brevity or intelligibility".[45]

Gender-neutral drafting is more than just a cosmetic or symbolic matter. It can actually affect the way we perceive ourselves. And it can affect the way we act, or influence others to act. This point was made forcefully at a plain language conference held in Vancouver in 1992.[46] A (female) judge told the conference how, for 10 years, she had instructed juries that they should appoint a "foreman". Then one day she decided to say instead that they should appoint a "foreperson". For the first time in her 10-year experience of instructing juries, they appointed a woman.

The drafters of the South African Constitution recognised this too. In some provisions they decided to refer specifically to gender. For example, in section 86(1) they made the point that women may also hold high office:

---

41   Section 18B.

42   Commonwealth OPC *Drafting Direction No 2.1* <http://www.opc.gov.au/about/drafting_series/DD%202.1.pdf>.

43   Section 19.

44   For more on "Chairs", see Asprey, M, "A 'chair' with no leg to stand on", *Clarity* No 41, April 1998, p 9 and *Australian Style*, Vol 6, No 2, Dec 1998.

45   *Drafting Techniques Group Paper 23*, Dec 2008, p 1 <http://www.cabinetoffice.gov.uk/media/190043/gnd.pdf>.

46   *Just Language*, 22-24 Oct 1992, organised by the Plain Language Institute of British Columbia.

At its first sitting after its election, and whenever necessary to fill a vacancy, the National Assembly must elect a woman or a man from among its members to be the President.[47]

In George Orwell's essay "Politics and the English Language",[48] he expresses the view that language can influence thought. This is a view shared by Glanville Williams in his essay "Language and the Law".[49] The linguist Edward Sapir expressed the same view in 1929. He said:

> Language is a guide to social reality ... it powerfully conditions all thinking about social problems and processes ... The fact of the matter is that the real world is to a large extent built upon the language habits of the group.[50]

Another linguist, Benjamin Lee Whorf, has described language as a "vast pattern" by which a person:

> not only communicates, but also analyses nature, notices or neglects types of relationships and phenomena, channels his reasoning and builds the houses of his consciousness.[51]

If language can shape thought, then it is important not to be careless with it. We should not ignore the issue of gender in our writing. Even if gender-neutral drafting requires extra effort, it is important we make that effort. As with most things, the effort diminishes with practice.

Be flexible

That deals with the most common of the strange grammatical structures that we need to avoid if we want to write in plain language. But we must be flexible.

Nearly every grammatical structure I have criticised in this chapter can be used correctly, if we are selective. There are times when we must use the passive voice or draft in the negative. There are times when putting an adverbial clause before a verb is the most natural

47 The same technique is used in section 174(1) concerning judicial appointments.
48 Orwell, G, "Politics and the English Language" (cited at note 29).
49 (1945) 61 *LQR* 71.
50 Sapir, E, 1929, in Mandelbaum, DG (ed), 1949, *Culture, Language and Personality, Selected Essays*, University of California Press, Berkeley and Los Angeles, pages 68-69.
51 Carroll, JB (ed), 1956, *Language, Thought and Reality: Selected Writings of Benjamin Lee Whorf*, The MIT Press, Cambridge, Mass, p 252.

way of expressing a thought. If these things are done thoughtfully and sparingly they do not make our writing cluttered or unclear.

On the other hand, it is difficult to think of an occasion when using a proviso would be acceptable, or when it is proper to use masculine words to refer to females, or males and females together.

The point of all this is not to lay down yet another set of rules to be slavishly followed in preference to the old rules of grammar. It is that if we want to improve and simplify our legal writing style, we should at least be alive to all these problem areas and be aware of their effect on what we write.

We now come to consider some habit-forming words and phrases that seem to affect lawyers in particular.

Chapter 9

Legal affectations and other nasty habits

Latin

We saw in Chapter 7, in the context of technical terms, that our clients do not come to us for Latin lessons. Latin is *sometimes* a useful short-hand among lawyers, though this is less so as the years go by. And it does tend to spread into documents and letters to clients. When it does that, it ought to be translated or cut out.

The only excuse for using Latin in a letter to your client is that your client is an ancient Roman.

Of course there are some Latin phrases and symbols that have entered the English language and their meaning is well known. For example: *de facto, versus, per cent, per capita, quid pro quo, ie* and *eg*. I am tempted to add *subpoena* to this list, but for two things: the difficult spelling, and the fact that the 1999 revision of the Civil Procedure Rules of England and Wales replaced it with *witness summons*. Against this is an anecdote I heard about a witness who, when faced with a *witness summons,* asked "What's this, a subpoena?"

Plain language does not require commonly used and well under-stood expressions to be eliminated.[1] But there are others that lawyers tend to use, believing that everyone either already knows what they mean or is dying to find out. Some of the common ones are:

ab initio	*in personam*	*re*
a fortiori	*mens rea*	*res ipsa loquitur*
bona fide	*mutatis mutandis*	*sui generis*
et al	*obiter dictum*	*sui juris*
ex parte	*per stirpes*	*uberrimae fidei*
	quantum meruit	

---

1   "Is *Magna Carta* to be translated and its real name abandoned?" John Gray misguidedly asks in the preface to *Lawyers' Latin*, Trafalgar Square Robert Hale Ltd, London, new edition, 2006, p 15.

All of these expressions, and the other Latin expressions we use when we write or talk to other lawyers, can be readily translated into English, and they should be.

Case references

How automatically case references seem to flow from our lips and pens. When you read our letters you would think lawyers are not allowed to refer to cases without giving the full citation.

It is appropriate to give a full citation when one lawyer quotes a case to another. In fact, it would be discourteous not to. But when we write to or for non-lawyers, there is no need to clutter up the letter with citations. By all means refer to the case by name. It is often helpful, and even interesting to do so. But don't bother to give the client the details that would enable them to look the case up for themselves – unless of course you know they would like to do so.

The client who sees the citation will not be impressed, because they know it is your job to know these things. The client will probably suspect what we all know – that you are just putting the citation down so that it is in the file for next time you want to look it up.

Don't waste your client's time by using their letters as memo pads. Use a memo pad!

Where

This is another word that lawyers love to use in a peculiar way. To most people, *where* is a word to describe a physical or geographical location. But not to lawyers. Lawyers like to use it to describe a circumstance. Nearly everyone else writes *when* or *if* to describe a circumstance, but lawyers love *where*. Even worse than *where* on its own, is *in cases where* or *in cases in which*.

Legal drafting books have tried to teach lawyers the distinction that was made in the past between *where* and *when*, but there are problems with that distinction, and it just doesn't come naturally. Dick says that *where* may be used if "frequent occurrence of an event is contemplated", and *when* may be used if the event is only expected to happen once, or rarely. But Dick admits it is often hard to tell how often something will happen.[2]

---

2   Dick QC, RC, 1995, *Legal Drafting in Plain Language*, 3rd edition, Carswell, Toronto, p 145.

This sort of analysis ignores the fact that this use of *where* is drifting out of our language. And that drift has been recognised by our legislators. For example, in 1985 the Victorian Attorney-General directed that *where* should no longer be used as a synonym of *if* to introduce a condition.[3] The Australian Office of Parliamentary Counsel, in its *Plain English Manual*, says:

> The traditional style uses "where" to introduce a set of facts, but in common usage the word conveys the idea of place. Say "if" to introduce a set of facts. But if the event is so certain that "if" is inappropriate, use "when".[4]

Speaking of conditions, there are also those who say that the distinction between *where* and *when* ought to be kept, because they say *where* is the word that should be used for a case, and *when* is the word that signifies a condition.

It was George Coode who first formulated this idea of cases and conditions. We looked at Coode's rules in Chapter 6.[5] I mentioned then that Coode's analysis had been criticised by a several commentators, including Dr EA Driedger QC[6] and Robert Dick QC.[7] Dick has summarised what Driedger said about Coode's cases and conditions:

> there is no grammatical distinction between the case and the condition that Coode describes. Each is a clause or phrase that modifies the predicate and is joined to other parts of the sentence by a conjunction or a preposition. It is often impossible to identify a particular phrase or clause as the case or condition, using Coode's definitions.[8]

What is the point of reviving such artificial concepts?

The plain language approach has been summarised by Bryan Garner this way:

---

3   1987, Law Reform Commission of Victoria, Report No 9, *Plain English and the Law*, Appendix 1, p 45 – Drafting Manual.

4   Paragraph 86, p 20, online version dated 11 March 2003 <www.opc.gov.au/plain/docs.htm>.

5   Pages 124-126.

6   1976, *The Composition of Legislation, Legislative Forms and Precedents*, 2nd edition Department of Justice, Canada and 1982, *A Manual of Instructions for Legislative and Legal Writing*, Department of Justice, Canada, pages 3-4.

7   Dick QC, RC, 1995, *Legal Drafting in Plain Language*, p 60 and following pages (cited at note 2).

8   Same work, p 64.

The best word in stating a circumstance to which a statement relates is either *if* or *when*, the word *where* being archaic and legalistic to nonlegal readers ... One writer actually suggests a nuance between *when* and *where*, but actual usage has never reflected this distinction.[9]

Above and *below*

These words, when used in the sense of "clause 4 above" or "paragraph 6 below" are unnecessary. Perhaps they stem from the days when documents were only one page long, and there was a physical "above" and "below". Even worse, when they are used without a specific page, paragraph or clause reference (as in "see below") they are vague and unhelpful.

Any, each, every and *all*

Lawyers seem to have a fetish about these words. Most legal documents are littered with them. It looks as if the writers are afraid that unless they write *any applicant, all directors, each shareholder* and *every person,* one member of these groups will slip through the net.

Most commentators agree that the indefinite article "a" can often be used instead of these words. But sometimes it *is* appropriate to use them. For example, if you want to impose an obligation separately on each individual in a class, it is appropriate to use *each,* as in:

each applicant must complete the prescribed form.

In that example, because you wish to emphasise that there is an obligation on each individual applicant, it is best to use the word *each.* But it would have been possible to use the indefinite article instead, as in:

an applicant must complete the prescribed form.

You would have achieved the same meaning, but you wouldn't have achieved the emphasis.

Two other ways you could have achieved emphasis in that sentence are:

every applicant must complete the prescribed form

---

9   Garner, BA, 1995, *A Dictionary of Modern Legal Usage,* Oxford University Press, New York and Oxford, 2nd edition, under *where,* p 928. The writer he quotes is GC Thornton in *Legislative Drafting* (an earlier, 2nd edition, 1979).

or

     all applicants must complete the prescribed form.

But consider the effect on the reader if you *always* use *any, each, every* or *all,* when *a* would do. Emphasis is only emphatic if used sparingly.

Again, some commentators have tried to analyse when is the right time to use some of those words, and have come up with some rules. The rules stated by Dickerson[10] are:

1. Use *any* to give a right, privilege or power (eg: any applicant may complete the prescribed form).
2. Use *each* to impose an obligation (eg: each applicant must complete the prescribed form).
3. Use *no* to restrict a right, privilege or power (eg: no applicant may complete the prescribed form).

That is an interesting analysis, but it seems to me that the indefinite article does just as well. Here is my version of each:

1. *An* applicant may complete the prescribed form.
2. *An* applicant must complete the prescribed form.
3. *An* applicant may not complete the prescribed form.

Is there a difference in meaning from Dickerson's examples? If there is, I can't see it. The difference is in emphasis. That is all. So why not try to reserve *any, each, every* and *all* for emphasis?

The same, the said and *such*

These are words that are rarely seen outside legal and other "official" documents. They look strange to most readers and make writing stilted. We can replace them, or leave them out altogether. Here is what I mean:

The same:

Either replace those words with a pronoun, or leave them out and rephrase the sentence. For example, we can rewrite:

---

10   Dickerson, R, 1986, *The Fundamentals of Legal Drafting,* 2nd edition, Little, Brown and Company, Boston and Toronto, p 217.

> The property may be sold by the Executor auctioning *the same*.

either as:

> The property may be sold by the Executor auctioning *it*.

or:

> The property may be sold by the Executor by auction.

The said:

Replace *the said* with *the, that* or *those*. For example, we can rewrite:

> The stock must be counted and the price for *the said* stock is to be calculated using a unit price of $10.00.

as:

> The stock must be counted and the price for *the* stock is to be calculated using a unit price of $10.00

There can be no doubt about which stock we are pricing. When things get a little more complicated, you might be better to use *that* or *those*. For example:

> ABC Company may sell any shares the Borrower owns if the loan is not repaid on time and ABC Company may complete the transfer forms for *the said* shares on the Borrower's behalf.

becomes:

> ABC Company may sell any shares the Borrower owns if the loan is not repaid on time and ABC Company may complete the transfer forms for *those* shares on the Borrower's behalf.

There is no truth in the belief of some lawyers that *those shares* leaves doubt about which shares we are talking about. *Those* is a perfectly adequate referent, as is *that*.

Such:

The lawyer's beloved "defining" use of the word *such*, as in:

> … any such person must register an interest

can always be replaced by *the, that* or *those* or a pronoun. In that respect it is a mixture of *the same* and *the said*. The word *such* was traditionally used as a reference to a category or kind of persons or things. It can still do that job, if used carefully.[11] But less skilled writers use *such* to refer

---

11   See, Thornton, G, 1996, *Legislative Drafting*, Butterworths, London, 4th edition, p 106.

to *any* person or thing that has been mentioned before. In neither case is there a real need to use *such*. For example, take the sentence:

> Recipients of the invalid pension are not entitled to receive unemployment benefits in addition to *such* pension. *Such* recipients may apply for a supplementary benefit.

We could be said to be referring to a class of pension and a class of recipient. But we could get rid of both *such*es; we could replace the first with *the* or *that*, and the second with *those*:

> Recipients of the invalid pension are not entitled to receive unemployment benefits in addition to *the* pension. *Those* recipients may apply for a supplementary benefit.

The meaning does not change at all, and it does not create ambiguity to do without *such*.

Whereas and recitals

Using *whereas* in the sense of *but on the contrary* is not the problem. That sense of *whereas* is still in everyday use to show a contrast (for example, "He speaks fluent French, whereas I only remember a few words from my high school days").

The problem with *whereas* is its archaic use in the sense of *given the fact that*. That, and the way lawyers use it as a banner on the front of their documents, in the recitals:

> WHEREAS ...
> AND WHEREAS ...
> AND WHEREAS ...

But before we even begin to consider *whereas*, the question that we should ask is: why do lawyers still have so many recitals in their documents?

Recitals are the formal statements that come before the main body or "operative part" of an agreement. They are mostly used to set out background material.

For centuries, lawyers have used recitals in the deeds that form part of conveyancing transactions for land with common law title. There, recitals can have special significance; for example, when they give rise to a statutory presumption of the truth of matters concerning the relevant land.[12]

---

12 For example, see section 53(2) of the Conveyancing Act 1919 (NSW) and section 45(6) of the Law of Property Act 1925 (UK).

But contracts are completely effective without the need for recitals. Even deeds don't need them.[13] Yet many lawyers are reluctant to delete recitals from their documents. Some pack their documents full of facts that they think might possibly be useful, just in case they need to use them defensively. If the facts are all set out in the recitals, they say, they can use the recitals as evidence, or they can invoke the doctrine of estoppel and stop the other party to the transaction from denying those facts.

But if the facts are so important, why aren't they in the main body of the agreement? If the operative provisions are clear and unambiguous, recitals become irrelevant.[14] Even the significance of setting up an estoppel by using recitals can be overstated.[15] And modern principles of interpretation allow an investigation into the background facts surrounding a contractual transaction anyway, even if they are not recorded in the document.[16]

If we do allow that sometimes it might be useful to have some background material set out in recitals, if only to give the reader the context of the transaction, it is better to give them a more useful name for a heading like **Background**, or, better still, **Introduction**.[17]

Pursuant to

This is an expression we are so used to that we barely notice we are using it. Yet to most non-lawyers it is one of the hallmarks of legalese. Ordinary people say *under* if they mean to refer loosely to something (eg: "*Under* the law, you must put in a tax return"). Or, if they are being more specific, they say *according to* (eg: "You must build the model *according to* the directions on the box").

There is no reason why lawyers cannot do the same. We should be able to say "Under the contract, you must indemnify the Buyer against

13   Norton, RF, 1928, *A Treatise on Deeds*, 2nd edition, Sweet & Maxwell, London, p 197, citing *Bath and Montague's Case* (1693) 3 Ch Ca 55.

14   *Mackenzie v Duke of Devonshire* [1896] AC 400 at 406 per Lord Halsbury LC; *Chacmol Holdings Pty Ltd v Handberg* (2005) 215 ALR 748.

15   Feltham, P, Hochberg, D & Leech, T, 2004, *Spencer Bower: The Law Relating to Estoppel by Representation,* 4th edition, LexisNexis, London, p 196.

16   See Chapter 12.

17   In *Lewis v Nortex Pty Ltd* [2001] NSWSC 511; (2001) 10 BRP 19,035, Justice Young held that a section headed "Introduction" in a deed was the plain English version of "Recitals".

claims by customers" or "You must complete the share transfer form *according to* rule 44 of the constitution".

In fact, the Federal Court of Australia has indicated that *pursuant to, in pursuance of, by virtue of* and *in the exercise of powers conferred by* mean the same thing as *under*.[18] The Australian Office of Parliamentary Counsel agrees, and recommends using *under*, or *because of* in place of *pursuant to, in pursuance of* and *by virtue of*.[19]

Moneys and *monies*

What are *moneys* and *monies*? Are they different from *money*? To the rest of the community, *moneys* and *monies* are archaic forms of the word *money*. Yet to lawyers and bankers they are mellifluous words we won't let go of. Somehow, we think, a mortgage or a loan document doesn't sound quite right if it deals with mere *money* rather than the more abundant-sounding and richer *moneys* or *monies*.

Moneys or *monies* did traditionally have a sense of "sums of money" about it. But it is by no means clear that this will come across to the reader. It would be better, if you want to refer to "sums of money", to do just that.

The Law Reform Commission of Victoria was short and sweet on the subject of *money*. It said:

> Use the word *money*. The form *moneys* or *monies* is obsolete and should not be used.[20]

The time problem

Lawyers are always worried about time. They never have enough time to do what they have to do. They keep slipping into the future when they draft,[21] or they talk about *at this particular point in time*, rather than *now*.

So they sometimes use expressions like *at any time* and *from time to time* and even *at any time and from time to time*. They use those expressions to save them from a court holding that when they refer to an action it should be read as occurring once only. For example, they may not be content with:

---

18   *Collector of Customs v Brian Lawlor* (1979) 24 ALR 307.
19   *Plain English Manual*, p 40, online version dated 11 March 2003 <www.opc. gov.au/plain/docs.htm>.
20   1987, Law Reform Commission of Victoria, *Report No 9*, "Plain English and the Law", Appendix 1, p 59 – Drafting Manual.
21   See p 149.

> If the Bank considers that the Mortgaged Property is in jeopardy it may appoint a receiver.

They worry that writing it that way might imply that the Bank can only act once. That it has one chance to consider and one chance to act. If it blows that, they think, it can't ever rely on the clause again.

So they might rewrite it as:

> If at any time and from time to time the Bank considers that the Mortgaged Property is in jeopardy it may at any time and from time to time appoint a receiver.

But do we really need the words *from time to time* and *at any time*?

I referred earlier to the principle that the law is "constantly speaking" and said that it generally applies to both statutes and private documents.[22] But several commentators have said that we can use words like *if at any time* if there is any doubt about the application of that principle.

The key point is to use those words *only if there is likely to be any doubt* about whether the provision should be interpreted as applying more than once. Remember that the commentators agree that, generally, anything that is expressed in the present or the past will be interpreted as applying whenever the circumstances occur and whenever the obligation has to be performed or the condition has to be satisfied.[23] They only recommend the expression *if at any time* for cases where there might be doubt. Normally it is not needed. That makes sense. Otherwise we'd have to use expressions like that constantly, and risk diminishing their effect when we really do need them. So there is no need to say:

> If at any time two or more members are present in person or by proxy, attorney or company representative and entitled to vote at a meeting of the Company, there is a quorum.

We can delete the reference to *If at any time* and simply write:

> Two or more members present in person or by proxy, attorney or company representative and entitled to vote at a meeting of the Company is a quorum.

Similarly, we don't need to say:

---

22   Page 150 and following.

23   For example, see Aitkin, JK & Butt, P, 2004, *Piesse: The Elements of Drafting*, 10th edition, Lawbook Co, Sydney, p 67; Dick QC, RC, 1995, *Legal Drafting in Plain Language*, pages 88-89 (cited at note 2); and Robinson, D, S, 1973, *Drafting*, Butterworths, Sydney, p 42.

> If there is any inconsistency at any time between the special conditions attached from time to time to this agreement and the provisions of this agreement, the special conditions prevail.

We just say:

> If there is any inconsistency between the special conditions attached to this agreement and the provisions of this agreement, the special conditions prevail.

If we are sparing in our use of these time expressions, we can insert them for emphasis when the normal implication would be that the provision operated once only, as for example it might be with certain kinds of payments or the giving of unusual powers. But normally, as the commentators say, that is not necessary.

Incidentally, there is another problem with the expression *at all times*. Its misuse can lead to ludicrous results. The 5th edition of *Stroud's Judicial Dictionary* dryly pointed out one example:

> A covenant in a mining lease to work the mine "at all times", is frequently incapable of literal performance.[24]

Another good example is a clause I have seen, also in a lease, under which the tenant was obliged to "make a reasonable amount of noise at all times". One wonders what sort of noise would qualify ... perhaps a constant low hum?

Hereafter, hereinafter and *heretofore*

I mentioned these expressions earlier in the context of archaic words.[25] The problem with these three, and the other archaic "time" words, is that they are imprecise. When does *hereafter* begin? When or where is *heretofore*? Professor Mellinkoff points out that the starting point can vary. He says:

> When legislators say hereafter, it sounds as if they mean as-soon-as-we-pass-this-law, and sometimes they do. More often, the courts say they mean after-this-law-becomes-effective. And so, when a

---

24 James, JS, *Stroud's Judicial Dictionary*, 5th edition, Sweet and Maxwell Ltd, London Vol 1, A-C, p 212. Example quoted in *Clarity* Newsletter No 17, June 1990, p 9. Sadly, this observation is missing from the 6th & 7th editions, which seem to have a diminished sense of humour: Greenberg, G and Milbrook, A, 2000, *Stroud's Judicial Dictionary*, 6th edition, Sweet & Maxwell, London, Vol 1, A-F and Greenberg, D, 2006, *Stroud's Judicial Dictionary*, 7th edition, Sweet & Maxwell, London, Vol 1, A-E.

25 Pages 136-137.

statute is amended and republished, the hereafter may refer to two effective dates, one for the old part and one for the new.[26]

Hereafter is clearly so uncertain that we should avoid it altogether. The same applies to *heretofore.*

Now

Another "time" word that creates the same sort of problem (when does it start?) is *now*. It is not an archaic or difficult word, of course, but it can create difficulties in legal documents. When is *now* in a document? *Now* when I'm drafting it, *now* when you're signing it, *now* when the event we are talking about is occurring or *now* when we are in court?

We often see *now* in documents. For example in "all money" mortgages and other securities, which secure the repayment of:

all amounts now or in the future owing to the Lender

or some similar formula. The question I always ask when I see those provisions is: when is *now*? And when, for that matter, is *the future*? When does it start? When is *the past*? Is it anything that happened before we ended up arguing in court? Or was it before we began to talk about the deal? We need to be more precise.

A starting point

In each of these cases: *hereafter, hereinafter, heretofore, now, the future* and *the past,* we are creating problems for the reader and the later interpreters of the document. We should be providing the reader with a point of reference: giving them a way to measure the time.

The State of Victoria has recognised this problem in its Interpretation of Legislation Act 1984. Section 44(7) provides:

In a provision of an Act or a subordinate instrument the expression "now", "heretofore" or "hereafter" shall be construed as referring to the time when the provision in which the expression occurs came into operation.[27]

We need to give the reader similar help when we draft private documents. Give the reader a starting point to count from. If the relevant starting point is the date of the document, say so. Write "at the date of this agreement" or "after this agreement is signed by the

---

26   1963, *The Language of the Law*, Little Brown, Boston, p 312.
27   There's a similar provision in section 31(2) of the Interpretation Act (Northern Ireland) 1954.

parties", or "14 days from the date of this agreement" or "by 5pm on 30 June 2010". Be exact in your time measurements. And always give a clear starting point for any calculations.

Forthwith

Another "time" word that is most imprecise is *forthwith*. Like *heretofore* and *hereafter*, it is archaic. But it is also unclear. Bryan Garner, in *A Dictionary of Modern Legal Usage*, called it "a fuzzy word with no pretence of precision".[28] Professor Mellinkoff has traced its meanings from the Middle English, when it was *forth with*, and meant "along with, at the same time with something else",[29] through various shades of meaning, from *immediately*, through *such convenient time as the court shall judge reasonable*, and *without unnecessary procrastination or delay* to *a reasonable time*.

It is much better to specify a time limit if we can. For example, "By 5pm that day" or "By the close of business".

The word *immediately* is often suggested as a better alternative to *forthwith*. And it certainly is more common in general usage outside law, so it is more in keeping with the aims of plain language.

Piesse[30] dislikes *forthwith*, saying:

> In vernacular English, *forthwith* may be seen as having overtones of undue formality. For that reason, *immediately* is preferable.

Time and again we see statements that *forthwith* means the same thing as *immediately*. For example, in *Halsbury's Laws of England*:

> There appears to be no material difference between the terms "immediately" and "forthwith". A provision to the effect that a thing must be done forthwith or immediately means that it must be done as soon as possible in the circumstances, the nature of the act to be done taken into account.[31]

But according to *Halsbury's Laws of Australia*, their meanings are different:

---

28   1995, 2nd edition, Oxford University Press, New York and Oxford, p 372.
29   Mellinkoff, D, 1963, *The Language of the Law*, p 310 (cited at note 26).
30   Aitken, JK, & Butt, P, 2004, *Piesse: The Elements of Drafting*, p 133 (cited at note 23).
31   LexisNexis, *Halsbury's Laws of England* 45(2) (Reissue) (at 11 Sept 2009), 2 Computation of Time, 7 Construction of Expressions Limiting Time [251] Meaning of "immediately" and "forthwith".

The term 'immediately' takes its meaning from the context in which it is used … 'Forthwith' does not mean instant or immediately; an undertaking or order to the effect that something must be done forthwith means that it must be done as soon as reasonably possible, or within a reasonable time, taking into account the circumstances existing or in the contemplation of the parties at the time the agreement or order was made. Use of the term 'forthwith' in a notice may not satisfy a requirement in a deed that such notice specify a date of termination, but in certain circumstances it may constitute a sufficiently clear delineation of time within which a relevant act must be performed.[32]

The footnotes to this quotation from *Halsbury's Laws of Australia* are too lengthy to reproduce here verbatim, but the cases cited there are instructive, because they confirm that although *forthwith* does not mean *immediately*, neither does *immediately* always mean *immediately*, and the meanings of both depend on their context and circumstances.

So *forthwith* is a prime example of a word that pretends to be precise, with a time-honoured meaning, but whose meaning is actually fuzzy. The plainer alternative, *immediately*, whose meaning also depends on its context, at least has the virtue of being in more general usage. But neither has a precise, unchangeable meaning in law. If you want to specify immediacy, it would be better to avoid both words and write something like "the instant that". If you want to allow a period of time, say "within x days", and be sure to specify a starting point.

On demand

The expression *on demand* suffers the same problem. It is a "time-honoured" expression in the law, and we can find it in countless loan and security documents, but the common law tells us that a loan payable *on demand* does not actually have to be repaid the minute the demand is made.

Australian law on this question has come into line with the law of the United Kingdom[33] and New Zealand.[34] All three jurisdictions apply what is called the "mechanics of payment" test, and say that the debtor

---

32   LexisNexis, *Halsbury's Laws of Australia* (at 11 Sept 2009), 410 Time, (2) Computation of Time, (D) Construction of Expressions Prescribing Time, [410-220] Meaning of "immediately", "upon" and "forthwith".

33   *Bank of Baroda v Panessar* [1987] 1 Ch 335.

34   *Gibson v ANZ Banking Group (NZ) Limited* [1986] 1 NZLR 556.

who must pay *on demand* must have an opportunity to get funds from a convenient place. In *Bond v Hongkong Bank of Australia*,[35] the New South Wales Court of Appeal held that a guarantor who had to pay *on demand* had to be given the time to organise whatever "mechanics of payment" it needed to discharge the debt.

In Canada, the question of what is a reasonable time to make an *on demand* payment is a question that has to be determined on the individual facts of every individual case.[36] It seems that in Canada the expression has *no* meaning that can be anticipated.

The point of all this is that some of the "time" words we use in order to be precise, are actually imprecise or misleading. Often they do not mean what they appear to mean. *Immediately* doesn't always mean *immediately* – it can mean *as soon as possible*. In Australia, the United Kingdom and New Zealand, payment *on demand* may not mean immediately on demand – the mechanics of payment need to be considered.

As lawyers, it is our job to know how the courts have bent the meanings of words in the interests of justice. We must choose our words carefully, so that they accurately reflect the aims of the parties (or the legislators) *and* so that – as far as possible – readers cannot be mislead.

The best way to deal with the time problem, if you need to be precise, is to *specify a time limit* in concrete, measurable terms. Or if you are being lenient, you can use a flexible phrase like *as soon as possible* – but don't expect it to give you speed or precision. We should avoid, if we can, those words that mean something other than they appear to mean.

Amounts of time and other commodities

We lawyers also have some difficulty describing numbers and amounts – amounts of time, numbers of people, amounts of things. For example,

---

35   (1991) 25 NSWLR 286.

36   *Mister Broadloom Corporation (1968) Ltd v Bank of Montreal* (1979) 101 DLR (3d) 713 at 723; *Ronald Elwyn Lister Ltd v Dunlop Canada Ltd* (1982) 135 DLR (3d) 1; *Waldron v Royal Bank of Canada* [1991] 4 WWR 289 (BC Court of Appeal). In addition, the Bankruptcy and Insolvency Act 1992 (Canada), section 244, requires a secured creditor to give 10 days notice to the debtor before enforcing its security.

when we try to describe the number of days notice in a document like a lease, we might write something like:

> The Tenant must give not less than six months notice of its intention to terminate the lease.

What does the *not less than* do in that sentence? Does it help us with the real problem in that sentence, which is: when does the six months start and finish? No. It begs that question, and adds words that don't tell us any more than "six months" on it own told us. If you must give six months notice then you've given six months notice if you give seven months. *That* is not what is confusing about the sentence. If you want to give the reader some *real* help, tell the reader whether a month is 30 days long and so six months is really 180 days, or whether a month is counted from one day in a month to the corresponding day in the next month.

The same thing can be said if we had used the words *at least* in the last example. They too could be deleted.

Strangely enough, *not more than*, which is parallel to *not less than*, does not suffer from the same problem because those words are usually intended to prohibit the additional time or other items. For example:

> This lift is licensed to carry not more than 15 people

has a point to make, because it is when we pass the limit of 15 that trouble can occur.

But the structure *not more than* isn't easy to comprehend, and there is a plainer way to say the same thing. "This lift is licensed to carry a maximum of 15 people" is easier to comprehend, probably because it is framed in the positive, rather than the negative *not more than*.

The time between dates and times can cause similar problems. For example, if we can take up an option to purchase land *between* 30 June and 31 December, can we take up the option on 30 June? Or on 31 December? Is *from* 30 June *to* 31 December any clearer? Perhaps, but if we added the word *inclusive* it would be crystal clear.

And then, would 1 minute to midnight on 31 December be an acceptable time to take up the option?

If that is likely to be a problem, specify the time (for example, 5pm on 31 December). Or if the time at which notice may be given is very important in your agreement, then you might want to put in an interpretive clause that makes it clear that notice may only be given after, say, 9am and before 5pm

In other words, when you are drafting provisions that relate to time or dates, or provisions for which time or dates might be important, you should try to anticipate the problems that the parties might have in working out the time and dates, and clarify anything that might be ambiguous or left unsaid.

Put yourself in the shoes of the party trying to work out how much notice to give or whether the right amount of notice has been given. Make it easy to work out.

This also applies to numbers. Try to be definite if you can. If it is possible to be specific, then be specific. When it comes to numbers, some writers seem to have a morbid fear of the specific. One of my favourite clauses along these lines is this one:

> The Borrower must give more than one and less than three days notice of its intention to prepay interest.

Did the writer mean two?

Drafting by stealth

Lawyers are often accused of saying very little and making it sound like something more than it is. But there is a worse sin: saying something and making it look like nothing. Or hiding it among clauses that deal with a different issue. I call that "drafting by stealth".

The proviso is one way that lawyers sometimes intentionally or unintentionally hide provisions in documents. The afterthought doesn't fit too well into the existing structure of the document, so they put it in a proviso.

Poor organisation is another reason people unintentionally draft by stealth. They have not organised the document well enough to get all the issues that relate to each other in the same place. And they haven't given adequate cross-references and other guides to the reader. So material is hidden from the reader.

Sometimes material is hidden in unexpected places, like schedules that relate to different matters entirely. The bonus the stealthy drafter sees is that the lawyers for the other side might miss the hidden tough provisions and allow their client to sign up without asking for amendments. But these days the courts are examining documents more closely to see if the parties were aware of all their obligations. I've already mentioned several cases in which that was done: *Commercial Bank of*

Australia v Amadio,[37] *National Australia Bank Ltd v Nobile,*[38] *Goldsbrough v Ford Credit Aust Ltd,*[39] *Houlahan v Australian & New Zealand Banking Group Ltd,*[40] and *Garcia v National Australia Bank Limited.*[41] In that sort of climate, the person who drafts by stealth takes a great risk.

This chapter has dealt with some of the words, phrases and other habits that lawyers have adopted as their own. The next chapter looks at some ordinary words and phrases that aren't the exclusive property of lawyers, and can be overused by anyone.

---

37   (1983) 151 CLR 447.
38   (1988) 100 ALR 227.
39   (1989) ASC¶55-946.
40   (1992) 110 FLR 259.
41   (1998) 194 CLR 395.

Chapter 10
Overused words and formulas

Accordingly

This word is useful. It is so useful that it has been worn out with over-use. It is a grander-sounding alternative for *therefore* and *so*. Gowers suggests we should prefer those two words.[1] Even if we don't give up *accordingly* altogether, we should remember that *therefore* and *so* are simpler (and shorter) alternatives.

The writer

I'm thinking here of that expression when used in this sort of context:

> Should you need any more information, please contact the writer.

How coy it sounds! "I" am the writer, if the letter is written in the first person singular, so I should say so: "please contact *me*".

If the letter is written in the first person plural (we) and the writer writes, "please contact us", the writer might not be being coy, but isn't being too helpful either. Who is "us"? How can the reader telephone or write to "us"?

Of course, pure politeness tells us that we should give the reader a name. And just a name. Not "our Ms Smith". Just Ms Smith, or Mary Smith. And while we're on the subject, how about giving the reader a direct telephone number or email address if they are different from the ones on the letterhead? The aim of the game is to help the reader to contact you ... not to make it difficult. Each letter you write is a potential market-ing tool. Why not make it easy for your clients to give you more work?

Tired openings

Even though most lawyers are not writing purely for the joy of crea-tion, there is no need for our writing to sound as if it comes from a

---

1   Gowers (Greenbaum and Whitcut eds), 1987, *The Complete Plain Words*, 3rd edition, Penguin Books, London, p 199.

machine. Most lawyers begin their letters in exactly the same way each time, no matter whom they are writing to or what it's about. Here are a few of the classics.

1. We act for … and are in receipt of your letter of …
2. We refer to your letter of …
3. Please find enclosed …
4. We refer to previous correspondence in this matter …

These openings are so hackneyed that it is doubtful anyone reads them. If that is the case, why use them at all?

Lawyers often say that it is necessary to refer to earlier correspondence, and it is customary to do that by referring to the date. This enables anyone looking through the file to see the string of correspondence.

That may be true, but it doesn't have to be done by using tired old formulas.

How about trying something a little livelier, like:

1. Thank you for your letter asking us to advise you about land tax. We would be delighted to help.
2. In your letter dated 17 July 2010, you asked four questions about your family trust. Here are the answers:
   1. …
   2. … [etc].
3. Here is the document you asked us to prepare …
4. Over the last few weeks we have been gathering evidence for the case …

The overwhelming impression you will give with this sort of fresh approach is not that you are unprofessional, but that you are actually interested in your client's matter or the other business to hand.

Tired endings

If we are tired when we begin a letter, by the time we get to the end we are positively exhausted. We abdicate all control of our writing and switch to automatic pilot. This is the sort of thing we like to finish with:

1. If you have any queries, please do not hesitate to contact the writer.
2. If you require any clarification of the foregoing, please let us know.
3. We trust the foregoing is of assistance to you.
4. We hope that the above meets with your satisfaction.

These phrases are not only hackneyed, they are so hackneyed that they sound insincere. Imagine the impression they make on the client.

And do we think that our clients are so shy that they need to be coaxed to call us or write back? Occasionally that might be so, but there are plenty of clients who would ring up straight away if they had questions, thought the advice was unclear (heaven forbid!), needed more help, or were unsatisfied. And what's more, clients know it is most unlikely that the service will be free.

Understating and equivocating

Lawyers hate to stick their necks out. It seems ironic that a profession that is in the business of giving advice is so reluctant to take a firm view.

Of course, we would hate to be wrong about anything, and for our clients to suffer as a result. So we couch our advice in equivocal language. We say:

> It would appear that …
> It may be that …
> It seems that …
> The court may very well hold that … on the other hand it may hold that …

and it is quite clear that we are trying to avoid taking a stand.

Admittedly, lawyers do have a problem. If we are advising on an uncertain area of law we cannot say:

> The law is that …

or

> It is a fact that …

but there is nothing to prevent us from saying:

> We think that you should …

or

> In our opinion …

or

> The better view is …

or

> We recommend that …

If we use that sort of language, it is still clear that it is only an opinion and not gospel. But at least we express an opinion, rather than an each-way bet. The client is entitled to that opinion because the client is paying for it. Couching the opinion in the language of understatement and equivocation only makes us look weak and incompetent.

As we saw in Chapter 5,[2] writing in a more direct manner can actually help our relationship with the reader. A story reported in the South African journal *De Rebus* in 1993 illustrates this.[3] A lawyer wrote to a government department, in a letter headed "without prejudice", to suggest that a case should be settled. His letter ended:

> Civil servants do not usually reply to letters, but please prove the exception to the rule by replying. If you are not prepared to say "yes" or "no", at least say something, even if it is only "goodbye".

The government department replied, also "without prejudice":

> We are not prepared to say "yes" or "no" and accept the alternative of saying "goodbye".

The lawyer responded:

> You amaze me! Since when has a civil servant had a sense of humour? Instead of marking your letter "without prejudice" you should have marked it "without precedent".

Choosing the right words

It is not always easy to choose the right words, especially when you have all the constraints on you that lawyers have. So much is riding on our choice. And yet, as I've said several times in this book: it is our job to know the right words.

George Orwell, writing about the English language in 1946, described the problem this way:

> prose consists less and less of *words* chosen for the sake of their meaning, and more of phrases tacked together like sections of a pre-fabricated hen-house.[4]

Orwell's theory is that if you avoid the bad habits that he saw in modern written English, you can actually *think more clearly*. This is a view shared by Glanville Williams who wrote:

---

2   Pages 99-100.

3   Reported in "Outside View" (1993) 31(2) NSW *Law Society Journal* 96.

4   "Politics and the English Language", in 1985, *The Penguin Essays of George Orwell*, Penguin Books, London, p 356.

Language is perhaps the greatest of all human inventions. Most people think of it merely as the chief means of communication, but it is much more than that: it is the chief medium of thought.[5]

Whether or not this is true as a technical matter, there is no doubt that the care we take in choosing our words and arranging our thoughts is obvious to the reader. Weak, confused or tangled writing makes the reader suspect that it comes from a weak, confused or tangled mind.

The next chapter focuses on some of the little words that have caused problems for lawyers over the years and offers a few suggestions on how to deal with them.

---

5   "Language and the Law" (1945) 61 *LQR* 71.

Chapter 11
Little words: big problems

And and *or*

Though they are small words, *and* and *or* create many problems. Even very experienced drafters have problems with these words, and often have to think twice before deciding whether to use *and* or *or* in a particular case.

The last two sentences illustrate how *and* and *or* are used in the simplest cases. *And* usually shows we are talking about two things together: *both* apples *and* pears (together). *Or* usually shows we are talking about two things separately: *either* apples *or* pears (but not both). For example:

    1.   "Here is $10.00. Buy apples and pears"

means buy *both* apples *and* pears (together), but

    2.   "Here is $10.00. Buy apples or pears"

means buy *either* apples *or* pears (but not both).

Unfortunately, when *or* is used in legal drafting, it is not always clear what the writer meant. For example, in the sentence:

    3.   "You or your sister may buy the apples"

it looks like the writer intends to give *both* of you permission to buy, but probably only intends *one* of you to go to the shops. But it could also mean that *only one* of you (that is, *either* you *or* your sister) has permission to buy the apples. So there are four possible meanings: you may buy the apples, your sister may buy the apples, both of you may buy the apples, and only one of you may buy the apples.

But look what happens if we decide to use an *and*, since the *or* was so confusing in that sentence:

    4.   "You and your sister may buy the apples".

Is it any clearer? It seems to mean that both of you, *both* your sister *and* you, must go together. That is consistent with the simplest meaning of *and* that I described first. Apples and pears together. You and your sister together. But did the writer intend merely to give permission to both you and your sister, without intending to tell you who should act? It is not clear. The first possibility is the more likely, but can we rule out the other possibility?

Dick[1] points out that many of the cases on the interpretation of *and* and *or* concern wills. He cites cases in which courts have been forced to hold that *and* meant *or*, and *or* meant *and*.[2] The courts were forced to rewrite the provisions to give effect to the presumed intentions of the will makers. This does not show that *and* and *or* are uncertain or treacherous words: just that sometimes, on their own, they are not enough to make things clear.

A recent case in the Supreme Court of NSW considered the meaning of the word *and*. In *Shepherds Producers Co-op Ltd (in liq) v Lamont*,[3] Einstein J said that the ordinary meaning of *and* was conjunctive, and quoted *Adbooth Pty Ltd v Ryde City Council*[4] as authority for the comforting proposition that *and* generally does not mean *or*.

But in the *Adbooth* case, Preston CJ noted that there were two exceptions to that rule:

1. If "the result would be so extraordinary that ... the Court would be obliged to read the word 'and' as if it had been 'or'."

2. If the items in a list "are joined by 'and', and the list is governed or affected by words that showed that the list was a list of alternatives".[5]

Sometimes it helps to add a few words to make it clear. We can rewrite all the four "apples" examples quoted earlier by adding words to make their meanings clearer:

1. "Here is $10.00. Buy both apples and pears"
2. "Here is $10.00. Buy either apples or pears"
3. "Either you or your sister, or both of you, may buy the apples"
4. "You and your sister must both buy the apples together"

Examples 1 and 2 were both clear enough before the rewrite. And you can see that only a word or two was enough to make the meaning

---

1   Dick QC, RC, 1995, *Legal Drafting in Plain Language*, 3rd edition, Carswell, Toronto, pages 104-107.

2   *Re Metcalfe* [1946] OR 882; [1947] 1 DLR 567 and *Re Ingram* (1918) 42 OLR 95.

3   [2009] NSWSC 294.

4   [2006] NSWLEC 783.

5   [2006] NSWLEC 783 at [18]-[20].

iron-clad. But examples 3 and 4 ended up needing a few extra words to make them clear.

In particular, example 4 needed a change from *may* to *must* to make it absolutely clear that both you and your sister are to act together. If we had left it at "You and your sister may both buy the apples together" we are still left wondering whether giving us permission to act together is the same thing as forbidding us to act alone. It is still ambiguous, and therefore we need to strengthen it by making the obligation clear by changing *may* to *must*. There is more about those words later in this chapter.

Another way of illustrating that point about whether that *and* implied permission to act together and alone is this question: in the sentence "soldiers and scholars will be rewarded by their countries", do you qualify for reward if you are a soldier but not a scholar, or a scholar but not a soldier? Or is it a requirement that you be both a scholar and a soldier?

The answer is that it is unclear. It is best to use additional words. Depending on what is intended, it would be better to write either "those who are both soldiers and scholars will be rewarded by their countries" or "soldiers, scholars and those who are both soldiers and scholars will be rewarded by their countries". But this last phrase might be better as a tabulated list, as we're about to see.

Some of the legal drafting textbooks analyse the different functions of *and* and *or* in detail and come up with various labels such as the "conjunctive" and "disjunctive" and "inclusive" and "exclusive" *ands* and *ors*. This is a useful analysis, but the rules are not easy to learn, and can be confusing to apply. When it comes to choosing the words to convey the appropriate meaning, in the interests of clarity and plain meaning, it is easier to add of few words of clarification.

Here are some of the useful ones:

    either A or B or both
    either A or B but not both
    any one of the following: A, B, C
    any one or more of the following: A, B, C
    each of the following, together or separately: A, B, C
    all of the following, together but not individually: A, B, C

Notice that the last four examples are lists. Because the opening words are so clear, there is no need to use *and* or *or* in the list itself. The paragraphs do not need to be separated by either word.

Let's now look at the classic arrangement of a series of sub-paragraphs we see in legal documents, with an *and* or an *or* between the last two paragraphs. For example:

The Seller warrants that:
    (a) the Seller has the power to enter into this agreement and transfer the property sold under this agreement to the Buyer;
    (b) as at the Completion Date the property agreed to be sold will be owned by it;
    (c) as at the Completion Date all the equipment and other assets described in Schedule A will be in good working order;
    (d) all the liabilities of the Business have been disclosed to the Buyer; and
    (e) the Seller has no knowledge of any claims against it that relate to the Business, which have not been disclosed to the Buyer.

Clearly, these warranties are meant to operate together: the Seller is making *all* the warranties, not just one or two of them. The word *and* is appropriate, but we have to wait until the end of the second-last paragraph before we find that out.

It is often even worse when the conjunction is *or*. For example:

The Cashier will not accept a cheque in payment without proof of identity. Identity may be proved by tendering:
    (a) a passport;
    (b) a certified copy of a birth certificate;
    (c) a driver's licence;
    (d) a bank passbook;
    (e) a bank identity card; or
    (f) two credit cards.

We are left in suspense until the end of the list as to whether the list is a list of alternatives or a cumulative list. It is much fairer on the reader to indicate your intentions up-front, by using the conjunction between each paragraph or item on the list. For example:

The Seller warrants that:

- (a) the Seller has the power to enter into this agreement and transfer the property sold under this agreement to the Buyer; and
- (b) as at the Completion Date the property agreed to be sold will be owned by it; and
- (c) as at the Completion Date all the equipment and other assets described in Schedule A will be in good working order; and
- (d) all the liabilities of the Business have been disclosed to the Buyer; and
- (e) the Seller has no knowledge of any claims against it that relate to the Business, which have not been disclosed to the Buyer.

and:

The Cashier will not accept a cheque in payment without proof of identity. Identity may be proved by tendering:

- (a) a passport; or
- (b) a certified copy of a birth certificate; or
- (c) a driver's licence; or
- (d) a bank passbook; or
- (e) a bank identity card; or
- (f) two credit cards.

While some have criticised this practice as being repetitive or irritating, there is no doubt that it makes it abundantly clear whether the paragraphs are alternatives or cumulative. The Australian Parliamentary Counsel's Office agrees. It adopted the practice in 1989. Its *Plain English Manual* recommends:

127. If you need to show whether paragraphs are cumulative or alternative, put "and" or "or" at the end of each one (but don't mix "ands" and "ors" in the same string of paragraphs).

128. If there are a lot of short paragraphs, the "ands" or "ors" can look awkward. You can avoid using them altogether by dealing with the matter in the introductory words.

　　　Example　say "each of the following:", "any one of the following:", or "any or all of the following:".

129. Sometimes it's unnecessary to show whether the paragraphs are alternative or cumulative. The sense makes it clear, or it doesn't matter which way they're read. However if there's any chance of confusion, make the meaning clear as described above.

130.   Definitions are obviously independent, so there's no need to include "ands" or "ors" at the ends.[6]

I said that sometimes there is no need for any conjunction. If we have already used clear words to show whether our list is a list of alternatives or a list of items that accumulate together, then we don't always need to write *and* or *or* as well. For example:

The Buyer agrees not to carry on business in any of the following places for one year:
>   (a) Brisbane
>   (b) Sydney
>   (c) Melbourne
>   (d) Auckland
>   (e) Wellington
>   (f) Christchurch.

or

"Insolvency" means the occurrence of any one of these things:
>   (a) someone applies to a court for a winding up order
>   (b) someone applies to a court for an order appointing a liquidator
>   (c) a court makes a winding up order
>   (d) a receiver is appointed
>   (e) an official manager is appointed
>   (f) a body corporate resolves to wind itself up
>   (g) a body corporate enters a scheme of arrangement.

In cases like those, adding *and* or *or* doesn't add anything to the meaning, which is already clear.

Incidentally, in the last two examples, you'll notice that I removed the semi-colons as well. As we saw in Chapter 6, they do not add anything to the readability of the items in each list.[7] We could have done the same for the other lists with the *and*s and *or*s. But it is probably better to leave some punctuation before the *and* or *or*, just as you would pause before those words if you read the list aloud.

---

6   Paragraphs 127-130, p 28 online version dated 11 March 2003 <www.opc.gov.au/plain/docs.htm>.
7   See pages 123.

And/or

This expression has been reviled over the years as "unfortunate",[8] an "ugly device",[9] "verges on the inelegant",[10] "ugly and unnecessary",[11] and a "bastard".[12] It also has its supporters. And most obviously, it has its users.

The real problem with *and/or* is not its "ugliness", but its ambiguity. We know *and/or* means both *and* and *or*: but what does that mean? Mellinkoff catalogued five possible meanings for *and/or*.[13] Most often it is a sign that the writer has been unable to choose between *and* and *or*, and takes the easy option. In that sense, writing *and/or* is a bit like writing *means and includes*. The writer wants to have it both ways but ends up by creating even more confusion.

If *and/or* can have at least five possible meanings, it is a most unwise and uncertain option to take. If what you mean is **both** *and* **and** *or*, as in apples *or* pears **as well as** apples *and* pears, then you should write:

> Apples or pears or both.

The New Fowler's Modern English Usage endorses this suggestion as "a more comfortable way of expressing the same idea", and notes that, in many contexts, just "or" would be sufficient.[14]

Shall **and** *must*

When I dealt with the future tense, I mentioned the way lawyers use the word *shall* for the "imperative".[15] I explained that lawyers like to use the word *shall* in a special sense – to express an obligation or to state a command. I said that when lawyers use the imperative *shall* and also draft in the future tense, things can become confusing. I said that

---

8   *In re Lewis* [1942] Ch 424 at 425.
9   Gowers (ed), 1965, *Fowler's Modern English Usage*, 2nd edition, Oxford University Press, Oxford, p 29.
10   Burchfield, RW, 1998, *The New Fowler's Modern English Usage*, revised 3rd edition, Oxford University Press, Oxford, p 53.
11   Gowers (Greenbaum and Whitcut eds), 1987, *The Complete Plain Words*, 3rd edition, Penguin Books, London, p 16.
12   *Bonitto v Fuerst Brothers & Co Ltd* [1944] AC 75 at 82 per Viscount Simon LC; Davis, JW in "An And/or Symposium" (1932) 18 *ABAJ* 574 at 575 and *Extraman (NT) Pty Ltd v Blenkinship* (2008) 155 NTR 31 at [43].
13   Mellinkoff, D, 1963, *The Language of the Law*, Little Brown, Boston, p 308.
14   Burchfield, RW, 1998, *The New Fowler's Modern English Usage*, p 53 (cited at note 10).
15   Page 153.

to avoid this confusion, we should draft in the present tense – which gets rid of all the "future" *shalls* – and I said that it is also possible to avoid the imperative *shall* altogether. One way we can do that is simply by using *must*, instead of *shall*, to impose an obligation.

Must imposes an obligation

Must fits everywhere that *shall* does when it is used to impose an obligation. And no one can get *must* confused with the future. Therefore, our prime plain language principle – consider your reader – requires that we adopt *must* to prevent our reader becoming confused.

Compare the merits of *shall* and *must*. *Must* is a clear and definite word that imposes an obligation with certainty. It cannot be confused with the future. *Must* is also a commonly used word. We all know what it means. It is the word most people use when they speak about obligations.

Shall is ambiguous – and often misused

Shall, on the other hand, is used less and less these days. It is not surprising. It is difficult enough to work out when to use *shall*.

There is a set of rules for *shall*, which applied traditionally in England (but not, according to Gowers,[16] in Scotland, Ireland or America). The rules told the English when to use *shall* for the "plain future" (in the first person: *I shall go, we shall go*) and when to use it for volition, permission or obligation – the "imperative" *shall* (in the second and third person: *you shall go, he, she, it, they shall go*). In all the other cases the rule was to use *will*. But, according to the leading commentators and dictionaries,[17] those rules have been on the way out, even in England, for quite some time.

Still, lawyers have tended to use *shall* to show a legal obligation. And they often forget the English rules, using the "imperative" *shall* for first, second *and* third persons. This, combined with their tendency to draft in the future tense, produces a repository of *shalls* unrivalled elsewhere in the language!

---

16   Gowers, 1987, *The Complete Plain Words*, pages 141-142 (cited at note 11).
17   Quirk, Greenbaum, Leech and Svartvik 1985, *A Comprehensive Grammar of the English Language*, London, Longman, pages 229-230; Gowers, 1987, *The Complete Plain Words*, pages 141-142 (cited at note 11); *Oxford English Dictionary, Macquarie Dictionary; Merriam Webster Third International Dictionary* and *Random House Dictionary of the English Language*.

Dr Robert Eagleson, who is a linguist, said this about the tendency of lawyers to misuse *shall:*

> Authorities on drafting ... bemoan the failure of lawyers to use *shall* correctly. Strangely, they never seem to consider that it might be *shall* itself that is the root of the problem. Its use to express obligation is archaic.[18]

Shall is on the way out

In 1992 the US federal government's Style Subcommittee decided to abandon *shall*. The Style Subcommittee is part of the Standing Committee on Rules and Procedure, which works on all amendments to all the US federal court rules. The Subcommittee believes that this move led to the rules becoming sharper, because the drafters now have to think more specifically about the meaning of each rule.[19] As we saw in Chapter 4, the Federal Rules of Appellate Procedure, and of Criminal Procedure, were first to be restyled, the revisions taking effect in 1998 and 2002 respectively. There is no *shall* left in any of those restyled rules.[20]

The US Federal Rules of Civil Procedure were next to be rewritten, and they came into effect on 1 December 2007, with all but one *shall* eliminated. Following them, the restyled Federal Rules of Evidence – with no *shall*s as currently drafted – were published for public comment in August 2009. They should come into effect in December 2011.[21]

In the rewritten South African Constitution, there is not a single *shall*. Wherever *shall* appeared in the earlier, interim Constitution, it has been replaced by *must* or the present tense, as in:

Interim Constitution
The executive authority of the Republic shall vest in the President, who shall exercise and perform his or her powers subject to and in accordance with the Constitution ...[22]

---

18 *Clarity*, No 11, Dec 1988, p 6 <http://www.clarity-international.net/journals/11.pdf>.

19 Garner, BA, 1995, *A Dictionary of Modern Legal Usage*, 2nd edition, Oxford University Press, New York and Oxford, p 940.

20 See pages 78-79.

21 Professor Joseph Kimble, who had been drafting consultant on the earlier restylings, was the main drafter here.

22 Interim (1993) Constitution, section 75.

New Constitution
The executive authority of the Republic is vested in the President.[23]
The President must uphold, defend and respect the Constitution …[24]

And in:

Interim Constitution
Every person shall have the right to life.[25]

New Constitution
Everyone has the right to life.[26]

The clarity here is almost poetic.

In the United Kingdom, the legislation that has emerged as part of the Tax Law Rewrite Project has generally used *must* in place of *shall* for the imperative. However, *shall* does appear from time to time in other recent UK legislation, as does *must*.

There is, at the time of writing, no formal stylebook for the UK Tax Law Rewrite Project. But there is a set of guidelines that "bring out some of the principles that we expect the drafters to consider".[27] Many of these guidelines follow what many would consider plain language principles.

On *shall*: the guidelines do not prohibit using *shall* to impose a statutory duty; they allow the use of *must* then. They also discourage the use of *shall* when the present tense and indicative mood is an alternative.[28] In practice, I'm told the Tax Law Rewrite drafting team avoids using *shall* in substantive provisions. At the time of writing, the latest Act passed (the Corporation Tax Act 2009) and one of the two latest drafts (a second Corporation Tax Bill planned for enactment in 2010) don't use *shall* at all in their substantive provisions. But consequential amendments to older Acts tend to adopt the style of the Act being amended.[29]

---

23 Constitution of the Republic of South Africa 1996, section 85(1).
24 Section 83(b).
25 Interim (1993) Constitution, section 9.
26 Constitution of the Republic of South Africa 1996, section 11. For more information, see Viljoen, F, "Baring the nation's soul through plain language", *Clarity* No 46, July 2001, p 15.
27 HM Revenue & Customs, *Tax Law Rewrite: The Way Forward*, Annex 1: Guidelines for the rewrite <http://www.hmrc.gov.uk/rewrite/wayforward/tlra1.htm> p 1 (as at 17 Sept 2009).
28 Same work, p 4.
29 Email from Guy Lawrenson, CenPol Tax Law Rewrite, to M Asprey, 21 July 2009.

The UK Office of Parliamentary Counsel's Drafting Techniques Group[30] has a new published policy on *shall*, which applies to bills presented to Parliament from the 2008-09 session onwards. That policy is "to minimise the use of the legislative *shall*."[31]

The group suggests that *shall* might have to be retained in text that is inserted near existing provisions that use *shall* in the same sense, or where using an alternative might suggest that a different meaning was intended in the existing provision. I venture to suggest that this is overly cautious, given the published policy of avoiding *shall*. But amending old laws (and old documents) can be tricky, and we must remain flexible if the circumstances demand it.

British Columbia, which had been using *must* (to impose obligations) in its statutes for some years, formally adopted *must* in April 1997 as part of its 1996 statute consolidation and revision. To make their intentions absolutely clear, they added a statement to their Interpretation Act that "must is to be construed as imperative", mirroring the existing provision "shall is to be construed as imperative".[32]

Must is a better alternative for the imperative

There is no doubt that *must* is an appropriate equivalent for the imperative *shall*. Gowers says so.[33] The Attorney-General of Victoria said so in 1985,[34] and instructed all parliamentary counsel in Victoria to use *must* instead of *shall* to impose an obligation. The Law Reform Commission of Victoria tells us to use *must,* rather than *shall,* to describe obligations.[35]

---

30   The UK OPC is the main source of UK primary legislation. But there are separate drafting offices for Scotland, Northern Ireland and Wales.

31   Drafting Techniques Group recommendations <http://www.cabinetoffice. gov.uk/parliamentarycounsel/drafting_techniques.aspx> p 8.

32   Interpretation Act [RSBC 1996] chapter 238, section 29. Strangely, after the 1996 revision, Spencer J in *Lovick v Brough* ((1998-03-10) BCSC F970404, para [7] <http://www.courts.gov.bc.ca/jdb%2Dtxt/sc/98/03/s98%2D0356. txt>), thought that the purpose of the change from *must* to *shall* was to "strengthen" the imperative quality of *shall*, and he did not seem to recognise that the BC Interpretation Act says both *must* and *shall* are to be construed as imperative, without drawing a distinction between them.

33   Gowers, 1987, *The Complete Plain Words*, p 142 (cited at note 11).

34   Ministerial Statement of Mr JH Kennan MLC to Victorian Legislative Council on 7 May 1985.

35   1987, Law Reform Commission of Victoria, Report No 9, *Plain English and the Law*, p 61.

The Australian government tells us that *must*, not *shall*, is the word for writers to use to express an obligation.[36] Both the Australian and the New South Wales Parliamentary Counsel's Offices also use *must* (or occasionally other expressions like *is required to* or *is to*) rather than *shall*, to impose an obligation or express a duty. The eminent legislative drafting expert GC Thornton has advised:

> It is preferable to use 'must' instead of 'shall' to impose an obligation. This is more in line with ordinary speech and avoids the confusion that the use of 'shall' may introduce.[37]

In the United States of America, the Practising Law Institute warned its members way back in 1981 not to use *shall*, and advised that *must* should be used to indicate a requirement.[38] And in Canada, in 1979, the Ontario High Court, Divisional Court, said this:

> The question of the interpretation of the word 'must' in a collective agreement has come before the Courts on only two occasions known to counsel … In both of these cases it was held that 'must' was mandatory. No case has been cited to us in which 'must' has been otherwise interpreted. The word "must" is a common imperative. It is hard to think of a commoner.[39]

Many lawyers in private practice have now adopted *must*. In 1990 the English Law Society published a text on legal writing, which recommended using *must* for the imperative *shall*.[40] Mellinkoff, in his *Dictionary of American Legal Usage*, says "unless the context can be made crystal clear, prefer *must* or *required to* shall".[41] And it has been standard practice since the early 1990s in many of Australian law firms to use *must* to impose an obligation.

We know that *must* is sufficient to create a covenant. *Halsbury's Laws of England* tells us that:

---

36   Eagleson, R, 1990, *Writing in Plain English*, AGPS Press, Commonwealth of Australia, Canberra, p 118.

37   Thornton, GC, 1996, *Legislative Drafting*, 4th edition, Butterworths, London, p 104.

38   Practising Law Institute Course Handbook, 1981, *Drafting Documents in Plain Language*, p 253.

39   *Re UAW and Massey-Ferguson Industries* (1979) 94 DLR (3d) 743 at 745.

40   Adler, M, 1990, *Clarity for Lawyers*, The Law Society, London, p 43. Adler's 2nd edition (2007) describes using *must* instead of *shall* to express the imperative, as "current normal use" for both non-lawyers and plain language lawyers (p 112).

41   1992, West Publishing Co, St Paul, Minn, p 403.

No particular technical words are necessary for the making of a covenant. Any words which, when properly construed with the aid of all that is legitimately admissible to aid in the construction of a written document, indicate an agreement constitute, when contained in an instrument executed as a deed, a covenant.[42]

Halsbury's Laws of Australia says, similarly:

No particular technical words are necessary for making a covenant. To charge a party with a covenant, it is not necessary that there should be express words of covenant or agreement although, the intention of the parties to create a covenant must be apparent.[43]

In fact, the statutes of some Australian states have for many years told us that *shall* means *must*. For example, section 9(2) of the Interpretation Act 1987 of New South Wales says:

In any Act or instrument, the word "shall", if used to impose a duty, indicates that that duty *must* be performed.[44]

This is not new – a corresponding section appeared in the predecessor of the 1987 Act: the Interpretation Act 1897.[45] The same sort of provision is in the Victorian Interpretation of Legislation Act 1984. Section 45(2) says:

Where in this Act or any Act passed or subordinate instrument made on or after the commencement of this Act the word "shall" is used in conferring a power, that word shall be construed as meaning that the power so conferred *must* be exercised.[46]

A few years ago the High Court of Australia had to deal with legislation that appeared to authorise the unlimited detention of immigrants.[47] The relevant words in the legislation were:

- An officer "must detain" an unlawful non-citizen.
- An unlawful non-citizen "must be kept in immigration detention until he or she is … removed from Australia".

- "An officer must remove, as soon as reasonably practical, an unlawful non-citizen" after a request for removal.

The High Court held that the words were "clear", "unambiguous" and "intractable".[48] There was no room for any "purposive limitation". Detention was mandatory, however that might interfere with human rights.

Objections to *must*

Despite all this, there is still some reluctance by lawyers to abandon *shall* in favour of *must*.[49] One of the most common arguments against the use of *must* is that it is "too harsh" – which implies that *shall* is somehow softer. If that is true, what are these "soft" obligations we lawyers have been writing about all these years, and how they are different from the new harsh ones? It is an argument that is impossible to answer, because it is based on taste, not logic. It really must be translated as: "we are not used to it", which of course is not an argument at all, but a complaint.

The Australian Office of Parliamentary Counsel has taken a robust approach to the problem. In its *Plain English Manual* it advises:

> We shouldn't feel any compunction in using "must" and "must not" when imposing obligations on the Governor-General or Ministers, because "shall" and "shall not" were acceptable in the past.[50]

Moreover, if we eliminate all of the "mistaken future" occurrences of *shall* and draft in the present tense, there will be fewer *musts* in the average document than there were *shalls*.

Some commentators believe that *shall* is still appropriate for "commercial" contracts, and that *must* is more appropriate for "consumer" contracts.[51] But that argument assumes that "consumers" are

48   Same case at [33] per McHugh J, at [241] per Hayne J (with whom Heydon J agreed) and at [298] per Callinan J.

49   See, for example, the exchange of views in the *Australian Law Journal*, at (1989) 63 *ALJ* 75, (1989) 63 *ALJ* 522, (1989) 63 *ALJ* 726 and (1990) 64 *ALJ* 168.

50   Para 83, p 19 online version dated 11 March 2003 <www.opc.gov.au/plain/docs.htm>.

51   See, for example, Doonan, E and Foster, C, 2001, *Drafting*, 2nd edition, Cavendish Publishing Limited, London, p 181. *Piesse: The Elements of Drafting*, used to make this distinction in its earlier editions, but with the advent of the current edition, *must* is now recommended for use by "modern drafters" for the obligatory sense of *shall*: Aitken, JK & Butt, P, 2004, *Piesse: The Elements of Drafting*, 10th edition, Lawbook Co, Sydney, p 71.

the only ones confused by *shall*, when there is plenty of evidence that even lawyers are confused. It also assumes that "consumers" are an identifiable sub-group, when in fact *every* client is a consumer of a lawyer's legal services. And it does not acknowledge the argument of the plain language movement that every document must take into account the needs of its readers, no matter what its purpose.

Other commentators still see a modest place for *shall* in legal writing. Some point to the origin of the command, noting that traditionally, *must* was used to *describe* a command that had its origin elsewhere, and that *shall* was used to *express* the command. So a sign might say, "Dogs *must* be on leashes in the park" (*describing* the command) but the Dog Regulations themselves would say, "Dogs *shall* be on leashes in the park" (*expressing* the command).[52] But the distinction is evident to the drafter, and not to the reader, who sees only the obligation.

Professor Joseph Kimble has long argued that *shall* is the most misused word in the legal vocabulary. However, in a 1992 article,[53] he had suggested that there might still be some virtue in retaining *shall,* but defining it in certain documents and legislation, along with *must* and other words of permission or authority. This, he felt, would enable us to retain some of the finer shades of meaning, such as whether an obligation is "mandatory" or "directory". But I countered by saying that retaining the shades of meaning is not the important thing. It is better to have a simple obligation, and *state the consequences of not obeying that obligation*, than to rely on definitions to tell you what degree of obligation there is.[54]

Professor Kimble is now one of the champions of *must*. In a more recent essay, "A Modest Wish List for Legal Writing", one of the wishes was "Give *shall* the boot; use *must* for required actions".[55]

---

52   For example, see the note from Nick Horn in "And yet more on the Thorny Business of Auxiliary verbs ....", *Clarity* No 48, Dec 2002, p 35, and "A Dainty Dish to set before the King: Plain Language and Legislation", *Plain Language Association International (PLAIN) Fourth Biennial Conference Proceedings Toronto, Canada, 26-29 Sept 2002* <http://www.plainlanguagenetwork.org/conferences/2002/ dish/1.htm>.

53   "The Many Misuses of *Shall*" (1992) 3 *Scribes J Legal Writing* 61.

54   "*Shall* Must Go" (1992) 3 *Scribes J Legal Writing* 79. See also "Must we Continue with *Shall*?" (1989) 63 *ALJ* 75.

55   Kimble. J, 2006, *Lifting the Fog of Legalese*, Carolina Academic Press, Durham, North Carolina, p 159.

Objections to *shall*

The fundamental objections to the word *shall* are that it is confusing, and out-of-step with current language usage. *Shall* is difficult to use correctly. We know that lawyers make mistakes when they use *shall*. It is difficult to teach them the correct usage. Legal drafting experts, including judges, have been complaining about its misuse for years. Commentators have also complained that it is imprecise and ambiguous. Professor Kimble identified hundreds of cases showing that *shall* can be strong or weak, as the court decides[56]. Dr Robert Eagleson and I listed six different legal uses of *shall*.[57] Bryan Garner listed eight shades of meaning – most from a single set of court rules.[58] Peter Butt and Richard Castle identified at least 10 separate uses of *shall* in private legal documents, including:

- to impose a duty
- to grant a right
- to give a direction
- to state circumstances
- to create a condition precedent
- to create a condition subsequent
- to express the future
- to negate a duty or discretion
- to negate a right
- to express intention.[59]

The potential for confusion on the part of both reader and writer is obvious. It is safer to avoid *shall* altogether.

Must is one word that can do the same work as the *imperative shall*. There are other words and phrases that might do in some circumstances. But those of us who have been working with *must* for 25 years find that it works. The obligations in our contracts have held firm. Since we banished *shall*, we have had no difficulty in expressing obligations, (whether directory, mandatory, declaratory or in any other sense) and our documents are better for it. Clients have noticed the change, and they like it. It is far too late to resuscitate *shall*.

---

56   "The Many Misuses of *Shall*" (1992) 3 *Scribes J Legal Writing* 61.
57   "Must we Continue with *Shall*?" (1989) 63 *ALJ* 75 at 77.
58   Garner, BA, 1995, *A Dictionary of Modern Legal Usage*, p 940 (cited at note 19).
59   Butt, P and Castle, R, 2006, *Modern Legal Drafting*, 2nd edition, Cambridge University Press, Cambridge, p 131.

Replacing *shall* when it is not imperative

One last word of warning on *shall* and *must*. *Must* replaces *shall* in *shall*'s imperative sense. But you cannot simply replace every *shall* with *must*. Remember that drafters have used *shall* to cover a multitude of sins. One of the reasons you find *shall* in documents is that lawyers have mistakenly drafted in the future tense. The way to correct that is to draft in the present tense. So:

> This agreement *shall be* governed by the law in force in New South Wales

is a mistaken future, and we should rewrite it in the present tense, like this:

> This agreement *is* governed by the law in force in New South Wales

and *not* as:

> This agreement *must be* governed by the law in force in New South Wales.

But, by contrast:

> The borrower shall pay interest at a rate of 10% per year

is imperative – states an obligation – so it becomes:

> The borrower m*ust* pay interest at a rate of 10% per year.

So it is not a question of mechanical substitution: it is a question of selecting the meaning you need. The UK Office of Parliamentary Counsel, in seeking to minimise the use of the legislative *shall*, has suggested a range of alternatives, including the following, depending on the drafter's intention:

- *must* for obligations (or sometimes *is to be* and *it is the duty of*)
- *there is to be* (to establish new statutory bodies etc)
- the present tense
- *is to be* (for provisions relating to statutory instruments).[60]

During the rewriting of the US Federal Rules of Civil Procedure, Professor Joseph Kimble reports that *shall* had to be changed to *may* in over 20 instances. The process of rewriting those rules uncovered problems in the drafting that needed correction.

Surely this sort of drafting confusion, and the need to choose the correct alternative to the word *shall*, only demonstrates yet again

---

60   For the full list of alternatives, see <http://www.cabinetoffice.gov.uk/ media/190037/dtg_recommendations250700.pdf> p 8.

the many misuses of *shall*, and strengthens the case for eliminating it entirely from legal writing.

Will

I must refer again to *will*, because even though we should be able to eliminate almost all instances of the word *will* (in its sense as the future auxiliary) from our documents by drafting in the present tense, some people argue that it is a word of promise and therefore should be used in legal drafting to express a promise. Holders of this view would write:

> The Lender will lend $100,000 to the Borrower and the Borrower will repay it within 30 days

in order to create mutual promises.

I can find no authority for this proposition as a matter of law. It may stem from a misreading of the advice of FH Callaway, QC, who wrote in 1975 on his view of the correct use of *shall* in these terms:

> Where it is necessary to use the future tense, "will" and not "shall" should be used, except in the rare case where a document speaks in the first person.
>
> The correct use is illustrated by contrasting the following clauses:
>
>> The goods shall be manufactured in accordance with the specifications set out in the Schedule.
>>
>> The goods will be manufactured in accordance with the specifications set out in the Schedule.
>
> Strictly speaking the former is suitable for a covenant to manufacture the goods and the latter to express a warranty that they will comply with a certain description.[61]

Callaway was clearly referring to a warranty in these terms:

> The Seller warrants that the goods will be manufactured in accordance with the specifications set out in the Schedule.

The warranty is expressed in the present tense: *The Seller warrants that* and then describes the future manufacture of the goods in the future tense: *The goods will be manufactured.*

But a warranty need not always refer to the future. If it relates to a present state of affairs it is expressed in the present tense. For example:

> I warrant that I am the owner of the Land.

---

61   Callaway, FH, 1975, *Drafting Notes*, Law Institute of Victoria, p 9.

Will has the same problem as *shall*: in fact it looks even more like a mere prediction of the future. We must be careful to use it only when we write in the future tense. And we must remember to write in the future tense only when the present is inappropriate.

May

If *shall* traditionally implied obligation or command, then *may* is the language of permission. *May* states what is allowed. This is consistent with normal language use and is not liable to be confused with the future.

Unfortunately, the courts sometimes say that *shall* means *may* and *may* means *shall*. This is not due to any defect or ambiguity in either word: it is only done to correct poor drafting. *Black's Law Dictionary* notes that:

> In dozens of cases, courts have held *may* to be synonymous with *shall* or *must*, usu. in an effort to effectuate legislative intent.[62]

GC Thornton also recognised this point, when he wrote:

> Not infrequently, courts have been obliged to construe "may" as obligatory but these instances amount rather to judicial amelioration of drafting errors than to a licence to drafters to say one thing and mean another.[63]

So if justice must bend the rules of grammar occasionally to correct the poor drafting of lawyers, we should be all the more careful in our choice of words. We should be careful to use *must* only when we wish to impose an obligation. When we want to give permission we should use *may*. If there is no obligation, but only a discretion, *may* is the word to use. So, for example:

> The Secretary may call a meeting of shareholders if the Directors propose to create a new class of shares

is permissive and gives the Secretary a discretion. The Secretary does not *have* to call the meeting, but if the Secretary wishes, the Secretary may do so. On the other hand,

> The Secretary must call a meeting of shareholders if the Directors propose to create a new class of shares

---

62   Under *May*, 9th edition, 2009, West Group, p 1068.
63   Thornton, GC, 1996, *Legislative Drafting*, 4th edition, Butterworths, London, p 104.

is mandatory. The Secretary is obliged to call a meeting. The Secretary has no discretion, no choice. Again, it illustrates the beauty of *must* in conveying the sense of obligation. But the main point to be made here relates to *may*: use *may* when you give permission – not when you impose an obligation, unless you add the word *only*.[64]

Shall not, may not and must not

If we should not be using *shall*, we should certainly not be using *shall not*. It causes even more difficulties than *shall* does alone. So we have a choice between *must not* and *may not*. We could write either:

> The employee must not participate in a similar business.

or

> The employee may not participate in a similar business.

depending on whether it is a matter of command or permission. But what is the point of drawing a distinction between command (or obligation) and permission (or authority)? For all practical purposes, these two expressions mean the same thing. As Bryan Garner says, "these two are nearly synonymous".[65] In fact, as Garner points out, there is one other possible meaning for *may not* and that is *might not*, as in:

> The employee may not have time to participate in a similar business.

To avoid that potential ambiguity, and to continue the clear and definite meaning of the positive *must* into the negative, the plain language writer would usually choose *must not* over *may not*.

We have not yet finished with problem words and phrases, but we are learning what to avoid. In the next chapter, we look at the way the courts read and interpret our words. We focus on the principles the courts use to interpret what we write, and ask the question: do the principles of legal interpretation prevent us from drafting in plain language?

---

64   See pages 156-158 for a discussion of the meaning of *may only*.
65   1995, *A Dictionary of Modern Legal Usage*, p 942 (cited at note 19).

Chapter 12

What about the principles of legal interpretation?

How will our writing be read?

Lawyers are only too aware that our legal writing may be subject to interpretation by the courts, whether we have written a contract or played a role in drafting legislation. But the fact that judges may be called on to review the words we choose should not prevent us from simplifying and clarifying our writing. It is our business to know what our words mean and what to expect when they come under scrutiny.

Let's look first at what is involved in interpreting contracts, then legislation, and then ask the question: is using plain language a help or a hindrance in this process?

Interpreting contracts

Every day, in every civil court, judges are being asked to rule on the meaning of words used in contracts. How do they go about this task?

In Australia, the starting point is what Justice Gibbs of the High Court said in 1973:

> the primary duty of a court in construing a written contract is to endeavour to discover the intention of the parties from the words of the instrument in which the contract is embodied. Of course the whole of the instrument has to be considered, since the meaning of any one part of it may be revealed by other parts, and the words of every clause must if possible be construed so as to render them all harmonious one with another. If the words are unambiguous, the court must give effect to them ...[1]

But even though clear, unambiguous language is essential, the matter does not end there. The High Court has more recently said:

> The meaning of the terms of a contractual document ... normally requires consideration not only of the text, but also of the

---

[1]   *Australian Broadcasting Commission v Australasian Performing Right Assn Ltd* (1973) 129 CLR 99.

surrounding circumstances known to the parties, and the purpose of the transaction.[2]

This approach now conforms more closely with the approach taken by courts in the United Kingdom. For some time those courts have looked at the background facts to help them interpret contracts.[3] The same approach is taken by the courts of Ireland.[4]

But does this mean that no matter how clear the words of a contract appear to be, judges can nevertheless delve into all the background circumstances of the contract in search of some other meaning? Probably not, according to the New South Wales Court of Appeal.

In *Ryledar Pty Limited v Euphoric Pty Limited*,[5] Justice Tobias agreed with what the first instance judge had to say about when courts should go beyond the words used by the parties:

> When the court is construing a commercial contract, it begins with the words of the document: there it often finds expressed the factual context known to both parties and the common purpose and object of the transaction. But the Court is alive to the possibility that what seems clear by reference only to the words on the printed page may not be so clear when one takes into account as well what was known to the parties but does not appear in the document. When that is taken into account, the words in the contract may legitimately have one or more of a number of possible meanings.

So in some cases, language that *seems* clear enough on the printed page, but has not gone far enough to express the real nature of the transaction in context, can cause problems.

The Full Court of the Federal Court of Australia has explained it this way:

> In context, a word or phrase may have 'a' plain meaning in the sense of a clearly applicable meaning even though that meaning is not the only possible meaning. To take a trivial example, it could not seriously be suggested that the warning on a box of matches 'keep away from children' is unclear or obscure or even capable of

---

2   *Toll (FGCT) Pty Ltd v Alphapharm Pty Limited* (2004) 219 CLR 165 at [40]; See also *Pacific Carriers Ltd v BNP Paribas* (2004) 218 CLR 451 at 461-462.

3   *Prenn v Simmonds* [1971] 1 WLR 1381 at 1383-1384; *Investors Compensation Scheme Ltd v West Bromwich Building Society* [1998] 1 WLR 896; *Bank of Credit and Commerce International SA v Ali* [2002] 1 AC 251.

4   *McCabe Builders (Dublin) Ltd v Sagamu Developments Ltd, Laragan Developments Ltd and Hanly Group Ltd* [2007] IEHC 391.

5   (2007) 69 NSWLR 603 at 626.

more than one meaning… in contrast, the same words in written directions by a doctor to a patient might have an entirely different but plain meaning, especially if the document indicated that the patient had a compromised immune system.[6]

Or, as Chief Justice Spigelman of the New South Wales Supreme Court has put it:

> Context is always important. Take the example of the statement: "The chicken is ready to eat". This can either refer to a cooked chicken or a hungry chicken. The context alone will determine the meaning.[7]

So Australian Courts will not always confine the process of interpretation to a simple reading of the words written in a contract. A different meaning might emerge, depending on the background. Nevertheless, if contractual language is clear and, in context, unambiguous, Australian judges are prepared to give effect to the words the parties have chosen.

Interpreting statutes

Courts are also constantly dealing with arguments about what the words of an Act or Regulation might mean. What is the modern approach to resolving these arguments?

Once again, in Australia, the starting point is the wording and grammar the drafter has used. The clearer the better. In *Project Blue Sky Inc v Australian Broadcasting Authority,*[8] the High Court of Australia said:

> the duty of a court is to give the words of a statutory provision the meaning the legislature is taken to have intended them to have. Ordinarily, that meaning (the legal meaning) will correspond with the grammatical meaning of the provision.[9]

The High Court went on to say that in some cases this will *not* be so, for reasons including context and the purpose of the statute. But in a

---

6   *Colby Corporation Pty Ltd v Commissioner of Taxation* (2008) 165 FCR 133 at [44].
7   Spigelman, JJ, "The Principle of Legality and the Clear Statement Principle", address to NSW Bar Association conference, 18 March 2005 <http://www.lawlink.nsw.gov.au/lawlink/supreme_court/ll_sc.nsf/pages/SCO_speech_spigelman180305>.
8   (1998) 194 CLR 355.
9   Same case at 384.

later case, the same court was in no doubt that clear and unambiguous drafting would be given its plain meaning:

> where the language of a statutory provision is clear and unambiguous, and is consistent and harmonious with the other provisions of the enactment, it must be given its ordinary and grammatical meaning.[10]

This was also the approach taken by the Court of Appeal of the Supreme Court of Queensland in *Amos v Brisbane City Council*.[11]

There are many other cases where the courts have quickly discerned the legislative intention from the words used, even when confronted with the argument that a recognised presumption or "canon of construction" (which we will discuss later in this chapter) demanded a different outcome. In *Al-Kateb v Godwin*[12] the High Court of Australia had to deal with legislation that appeared to authorise unlimited detention of illegal immigrants. Counsel for the illegal immigrants argued that this was at odds with a presumption that legislation should be consistent with the maintenance of fundamental rights, sometimes called the "principle of legality".[13] The court did not agree. It held that the words authorising the detention were unambiguous and "too clear" to be read in any other way.

This is a far cry from what Justice Kirby complained about in 2002:

> In statutory construction, there is a tendency, noted in several recent cases, for judges and others to look first to a number of external sources for guidance, including judicial generalities or legal history. It is as if some who have the responsibility of interpretation of legal words find the reading and analysis of the texts themselves distasteful, like dentists happy to talk about the problem but loath to pull a tooth. In statutory construction this error of approach must be rooted out. The proper place to start is the statute ... .[14]

---

10   *WACB v Minister for Immigration and Multicultural and Indigenous Affairs* (2004) 210 ALR 190 at 200.

11   [2006] 1 Qd R 300. An application to the High Court of Australia for leave to appeal from this decision was dismissed, the High Court ruling that in light of the clear terms of the legislation in question, the decision of the courts below was correct: *Amos v Brisbane City Council* [2006] HCATrans 224.

12   (2004) 219 CLR 562.

13   *R v Secretary of State for Home Department; Ex parte Simms* [2002] 2 AC 115 at 131. See also Spigelman, JJ, "The Principle of Legality and the Clear Statement Principle" (cited at note 7).

14   *Royal Botanic Gardens and Domain Trust v South Sydney City Council* (2002) 186 ALR 289 at 307.

In the United States, the Supreme Court has also endorsed an approach that first looks to the language of a statute. If it is plain and unambiguous, then the court must enforce it according to its terms. The Court said:

> It is elementary that the meaning of a statute must, in the first instance, be sought in the language in which the act is framed, and if that is plain, and if the law is within the constitutional authority of the lawmaking body which passed it, the sole function of the courts is to enforce it according to its terms.[15]

But then again US judges can still find reasons to look beyond the plain meaning of a statute. In *United States National Bank of Oregon v Independent Insurance Agents of America, Inc*,[16] a case about misplaced punctuation, Justice Souter said:

> A statute's plain meaning must be enforced, of course, and the meaning of a statute will typically heed the commands of its punctuation. But a purported plain-meaning analysis based only on punctuation is necessarily incomplete, and runs the risk of distorting a statute's true meaning. Along with punctuation, text consists of words living "a communal existence," in Judge Learned Hand's phrase, the meaning of each word informing the others and "all in their aggregate tak[ing] their purport from the setting in which they are used." *NLRB v Federbush Co*, 121 F 2d 954, 957 (CA2 1941).[17]

Interpretation legislation

Modern judges faced with the task of statutory interpretation (if they need to go outside the words of the instrument) also have the benefit of interpretation legislation. In Australia, each jurisdiction has an interpretation Act. These Acts lay down various methods of interpretation, set out definitions of words that are commonly found in statutes, and elaborate on concepts such as time and distance and how to measure them. They govern the interpretation of the Acts of the relevant jurisdiction (often permitting recourse to extrinsic materials such as explanatory memoranda and parliamentary speeches), and most of them also apply to subordinate legislation (like regulations and statutory rules) and executive instruments (issued under the legislation of the jurisdiction).

---

15   *Caminetti v United States* 242 US 470 at 485 (1917).

16   508 US 439 (1993).

17   Same case at 454–455.

Of course, the interpretation Acts don't apply to private documents, but there are a few other laws that do contain interpretive provisions.[18]

What about the "maxims" and "canons" of interpretation?

Most lawyers have come across these epithets – often written in Latin. Do they still have a role to play in modern legal interpretation?

I have already mentioned a couple of these: the *ejusdem generis* and *expressio unius* rules.[19] But there are many others. They are collected in such venerable books as *Broom's Legal Maxims*, which was first published in 1845. The latest edition – the 10th – was published in 1939. The fact that there has been no update since then may in itself say something about the relevance and usefulness of "maxims" to modern lawyers. Nevertheless some lawyers still regularly quote them. For example:

- *Contra proferentem* – in full, the maxim *verba chartarum fortius accipiuntur contra proferentem* – which says that the party responsible for choosing the language will have the document construed against them. Obviously that rule does not apply automatically. It is subject to the overriding principle that words that (in their context) are clear and unambiguous, prevail.

- The "reasonable construction" rule, which says that in any case of ambiguity, if words are capable of two constructions, the reasonable construction is to be preferred on the basis that the court will presume that would be intention of the parties.

- A related rule is that words are to be construed so that the object is carried out, and does not fail – *verba ita sunt intelligenda ut re magis valeat quam pereat.*

- Words must be interpreted so as to give them some effect – *verba cum effectu accipienda sunt.* In other words, the court presumes if the writer of a document used a word, it was intended to mean something. Of course, this rule should encourage us to use fewer words, but choose them more carefully. Any unnecessary words – any padding – could alter the effect of the necessary or precise words. So we must avoid "elegant variation".

- Words are interpreted subject to the intention of the parties, not the other way around – *verba intentioni, non e contra, debent inservire.*

---

18   For example, Conveyancing Act 1919 (NSW), section 181(1).

19   See pages 133-134.

- Words are to be interpreted in keeping with the subject matter – *verba accipienda sunt secundum subjectam materiam*. This is similar to the *noscitur a sociis* rule (literally, something is known by its associates) – which says that the meaning of a word can be gathered from its surroundings.

- Another similar rule is *verba generalia restringuntur ad habilitatem rei vel aptitudinem personae* – general words are to be limited to the nature of the subject-matter or the aptitude of the persons affected by them.

- Words that are referred to in a document have the same meaning in that document as if they appeared there – *verba relata hoc maxime operantur per referantiam ut in eis inesse videntur*. This maxim applies to words that are referred to in a document, no matter whether they are outside the document, or elsewhere in the document. This of course means that the courts presume that the writer uses words consistently, so words used more than once in a document are assumed to bear the same meaning each time they are used. This is more incentive to choose words carefully and stick to them. This rule, combined with another rule I've mentioned – *verba cum effectu accipienda sunt* (words are presumed to have a meaning) means that inconsistency or elegant variation might be fatal.

There are many more of these so-called "rules" of interpretation or "canons" of construction, which the courts have employed over the years when considering unclear or ambiguous legal writing. But ancient maxims and so-called "rules" of interpretation have long been criticised.

In 1887 Lord Esher expressed his doubts about the utility of legal maxims saying:

> They are almost invariably misleading: they are for the most part so large and general in their language that they always include something which really is not intended to be included in them.[20]

The position seems to be much the same in the United States. Mellinkoff, in his *Dictionary of American Legal Usage*, describes the rules of interpretation as:

> a loose assortment of ways to discover the sense, if any, in a piece of legal writing. The label *rule* gives an aura of general standard to what are usually very personal conclusions of interpretation,

---

20   *Yarmouth v France* (1887) 19 QBD 647.

eg favouring intent ... avoiding absurdity ... The rules are not uniform and cannot be relied upon as guides to precise writing.[21]

In the same book, under the topic "maxims", Mellinkoff gives us a "maxim for maxims":

Take, for instance, the following: *Incivile est nisi tota lege perspecta una aliqua particula ejus proposita vel respondere,* cited by the authors at p 27. By all means try this over in your bath to the tune of Annie Laurie, but do not try to persuade me that it helps anyone to inter-

A maxim is to law as a fortune cookie is to philosophy.[22]

Other American legal writers have suggested that legal maxims should, in Bryan Garner's words, be deposited "into the dustbin of history".[23]

Commentators have also complained about the fact that they are written in "dog Latin". In a book review of the 11th edition of *Maxwell on the Interpretation of Statutes* (1962),[24] CP Harvey commented:

Take, for instance, the following: *Incivile est nisi tota lege perspecta una aliqua particula ejus proposita vel respondere,* cited by the authors at p 27. By all means try this over in your bath to the tune of Annie Laurie, but do not try to persuade me that it helps anyone to inter-pret anything.[25]

Moreover, the "rules" of statutory interpretation have been criticised on the basis that that the number of recognised exceptions to them make them anything but "rules". The Chief Justice of New South Wales has observed that, in interpreting laws, "rules" are often there to be broken:

In the field of statutory interpretation it may be best to never say "never".[26]

These days the courts are clearly shying away from maxims and "rules". In the same case, the New South Wales Court of Appeal held that using the *ejusdem generis* rule in statutory construction is rarely justified.[27] The corresponding court in Queensland has sounded a similar note of caution about *ejusdem generis,* agreeing with the trial judge's reference to earlier authority stating that this "rule" of construction:

is subordinate to the real intention of the parties, and does not control it; that is to say, that the canon of construction is but the

---

21   1992, West Publishing Co, St Paul, Minn, p 578.
22   Same work, at p 402, quoting from Mellinkoff, D, "The Myth of Precision and the Law Dictionary" (1983) 31 *UCLA Law Review* 423 at 434.
23   Garner, B A, 1995, *A Dictionary of Modern Legal Usage,* 2nd edition, Oxford University Press, Oxford, p 552.
24   Wilson QC, R, and Galpin, B, Sweet and Maxwell Ltd, London.
25   (1963) 26 *Mod LR* 104.
26   *Deputy Commissioner of Taxation v Clark* (2003) 57 NSWLR 113 at [126] per Spigelman CJ.
27   Same case at [127].

instrument for getting to the meaning of the parties, and that the parties, if they use language intimating such intention, may exclude the operation of this or, I suppose, any other canon of construction.[28]

In light of the contemporary approach to contractual interpretation, several judges have said that use of maxims such as the contra proferentem rule must be a "last resort".[29] Justice Mance of the English Court of Appeal has said so too.[30]

In the end it seems that the legal maxims and canons of construction were born of a time when the courts had few tools to aid them in the task of interpreting contracts and statutes. In the case of contracts, maxims would have been resorted to when judges were forbidden to go beyond the four corners of the written instrument. Modern judges are not so constrained.

Whatever role the maxims and canons of interpretation had to play in the past, it is clear that these days they may be called on only if what the parties have written is confused, contradictory, unclear, or does not reflect what they must have intended to write. If what is written is clear, the maxims and canons of interpretation are simply irrelevant.

How do the courts react to plain language?

Although some judges have been sceptical of "so-called plain English",[31] there are many others who favour it.[32]

---

28   *Cody v J H Nelson Pty Limited* (1947) 74 CLR 629 quoted in *Pepper v Attorney-General* [2008] 2 Qd R 353 at [22].

29   *Rava v Logan Wines Pty Limited* [2007] NSWCA 62 at [51]; *McCann v Switzerland Insurance Australia Ltd* (2000) 203 CLR 579 at 602 per Kirby J; *MLC Ltd v O'Neill* [2001] NSWCA 161 at [20].

30   *Sinochem International Oil (London) Co Ltd v Mobil Sales and Supply Corporation* [2000] EWCA Civ 47 at [27].

31   For example, Tadgell J of the Supreme Court of Victoria in *R v Roach* [1988] VR 665 at 670; Olney J of the Federal Court of Australia in *Secretary, Department of Social Security v Pellone* (1993) 47 FCR 130 at [18]; and Burchett J of the Federal Court of Australia in *Simon Graduate School of Business Administration Inc v Minister Administering the National Parks and Wildlife Act 1974 (NSW)* (1994) 51 FCR 243 at [9]. See also *Cultivaust Pty Ltd v Grain Pool Pty Limited* (2005) 67 IPR 162 at [6] although the words in question were undoubtedly convoluted.

32   For example, Justice Kirby in *Dousi v Colgate Palmolive Pty Ltd (No 2)* (unreported, NSWCA, 12 May 1989) where he called for a "plain English" redraft of the Limitation Act 1969 (NSW). The Hon Michael Kirby, now retired from the High Court of Australia, is a patron of the plain language organisation "Clarity". See also Mahoney JA of the NSW Court of Appeal in *Government Cleaning Services v Ellul* (unreported, NSWCA, 12 Aug 1996) and Wilcox J of

Judges are calling for expert reports in litigation to be written in plain language,[33] and for sentencing remarks in criminal cases to be expressed in plain language.[34] As we saw in Chapter 4, judges are attending courses on judgment writing that teach plain language principles. Joseph Kimble and Barbara Child have each done research in the US that indicates that judges prefer documents written in plain language.[35] And in a recent research project undertaken in Australia by Kathryn O'Brien, 23 senior judges were asked in detail about their views on plain language, focusing on three main areas: barristers' submissions, judgment writing and legislative drafting. O'Brien's article in the *Australian Bar Review*[36] describes "the remarkable degree of judicial support for the use of plain language in all three areas".

The fear that courts will seize on plain language changes in statutes and documents to alter "well settled" meanings has not come true. In *Boehm v Director of Public Prosecutions*,[37] archaic language used in the Supreme Court Act 1958 of Victoria had been rewritten in plain language. The question was whether this removed a right of appeal that existed under the old legislation. The Supreme Court of Victoria ruled that it did not:

> Provisions rewritten in plain English, like mere amending provisions, should not be treated as altering the character and operation of the previous provisions unless that intention is clearly indicated[38]

The same court took the same approach in *R v SA*.[39]

But a majority of the Supreme Court of South Australia took a step backwards in *Hanel v O'Neill*.[40] Changes had been made to the

---

the Federal Court of Australia in *McMullin v ICI Australia Operations Pty Ltd* (1998) 156 ALR 257, where he required a class action notice to be written in "plain English".

33 *Dagenham Nominees Pty Limited v Shanks* [2007] SASC 242 at [177].

34 *R v Becker* [2005] SASC 186.

35 Kimble, J, "Plain English Wins Every Which Way" (1987) 66 *Michigan Bar Journal* 1024; Kimble, J and Prokop, J, "Strike Three for Legalese" (1990) 69 *Michigan Bar Journal* 418 and Child, B, "Language Preferences of Judges and Lawyers: A Florida Survey" (1990) 64 *Florida Bar Journal* 32. See also Palyga, S, "Is it Safer to Use Legalese or Plain English? What the Judges Say", *Clarity* No 43, May 1999, p 46.

36 "Judicial attitudes to plain language and the law" (2009) 32 *Aust Bar Rev* 204.

37 [1990] VR 494.

38 Same case at 498.

39 [2001] VSCA 117.

40 (2003) 180 FLR 360.

Corporations Act to "make the law more user friendly".[41] The Court ruled that this had the effect of making a substantive change to the pre-existing law. This ruling was roundly criticised by other Courts. Justice McDougall of the Supreme Court of New South Wales found it difficult to accept that a substantive change was intended in the face of a "plain English rewrite".[42] Justice Windeyer of the same court, and Justice Douglas of the Supreme Court of Queensland, were even more critical: they thought the *Hanel* decision was "plainly wrong".[43] The matter was put beyond doubt by a further amendment to the legislation making it clear that no substantive change had ever been intended.[44]

Even if the courts are tempted to treat plain language redrafts as altering the pre-existing law, in some jurisdictions there is now legislation to pre-empt this. For example, the Acts Interpretation Act of Queensland 1954 says:

14C Changes of drafting practice not to affect meaning
If –

    (a) a provision of an Act expresses an idea in particular words; and

    (b) a provision enacted later appears to express the same idea in different words for the purpose of implementing a different legislative drafting practice, including, for example –

        (i) the use of a clearer or simpler style; or

        (ii) the use of gender-neutral language;

the ideas must not be taken to be different merely because different words are used.

And the Commonwealth Acts Interpretation Act includes this provision:

15AC Changes to style not to affect meaning
Where:

    (a) an Act has expressed an idea in a particular form or words; and

---

41   Explanatory Memorandum to the *Corporate Law Economic Reform Program Bill* 1998 para 2.12.

42   *Intagro Projects Pty Ltd v Australia and New Zealand Banking Group Ltd* (2004) 183 FLR 462.

43   *Saffron Sun Pty Ltd v Perma-Fit Finance Pty Ltd (In Liq)* (2005) 65 NSWLR 667; *RJK Enterprises Pty Limited v Webb* [2006] 2 Qd R 593.

44   Corporations Amendment Act (No 1) 2005, section 3 and Schedule 1.

   (b) a later Act appears to have expressed the same idea in a
        different form of words for the purpose of using a clearer
        style;
the ideas shall not be taken to be different merely because different
forms of words were used. [45]

Can black mean white?

One last thing on interpretation: some people make the mistake of
assuming that, because the courts sometimes say that *black* means
white, or *shall* means *may*, or *may* means *shall*, or other ordinary words
have extraordinary meanings, we should not use ordinary words in
drafting. They say we cannot be sure that words will always mean
what they seem to mean, and therefore plain language is dangerous.

That is a mistaken analysis. It makes the exception govern the rule.

For example, it is true that in a case from the 19th century, the
English Court of Appeal ruled that *black* could mean *white*, at least
among cloth manufacturers.[46] But, as explained by more recent
authority,[47] what the court did – as modern courts now do – was
simply construe a word against the background factual matrix, namely,
that the parties were cloth manufacturers in whose particular trade
vernacular *white* had a special meaning.

As we have seen, the courts interfere only if they must, in order to
give effect to the intention of the parties or the legislature. They give
ordinary words extraordinary meanings only if they must.

This happened in the High Court of Australia some years ago,
when the court held that the word *entry* meant *entry by means of which
the offender takes possession or intends to take possession of the premises.*[48]
But the court did that only in the context of section 207(1) of the Crimes

---

45 Note however that using plain language may actually make laws more potent.
    On p 209 at note 32, I mentioned that Spencer J of the British Columbia
    Supreme Court found in *Lovick v Brough* ((1998-03-10) BCSC F970404) that
    the replacement word *must* was "more mandatory" than the original *shall*
    in a revised statute, despite the Interpretation Act stating that both *shall* and
    must are to be construed as imperative.

46 *Mitchell v Henry* (1880) 15 Ch D 181. See also *Jones v Evans* [1944] 1 KB 582 in
    which it was held that a married woman was within the definition of "single
    woman" and *Smith v Wilson* (1832) 3 B & Ad 728; 110 ER 266 where 1000
    rabbits actually meant 1200.

47 *LMI Australasia Pty Ltd v Baulderstone Hornibrook Pty Ltd* [2003] NSWCA 74.

48 *Prideaux v Director of Public Prosecutions (Vic)* (1987) 163 CLR 483.

Act 1958 (Vic) to give the intended effect to that section. The court did not prevent the rest of us from using the word *enter* in its simple sense in our writing.

The real problem in that case was that the drafter of the section used the word *entry* without explaining the special sense in which it was used. The very fact that the case came to court indicates that more words were needed to make the meaning of the section clear.

In summary, the approach of the courts to interpretation is perfectly compatible with a practice of plain language drafting. And the case histories of those who have adopted a policy of plain language drafting bear this out.[49] They have consistently reported less time, not more, spent by courts interpreting documents.

Now we can be confident that the courts are prepared to give ordinary words their ordinary meanings. So let's list some of the words we want to avoid in our drafting, and look at the plainer alternatives.

---

49   See Chapters 3 and 4.

Chapter 13
A plain language vocabulary

Plain language drafting is more than just a matter of using simple words. Less than half this book is devoted to words. The rest looks at writing for your audience, choosing the appropriate tone, planning, structure, design and layout, readability, devices to help your reader find things, the new electronic writing media, testing documents, and some "philosophical" matters.

But throughout this book I have singled out some particular words and phrases for criticism. Sometimes it is because they are imprecise or inaccurate. Other times it is because they are archaic, not English, or not used by anyone but lawyers. Sometimes they're just plain difficult.

What follows is an alphabetical list of problem words and phrases, with a corresponding list of words you could use as alternatives. The alternative words might not mean exactly the same thing as the problem words in all cases. Sometimes it is because the word we're trying to avoid is unsatisfactory, and sometimes it is because it is difficult to anticipate the meanings of a word in every set of circumstances. Sometimes the word in the "Avoid" list is perfectly fine in some circumstances (like *any*, or *all*, for instance) but should be avoided in others.

It is difficult to be dogmatic when we are talking about a list of words without a context. That's why I've suggested the words as *alternatives* rather then *equivalents*.

But in *every* case the alternative is an alternative you should consider. The alternative is easier to understand and often it means exactly the same thing as the word I recommend you avoid. You may find that you consider both words and still choose the word I recommend you avoid. The point is that if you do that you must know *why* you've chosen it and *why* the alternative is not appropriate in your case. And tradition is not a good enough reason.

One last lawyerly disclaimer: it isn't a complete list. No doubt you'll be able to add to it. I encourage you to do so.

Avoid	Alternative
abatement	*suspension*
ab initio	*from the start*
above (as in *see above*)	be specific instead
abovementioned	be specific instead
accordingly	*so, therefore*
adduce	*bring, produce*
affix (seal)	*place*
afforded	*given*
aforementioned	be specific instead
aforesaid	*omit*
aggregate	*total, sum*
agreeance	*agreement*
albeit	*although, even though*
all	*the*
all and singular	*all*
allege	*claim*
amend	*alter*
ancillary	*associated*
and/or	*and, or, either … or … or both*[1]
annex	*attach, add, include*
any	*the*
appurtenant to	*relating to, concerning*
a priori	*from assumed principles*
as a result of	*because of*
assist	*help*
at any time	*omit*
at this point in time	*now*
beforementioned	be specific instead
below (as in *see below*)	be specific instead
bequeath	*give*
bona fide	*good faith, genuine, honest*
by virtue of	*because of, under*
cease	*end, stop*

---

1   See pages 199-204.

Avoid	Alternative
chattels	*goods*
commence	*begin/ start*
consequently	*so*
considers expedient	*thinks fit*
construe	*interpret, find meaning*
contained in	*in*
covenant and agree	*agree*
curial	*of* or *by a court*
the day and year first hereinbefore written	*on the date of this agreement,* (or state the date)
deem to be	*treat as, consider to be, take to be*
demur	*object, disagree*
derive	*come from*
determine (as in *terminate*)	*end, finish*
devise	*give*
dictated by	*required by*
disbursements	*money spent, out-of-pocket expenses*
each	*the*
effected	*made, done*
employ	*use*
enclosed please find	*we enclose, here is*
endeavour	*try*
estop	*stop, prevent*
et al	*and the others, the rest*
et seq	*and those following*
every	*the*
exceeding, in excess of	*more than, over*
expeditiously	*quickly, as soon as possible* (or state a time limit)
expend	*spend*
expiration	*end*
extinguish	*end*
extraneous	*external, outside*
facilitate	*help, assist*
fails to	*does not*
for and on behalf of	*for*

Avoid	**Alternative**
foregoing	*earlier*, or be specific
for the duration of	*during*
forward	*send, give*
forthwith	*immediately, as soon as possible, now* (or state a time limit)
from time to time	omit
furnish	*give*
gift (verb)	*give*
give consideration to	*consider*
give devise and bequeath	*give*
grant	*give*
hence	*therefore*
henceforth	*from now on*
hereafter	*after* (and state date or time)
hereby	omit
herein	*in this agreement* (or other document)
hereinafter	*after* (and state date or time), *from the date of this agreement*
hereinafter called	omit, or use *called*
hereinbefore	*before* (and state date or time), *before the date of this agreement*
hereof	*of it*
hereon	*on it*
hereto	*to it*
heretofore	*before* (and state date or time), *before the date of this agreement* (or other document)
hereunto	*on it* (or omit)
herewith	omit, or use *with it* or *with this* (and specify)
hitherto	*before* (and state date or time), *before the date of this agreement* (or other document)
howsoever	omit, or use *however, no matter how*
implement	*carry out, fulfil*
in accordance with	*following, according to*
incur	*become liable for, run up*

Avoid	Alternative
indicia	*features, indicators*
indemnify, keep indemnified and save harmless	*indemnify* (plus a clause stating that there is no need for the indemnified party to suffer loss before requiring payment)
indicate	*show, tell, say*
initiate	*begin, start*
in personam	*personal, personally*
in pursuance of	*because of*
in regard to	*about*
in relation to	*about, for, as to*
in respect of	*about, for, as to*
insofar as	*as far as*
institute proceedings	*begin* or *start proceedings, sue*
instrument	*document*
inter alia	*among other things*
interlocutory	*temporary, pending a final hearing*
in the event of	*if*
in the event that	*if*
in the future	*after the date of this agreement* (or state date or time)
in the past	*before the date of this agreement* (or state date or time)
in witness whereof the parties have hereunto set their hands and affixed their seals	*executed as a deed*
irrespective of	*whether or not, even if*
is authorised to	*may, can*[2]
is entitled to	*may, can*[2]
is not entitled to, has no power to	*cannot,*[3] *must not*
is not permitted to	*may not, must not*
is not required to	*need not*

---

2 But use *may* with care: see pp 202-203.
3 This usage is recommended by the Australian Parliamentary Counsel's Office (*Plain English Manual* p 39 online version dated 11 March 2003 <www opc.gov.au/plain/docs.htm>).

Avoid	Alternative
is required to	*must*
is permitted to	*may*
is prohibited from	*must not*
issue (verb)	*give, publish, produce, deliver, start* (depending on context)
it is important to note that	omit
it is lawful for	*may, can*
it may necessitate	*you may have to*
last will and testament	*will*
lodge	*send in, put in, file*
loss occasioned thereby	*resulting loss*
make an application	*apply*
make a statement	*state*
make payment	*pay*
make provision	*provide*
manifest (verb)	*show*
manifest (adjective)	*clear, obvious*
material (facts, evidence)	*relevant*
means and includes	*means, includes*
mens rea	*state of mind*
mitigate	*lessen, reduce*
moneys	*money*
monies	*money*
mutatis mutandis	*with the necessary changes*[4]
mutually agree	*agree*
nothing in this clause (document)	*this clause (document) does not*
not less than	*at least*
not more than	*at most*
notwithstanding	*despite, even if*
now	*on the date of this agreement,* or state date

---

4   In *Ho Song Lu v Minister for Immigration and Multicultural and Indigenous Affairs* [2004] FCAFC 340 at [95], Sundberg, J, in the Federal Court of Australia, said: "'in a corresponding way' is only putting in plain English what until comparatively recently would have been rendered as 'mutatis mutandis'."

Avoid	Alternative
now therefore this agreement witnesseth	omit, or use *the parties agree*
null void and of no effect	*has no effect*
obiter, obiter dictum	*part of the judgment not essential to the decision in the case, passing remark, incidental comment*
on behalf of	*for*
on each occasion when	*whenever*
onus	*responsibility*
otherwise than	*except*
pari passu	*equally*
per stirpes	*the share of a deceased parent is divided equally among their children, with descendants of a deceased child dividing the deceased child's share between them*
peruse	*read*
the premises (in the sense of "the matters")	*this agreement, this deed*
prima facie	*at first glance*
prior to	*before*
propound	*propose, put forward*
proscribe	*prohibit, forbid, not allow*
provide	*give*
provided that	*but, if*
punctually	*on time*
purchaser	*buyer*
pursuant to	*under, according to*
quantum	*amount*
ratio decidendi	*reasons for decision*
re	omit, or use *about*
rectify	*make good*
relating to	*about*
release remise and forever quitclaim unto	*release*
remit	*send*
render	*make, give*
request	*ask*

A PLAIN LANGUAGE VOCABULARY

Avoid	**Alternative**
requisite	*required, necessary*
res ipsa loquitur	*it speaks for itself*
rest residue and remainder	*rest, balance*
retain	*keep*
said, the	*the, that, those*
same, the	use a pronoun
save	*except*
save and except	*except*
shall (present)	draft in the present tense
shall (future)	*will*
shall (imperative)	*must*
sounding in	*resulting in, reflected by, leading to*
submit	*propose, put forward*
subsequently	*then, after, later*
subsequent to	*after*
such	*the, that, those* (or use a pronoun)
sui generis	*the only one of its kind*
sui juris	*of full legal capacity*
terminate	*end, finish*
terms and conditions	*terms*
testament	*will*
testamentary disposition	*will*
thence	*afterwards, then*
thenceforth	*afterwards, from then on*
thereby	*by it*
therefor	*for*
therein	*in it*
thereinafter	*afterwards, from then on, later*
thereof	*of it*
thereon	*on it*
thereto	*to it*
therewith	*with it*
these presents	*this agreement, this deed*
to the effect that	*so*
to wit	*namely*

Avoid	Alternative
uberrimae fidei	*utmost good faith*
undermentioned	omit, or use *as mentioned later*, or be specific
undersigned (the)	*me* (or use a name)
undue	*inappropriate, not called for*
until such time as	*until*
unto	*to*
upon	*on*
upon the expiration	*at the end*
upon the {occurrence of X {happening	*when X happens*
utilise	*use*
vendor	*seller*
we should point out that	omit
whatsoever	omit, or use *whatever, no matter what*
where (case)[5]	*when, if*
WHEREAS	*RECITALS, BACKGROUND, INTRODUCTION*
whereby	*by it, by which*
whereof	*of it*
whereon	*on it*
wheresoever	omit, or use *wherever, no matter where*
whilever	*while, whenever, as long as*
whosoever	omit, or use *whoever*, or *no matter who*
will suffice	*will do*
with a view to	*to*
with regard to	*about*
with respect to	*about*
with the result that	*so that*
will and testament	*will*

---

5   See pages 177-179.

Chapter 14
Email and the internet

Email is ubiquitous. It is the most used aspect of the internet.[1] The number of emails sent in 2009 is estimated at 247 billion per day. By 2013, that total is expected to almost double, to 507 billion emails per day.[2]

Lawyers today routinely write to their clients and to each other by email. Email messages are even replacing telephone conversations: it is often easier to contact someone by email than to play "telephone tag" with them. Letters written on paper are becoming less common, and are reserved for the more formal pieces of communication: letters of advice, opinion and instruction, letters of agreement that have contractual effect, letters that threaten litigation or other dire consequences, briefs for barristers and so on.

For some time now, Australian courts have recognised the trend, allowing litigants to serve documents by fax, email,[3] even telephone text message.[4] Recently in Australia – in what has been described as a possible "world first" – legal process was served by email to the social networking website, Facebook.[5] Even more recently, a liquidator was allowed to post an explanatory statement on the liquidator's website, rather than sending a copy to each creditor, as the law required.[6]

---

1   Collins, Dr M, 2005, *The Law of Defamation and the Internet*, 2nd edition, Oxford University Press, Oxford, para 2.27.

2   The Radicati Group, Inc, *Email Statistics Report 2009-2013* <http://www.radicati.com/wp/wp-content/uploads/2009/05/email-stats-report-exec-summary.pdf>.

3   *Equititrust Ltd v Bosiljevac* [2007] FCA 323 (bankruptcy notice sent by pre-paid post, fax, and email); *Mort v Lois* [2007] FamCA 1294 (service of all documents in proceedings by email).

4   See p 243. And Part 6 of the UK Civil Procedure Rules and Practice Direction 6A allow service by fax, email or text message.

5   *MKM Capital Pty Limited v Corbo & Poyser* (unreported ACTSC, Master Harper, 12 Dec 2008). See Towell, N, "Lawyers to serve notices on Facebook", smh. com.au 16 Dec 2008 <http://www.smh.com.au/news/technology/biztech/lawyers-to-serve-notices-on-facebook/2008/12/16/1229189579001.html>.

6   *In the matter of Opes Prime Stockbroking Limited* [2009] FCA 813.

Email and the internet do not, of themselves, require a different kind of writing. They are simply different media for the writer to work in. But lawyers writing today – whether in plain language or not – often write by means of email, or use the internet to publish written material on websites or electronic bulletin boards. Different conventions are emerging in email writing. Email and the internet have special features that have implications for the way we write.

Immediacy

Email communication is almost immediate. In fact, with "instant messaging" it *is* immediate. (Instant messaging allows you to find out if the intended recipient of your message is logged onto the internet and, if so, you can send a message that is received instantaneously.) Laptop computers and handheld devices such as BlackBerries, iPhones and the like mean we can send and receive email and use the internet anytime, and almost anywhere.

Perhaps because of the immediacy of delivery, people tend to respond to email more quickly than they would to a letter. That immediacy can have undesirable consequences, which I deal with later in this chapter.[7] But it has major advantages for efficiency in communication. It is even possible to refer readers directly to information on the internet by means of a "hyperlink".[8] This saves them the trouble and time of having to locate the reference themselves. By using a hyperlink (written as "http://www.hyperlink.com", for example) we can allow the reader to see instantly the additional information we want them to see.

Internationality

Email is international. It is just as quick and easy to exchange messages with a friend or colleague in another country and another time zone, as it is to do so with the person in the next room. We can post a message on a website and we have no idea who may stumble across it. They

---

7   See p 252 (**Defamation**).

8   A hyperlink is a set of characters or a symbol or image in a "hypertext" document, which links (by means of a mouse click) to another place in the same or another document. A hypertext document is one that is designed to allow those links.

could live anywhere. This in itself raises issues of communication: will the reader of the email or website understand the way we use the language, even if it is a language we have in common? It is not just a question of slang. Some words that belong to the formal lexicon could also be misunderstood by an audience unfamiliar with them. What is a hire car? A thong? A flat? We can even cause confusion with things such as dates (is 4/5/09 the 4th of May or the 5th of April 2009?), or measurements (how many kilometres – or kilome*ters* – in a mile?). Conventions of spelling and notation may vary. Communicating with an international audience reminds us yet again to focus on the prime directive of plain language – consider your reader.

The international nature of email and the internet can have undesirable consequences too, as we'll see later in this chapter.

Informality

Email sits somewhere on the formality scale between the phone call and the letter. Writers tend to use a conversational manner in email – sometimes using contractions like "yr" for "your" and "pls" for "please". They may begin with "Hi" rather than "Dear" and they can make up their own "letterhead" and "signoff".

"Texting", or sending short text messages by mobile phone (SMS) is even more informal. Texting has its own convention of abbreviating words. Single letters or numerals can replace words (*see* becomes *c*, *to* or *too* becomes *2*). Single letters or numerals can replace a syllable (*great* becomes *gr8*). And they can be combined (*tomorrow* becomes *2mro*). These conventions are even beginning to creep into email.

Some lawyers have rejected this kind of informality. A number of law firms do not allow their employee (or junior) lawyers to send email – just as they do not allow their employee (or junior) lawyers to sign mail. Instead, they may require a superior lawyer or a partner to sign a traditional letter, which is then scanned and sent by email. This is to ensure that the partners retain control over all of the significant communication that takes place in the firm's name.

They have a point: communicating by email and the internet means that everyone is now a potential international publisher. Type up an email, press the send button, and in a flash your message can be broadcast worldwide. There's no "cooling-off" period. There's no secretary to type up a draft for careful checking. There's no time lag in which errors and intemperate words can be picked up and altered. Email delivery is not only almost instantaneous, it is practically irrevocable. As author William Zinsser put it in his book *On Writing Well*:

> Email is an impromptu medium, not conducive to slowing down or looking back.[9]

What is the significance of this for the way we write?

Earlier in this book[10] I discussed "tone" in legal writing, and observed that when lawyers write letters in the course of their work, they tend to adopt only one, quite formal, tone. This does not necessarily apply to email – email style tends to be less formal. And the immediacy of email tends to mean that the writing style of email is more shorthand, even abrupt, and sometimes breathless.

Typeface choice

In Chapters 15 and 16, we will look in detail at various aspects of document design, both for paper documents and for the screen. But in this chapter on email it is appropriate to flag the issue of typeface choice. The typeface you choose for your emails can be quite significant, not just for legibility, but also for reader perception of the writer. This has been known for some time in the context of paper documents, but a 2007 study has looked at the effect of typeface choice in emails.[11]

An earlier study had rated the "appropriateness" of 20 typefaces for 25 different uses, including business documents, web pages and email. Calibri was rated the most appropriate typeface for emails. Comic Sans had a medium level of appropriateness, and *Gigi* (a whimsical handwritten style of typeface) was rated low in appropriateness.[12]

Using those three typefaces, the 2007 study found that that the writer using the least appropriate typeface, *Gigi*, was seen as "less stable, less practical, more rebellious, and more youthful" than either

---

9   2006, 7th (30th anniversary) edition, HarperCollins Publishing, New York, Introduction, p xii.
10   Pages 13 and 98-100.
11   Shaikh, AD, Fox, D, & Chaparro, BS, 2007, "The Effect of Typeface on the Perception of Email", *Usability News*, Vol 9, Issue 1 <http://psychology. wichita.edu/surl/usabilitynews/91/POF2.asp>.
12   Shaikh, AD, Chaparro, BS, & Fox, D, 2006, "Perception of fonts: Perceived personality traits and uses", *Usability News*, Vol 8, Issue 1 <http://psychology.wichita.edu/surl/usabilitynews/81/PersonalityofFonts.asp>.

of the other two writers. There was no real difference in reader perception between the emails written in Calibri (highly appropriate) or Comic Sans (moderately appropriate).

The researchers concluded that:

> Typefaces should be chosen to reflect the message of the content and care should be taken to ensure that the typeface does not conflict with the intentions of the reader.[13]

Symbols, emoticons and abbreviations

There is another emerging difference between email writing and other writing. Email writers have found new uses for certain symbols to enhance communication. They may use asterisks for *emphasis*, angled brackets to convey a <different> shade of meaning, or underscoring_to_make_a_point.

Email writers have also developed symbols that they use to convey emotions. These symbols are known as "emoticons" (from the words "emotion" and "icon"). Originally a writer would arrange standard keyboard characters – often sideways – to form pictures. For example, a smile is arranged like this:

:-)

More recently, with increased computer power it became possible to use pictures as well:

☺

Emoticons give clues to the subtext of the writing and the intention behind it. This brings the writing closer to verbal communication, where we have the advantage of facial expression and body language to help us make our intentions clear.

The website "Emoticon.com" describes the role of the emoticon this way:

> The very nature of communicating on the Internet allows people to express thoughts and feelings with an openness and frankness unusual in face to face or phone conversations. The trouble is that on-line conversations are really a cross between a letter and a phone call. The potential for misunderstandings, without the tone and expression of a voice, or signals given out by body language, are considerable. Email, newsgroups, Facebook, MSN – all rely on

---

13   Shaikh, AD, Fox, D, & Chaparro, BS, 2007 (cited at note 12), p 7.

the written word – and the written word is so easy to misinterpret (ask lawyer$!).

As a result of this, a shorthand version of expressing moods has emerged on the Net and together with certain behavioral rules form *netiquette*.[14]

Other emoticons include:

:-(	Sad
:,(	Crying
:-D	Laughing
:-0	Yelling
:-@	Screaming
:-X	A kiss (or my lips are sealed)
:-y	Said with a smile
:-|	Frowning, or grim
;-)	Winking, just kidding
|-o	Bored
:-r	Sticking tongue out
:-&	Tongue-tied
# –)	Oh, what a night!

Many would say that emoticons are completely inappropriate to use in legal correspondence. However, because of the effect they can have on the tone of our writing, they can be an important element in the communication mix. For example, as Dr Matthew Collins points out in his book *The Law of Defamation and the Internet*:

> Tone of voice and facial expression will sometimes neutralize words which would, if read in print, convey a defamatory meaning ... emoticons can be used to neutralize words which would otherwise be defamatory.[15]

---

14   <www.emoticon.com>. For more on linguistic "netiquette" and style, see Hale, C and Scanlon, J, 1999, *Wired Style: Principles of English Usage in the Digital Age,* Broadway Books, New York and Walker, JR and Taylor, T, 2006, *The Columbia Guide to Online Style*, 2nd edition, Columbia University Press, New York.

15   Collins, Dr M, 2005, *The Law of Defamation and the Internet*, paras 7.18 and 7.19 (cited at note 1). See also the section on defamation later in this chapter (p 252).

Some of the abbreviations used in email are known as "TLAs" (three-letter acronyms). This label is misleading though, because most TLAs are not acronyms, strictly speaking. (Acronyms are *words* formed from the initials or parts of several words.) And some of the TLAs do not have just three letters.

For example:

AAMOF	As a matter of fact
BTW	By the way
CMIIW	Correct me if I'm wrong
EOL	End of lecture
FAQ	Frequently asked question(s)
FITB	Fill in the blank
FWIW	For what it's worth
FYI	For your information
HTH	Hope this helps
IAC	In any case
IAE	In any event
IMHO	In my humble opinion
IMO	In my opinion
IOW	In other words
NRN	No reply necessary
OIC	Oh, I see
OTOH	On the other hand
TIA	Thanks in advance
TIC	Tongue in cheek
TTYL	Talk to you later
TYVM	Thank you very much
WYSIWYG	What you see is what you get.
<G>	Grinning
<J>	Joking
<L>	Laughing
<S>	Smiling
<Y>	Yawning[16]

---

16   These emoticons and "TLAs" were collected from urls: <www.emoticon. com>, <www.windweaver.com/emoticon.htm> and <www.pb.org/emoti- con.html>,

The informality of email can also lead to other breaks with convention, such as using upper case for emphasis, or even for the whole message. Some email writers also feel free to abandon punctuation. But these things can have a serious effect on readability, and can even cause offence in the reader. So they are habits best avoided. I touch on these issues again in Chapter 16 in the context of electronic document design.[17]

Spelling and typing errors

Another result of both the informality and the immediacy of email is the fact that spelling and typing errors are rife. The trend seems to be to tolerate this to a degree, in the interests of quick and efficient communication. "No one reads email with red pen in hand", say the authors of *Wired Style*, an English usage guide for the digital age.[18] That's a sensible approach – but only if it is appropriate to the relationship between the parties. If the parties have an informal relationship, minor errors may not be a problem. If the relationship is more formal, or if accuracy and attention to detail is an issue (as it often is), spelling errors should not slip through. As lawyers, it reflects badly on the skill and care we bring to the affairs of our clients if we ignore this.

A related issue, while we are considering the new writing technology, is the spell checker. This handy time-saver can lull the writer into a false sense of security, as this poem illustrates:

CANDIDATE FOR A PULLET SURPRISE

I have a spelling checker,
It came with my PC.
It plane lee marks four my revue
Miss steaks aye can knot sea.
Eye ran this poem threw it,
Your sure reel glad two no.
Its vary polished in it's weigh.
My checker tolled me sew.
A checker is a bless sing,
It freeze yew lodes of thyme.
It helps me right awl stiles two reed,
And aides me when eye rime.

---

17   See pages 289, 292 and 302-303 for example.
18   Page 3 (cited at note 14).

Each frays come posed up on my screen
Eye trussed too bee a joule.
The checker pours o'er every word
To cheque sum spelling rule.
Bee fore a veiling checker's
Hour spelling mite decline,
And if we're lacks oar have a laps,
We wood bee maid too wine.
Butt now bee cause my spelling
Is checked with such grate flare,
Their are know fault's with in my cite,
Of nun eye am a wear.
Now spelling does knot phase me,
It does knot bring a tier.
My pay purrs awl due glad den
With wrapped word's fare as hear.
To rite with care is quite a feet
Of witch won should bee proud,
And wee mussed dew the best wee can,
Sew flaw's are knot aloud.
Sow ewe can sea why aye dew prays
Such soft wear four pea seas,
And why eye brake in two averse
Buy righting want too pleas.[19]

There's no avoiding proofreading, unfortunately, no matter what form our writing takes.

Does informal = plain?

If email writing is less formal and more flexible in tone than other forms of legal writing, and if it uses symbols, emoticons and abbreviations to help get the message across, does that make it plain? Not necessarily.

---

19   Poem by Emeritus Professor Jerrold H Zar, the Graduate School, Northern Illinois University, DeKalb, Illinois, USA. Title suggested by Pamela Brown. Based on opening lines suggested by Mark Eckman. Originally published in *Journal of Irreproducible Results*, Jan/Feb 1994, p 13. Reprinted ("by popular demand") *Journal of Irreproducible Results*, Vol 45, No 5/6, 2000, p 20. Reproduced with the kind permission of the author, and *Journal of Irreproducible Results*.

As we have seen, plain language involves more than questions of tone and formality. Plain language must be clear, straightforward and unambiguous. It must take into account the needs and abilities of its audience, and the purpose of the writing. There are questions of vocabulary, structure, sentence length and punctuation. But there are no hard-and-fast rules. What is clear to one reader may not be clear to another. The medium of email may suggest that a less formal style is appropriate, but the information itself still needs to be conveyed in the clearest way possible. If informal language, contractions, abbreviations and even emoticons help to get the message across effectively, then they are useful aids to communication.

But the informal, one-to-one nature of email can also be misleading: will the recipient of your email be its only reader? Forwarding email is only a matter of a click of the mouse. Will there be more than one audience for the email? Will the email have to be looked at later, after some time, when the context and surrounding circumstances are not as clear as they are at the time of writing? Could a shorthand means of writing become a hindrance to communication? Could the reader misunderstand you?

And what about mistakes? If email and the internet make everyone a potential international publisher, they also make everyone potentially internationally negligent – and, as we'll see later in this chapter, potentially an international defamer. So it is important to plan, draft, scrutinise, check and double-check email, just as you would a letter. In fact, it is probably *more* important, since it is possible to retrieve a letter that has not yet been posted. Email is posted with the touch of a finger, and it is virtually impossible to get it back.

It is also important to be sure where your email is going. It is very easy to send email to the wrong person by misaddressing it, or pressing *send* or *reply* by mistake. The results could be disastrous. In addition, the recipients of email can easily forward your email messages on to others. As Dr Matthew Collins has pointed out, an email message intended for one reader can easily be republished to a different, unintended, worldwide audience.[20]

The immediate and universal nature of email is a blessing for clear communication, but it can also be a curse.

---

20 Collins, Dr M, 2005, *The Law of Defamation and the Internet*, para 2.32 (cited at note 1).

The myth of the paperless office

A subsidiary point about email and the internet is the one about the paperless office. It used to be said that computers would mean that paper and filing would become a thing of the past. But most of us have discovered (sometimes painfully) that it is wise to keep emails for later reference, or even as evidence, and that you cannot assume that they will stay on your computer. They can be deleted in error, or at the end of a set period after which the system administrators automatically delete them. Even back-up tapes are regularly destroyed. The cost of calling in forensic technicians to try to retrieve email can be staggering. Prudent lawyers always print out and file important emails for the record.

Websites

So far in this chapter we have been considering the special features of email, but that is not the only writing lawyers do for publication on the world wide web. Law firms, barristers' chambers, courts, law societies, legal aid organisations, community legal centres and other law-related groups now have websites and "home pages". There they project their images, publish newsletters, give commentary on legal issues and otherwise communicate with clients, potential clients and the world at large. They write the documents to be published on those websites. And they publish them to the world at large.

As with email, the special feature setting apart material published on websites, including social networking sites such as Facebook and MySpace, is the immediate and international nature of the internet. "This is the only media context in which your audience is sitting at a keyboard, ready and able to respond now", says Scott Rosenberg, of *Salon.com*.[21] And if you post a document to a website, or send an email, you have no control over who might read it, or where. An intemperate thought hastily written and sent, or an ill-judged assertion, could be read by anyone with access to the internet. Even an email directed specifically to one person can be copied or forwarded on to countless recipients in many jurisdictions in an instant, with one click.

---

21   Quoted in Hale, C and Scanlon, J, 1999, *Wired Style: Principles of English Usage in the Digital Age*, p 5 (cited at note 14).

PLAIN LANGUAGE FOR LAWYERS

Defamation

I've suggested that using email and the internet makes everyone potentially liable for international defamation. This issue has been considered in the past few years by the courts in Australia and various other countries. These cases have often concerned publications on the world wide web of online versions of newspapers or magazines, or messages posted on electronic bulletin boards. But the same general principles apply to publishing email, since that is also published via the internet, passing from server to server. The sender of a defamatory email can be sued for the email sent to the intended (direct) recipient, *and* for republishing the email to others, if it was reasonably contemplated that the email could be republished by being sent on to others.[22]

The High Court of Australia ruled on some of these issues in 2002 in *Dow Jones & Company Inc v Gutnick*.[23] That case was the first time a court of ultimate appeal had decided on jurisdiction in a case of alleged internet defamation.

Australian law

In the *Gutnick* case an Australian businessman sued Dow Jones & Company Inc, the publisher of the *Wall Street Journal*, *Barron's* magazine and *Barron's Online*, for defamation in the Australian State of Victoria. In October 2000, *Barron's* magazine published an article that was critical of Mr Gutnick. He denied the allegations made in the article. The article was also published in the electronic version of *Barron's* magazine, *Barron's Online*. Mr Gutnick resides in Victoria, and that is where he alleged his reputation was damaged by the *Barron's* article. He undertook to the court that he would sue only in Victoria for the damage to his reputation there.

Dow Jones & Company Inc argued that "publication" on the internet takes place once only – in the place where the item is first "published" on computer servers. In this case the relevant servers were maintained by Dow Jones in New Jersey, USA. Dow Jones argued that the internet article was published only in New Jersey.

---

22   It would be "reasonably in contemplation" that someone would republish, or send on, an email if it contained information that might be interesting to others.

23   (2002) 210 CLR 575.

The High Court held that the law of defamation in Australia applied to the internet just as it applies to all other media of publication. The defamation occurs where the damage to the reputation occurs. Normally that is where the defamatory material is available in comprehensible form. Material from the internet is not available in comprehensible form until a person downloads it to a computer. That had happened in Victoria, even though there were only 300 Victorian subscribers to *Barron's Online,* and just 14 print copies had been sold there. The High Court ruled that publication had taken place in Victoria and Mr Gutnick was entitled to sue Dow Jones & Company Inc there.

The judges of the High Court were well aware of the potential logistical problems this creates for anyone publishing anything on the internet. It did not daunt them. In the majority judgment, they said:

> the spectre which Dow Jones sought to conjure up in the present appeal, of a publisher forced to consider every article it publishes on the World Wide Web against the defamation laws of every country from Afghanistan to Zimbabwe is seen to be unreal when it is recalled that in all except the most unusual of cases, identifying the person about whom material is to be published will readily identify the defamation law to which that person may resort.[24]

After the *Gutnick* case, according to Australian law, internet writers publish at their own peril. So, potentially, do senders of email. They publish not in a single place, but potentially in every place where, and at every time when, the published material is comprehended by the reader, listener or observer, and causes harm to someone's reputation.

English and Canadian law

The High Court of Australia's decision in the *Gutnick* case is not as astonishing as media commentators made out at the time. Defamation law in Australia remained essentially unchanged. Dr Matthew Collins has pointed out that the case is:

> part of a growing body of international jurisprudence. It is consistent with the approach adopted so far by courts in England and Canada.[25]

---

24   Same case at 609.
25   Collins, Dr M, 2003, *Defamation and the Internet after Dow Jones v Gutnick* (paper delivered at a Centre for Media and Communications Law (University of Melbourne) seminar, 31 March 2003, Sydney) p 17.

He noted that courts in England and Canada had previously applied the same principles as those applied in *Gutnick*, to both print and internet publications.[26]

The starting point of English law on the issue of publication was neatly summarised in 2002 by The Law Commission in its paper *Defamation and the Internet*:

> each communication to a third party constitutes a separate tort which takes place in the country in which the statement is heard, read or seen.[27]

This long-standing principle is consistent with Australian law, and the decision of the High Court in *Gutnick*. It has been applied in various recent cases involving publication on the internet.[28]

In Canada, too, the tort of defamation is committed where the publication takes place. Publication occurs when the words are heard, read or downloaded.[29]

United States law

However, the position in most of the United States is quite different. Most American states follow the "single publication" rule, so that only one cause of action arises out of one publication, such as one edition of

---

26   Same paper, pages 7-10, noting *Berezovsky v Michaels* [2000] 2 All ER 986; *Scapira v Ahronson* [1999] EMLR 735; *Chadha v Dow Jones & Company Inc* [1999] EMLR 724; and *Kitakufe v Oloya* (unreported, Ontario Court of Justice, Himel J, 2 June 1998).

27   *Defamation and the Internet, A Preliminary Investigation:* Scoping Study No 2, Dec 2002, para 4.4 <http://www.lawcom.gov.uk/docs/defamation2.pdf>. See also *Duke of Brunswick v Harmer* (1849) 14 QB 185.

28   For example, *Loutchansky v Times Newspapers (Nos 4 & 5)* [2002] QB 783; *Harrods v Dow Jones & Co Inc* [2003] EWHC 1162 (QB); *King v Lewis* [2004] EWHC 168 (QB); *King v Lewis* [2005] EMLR 4.

29   Raymond E Brown, *The Law of Defamation in Canada*, 2nd ed (1999) at 7.2-7.8, 10.11-10.14 and 16.5-16.7, cited in *Black v Breedon* 2009 CanLII 14041 (ON SC) 31 March 2009. Three recent Canadian cases involving internet publishing have applied these principles to achieve different results, depending on the facts of each case: *Burke v NYP Holdings Inc (c o b New York Post)*, [2005] BCJ No 1993 (SC); *Bangoura v Washington Post* [2005] OJ No 3849 (CA); *Black v Breedon* 2009 CanLII 14041 (ON SC) 31 March 2009. See also GJH Smith, 2007, *Internet Law and Regulation*, 4th edition, Sweet & Maxwell, London, para 6-131.

a book, one issue of a magazine, or one broadcast of a program.[30] The American position on jurisdiction is quite different as well.

Just three days after judgment in the *Gutnick* case was delivered, the US Fourth Circuit Court of Appeals decided a case that illustrates just how far apart US law stands from Australian, English and Canadian law on this issue.

In *Young v New Haven Advocate et al*,[31] the court held that a Virginia prison warden could not sue the publishers of two Connecticut newspapers for defamation in his home State of Virginia. Two small Connecticut newspapers had published articles on the internet that allegedly defamed the prison warden. The court applied its "traditional standard for establishing specific jurisdiction" as adapted for the internet by the court in *ALS Scan, Inc v Digital Service Consultants, Inc*.[32] That standard involves more than simply allowing publication in a particular place. In order to establish specific personal jurisdiction over a "foreign" defendant, the plaintiff must show that the defendant:

(1) directs electronic activity into the State,
(2) with the manifested intent of engaging in business or other interactions within the State, and
(3) that activity creates, in a person within the State, a potential cause of action cognisable in the State's courts.[33]

None of these connections was established: one of the publications had no subscribers in Virginia, and the other had only eight. The publishers did not target Virginia readers and they didn't even send a reporter to Virginia to cover the story – they got their story by phone interviews.

Another decision of the US Court of Appeals only a couple of weeks after the *New Haven Advocate* case followed the same reasoning. In *Revell v Lidov*,[34] an item that was allegedly defamatory had been published on a bulletin board on the website of the School of Journalism of New York's Columbia University. The plaintiff, who lived in Texas, claimed to have been defamed, and sued in Texas. The court held that the publisher

---

30   American Law Institute's Uniform Single Publication Act, adopted in many US states. See also Collins, Dr M, *The Law of Defamation and the Internet*, para 13.22 (cited at note 1).

31   315 F 3d 256 (4th Cir, 2002).

32   293 F 3d 707 (4th Cir, 2002).

33   293 F 3d 707 at 714 (quoted in 315 F 3d 256 at 263).

34   317 F 3d 467 (5th Cir, 2002).

must be shown to have conducted business in Texas or otherwise have sufficient connection with Texas, so that it would reasonably anticipate being sued in Texas. The court held that the publisher did not have that kind of connection with Texas and so jurisdiction was denied: the plaintiff could not sue for defamation in Texas.

A global problem

Given the global nature of the internet, the gradual development of case law in each jurisdiction is not going to settle the issue quickly. As the UK Law Commission concluded:

> Although we have some sympathy with the concerns expressed about "unacceptable levels of global risks", any solution would require an international treaty, accompanied by greater harmonisation of the substantive law of defamation. We do not think that the problem can be solved within the short to medium term. We do not therefore recommend reform in this area at the present time.[35]

Justice Kirby of the Australian High Court acknowledged the global nature of the problem in his judgment in the *Gutnick* case:

> In default of local legislation and international agreement, there are limits on the extent to which national courts can provide radical solutions that would oblige a major overhaul of longstanding legal doctrine in the field of defamation law. Where large changes to settled law are involved, in an area as sensitive as the law of defamation, it should cause no surprise when the courts decline the invitation to solve problems that others, in a much better position to devise solutions, have neglected to repair.[36]

Lawyers and publishers have struggled to reach some kind of consensus on the issues of jurisdiction raised by these cases. A group of media lawyers, meeting in Durban, South Africa, in October 2002 produced a draft set of principles (the "Durban Principles") which deal with forum and jurisdiction issues applying to material posted on the internet. The "preliminary" *Draft Hague Convention on Jurisdiction and Foreign Judgments in Civil and Commercial Matters*[37] proposed a

---

35 *Defamation and the Internet, A Preliminary Investigation:* Scoping Study No 2, December 2002 para 1.16 <http://www.lawcom.gov.uk/docs/defamation2.pdf>.

36 (2002) 210 CLR at 643.

37 Adopted by the Special Commission on 30 Oct 1999, See <http://www.hcch.net/index_en.php?act=events.details&year=1999&varevent=66> and <http://www.hcch.net/upload/wop/jdgmpd11.pdf>.

scheme for deciding jurisdiction in cases of international defamation among the Contracting States to that Convention. Their negotiations stalled in 2001, and all that resulted was a limited *Convention on Choice of Court Agreements*, dated 30 June 2005.[38]

Summary

Email and the internet are now a common methods of communication used by lawyers. The immediacy and informality of email require special attention. What we think may be clear at the time of writing, and in the context available to the writer, may not be at all clear to the recipient or to other, subsequent readers. Informality does not necessarily produce plain language communication. And we can send unintended messages, just by choosing a particular typeface, or by typing poorly.

Our ability to communicate immediately and internationally by email and the internet poses special problems, such as:

- the potential for mistakes that cannot be undone
- the inability to limit or control who may receive our emails
- international defamation.

But while the internet and email communications revolution has brought us problems we had not dreamed of a few decades ago, it is also important to keep things in perspective. As William Zinsser reminds us:

> I don't know what still newer marvels will make writing twice as easy in the next 30 years. But I do know they won't make writing twice as good. That will still require plain old hard thinking … and the plain old tools of the English language.[39]

One of the other "tools" of writing is document design. We'll look at the basic principles of document design in Chapter 15. After that, in Chapter 16, we'll focus on the special way those principles apply to documents designed to be read on the computer screen.

---

38   <http://www.hcch.net/index_en.php?act=conventions.text&cid=98>.
39   2006, *On Writing Well*, 7th (30th anniversary) edition, HarperCollins Publishing, New York, Introduction, p xiii.

Chapter 15
Document design basics

Why worry about document design?

In the past, very few lawyers thought much about the design or look of their documents. Apart from giving a little thought to a numbering system, they often left all matters of style and layout to the typist. And of course, there were some documents that had to be in a prescribed format, or typed on a set form. But communications experts have long known that document design has an important effect on the reader's ability to read, find, understand and use the information in a document. That makes good design an essential element of plain language writing.

Even the most wonderfully thought-out and structured document can be difficult to read if it is poorly designed. For example, large blocks of print discourage readers. So does small print. So does an inappropriate typeface.

But good document design can encourage readers, and make them more efficient in extracting information from a document. Legal writing is hard enough to understand as it is. Legal writers who want to give their writing its best chance of being read and understood will pay attention to document design.

For the average lawyer, it is not too difficult to dabble in document design. Wordprocessing software gives you plenty of options. With laser printers and desktop publishing we can now produce a professional product with a minimum of effort.

And yet, putting all those choices and opportunities in the hands of amateurs can result in documents that are so packed full of features that they are just as difficult to read as the old "undesigned" documents. It is very easy (and tempting) to produce a document that is too busy, or contains a design feature that actually *hinders* comprehension.

So we should either consult an expert, or at least learn the basics of document design, before we start to dabble in publishing. At the same time, we should realise that simply putting material in upper case, or bold, or italics, or colour, or in a box, or – heaven forbid – using all of these things at once, will not cure poor written expression.

The starting point in document design is the same as it is in writing: consider your reader. In designing a document we need to make the information clear, relevant and usable, and select techniques and design elements that support those aims and that are appropriate for the purpose.

Here are some of the basic things the experts will tell you about documents designed for printing on paper.[1] If you are not interested in the detail, just skip to p 286 and read the summary.

Legibility and readability

First, we must distinguish between two specific qualities in the context of typography: legibility and readability.

Legibility is the characteristic of letters, numbers and other symbols that enables us to tell them apart by shape. This depends on several factors, including the form of the characters, the width of their strokes, and the spaces between the characters. If it is easy to tell the shapes of different characters apart, their typeface is said to be highly legible. If the text is not very legible, readers will be slower to read it and reading will be more fatiguing.

Readability, by contrast, is an attribute that enables us to extract meaningful information from characters and groups of characters (words, sentences, tables, footnotes and other forms of text). Material is said to be highly readable when the composition of the text allows a reader to extract information from it easily. Readability also depends on factors like vocabulary, sentence structure and many of the other topics covered in this book.

Thus, a random grouping of letters like jwrtidf may be legible, but it is not readable.

It is the quality of legibility that we look for as we consider some of the mysteries of typography. For readability, we need to look at other aspects of document design.[2]

---

1   Chapter 16 covers design for documents to be read on a computer screen.
2   For more about legibility and readability, see Beaufort Wijnholds, A de, 1996, "Using Type: The Typographer's Craftsmanship and the Ergonomist's Research" <http://www.plainlanguagenetwork.org.type/type.htm>.

Typeface

There's a bewildering array of typefaces, or fonts,[3] available to anyone with a computer and wordprocessing software. And they come in all sizes and styles. Do you just choose the one that you like best? No. Typography is a technical area, and there is now a body of research about the effects of different typefaces on legibility and comprehension. An Australian, Colin Wheildon, has been influential in this field. This is what he said about typography:

> Typography must be clear. At its best, it is virtually invisible to the reader![4]

Serif or sans serif?

Although there are various ways to classify typefaces, one of the distinctions that is easiest for the novice to understand is the one between "serif" or "sans serif" typefaces. Serifs are the little extensions at the end of each letter. They originated in Roman times. The other defining characteristic of serif letters is that each letter is usually made up of both thick and thin strokes. The body text in this book is printed in a serif typeface, called "Book Antiqua".

Sans serif typefaces are, literally, "without" the serifs, and the letters usually have uniform strokes. The chapter numbers and titles in this book are printed in a sans serif typeface.

The experts have long said that, in large amounts of text, serif typeface is easier to read than sans serif text. This was thought to be either because the serif lines "lead" the eye across the page, or because the serifs, together with the thick and thin strokes, make serif letters easier to recognise. But this reasoning has been questioned, even going back to 1878.[5]

---

3   "Font" is the word for the individual members of a typeface family. For example, in the Bodoni family there are various fonts, including Bodoni condensed, Bodoni bold, Bodoni italic bold, etc. Boldness and italics are "type styles".

4   Wheildon, C, 2005, *Type & Layout: Are you communicating or just making pretty shapes*, The Worsley Press, Hastings, Australia, p 23.

5   Poole, A, 2005, "Which Are More Legible: Serif or Sans Serif Typefaces?" <http://www.alexpoole.info/academic/literaturereview.html>, p 5, quoting Spencer, H, 1968, *The Visible Word*, Lund Humphries, London, p 13 and Rayner, K. & Pollatsek, A, 1989, *The Psychology of Reading*, Prentice-Hall Inc, Englewood Cliffs, pages 113-187.

Colin Wheildon's research supported using serif typeface in blocks of text. In his tests, five times as many readers showed "good" comprehension of text when it was printed in serif type, as opposed to sans serif.[6] But doubt has been cast on Wheildon's methodology, and on how far his conclusions apply as a general rule.[7]

Much of the research about the legibility of serif typefaces was done in the 1920s and 1930s, and often involved comparing only a limited number of typefaces, so that research is not necessarily conclusive for today. Readers in the 1920s and 1930s were not as familiar with sans serif typefaces as we are today. One theory is that we read most easily that which we are most used to. Research by the Communications Research Institute of Australia in the 1990s suggests that readers in Australia are familiar with sans serif typefaces and have no problem reading them efficiently.[8]

In 2005, "Interaction Designer" Alex Poole reviewed much of the literature on the question of serif v sans serif and came to the conclusions that:

1. It is likely that the effect of serifs on legibility is so peripheral to reading that it is not worth measuring.
2. Other factors, such as x-height, size, spacing and stroke width might be more significant.
3. Most reasonably designed mainstream typefaces will be equally legible.
4. The choice of serif v sans serif is more an aesthetic one that a question of legibility.[9]

Sans serif typefaces are often used for headings or headlines because they provide a contrast to serif body text. Some claim that they are easier to read when the type is very small, and that their

---

6   Wheildon, C, 2005, *Type & Layout: Are you communicating or just making pretty shapes*, p 47 (cited at note 4).

7   Poole, A, 2005, p 4 (cited at note 5), quoting several articles by O Lund, including: 1999, "Knowledge Construction in Typography: the case of legibility research and the legibility of sans serif typefaces", PhD Thesis submitted to University of Reading.

8   MacKenzie, M, 1994, "Our changing visual environment: Questions and challenges", *Communication News*, 7, No 4, Communications Research Institute of Australia, Hackett, Australia, pages 11-14.

9   Poole, A, 2005 (cited at note 5).

"clean" look can be useful for material that may have to be reduced, or photocopied many times,[10] or that will be shown on a computer screen.[11] They may also be more legible against moving or complex backgrounds.

But today most the experts agree that the choice between serif and sans serif typefaces is not as significant as it was once thought to be. We can choose between any number of highly legible typefaces. I often choose a sans serif typeface like Arial or Verdana, especially if I am working on a computer screen. But sometimes I prefer a serif typeface like Georgia or this book's Book Antiqua, which I think looks more elegant on paper. As always in plain language writing, my choice depends on my audience and the document's purpose. And as we are about to see, there are other factors that affect legibility.

Typeface choice can have unexpected effects too. Psychologists at the University of Michigan tested students, using two sets of instructions for exercising. One set was typed in the "plain, unadorned" typeface, Arial. Another set was typed in a *Brush* typeface, which looks like hand-panted Japanese brush strokes. The researchers found that the students were more likely to accept the instructions typed in Arial, and were more willing to act on them, than were the students reading the instructions typed in *Brush*. It seems the students mistook the ease of reading the instructions for the act of actually doing the exercises.

The researchers repeated the experiment, this time using cooking instructions, and the results were virtually the same.[12] So it may be that ease of reading leads directly to action, or at least to intention to act. If we want our writing to be acted on, we should choose a plain and simple typeface.

Type size

Type size is usually measured in points. A point is approximately 1/72 of an inch or 0.353mm. The older research on type size suggests that a type size of between 9-12 points is best for reading.

10   See Felsenfeld, C and Siegel, A, 1981, *Writing Contracts in Plain English*, West Publishing Co, St Paul, Minn, p 192.

11   See Chapter 16.

12   Wray, H, "A Recipe for Motivation: Easy to Read, Easy to Do", *Scientific American Mind*, 19 Feb 2009. <http://www.scientificamerican.com/article.cfm?id=a-recipe-for-motivation>.

Colin Wheildon originally wrote that, from a sample of 4000 people, around 75% found it easy to read type from 10-12 points.[13] However, in the latest edition of his book, he restated his findings. This time he reported that the overwhelming majority preferred typeface from 9-14 points (which is not surprising). But then, when he introduced one or two points of interlinear space (leading),[14] he reported that many more readers preferred type from 10-12 points.[15]

Felsenfeld and Siegel recommended a 10 point type, with a moderate "x-height" (which is another measure of the height of letters, based on the height of the letter x).[16] But Dr Janice Redish has pointed out that much of the older research is based on measurement for old type set in cold metal. Reproduction on a laser printer is not as good. She has stated that the modern thought on the optimal type size for desktop publishing is from 12-14 points.[17]

The Australian government *Style Manual* recommends using type with a size between 9-12 points for continuous reading, and larger type (between 14-20 points) for older or visually impaired readers.[18] This book is set in 10 point (Book Antiqua) for the main body text.

Here is the same typeface in some different type sizes:

This line is in Book Antiqua 9pt.

This line is in Book Antiqua 10pt.

This line is in Book Antiqua 11pt.

This line is in Book Antiqua 12pt.

This line is in Book Antiqua 13pt.

This line is in Book Antiqua 14pt.

---

13   Wheildon, C, 1995, *Type & Layout: How typography and design can get your message across – or get in the way*, Strathmoor Press, Inc, Berkeley, California, pages 140-146.

14   See p 269.

15   Wheildon, C, 2005, *Type & Layout: Are you communicating or just making pretty shapes*, pages 109-112 (cited at note 4).

16   Felsenfeld, C and Siegel, A, 1981, *Writing Contracts in Plain English*, p 193 (cited at note 10).

17   See Krongold, S, "Writing Laws: Making them Easier to Understand" (1992) 24 *Ottawa L Rev* 495 at 539. Dr Redish wrote the section of the article which deals with document design.

18   2002, *Style Manual for Authors, Editors and Printers*, 6th edition, John Wiley & Sons Australia Ltd, p 330. For more information about designing text for older readers, see Hartley, J, 1994, *Designing Instructional Text*, 3rd edition, Kogan Page, London, Chapter 12.

But not all typefaces *look* the same size, even if they have the same point rating. This is because of variations in letter shapes, and because point size refers, not to the size of the letter, but to the metal block on which the letters used to be placed in the old metal-type system.

Here are some different typefaces, all in 10pt. You can see how each looks a different size. I think the smaller ones are too small:

This line is in Book Antiqua 10pt.
This line is in Palatino Linotype 10pt.
This line is in Times New Roman 10pt.
This line is in NewCenturySchoolbook 10pt.
This line is in Bookman Old Style 10pt.
This line is in Arial 10pt.
This line is in Myriad Pro 10pt.
This line is in Courier New 10pt.

Legibility also depends on the amount of space around the letter, which is another thing that can easily be manipulated in word-processing systems. Recent research in neuroscience at New York University has shown that the spacing between letters – and not letter size – is the crucial factor in visual recognition. And this is the same for all objects, including letters, animals and furniture. We recognise letters – and words – only if there is enough space around them.[19]

Line length

Lines of type that range too far – or not far enough – across a page are hard to read. That is why so much reading material is presented in columns. Lawyers don't often use columns in their writing, and columns don't suit numbered paragraphs too well – the eye can't always range down one side of a page to get an idea of the total of the listed items. But double columns can make text more readable. For example, if you need to fit more words on a page, and are forced to reduce type size to achieve the result you want, the smaller print will be more readable in columns.

Lawyers who are looking to make their documents more "interesting" – and in particular, lawyers who dabble in PowerPoint – are often

---

19   Pelli, DG & Tillman, KA, 2008, "The Uncrowded Window of Object Recognition", *Nature Neuroscience*, 1129-1135 <http://nature.com/neuro/journal/v11/n10/abs/nn.2187.html>.

tempted to use "landscape" format, rather than the "portrait" format (in which this book is presented). They want to turn the page sideways, and write across it. But, unless you use a table or columns, this will give you lines that are much too long to read easily. It can also annoy readers, who have to turn the page sideways to read it, and then turn it back again to read the rest of the document.

For text presented in one single column (like this book), the experts recommend a line that is anything from 40 – 72 characters of type.[20] Wheildon found that 38% of readers found text hard to read if it was set wider than 60 characters.[21] This also means that the smaller the typeface you use, the shorter the line should be.

In the previous two paragraphs of this book, which are printed in Book Antiqua 10pt type, the full lines of type range between 54 and 59 characters in length.

Justified or ragged?

Text can be set in four main ways:

1. Justified. That means extra spaces are inserted between words so as to leave no gap at the left or right margin (as in this book).
2. Flush-left and ragged-right. That means the left margin is straight, and the right margin is allowed to finish as the words require, whether it forms a straight right margin or not.
3. Flush-right and ragged-left. That means the reverse of 2.
4. Centred. That means both margins are ragged, and there is no straight margin.

Here are examples of justified and ragged text:

---

20 Dr Redish recommends 50-70 characters: see Krongold, S, "Writing Laws: Making them Easier to Understand" (1992) 24 *Ottawa L Rev* 495 at 530. So does Martin Cutts: Cutts, M, 2000, *Lucid Law*, 2nd edition, The Plain Language Commission, High Peak, England, p 42. So do Felsenfeld and Siegel: Felsenfeld, C and Siegel, A, 1981, *Writing Contracts in Plain English*, p 197 (cited at note 10). The Australian government *Style Manual* recommends 40-80 characters, or 6-12 words per line for readability (varying according to typeface and size): 2002, *Style Manual for Authors, Editors and Printers*, p 332 (cited at note 18).

21 Wheildon, C, 2005, *Type & Layout: Are you communicating or just making pretty shapes*, p 99 (cited at note 4).

PLAIN LANGUAGE FOR LAWYERS

Justified

This text is justified. Both edges are straight. This text is justified. Both edges are straight. This text is justified. Both edges are straight. This text is justified. Both edges are straight. This text is justified. Both edges are straight. This text is justified. Both edges are straight.

Flush-left and ragged-right

This text is flush-left and ragged-right. This text is flush-left and ragged-right. This text is flush-left and ragged-right. This text is flush-left and ragged-right. This text is flush-left and ragged-right. This text is flush-left and ragged-right. This text is flush-left and ragged-right.

Flush-right and ragged-left

This text is flush-right and ragged-left. This text is flush-right and ragged-left. This text is flush-right and ragged-left. This text is flush-right and ragged-left. This text is flush-right and ragged-left. This text is flush-right and ragged-left. This text is flush-right and ragged-left.

Centred

This text is centred. Both edges are irregular. This text is centred. Both edges are irregular. This text is centred. Both edges are irregular. This text is centred. Both edges are irregular. This text is centred. Both edges are irregular. This text is centred. This text is centred. This text is centred.

In most documents that lawyers use or write, body text is set flush left, so that there is a straight line of text down the left margin. Then the question is whether to do the same on the right margin. Most books are justified: it has been the tradition with printers.

The experts are divided on which is easier to read: text that is justified, or flush-left with ragged-right margin. Wheildon's research comes down heavily in favour of justified text for better comprehension.[22] But that research involved text set in multiple columns, newspaper style Redish prefers left justified text with ragged-right margins, because she says, the different shapes of the lines help the reader to move from line to line of text. It also avoids too many hyphens, which can result from spreading out text to fill a line of justified text. And it avoids

---

22   Same work, p 59.

the extra spaces between words that you sometimes see in poorly justified text, particularly in newspaper columns: the so-called "rivers" (and "lakes") of white.[23] Too much space between words makes a line difficult to read. It stops the eye from taking in several words at once.

On the other hand, some people say justified text looks "neat" and "professional". And if it is well done, for most documents, the problems are not great. But professional publishers use typesetting algorithms to help them achieve the best arrangement of words, and avoid excessive spaces between them. Ordinary wordprocessing software is not very good at this.

The team working on the redesign of New South Wales legislation in 1994 reviewed the literature on this issue and decided to stay with justified text for main body text.[24] In 1999 when the Connecticut General Assembly adopted a new style and format for Bills and amendments, they carefully considered the recommendation of their document design consultant to use ragged-right margins. However, some legislators and staff were not comfortable with it, and the Assembly went with justified text instead.[25]

Typographers are still arguing about whether ragged-right margin or justified text is "better", and there does not appear to be conclusive proof either way. It is more a matter of personal preference, and whether you want a more relaxed (flush-left and ragged-right margin) or formal (justified) look to your document. There seems to be no significant difference in readability, except for poor readers.[26] Studies have shown poor readers are faster readers of text that has ragged-right margins.[27]

---

23 Krongold, S, "Writing Laws: Making them Easier to Understand" (1992) 24 *Ottawa L Rev* 495 at 542.

24 Parliamentary Counsel's Office & Centre for Plain Legal Language, 1994, *Review and Redesign of NSW Legislation*, New South Wales Government, Sydney, pages 21-22.

25 Shapiro, L, "Legislative document design in Connecticut", *Clarity* No 45, Dec 2000, p 18.

26 Hartley, J & Burnhill, P, 1971, "Experiments with unjustified text", *Visible Language*, 5, 265-278, quoted in Beaufort Wijnholds, A de, 1996 (cited at note 2), at 3.3.2.

27 Zachrisson, B, 1965, *Studies in Legibility of Printed Text*, Almqvist & Wiksell, Stockholm and Gregory, M & Poulton, EC, 1970, "Even versus uneven right-hand margins and rate of comprehension in reading", 13(4) *Ergonomics* 427-434, quoted in Beaufort Wijnholds, A de, 1996 (cited at note 2), at 3.3.2.

In the past, I have tended to use justified text in more formal legal documents, and flush-left text with ragged-right margins in letters. But the more I learn about the problems of readers, the more I lean towards ragged-right margins in non-professionally printed material.

One thing we do know is that it is not easy to read justified text in narrow columns. That arrangement produces too few words per line and odd spacing. And justification cannot be considered without also considering line length.[28]

White space

All the experts emphasise the importance of having plenty of white space around your text. It takes up space, it makes your documents longer, but it makes them easier to read and more inviting. One typographer recommends using wide margins on a page to allow the page to "breathe".[29]

You can draw attention to items (like the quotes in this book, for example, or the numbers in a margin) by surrounding them with white space. You can also indicate the structure of your material with white space. For example, you can signal to your reader that a particular section of text has ended, by leaving more white space at the end of that section than elsewhere. And you can tie a heading more effectively to the text it relates to, by leaving more space above the heading than below. The headings in this book follow that rule.

White space does one other important thing: it refreshes your reader. We all have personal experience of this from our reading. How often have you finished a chapter of a novel, seen the end of the page, turned over just to see what's next, or to mark your place, and then some time later realised that you *just kept reading?* Your interest is renewed by the new page and the white space.

One expert suggests you need to leave about 15-20% white space in page layouts – more on the outside to force items together rather than pushing them apart.[30] Other experts have suggested leaving up to

---

28 See p 264.

29 Tarbet, M, 1996, "Regarding text fonts for readability", *UTEST electronic subscription list*, quoted in Beaufort Wijnholds, A de, 1996 (cited at note 2) at 3.3.

30 "Producing Successful Publications: Layout and Design Points", *B & C Business and Communication Papers*, excerpts reprinted in *Rapport* No 11 Spring 1994, p 14.

50% of a page for margins or other white space.[31] Whatever the proportions, one thing is certain: white space is not usually wasted space. Even if it makes your documents longer, it will make them more likely to be read, and better understood. Do not forget the space "between the lines". Typographers call this "leading" (pronounced "ledding"). It is also called "line spacing". Most wordprocessing software allows you to choose line spacing at standard measurements, or to specify your exact requirements. Setting the optimum line spacing involves a compromise that depends on the typeface and type size you are using, the line length, and whether or not your text is justified.[32]

Having plenty of space between the lines is handy for text that might have to be annotated by hand, but again there's a trade-off. The greater the space between the lines, the more probable it is that, after reading to the end of a line, the reader skips to the wrong following line. On the other hand, there is evidence that in the case of text with more "leading", or wider line spacing, readers judge type size to be larger, and reading comfort may increase.[33]

And if you increase the space *between paragraphs*, and decrease the space *between lines*, you can help the readers "skim" more easily. This technique was used for the new, reader-friendly style for Bills and amendments that the Connecticut General Assembly adopted in 1999. They increased paragraph spacing from 1.5 to 2.0 and decreased line spacing from 1.5 to 1.2,[34] and found it "dramatically" improved the readability of their documents.[35]

One final thought on white space: using more white space means using more paper. That not only costs more – and paper is *very* expensive, but there is also the environmental effect to consider. If we are too

---

31 See Parliamentary Counsel's Office & Centre for Plain Legal Language, 1994, *Review and Redesign of NSW Legislation*, New South Wales Government, Sydney, p 17, quoting separate works by Rubenstein (1988) and Conover (1990).

32 Martin Cutts has suggested setting leading at about a fifth of the type size (so 12 point type might have leading at 2.5 or 3 points): Cutts, M, "Lucid Layout", *Clarity* No 45, Dec 2000, p 6.

33 Beaufort Wijnholds, A de, 1996 (cited at note 2), at 3.5.

34 These measurements are in terms of line spacing rather than in points (1 line = 12 points).

35 Shapiro, L, "Legislative document design in Connecticut", p 17 (cited at note 25).

extravagant with white space, not only are we likely to use more trees, but we also risk alienating an environmentally conscious audience.

Diagrams, tables, charts and other graphics

Lawyers have traditionally dealt in words, and until recently have been reluctant to describe concepts in any other way. But things are changing. Now we can see not only tables and formulas in legislation,[36] but also flow charts, logic trees and boxes with yes and no or ticks and crosses in them.[37]

It happens in private documents too: some years ago, one of my legal colleagues decided that what her client needed was not a standard-form contract, but a contract in the form of a checklist. Lawyers are becoming more adventurous about presenting complex concepts in different formats.

But most of us are design amateurs, and most of us will need some help if we want to go beyond the absolute basics. You only need to go to seminars given by lawyers and look at the pictorial or graphic material they present in their handouts, slides and PowerPoint presentations, to see that most lawyers know next-to-nothing about how to present material visually. They fill their presentations with so many different graphics and other visual devices that it can become even more confusing for the audience. Sometimes, it is wiser to get expert help.

---

36 For various examples of financial formulas, see the (Qld) Consumer Credit Regulation 1995 Parts 3, 7, 8 & 8A. This regulation is to be replaced on 1 July 2010 as part of the National Consumer Credit Reform legislation. The proposed new National Consumer Credit Protection Regulations 2009 use corresponding formulas: see Parts 7-2, 7-6, 7-7 & 7-8.

37 For example, Local Government Act 1993 (NSW), Income Tax Assessment Act 1997 (Cth). See also the Australian Office of Parliamentary Counsel's *Plain English Manual*, pages 31-37 <http://www.opc.gov.au/plain/docs. htm> and *Working with the Office of Parliamentary Counsel: A guide for clients* 2nd ed, July 2002, pages 30-32 and 51-66 <http://www.opc.gov.au/about/ documents.htm> and Penfold, H, QC, 2001, "When words aren't enough: Graphics and other innovations in legislative drafting", a paper given at the *Language and the Law* conference, University of Texas at Austin, 6-8 Dec 2001 <http://www.opc.gov.au/plain/docs.htm>.

Finding things

We must remember that not all our readers will read our document from cover to cover. They may (or may not) do that the first time, but the *next* time they look at the document they will almost certainly dip into it to find the parts that they are interested in. So it will help them to use the document efficiently if we give them directions.

Some of the things we can use in our documents to give directions are:

- headings
- numbering
- symbols like asterisks, or the "bullets" I'm using now
- signals
- highlighting
- other reading and navigation aids
- colour
- indenting
- indexes and tables of contents.

Let me deal with each of those individually (using headings, of course).

Headings

It is obvious enough that headings can help readers find what they are looking for. It can also help them understand what they are about to read. But headings can only do that if they are *meaningful* headings. For example, how helpful is the heading **Introduction**? It tells you that something is being introduced, but it doesn't tell you what. The reader knows that it is likely that the writer will introduce the topic in some way, but has no idea what the writer has in mind.

In this book, when I wrote my plan, I had as the first heading **Introduction**. After that came Chapter 1. Then I thought again. I decided what I wanted to say by way of introduction. I devised a heading that explained it better than **Introduction**. That was how the first chapter in this book came to be Chapter 1 – rather than an Introduction, and that is why Chapter 1 is called **What is this book about?**

You'll notice that Chapter 1's title is in the form of a question. I find that questions are often very useful as headings. They seem to make you focus your mind on the real issue, rather than describing things in the abstract. For example, I think a heading which reads **What income tax is payable?** is more descriptive and more precise than simply the words **Income tax**. Other times, a short label is all that is required. Whatever best helps the reader to decide whether this is the section they are interested in.

Another approach to headings is to give the answer in the heading. For example, **Income tax is payable**, **The case should be settled**, or **The facts do not establish negligence**. The heading then acts as a summary of what follows, so that readers not only know at a glance *where* the information they want is, but also, in brief, *what* it is.

Legislation in Australia has used questions as headings for some years now. A notable example is the New South Wales Local Government Act 1993, with headings for chapters, divisions and sections, such as: "What are the purposes of this Act?", "What activities require approval?" and "Who has the right to vote?" The Australian Parliamentary Counsel's *Plain English Manual* also recommends this practice, but warns against overdoing it, in case it becomes irritating, or narrows the scope of the headings.[38] This is an important point. Some readers do complain that having to deal with too many questions is annoying. Variety is the key to engaging writing.

Headings of all kinds can be very helpful to readers, but again, it is possible to overdo things. Not every paragraph needs a heading. Only use a heading when a new topic is introduced.

Be careful, too, when you use headings to summarise the text. There is no need to do this if the text itself is very short, or if it results in a heading almost as long as the text itself. You have probably seen the kind of thing I have in mind. You often see it in the company constitutions, where writers have felt compelled to put a heading on every clause, however short it may be. If you adopt that policy, then when it comes to very short clauses or paragraphs, the heading gives the whole show away. For example, I have seen things like this:

Calls paid in advance may be entitled to dividend
Dividends in proportion to the amount paid up may be paid on each share in respect of which any moneys have been paid in advance of calls.

Calls paid in advance give no participation in profits
Any moneys paid on shares in advance of calls shall not confer a right to participate in the profits of the company.

---

38   <http://www.opc.gov.au/about/docs/pem.pdf>, pages 25 & 33.

The headings say as much as, if not more than, the clauses themselves. The text becomes repetitive, superfluous.

If you are using numbering in your document, it helps the reader to find the information they are looking for if you include the number in the heading, hard over to the left margin, like this:

1.   What is this document for?

There is more on this technique later, under **Indenting**.[39]

Finally, for more complex documents, or for documents in which you have a multi-level structure, you may wish to have more than one level of heading – both headings and sub-headings. That can be a very effective way to show to your reader the logic underpinning your document. But if you do this, you must be consistent in the way you signify headings and sub-headings, so that the reader always knows which level of the structure they are in. Make sure that sections with comparable degrees of importance have the same style of heading, and that that style indicates the heading's level of importance.

In this book I have chapter headings, as in Chapter 3: **Why plain language?**, then subject headings, like **What's in it for me?** and occasionally sub-headings, like *Does it save money?*[40] All are in bold type, but the chapter heading is larger than the heading, which is larger than the sub-heading. Each has more "weight" than the next, which makes it is easy to see their order of importance, and that in turn indicates the significance of the text set out under each heading.

Numbering

Numbering is another thing that can help people find their way around a document. Like a heading, it acts as a sign post. The writer can use it to refer the reader to different parts of the document, both in the document itself, and later, if it is being discussed. It can also show the order in which things should be done, considered, and so on.

Numbering is good for lists, because it indicates how many things there are in a list. For that reason, it is essential to use numbering when you are listing in a document the things that need to be done or the items that are enclosed. Numbers are better for that purpose than other symbols, such as bullets (or dot-points) or asterisks. With numbers, the

---

39   See p 284.

40   See p 34.

reader can mentally (or even physically) check off the items as they are done or received.

When we write letters, we only need a simple numbering system. I think Arabic numbers (1, 2, 3 etc) are better than roman upper case (I, II, III) or lower case (i, ii, iii), because they are more common in non-legal drafting. Arabic numbers are also better for lists than alphabet characters because using letters of the alphabet makes it harder to work out how many things are in the list. What item number in a list is item (g)?

In other documents we might need a system with several "levels" of numbering. Like headings, numbering can show the reader the logic underpinning the document. There are plenty of numbering systems to choose from. But choosing a system of numbering is more than just a matter of taste. There are advantages and disadvantages to most systems.

Numbering systems for legislation

The old statutory system of numbering commonly used in the British Commonwealth is this:

- Sections have whole Arabic numbers (801).
- Subsections have bracketed whole Arabic numbers ((1)).
- Paragraphs have bracketed lower case letters ((a)).
- Sub-paragraphs have bracketed lower case roman numerals ((i)).
- Sub-sub-paragraphs have bracketed upper case letters (A) (these days most legislative drafters try not to use sub-paragraphs and sub-sub paragraphs).
- If the legislators need to squeeze another section in between two sections that already have numbers they use an unbracketed small upper case letter (section 801A).
- The whole number sequence does not appear for each subsection or paragraph (section 801(2) would be numbered as (2)).

But there are several disadvantages to this system:

- You have to memorise the order of the levels because they don't follow a "natural" sequence, as decimal numbers do.

- You can end up having to refer to sub-sub-paragraph (a)(i)(A) of section 801(1) or section 801(1)(a)(i)(A) for short.
- If you have a series of long subsections that go for several pages, you can lose track of what section you're in.

The Law Reform Commission of Victoria recognised these difficulties and recommended a new numbering system for our laws.[41] Its basic features are:

- Decimal numbering, but modified so that the main idea is given a whole number (805, 806 etc) and the subsidiary provisions – exceptions, qualifications and the like – are given a decimal point (805.1, 805.2 etc).
- A new number series (100, 200 etc) is adopted for each new part to allow room for amendments and to help readers find different sections.
- It only allows for three levels of numbering (801, 801.1, 801.1.1). After that it uses dots (·) or dashes, to be used sparingly, perhaps for items in a list.

Two disadvantages I can see with that system are:

- It is difficult to refer to the dots and dashes: the Law Reform Commission's Report recommended[42] the citation for a dot in a section be in this form: "first dot-point in section 41".
- The fact that numbering is not always sequential (because a new number series is used for each part) means that we could jump from, say, section 725 to section 800, and this might lead to confusion as to whether anything is left out.

These criticisms are minor, though, and I don't know of any numbering system that is perfect for all types of document.

Redesigning legislative numbering systems

The redesigned format of NSW legislation[43] did not adopt a decimal numbering system, although it was considered. It was decided not to

---

41   Law Reform Commission of Victoria, Report No 33, May 1990, *Access to the Law: the structure and format of legislation*, p 16.
42   Same work, p 21.
43   The Centre for Plain Legal Language worked with the New South Wales Parliamentary Counsel's Office to develop an improved design for NSW legislation. Almost all NSW Acts passed from 1995 are in the new format.

change from the traditional system, for several reasons. One reason was that full decimal systems do not work well for legislation that will be amended: what section number goes between sections 1.1 and 1.2 ? (1.1.1 is reserved for subsections). Another reason was that it can add clutter when the decimal numbers begin to add up. (They are working with a smaller B5 sized page). Another reason was the practical one that changing all legislation over to a new system would be very costly. In the end, the decision was that the other design improvements would mean the existing numbering system would work better. But occasionally decimal numbering crops up in subordinate legislation,[44] particularly if the "client"[45] asks for it.

In Canada, the legislative counsel considered and rejected full decimal numbering over 25 years ago. But decimal numbers are used in existing legislation in most Canadian jurisdictions for adding new sections and subsections.[46]

In Australia, the old Income Tax Assessment Act 1936 presented a special challenge to any numbering system. It is over 5000 pages long and has been amended many times. Its numbering system didn't handle those amendments well, so it ended up with strange section numbers like 159ZZZZA.

The Tax Law Improvement Project (known as TLIP)[47] experimented with several numbering systems in its rewrite of Australian tax laws. It came up with a new system with several of the features of the Victorian Law Reform Commission's system, and with other variations. The Project had a number of key objectives which the new system had to meet. They were:

1. Each unit of law should have a unique number to identify it.

2. For any two conceivable numbers within the system, it should be immediately apparent which one is higher.

3. Numbers should be easy to read.

---

44   For example, the Northern Territory's Work Health Court Rules.

45   The government department, instrumentality or other body that needs the drafting done for them.

46   Elliott, DC, 1994, *Writing Rules: structure and style*, paper given at the conference "Linguists and Lawyers – Issues we Confront", Århus, Denmark, 24-27 Aug 1994, p 19. Reconfirmed by email from David Elliott, Sept 2009.

47   See p 73.

4. Numbers should be able to be said aloud without being ambiguous.
5. The system should flow "naturally", and be predictable.
6. The system should follow existing drafting conventions unless there is a reason to abandon them, but allow change if they are causing problems.
7. Each number should identify the "building block" to which it belongs.
8. The system should cope well if a large amount new material is inserted later.[48]

The Project Team thought the new system they devised met all those objectives. They admitted that was not perfect, but they were confident that the system would work well in practice, especially for a law which is amended extensively and often. The rewritten Income Tax Assessment Act 1997 has chapters, parts, divisions, subdivisions, sections and smaller units, all numbered.[49]

One of the major innovations was inspired by objective no 7 – that numbers identify the "building block" to which they belong. This means that some numbers – section and part numbers – are "double-barrelled". For example, section 5-15 tells you it is section 15 in division 5. Part 5-6 tells you that it is Part 6 of Chapter 5. There are also gaps in numbering the divisions at the end of parts, and gaps in the part numbers at the end of chapters. This is to leave room to insert material without disturbing the number sequence.

These numbers are quite a change, and produce some of their own problems. For example, the gaps in the numbering of divisions and parts in the new tax laws are disconcerting to some. Others are more appreciative:

> while it may be difficult for some of the "old lags" to adapt to the new numbering scheme, the basic approach of the TLIP legislation does appear to offer a period of logic and order and a significant improvement over the old Act.[50]

---

48 Adapted, with minor changes, from Tax Law Improvement Project, 1995, Information Paper No 2, *Building the New Tax Law*, Commonwealth of Australia, Canberra, p 23.

49 There are some lists in the form of bullet points.

50 Woellner, Prof R and Zetler, J, 2000, "Tiptoe through the TULIPs: an Evaluation of the Tax Law Improvement Project", *Current Commercial Law eZine*, Vol 7, No 1, May 2000, p 16.

Interestingly, since the suspension of TLIP, very few pieces of the subsequently drafted tax legislation use the innovative numbering scheme developed by the TLIP.[51]

The rewrite of the New Zealand Income Tax Act[52] retains the alphabetical Part numbers of the existing Act (for example, Parts CE and CF), but it also employs a gap in the middle of the alphabet. Here, too, the aim is to allow leeway for the future so that drafters can avoid using subparts with three-letter identifiers (such as CEA between CE and CF).

I believe there is no one "right" answer on numbering. The system you choose should depend on the type of document and how it is used. I usually use the decimal system (for example, 1.1.1) or, depending on the document, I might use a hybrid system that is decimal at least at the section or clause level (for example, 1.1 (a)). For me, that emphasises the difference between the section and subsection, clause and subclause.

Numbering hints

Here are a few other practical hints to bear in mind when deciding on what numbering system best suits your document:

- keep it as simple as possible – so it is easy to remember
- don't mix too many styles
- if sequence or counting is important, numbers are better
- check what automatic numbering systems your wordprocessing software has; if one is suitable it will save time and effort. It can also make it easier to transmit documents to other computers. If you have used a modified or customised numbering system, documents can crash or be corrupted when they are transferred to another computer system
- bear in mind the effect the system you choose will have on the margins and tabs in your document
- it is also important *where* you place your numbers: usually hard against the left margin.

---

51 Except for, for example, A New Tax System (Goods and Services Tax) Act 1999 and Income Tax (Transitional Provisions) Act 1997 (both Cth). But perhaps this is simply because most Acts are not long enough to justify it.

52 See pages 73-74.

Symbols

If it is not important to keep your list sequential, or if the document is less formal, or unlikely to be discussed at great length or dissected, you might prefer not to number your list, and instead use other symbols like asterisks, dashes, arrows or the bullets I've been using over the last few pages. They are a bit more "graphic" than numbers, and less formal, so in some circumstances they might be better for attracting attention.

Signals

There's another thing you can do to help the reader find their way around the document. Give them signals that point the way to additional information that might help them understand the material better.

For example, many legal documents use definitions for special words and phrases. The traditional way of indicating that a word or phrase is defined is to use an initial capital for the defined expression each time in appears, and the first time it appears it has inverted commas around it. But, as we saw in Chapter 7, this system has some disadvantages.[53] One alternative to the initial capital is to use a numbered footnote, asterisk, icon (representative picture) or some other marker in the text, which cross-refers either to a note at the foot of the page or the end of a section, or to a marginal note.

This method works well to draw the reader's attention to all sorts of subsidiary information. But it has its disadvantages, especially if there are too many signals on each page. One commentator has remarked that too many asterisks can look like "fly spots".[54]

Highlighting

I like to use **bold type** for my headings because it is dramatic. That is my choice. But I don't use underlining or upper case in my text unless I am quoting something that is underlined or in upper case. There is a reason for that.

---

53   Page 145.

54   Bennett, J, 1993, "Slaying Small Print: The St George Mortgage", in *Plain Language in Commercial Documents*, BLEC Books, Melbourne, p 50.

Words that are underlined are more difficult to read because the eye is distracted from the letters by the line. Words written in upper case are more difficult to read than words in lower case. When we read a line of type, we recognise letters by the shapes of the top half of the letters. In lower case, the top half of letters are more distinctive, and surrounded by more white space. The vertical extensions on lower case letters ("ascenders", as in b and d, and "descenders", as in y and p) help us to recognize them. In upper case, the letters are squarer, and we need more effort to distinguish them.[55] Upper case also takes up as much as 30% more room. Compare these examples.

DEAR MR SMITH,
I AM SORRY TO INFORM YOU THAT YOUR APPLICATION FOR THE POSITION HAS BEEN UNSUCCESSFUL. HOWEVER, IF YOU AGREE, WE WILL KEEP YOUR CURRICULUM VITAE ON FILE AND CONTACT YOU SHOULD ANY SIMILAR POSITIONS BECOME AVAILABLE IN THE FUTURE. THANK YOU FOR YOUR APPLICATION AND YOUR INTEREST IN OUR COMPANY.

Dear Mr Smith,
I am sorry to inform you that your application for the position has been unsuccessful. However, if you agree, we will keep your curriculum vitae on file and contact you should any similar positions become available in the future. Thank you for your application and your interest in our company.

Dear Mr Smith
I am sorry to inform you that your application for the position has been unsuccessful. However, if you agree, we will keep your curriculum vitae on file and contact you should any similar positions become available in the future. Thank you for your application and your interest in our company.

Dear Mr Smith
I am sorry to inform you that your application for the position has been unsuccessful. However, if you agree, we will keep your curriculum vitae on file and contact you should any similar positions become available in the future. Thank you for your application and your interest in our company.

---

55 Wheildon, C, 2005, *Type & Layout: Are you communicating or just making pretty shapes*, p 62 (cited at note 4); Felsenfeld, C and Siegel, A, 1981, *Writing Contracts in Plain English*, p 194 (cited at note 10).

The first two examples are much harder to read than the last two. The last example also shows how the emphatic effect of bold type diminishes with overuse.

I sometimes use bold type for highlighting text because it draws the eye to the highlighted text, but there are alternatives. In fact, a 1992 study showed that bold type tends to draw *too much* attention to itself.[56] That is why typographers generally keep bold for headings and labels, and use italics and upper case for emphasis. Another alternative is using a different font or typeface.

In this book I have used italics for emphasis rather than bold type. That is because there is plenty of text, and there are quite a few headings in bold type for the reader to cope with. If I had used bold type for emphasis throughout the book, it might have become tiresome. Italics are a good alternative because they are easier to read than underlined words and they traditionally convey emphasis to the reader. But again, if they are overused their effect diminishes.[57]

With wordprocessing software it is just as easy to use bold type or italics as it is to use underlining. And both italics and bold type are much easier on the reader's eyes.

If you use a different typeface to highlight something, you need to choose carefully. For example, if you use a serif typeface for your body text, headings in sans serif typeface can make a good and effective contrast, depending on the typefaces you choose.[58] But if you want to highlight something in the body text itself, some typefaces won't give enough contrast, and some will be annoying. That is why people mostly choose the same typeface, but in italics or bold, to highlight body text.

Other reading and navigation aids

You could also consider putting some of your text in boxes. This was done in New South Wales in the Local Government Act 1993.

---

56   McAteer, E, 1992, "Typeface emphasis and information focus in written language", *Applied Cognitive Psychology* 6(4), pages 345-359.

57   Dr Janice C Redish has written that italics may be the best choice for highlighting definitions. She says italics are less obtrusive than upper case or bold type. See Krongold, S, "Writing Laws: Making them Easier to Understand" (1992) 24 *Ottawa L Rev* 495 at 540. See also Chapter 6, pages 145-147.

58   See pages 261-262.

Unfortunately, the drafters used boxes both for the "Introduction" information for each chapter, and for the "Notes" which give subsidiary information. That tends to give the impression that both these items are the most important information – and that both are equally important. It is probably wiser to use boxes for only one kind of information – the information you think your reader should read first. And for the record: that experiment was not repeated in later New South Wales legislation. In fact, the *Manual for the Preparation of Legislation* of the New South Wales Parliamentary Counsel's Office specifically says:

> **Do not use ...**
> • Boxes around text (a table can be used to create a blank box, say for a signature block, and a character used for a small box to be ticked).

Boxes and other innovative design techniques were also extensively used in the Income Tax Assessment Act 1997, which was the result of the Australian government's Tax Law Improvement Project. In that Act there are boxes at the beginning of various Divisions and Subdivisions of the Act that contain "theme statements" – text explaining what the Division or Subdivision is about. There are also boxes that contain "Method Statements" which give working examples of how to do the calculations required by the law. And there are boxes for text set out in tables. Theme statements in boxes have been used in much of the subsequently drafted tax legislation.

The Income Tax Assessment Act 1997 also has diagrams, including a picture of a pyramid explaining the underlying structure of the Act, and a diagram which gives a map of Subdivision 20-B of the Act. There are checklists, flow charts and other reader aids too. There are cross-references and explanatory notes sprinkled throughout the text. Some of these features continue to be used in later tax legislation.[59]

While there has been some criticism of the redrafted Act, there seems to be much appreciation for the improved layout, innovative design features and navigation aids. As two commentators put it:

> While immense effort was and will be required to "retool", at least one "old lag" finds the use of diagrams, flow-charts,

---

59 There is a list of these features in Attachment C to the Australian Parliamentary Counsel's *Drafting Direction no 1.8: Special Rules for Tax Code Drafting*, released 1 May 2006, p 37 <http://www.opc.gov.au/about/drafting_series/DD%20 1.8.pdf>.

cross-referencing, notes and checklists often generally useful and helpful as are the flow charts, diagrams, "Method Statements", the Map, Tables and the vastly improved Explanatory Memoranda.[60]

And:

> Combining tables, examples and notes in synergistic ways, embedded in a fundamentally restructured and more logical framework have, anecdotally, proven much simpler to teach and for students to understand, than their predecessors.[61]

Other Australian Commonwealth legislation features a wide variety of new reading and navigation aids. The redesign of New South Wales legislation also included some innovative navigation aids. There are now running headings on each page, which give the name of the Act and part, and the clause and part numbers. The page number is now in a running footer.[62]

However, most legislation is now available for viewing and downloading on various websites. These sites don't display the legislation in publishing layout", so many of the reading and navigation aids don't appear online. In fact, reading legislation in hard copy is becoming the exception rather than the rule.[63] And, as we will see in the next chapter, we navigate through documents quite differently on the internet.

Colour

Computers and photocopiers now allow us to consider the luxury of colour in our documents. But for amateurs in printing, it may be a luxury we don't need. Studies show that for legible text, as for the Model T Ford, you can choose any colour you like, as long as it is black.[64] Even text printed in very dark colours is nowhere near as

---

50 Woellner, Prof R and Zetler, J, 2000, "Tiptoe through the TULIPs: an Evaluation of the Tax Law Improvement Project", pages 22-23 (cited at note 50).

51 Same work, p 23.

52 See, for example, Retirement Villages Act 1999 and Callan Park (Special Provisions) Act 2002 (both NSW).

53 In NSW it is actually quite difficult to get hold of Acts in hard copy. Even NSW Parliament House doesn't hold hard copies any longer. The printing has been "outsourced" to a private printer which no longer has a bookshop, and prints and binds Acts to order. They still use the 1994 format.

54 Wheildon, C, 2005, *Type & Layout: Are you communicating or just making pretty shapes,* Chapter 7 (cited at note 4); Hartley, J, 1994, *Designing Instructional Text,* p 90 (cited at note 18).

legible as black type. If you want to print black text onto a coloured background, it had better be a background in a very light tint. Tests have shown that comprehension levels drop 7% if the background is not white. The darker the background tint, the lower the comprehension level.[65] Readers do *say* that they find a lightly tinted background more attractive. But that preference seems to give no boost to their comprehension levels.[66]

Colour works best when it is used for a purpose, not just to be decorative. For example, colour can be used to structure material: a block of colour behind text can indicate that it belongs together – that the material is related. On the other hand, randomly placed blocks of colour can confuse the reader or distract attention from the text. If the colour is poorly chosen it can make the text less readable. Don't forget that some of your readers may be colour–blind (5 – 8% of males and less than 1% of females). And don't forget that colour will only photocopy on a colour copier.

A recent study suggests that background colour choice may be significant for some cognitive functions.[67] But this research related to short advertising-type messages, and it may not translate to legal writing.

There is yet another factor to consider in terms of colour: cultural differences. For example, certain colours can be very significant for certain readers, and the meaning of colours can vary greatly from country to country. White may mean purity in many western cultures but in some eastern cultures it signifies death. Green can be the colour of environmental sensitivity, but it is also the colour of Islam.

Indenting

You can get a good idea of the difference that indenting can make by comparing the current and the old design of New South Wales legislation. In the current format, numbered sections are positioned to the left of the page, and subsections appear at the next indent. Text

---

65 Wheildon, C, 2005, *Type & Layout: Are you communicating or just making pretty shapes,* table 10, p 81 & table 17, p 87 (cited at note 4).

66 Same work, pages 79-88.

67 University of British Columbia, 6 Feb 2009, "Effect Of Colors: Blue Boosts Creativity, While Red Enhances Attention To Detail", *ScienceDaily* <http://www.sciencedaily.com/releases/2009/02/090205142143.htm>.

does not wrap around under the section numbers, as it did in the old format. The current format looks like this:

2. **Commencement**
   (1) This section commences on the date of assent to this Act.
   (2) Section 3 commences on a date to be proclaimed. Section 4 commences on 1 March 2010.

The old format had text wrapping right round, like this:

Commencement
   2. (1) This section commences on the date of assent to this Act.
       (2) Section 3 commences on a date to be proclaimed. Section 4 commences on 1 March 2010.

Notice how, in the second (old) version, the heading is aligned to the left margin, so that the section and subsection numbers are hidden by the heading on top of the numbers and the text below them. The system of indenting in the first (current) format allows you to scan down the left margin for section and subsection numbers to find the ones you want.

Indexes and tables of contents

Indexing is a very specialised field, and good indexing is quite an art.

Except for more "permanent" documents, such as laws, books and more "public" documents like company constitutions, public trusts, charters and constitutions, we have to face the fact that there is not enough time to index many legal documents. But our readers still need to be able to find their way around our documents. Wordprocessing software makes it possible to provide at least a table of contents or a list of headings. And that is all the more reason to use meaningful headings.

A table of contents isn't much use unless it gives page or paragraph numbers, but remember that if you insert the page numbers and then later amend the document, the page numbers may need to be altered. Wordprocessing software can automatically update tables as the document changes. In fact, many allow you to build a table of contents at the same time as you build your document, using it as a kind of framework to hang your words from. This is a useful feature for plain language writers, who like to begin their documents with an outline or plan.[68]

---

68   See pages 104-106.

Summary

- As lawyers we have always been concerned first and foremost with text. But we must also think about document design if we want our writing to be readable, and to give it its best chance of being understood.

- If you understand some of the basic design principles, you can make quite a difference to the readability of your document.

- Plain language lawyers consider carefully the typeface, font and size, line length, justification and white space they use in their documents. They will use diagrams, tables, charts and other graphics, as well as text, to explain the concepts they write about.

- If you choose a modern, legible typeface, it does not really matter if it is serif or sans serif. Today's readers are familiar with sans serif typefaces. I often use a sans serif typeface, especially to work on a computer screen (for example, Arial or Verdana). If I want something more elegant on paper, I use Georgia or something like this book's Book Antiqua. It depends on audience and purpose.

- Type size varies depending on typeface. Don't just pick a point size – see how it looks in the typeface you've chosen. 10-12 point type is usually legible, but legibility also depends on having adequate inter-linear space, or leading. Use larger type for older readers.

- Body text should always be set flush-left. It is debatable whether it is better to justify, or leave the text ragged right. But I am tending towards ragged right for reading ease.

- Plain language lawyers use meaningful headings, sensible numbering, symbols, signals, well-chosen highlighting, perhaps colour, and indenting, indexes and tables of contents to help their readers find things in their documents.

- There's no perfect numbering system for all documents, but Arabic numbers are easier to read, and better for lists. I use the decimal system (1.1.1), or sometimes a hybrid that is decimal to subclause level (1.1(a)).

- Don't use upper case or underlining to highlight body text. They are harder to read than bold or italics.

- Black type on white (or very lightly tinted) paper is the easiest combination to read. Use colour only for a specific purpose, such as background colour to group material.

And one final word on document design: lawyers who pay no attention to the way documents look have not completed the task of communication. Although they may have produced a document that works as a matter of law, they have not done their duty. They have not made sure that their document can be easily read. In this respect, they have even been compared to the Roman tyrant Caligula, who cruelly inscribed his laws on top of pillars too high for the people to read.[69]

In the next chapter we'll see that the principles of design that apply to documents printed on paper do not necessarily apply in the same way to documents designed for viewing on a computer screen. When you read something on paper you are looking a flat fixed surface that reflects light. When you read something on a computer screen you see a dynamic surface that emits light. Each surface has a different effect on your eyes. That has implications for document design, as we'll see in Chapter 16.

---

69   Felsenfeld, C and Siegel, A, 1981, *Writing Contracts in Plain English*, p 176
      (cited at note 10).

Chapter 16

Designing documents for the computer screen

Chapter 14 looked at the effect of the internet and email on our writing. Chapter 15 discussed the principles of traditional document design. This chapter brings the two topics together to deal with the special features of designing documents that will be viewed on a computer screen.

Websites

The internet has not only brought us email; it has also brought us websites. As we saw in Chapter 14, law firms, barristers' chambers, courts, law societies, legal aid organisations, community legal centres and other law-related organisations now have websites and "home pages" to communicate with clients, and the world at large. These websites are not just written, they are also "designed", often by professional website designers.

Also, web-based legal research is now the preferred method of many lawyers. So courts, judges and law reporters need to think about electronic document design when publishing judgments and other material on the internet.

The development of the internet, and in particular websites, has prompted document designers and others to look again at the design principles that were developed for material printed on paper.

Understanding design principles

I observed in Chapter 15 that the average computer gives the average lawyer plenty of design options. But I pointed out the pitfalls of "dabbling in publishing", without having a firm grasp of the basic principles of document design. The same warning applies with even more force in designing documents to be read on websites and on the computer screen. However, it helps to understand some of the issues that make designing for the computer screen a growing area of expertise.

Research suggests that established document design guidelines do not necessarily apply in the same way to material displayed electronically. And new research questions the validity of some of the old guidelines – even in the print context.[1] Much of the print-based research was done in the 1960s, and there is evidence that reading habits have changed since then, and that our reading habits can govern what we consider to be "readable".

The basic principles of information design that we saw in Chapter 15 remain the same: consider your reader, make the information clear, relevant and usable, and select techniques and design elements that support those aims and are appropriate for the purpose. But the computer screen brings into play new technical factors (such as the reflection of light and the phenomenon of pixels[2]) and human factors too. So the new medium has refocused attention on the basic assumptions of document design. If you are not interested in this detail, skip to p 307 and just read the summary.

Skimming or scanning

The first thing to question is the most basic assumption of all: that people *read* websites. According to several of the experts, they don't.[3] Web guru Jakob Nielsen says:

> People rarely read Web pages word by word; instead, they scan the page, picking out individual words and sentences. In research on how people read websites we found that 79 percent of our test users always scanned any new page they came across; only 16 percent read word-by-word.[4]

These findings are supported by research by Norwegian researcher Ann Mangen. Her theory is that the feeling of being literally "in touch" with the text is lost when we read digital text, which we do by clicking, pointing and scrolling. She concludes:

---

1   See p 261.
2   The dots of light that make up the images on a computer or TV screen. See p 295.
3   Spool, JM, Schroeder, W, Scanlon, T, Snyder, C, 1998, "Web sites that work: Designing with your eyes open", *Proceedings of CHI '98, Human factors in computing systems*, Los Angeles, California, ACM 18-23 <http://portal.acm.org/citation.cfm?doid=286498.286626>.
4   Nielsen, J, "How Users Read on the Web", *Alertbox*, 1 Oct 1997 <www.useit.com/alertbox/9710a.html>.

One main effect of the intangibility of the digital text is that of making us read in a shallower, less focused way.[5]

Nielsen has this advice:

Web pages have to employ **scannable text**, using

- highlighted **keywords** (hypertext links serve as one form of highlighting; typeface variations and color are others)
- meaningful **sub-headings** (not "clever" ones)
- bulleted **lists**
- **one idea** per paragraph (users will skip over any additional ideas if they are not caught by the first few words in the paragraph)
- the **inverted pyramid** style, starting with the conclusion.
- **half the word count** (or less) than conventional writing.[6]

This is actually good advice for plain language writing in general.

A new kind of document structure?

If most people are scanning rather than reading, they are probably not following a linear method of absorbing material. They are not reading from beginning to end, but are selecting chunks of information from different parts of the material available on the computer screen. They are also darting around from document to document, from web page to web page via hyperlinks, sometimes starting in the middle or end and working backwards. This suggests that on-screen documents might require a *completely different structure* from print documents.

To work out what structure will work best, the key, as always in plain language writing, is to think like the user. If you can work out how the user is going to come to your material and what they are going to want from it, then you are on the way to developing a usable structure for an on-screen document.

Organising material for the computer screen

The Australian government's *Style Manual* recommends authors and editors work closely with electronic publishing specialists to find the

---

5   Mangen, A, 2008, "Hypertext fiction reading: haptics and immersion", *Journal of Research in Reading*, Vol 31, Issue 4, pages 404-419 <http://www3.interscience.wiley.com/journal/121430985/abstract>.

6   Nielsen, J, "How Users Read on the Web" (cited at note 4).

best structure for on-screen publications. The *Style Manual* also gives some hints for organising material for use on the computer screen. In summary, it recommends that authors:

- Break content down into smaller logical units (to avoid forcing readers to scroll too much).
- Keep to a maximum of five A4 pages for any one section meant to be read independently.
- Use one heading per screen (or "window").
- Consider using a web-type structure rather than the sequential or hierarchical structures more common in print-based documents. Web-type structures arrange content in "associative" patterns, which allow readers to move from place to place within a document or between websites. This is a flexible structure, but it can also confuse, as the reader takes in information in a potentially random order.
- Use the various "signposting" techniques recommended for printed documents, as adapted for screen-based documents. For example, visually highlighting material on the screen, such as headings, lists, key words, text in boxes or margins, and captions.
- Use bridging words, cross-references and hyperlinks to link associated material.[7]

Structure to help your reader

In Chapter 15, we saw how headings can be a very effective way to show the reader the logic underpinning the document. This is especially important for documents designed to be read on a computer screen. The reader can get mentally lost if they lose track of the structure of the document. The hierarchy of information in the document is the way the reader will navigate through it and select information to read. A tight, well-organised and clearly labelled structure is vital.

Remember that the reader is coming into the document "cold". Categories, titles and other names used as headings and labels and options might mean something to you, but they can completely mystify the reader. Writing for the web means you must cater for those who are completely unfamiliar with your world.

---

7   See 2002, *Style Manual for Authors, Editors and Printers*, 6th edition, John Wiley & Sons Australia Ltd, p 42 and following pages for more detail.

Another technique already mentioned can help here. Summarising material at the beginning of each section, rather than at the end, helps two types of "skimming" or "scanning" reader. First, the summary may be enough for the person who needs only the minimum detail and does not want to have to read the full text. Second, it can help direct those who *are* looking for detail to the exact detail they want.

Write in a style that helps your reader

Because the web is a different medium from other print-based media, it actually requires a different style of writing too. The scanning reader not only needs a different structure in web writing, with lots of headings, lists, keywords and summaries, as we have seen. They need more.

Most of the time, the scanning reader is on a mission. They are searching for something specific, and therefore want facts, not filler. There is no time for storytelling, no time for gradual introductions, no time for setups. They may have arrived at your website after using a search engine like Google, and they may have a million or more "results" from their search, spread over many, many Google pages. They will want to quickly scan a limited number of results to see if any is relevant. They are not prepared for a leisurely or careful read. So here are a few more guidelines – this time for an effective web writing *style*, gleaned from the experts:

- Be brief and to the point.
- Make the first few words of any section particularly informative and concrete.
- Give web users "actionable" content. Help them achieve their goals quickly and move on.
- Use familiar words, rather than fancy, vague or, worse still, made-up words. Web users search using words they know, and they won't find your page if you don't use their language.
- Try to anticipate the various ways in which readers might use your writing. They could have any number of goals when they get to your web page. It's the fundamental rule of plain language writing again: consider your reader.
- If you want to demonstrate your expertise, and mark yourself as a leader in the field, don't do it by dashing off a piece of

disposable or shallow writing (such as a blog[8]). Be thorough, demonstrate your wisdom and experience, and write quality material to reflect that. Readers can tell the difference.[9]

Again, this is all just good plain language writing advice.

The F-pattern

A study done by Jakob Nielsen in 2006 showed in greater detail exactly how people read on a web page. Nielsen tracked how people's eyes move across the screen. He found that they read in an F-shaped pattern: the eyes pass across the screen in two horizontal stripes, then a vertical stripe. [10]

This confirms something we already knew about web-based reading: people don't read word-by-word. Thorough reading is rare on the web. But it also shows that the first two paragraphs of any web document are by far the most important – they should contain the most important information.

Also, if you use headings, paragraphs and bullet-points on your flush-left margin, users may well notice them as their eyes pass down the ascender (vertical line) of the F. Nielsen concludes: "they'll read the third word on a line much less often than the first two words". So it pays to make those first two words concrete and informative, if you want the reader to continue reading.[11]

---

8   "Blog" is contraction of the word "weblog", and refers to a kind of informal running commentary posted on a website. Blogs are usually maintained by an individual, but others may be invited to add their comments or post other material.

9   Nielsen, J, "Writing Style for Print vs Web", *Alertbox*, 9 June 2008 <http://www.useit.com/alertbox/print-vs-online-content.html>; "Use Old Words When Writing for Findability", *Alertbox*, 28 Aug 2006 <http://www.useit.com/alertbox/search-keywords.html>; "Write for Reuse", *Alertbox*, 2 March 2009 <http://www.useit.com/alertbox/writing-reuse.html>; "Write Articles, Not Blog Postings", *Alertbox*, 9 July 2007 <http://www.useit.com/alertbox/articles-not-blogs.html>.

10   Nielsen, J, "F-Shaped Pattern for Reading Web Content", *Alertbox*, 17 April 2006 <http://www.useit.com/alertbox/reading_pattern.html>.

11   Nielsen, J, "First 2 Words: A Signal for the Scanning Eye", *Alertbox*, 6 April 2009 <http://www.useit.com/alertbox/nanocontent.html>.

Other variable factors on the computer screen

According to Jim Byrne of Glasgow Caledonian University, reading speed and comprehension are 10–20% slower for web documents than those printed on paper.[12] So it is vital to make your documents easily readable. Byrne points out that when you prepare a document for display on a computer screen, you should consider these additional practical and technical matters:

- The same fonts are not available on all operating systems.
- Some typefaces are designed to look good on screen, some [are] designed to look good on paper. Those designed to look good on paper (particularly serif fonts) tend to look 'messy' on screen.
- Text size is dependent on screen resolution and operating system being used.
- The type of browser used can affect how the text looks.
- Users have their computers set up with different defaults and can change the preferences on their browsers.[13]

Now that we've looked at the more general design factors, let's consider typography and formatting.

Typeface

Not only does the typeface you choose look different on the screen from the way it looks on paper, you cannot even be sure that the reader will see the same typeface you have chosen. There are technical ways to get around that problem, but the safest and simplest course of action is to pick a typeface that is likely to be available on most operating systems.

As long as you choose a typeface that is reasonably readable (for example, not too fanciful, exaggerated or florid), typeface choice does not make a significant difference in either legibility or readability.[14]

---

12   Jakob Nielsen puts this figure as high as 25%. See <http://www.sun.com/980713/webwriting> and <http://www.useit.com/alertbox/9602.html>.

13   2009, *Accessible Web Typography, an introduction for web designers*, available in free pdf version at <http://www.scotconnect.com/webtypography/thwart php>.

14   Bernard, Mills, Peterson and Storrer, 2001, "A Comparison of Popular Online Fonts: Which is Best and When?" *Usability News* Vol 3, Issue 2 <http://psychology.wichita.edu/surl/usabilitynews/32/font.asp>.

But don't use too many different typefaces. If you use a few typefaces, use them consistently. Then you can use the same typefaces as an organisational tool – to group together similar information. This can help your reader to grasp the structure and logic of your document. You are using design to help the reader, not just to decorate the screen.

Typefaces designed for the screen

Some typefaces have been designed specifically for screen use. Pioneer web typeface designers saw that the relatively low resolution of the computer monitor was not suitable for print-based typefaces. There were simply not enough pixels to display the subtlety and style of those typefaces. So the designers developed the technique of "bit-mapping" to increase the readability of on-screen text.[15] In bit-mapping, pixels are arranged by the designer to maximise the clarity and legibility of each character. Bit-mapped typefaces include Geneva (taken from Helvetica), and Monaco (taken from Courier). The disadvantage of bit-mapped typefaces is that they do not always keep their clarity when the type size is increased, and you can get rough and jagged edges.

Certain typefaces were specifically designed from scratch for the computer screen: for example Verdana and Georgia. Verdana is a sans serif typeface and Georgia has serifs.[16] Both look as good on low-resolution screens and both are relatively readable and clear in smaller type sizes. Other typefaces recommended by web-based typographers include Arial (sans serif) and Times New Roman (serif). Arial seems to be the most popular typeface used on the web, but typographers recommend Verdana, especially for small-sized type on low-resolution screens, because Verdana has heavier lines than Arial. Web design expert Jim Byrne prefers Times New Roman for documents that will not be read on the screen, but will be printed and read later.[17] That is likely to be an important consideration for lawyers writing for the web.

---

15   Same work.

16   See p 260 for a description of serif and sans serif typeface.

17   2009, *Accessible Web Typography, an introduction for web designers,* http://www.scotconnect.com/webtypography/thwart.php> (under the heading "A selection of 'safe to use fonts'").

Serif or sans serif?

There is no strong evidence either way on whether serif or sans serif typefaces are better for on-screen reading. Some say that the "clean" lines or "clarity" of sans serif typefaces make them a good choice for type on the screen.[18] Others have found no significant difference in legibility, and very little difference in the reading time between serif and sans serif typefaces. However, it does seem that at smaller sizes sans serif typefaces are easier to read on the screen.[19]

Space between characters

One other important factor is the amount of space between the characters of a typeface. In some typefaces, the individual characters can touch, which reduces legibility. Both Georgia and **Verdana** (created for screen use) have been designed to ensure the individual characters never touch.[20]

Perception and preference

Several commentators point out that reader perception and preference can be important in web design, even though that preference may not be based on logic or fact. Jim Byrne puts it this way:

> The typeface used on a Web page, or indeed any document, affects the way we feel about the content … one page looks formal and serious, another informal and friendly, yet another may be modern and cool.
>
> Clearly the typography of a page designed to support a children's TV program should be different for one designed for a politics course in a university. Similarly the text on the Financial Times Website, if it is doing its job right, should be different from that of the Tate Modern.
>
> So typography, whether on the Web or otherwise has a job to do. This could be to support and re-enforce the message being presented by the content, or tell you something about the writer, or publication, that the page is part of.

18 2002, *Style Manual for Authors, Editors and Printers*, p 331 (cited at note 7).

19 Bernard, Mills, Peterson and Storrer, 2001, "A Comparison of Popular Online Fonts: Which is Best and When?" (cited at note 14); Will-Harris, D, 2002, "The Best Faces for the Screen", *Typofile Magazine* <http://www.will-harris.com/typoscrn.htm>.

20 For more information, see Will-Harris, D, 2002, "The Best Faces for the Screen", *Typofile Magazine* (cited at note 19).

The font chosen should give the reader clues about the nature of an article or content they are about to read. For example, the text from an old manuscript might usefully be presented in a cursive style font that reflects its ancient content.[21]

In Chapter 14, in the context of email, we touched on the issue of how a typeface can affect a reader's opinion of a writer.[22] Many researchers in this area have made the point that a typeface can set the mood of a document, and give information about the nature of its content.

Research also indicates that using typefaces that are considered "appropriate" for the subject matter can significantly affect reader perception. Participants in a 2007 study were shown a website for an online bookshop, and asked questions about 11 different typefaces. They reported that the websites with the more "appropriate" typefaces were more believable and trustworthy, and that they intended to use them to buy in the future. The question of whether a typeface was "appropriate" had been determined in earlier studies dating back to 1927. Calibri was perceived as the most appropriate typeface for the bookshop, with Cambria, Arial, Calisto and Georgia scoring highly too. Curlz was seen as least appropriate.[23]

A follow-up study in 2008 showed a similar effect on résumés prepared in different typefaces and read online.[24]

Type size

The evidence about type size on-screen suggests that there is no difference in the legibility of the most commonly used typefaces in 10pt, 12pt and 14pt. One 2002 study[25] showed no difference in accuracy and reading speed between four serif typefaces and four sans serif

---

21 2009, *Accessible Web Typography, an introduction for web designers* <http://www.scotconnect.com/webtypography/control.php> (under the heading "Why would you want to control the text on a Web page?").

22 Pages 244-245.

23 Shaikh, AD, 2007, "The Effect of Website Typeface Appropriateness on the Perception of a Company's Ethos", *Usability News,* Vol 9, Issue 2 <http://www.surl.org/usabilitynews/92/POF.asp>.

24 Shaikh, AD, & Fox, D, 2008, "Does the Typeface of a Resume Impact Our Perception of the Applicant", *Usability News,* Vol 10, Issue 1 <http://www.surl.org/usabilitynews/101/pof.asp>.

25 Bernard, M, Lida, B, Riley, S, Hackler, T and Janzen, K, 2002, "A Comparison of Popular Online Fonts: Which Size and Type is Best?" *Usability News,* Vol 4, Issue 1 <http:// www.surl.org/usabilitynews/41/onlinetext.asp>.

typefaces. Another study a year earlier supported this finding.[26] The Australian government *Style Manual*[27] recommends using a larger type size than you would use for documents printed on paper, usually 12pt or larger. And in an article called "The Best Faces for the Screen", web design expert Daniel Will-Harris writes:

> *The bigger the better.* You can use *any* typeface on-screen if you use it large enough.[28]

Of course, you can go too far. As information design expert Ron Scheer advised:

> You don't need super-sized fonts and graphics. Your message area is a small screen viewed at close range, not the side of a bus.[29]

Reader age is also a factor with type size. There is good evidence to show that older adults are more accurate with, and prefer, larger typeface sizes. Researchers have shown that 14pt typeface size is more legible for older adults, who also read faster, and prefer the 14pt to the 12pt typefaces. Interestingly, the same study showed that older adults preferred sans serif typefaces to serif typefaces.[30] The US National Institute on Aging and the National Library of Medicine have produced a checklist called "Making Your Website Senior Friendly", which sets out useful guidelines well-backed by research. That checklist recommends using sans serif typeface and 12 or 14 pt type size for body text. Much of the advice offered in the checklist applies to readers of all ages.[31]

However, because it is not possible to predict the specific print-size requirements of your reader, it is sensible to allow the reader to adjust your type size as it appears on *their* screen, to suit them.[32]

26   Bernard, M, Mills, M, Frank, T and McKown, J, 2001, "Which font do children prefer to read online?" *Usability News* Vol 3, Issue 1 <http://www. surl/usabilitynews/31/fontJR.asp>.

27   2002, *Style Manual for Authors, Editors and Printers*, pages 325 and 330 (cited at note 7).

28   2002, *Typofile Magazine* <http://www.will-harris.com/typoscrn.htm>.

29   Scheer, R, 2002, "Make your home page mean business" para 19 – originally posted at <http://saywhatyoumean.com/html/business.html>.

30   Bernard, M, Liao, C and Mills, M, 2001 "Determining the best online font for older adults" *Usability News* Vol 3, Issue 1 <http:// www.surl.org/usabilitynews/31/fontSR.asp>.

31   2001 <http://www.nlm.nih.gov/pubs/checklist.pdf>.

32   For information on how to do this, see Byrne, J, 2009, *Accessible Web Typography, an introduction for web designers* <http://www.scotconnect.com/

Colour and texture

The research into colour in web design confirms that background textures and colours do affect the readability of text. Text with a plain background is quicker for readers to search than text on a medium-textured background. But if the background is to be textured then the text will be more readable if there is a high contrast between the colour of the text and the background.

Most studies have shown that dark characters on a light background work better than light characters on a dark background. Hill and Scharff noted in a 1997 paper[33] that most website design books recommend the traditional colour combination of black text on a white background as the most readable combination. That is consistent with research done for readers of print on paper. Their study showed, somewhat surprisingly, that black on medium gray and black on dark gray had significantly faster reading times than black on white. Still, black on white was found to be one of the best colour combinations, and red on green was the worst.

We know that websites have other practical considerations that might militate against a pure white background: computer screens can flicker and there is the glare factor to contend with. So, as software usability researcher Michael Bernard points out, "it is common for websites (such as this one) to have an off-white background in order to reduce the flicker and glare associated with white backgrounds".[34] In addition, certain patterns can clash with the patterns of the screen's pixels, and certain colours can "strobe" or flare on-screen. Colours and patterns can be manipulated on the computer to avoid these effects.

The Australian government *Style Manual* states that dark text on light background has been found more readable than the reverse. It also notes that, on-screen only, white text on a black background ("negative text") has been found to be almost as readable. White on blue, and red on yellow rank "fairly highly". Red on green, and magenta

---

webtypography/thwart.php> (under the heading *Section 2: Accessible web text – sizing up the issues,*.

33   Hill, A and Scharff, LF, 1997, "Readability Of Websites With Various Foreground/Background Color Combinations, Font Types And Word Styles" <http://www.laurenscharff.com/research/AHNCUR.html>.

34   Bernard, M, 2002, *Criteria for optimal web design (designing for usability)* <http://www.hcomtech.com/documents/index.php?docid=5> under the heading "Background textures and colors can affect the readability of text".

on blue are said to be the least readable combinations. In choosing colour, remember that a proportion of the population (mostly male) is colour-blind, and that you need a colour printer to print colour. And regardless of colour, it is important to have a good level of contrast between background and foreground.[35]

I mentioned in Chapter 15 that colour works best in document design when it is used for a purpose, not just to be decorative. That is just as important when your document is designed for the computer screen. You can use colour to help the reader find what they are looking for, by using it to group related material together, and show logical connections. Also in Chapter 15 we saw that certain colours can be culturally significant for certain readers.[36]

White space

To enhance the readability of a document printed on paper, you should have plenty of white space around the text. But the limited research into the use of "white" space on websites shows that this is not necessarily so. One study actually found that websites with more white space "fared worse in terms of users' success in finding information" than websites with more dense text.[37] This may be stretching the point too far. Some researchers who were suspicious of those results conducted another study into white space on websites.[38] Their study showed, interestingly, that there was no significant difference in the time participants took to complete certain set tasks: the amount of white space did not affect performance. However, the researchers reported that while the participants found websites with too little white space difficult to read, they were annoyed by too much white space. They reported that too much space made the website feel "empty", and required too much scrolling.

A 2004 study conducted at Wichita State University showed that white space around text passages affected both reading speed and

35 2002, *Style Manual for Authors, Editors and Printers*, pages 341-342 (cited at note 7).

36 See p 284.

37 Spool, JM, Schroeder, W, Scanlon, T, Snyder, C, 1998, "Web sites that work: Designing with your eyes open" (cited at note 3).

38 Bernard, M, Chaparro, B and Thomasson R, 2000, "Finding Information on the Web: Does the Amount of Whitespace Really Matter?" *Usability News*, Vol 2, Issue 1 <http://www.surl.org/usabilitynews/21/whitespace.asp>.

comprehension. Readers read text surrounded by white space more slowly, but comprehended more. Readers also reported more "satisfaction" in reading the text with white space around it.[39]

The US Department of Health & Human Services' usability.gov website recommends "moderate" white space, noting that separating items too much might force users to scroll unnecessarily.[40]

It seems that readers of websites prefer "medium" levels of white space. But it is difficult to specify the optimal amount of white space because there are many factors at work in a website, and the content and layout can vary greatly.

Line length

Quite a few of the commentators recommend shorter over longer line lengths for material to be read on a computer screen. They suggest line lengths of between 40 and 60 characters, or 11 words per line. However, the studies so far show mixed results.

A 2005 study done at Wichita State University measured reading speed, comprehension and satisfaction, at four different line lengths – 35, 55, 75 and 95 characters per line. The longest line lengths (95cpl) resulted in the *fastest* reading speeds. Yet different readers indicated a strong preference for *either* the long *or* the short (35cpl) line lengths. And there were *no* differences in comprehension or satisfaction at any line length.

One thing we do know is that with a longer line length there is less "scrolling" down the page – and some studies have shown that readers resist excessive scrolling.[41] But one 2003 study found that readers may be becoming more accustomed to scrolling, and read faster online when scrolling than when "paging".[42] The Australian government *Style Manual* makes the point that it is hard to scroll efficiently on a

---

39   Chaparro, B, Baker, JR, Shaikh, AD, Hull, S, & Brady, L, 2004, "Reading online Text: A Comparison of Four White Space Layouts" *Usability News,* Vol 6, Issue 2 <http://www.surl.org/usabilitynews/62/whitespace.asp>.

40   <http://www.usability.gov/pdfs/chapter6.pdf> at para 6.11.

41   Bernard, M, 2002, *Criteria for optimal web design (designing for usability)* (cited at note 34) (under the heading "The optimal text line length is dependent upon several factors").

42   Baker, JR, 2003, "The Impact of Paging vs Scrolling on Reading Online Text Passages", *Usability News,* Vol 5, Issue 1 <http://www.surl.org/usabilitynews/51/paging_scrolling.asp>.

screen that displays text in two or more columns. Given that it also recommends using larger type size, it suggests using single column text for on-screen documents.[43]

Justified or ragged?

Perhaps because it is slower and more tiring to read on a computer screen, most people object to reading large sections of uniform text online. Large portions of justified text[44] look too formidable. They become what Dr Janice Redish calls a "wall of words." Online, she sees almost no use for justified text. "Our online expectation", she says, "is ragged right". She also warns against centred text, advising always to use the flush-left, ragged-right format.[45]

This is supported by Jakob Nielsen's eyetracking studies,[46] which show that users tend to read lists by moving their eyes rapidly down the left side of the list. They only read the rest of the list if something catches their eye in the first two words on the left. Thus, he recommends always having your menus (and, by extension, your lists and bullet points) flush on the left margin. A ragged-*left* margin severely reduces scanning speed.

Using upper case

In Chapter 15[47] I noted that words written in upper case are harder to read than words in lower case. However, the upper case seems to be having something of a resurgence in the age of email and the internet. This is probably because email requires us all to become typists, and the less competent typists are looking for shortcuts. Unfortunately, this only helps the writer, and makes life difficult for the reader. The following advice comes from social media consultant Meg Pickard:

> THERE IS ONE KEY ON YOUR KEYBOARD WHICH CAN IMPROVE YOUR COMMUNICATION SKILLS INSTANTLY

43 2002, *Style Manual for Authors, Editors and Printers*, p 332 (cited at note 7).
44 See pages 265-266.
45 Email to the PLAIN forum dated 9 March 2009. See also Redish, J, 2007, *Letting Go of Words: Writing Web Content that Works*, Morgan Kaufmann, San Francisco, pages 143-144.
46 Nielsen, J, "Right-justified Navigation Menus Impede Scannability", *Alertbox*, 28 April 2008 <http://www.useit.com/alertbox/navigation-menu-alignment.html>.
47 Page 280.

WITH A SINGLE TAP. IT'S NOT THE SPACE BAR – THOUGH THAT IS A PRETTY USEFUL KEY IN ITSELF, AND CERTAINLY HELPS TO PREVENT ALLYOURWORDSRUNNINGTOGETHER INABIG MESSLIKETHIS. THE KEY THAT WILL HELP PEOPLE UNDERSTAND – AND LIKE – YOU BETTER IS THE HUMBLE CAPS LOCK KEY WHICH TURNS A SHOUTY NONSENSE MAGICALLY INTO an ocean of reasoned calm. Ahhhhhhh. However, take note – a single tap is all that is required, uNlEsS yOu WaNt tO sEeM liKE a tWeLve yEAr OLd.[48]

Underlining

It is best to avoid underlining on websites, except to indicate a hyperlink.[49] Underlining is now a recognised web convention for that purpose.[50]

Numerals

Eyetracking studies done on website users by Jakob Nielsen in 2007 show that numerals often stop the wandering eye – even when they appear in a mass of words that readers are skipping over. Numbers represent concrete facts, and readers love concrete facts. Often people are looking for specific details on websites. So Nielsen recommends that, when writing for the web, you:

- Write numbers as numerals, not words (3, not *three*, and 2,000,000, not *two million*).
- Do this even if the number is the first word in a sentence or bullet point.
- If numbers get huge, you can compromise, as with *24 billion*.
- Only spell out numbers if they don't represent factual data. For example, write:

    Thousands of people all over the world …

    not:

    1000s of people all over the world …[51]

---

48 Originally posted at ickle.org: <www.ickle.org/archive/capslockkey.html>.
49 A hyperlink is a set of characters or a symbol or image in a "hypertext" document that links (by means of a mouse click) to another place in the same or another document. A hypertext document is one designed to allow those links.
50 See p 305 (**Web Conventions**).
51 Nielsen, J, "Show Numbers as Numerals When Writing for Online Readers", *Alertbox*, 16 April 2007 <http://www.useit.com/alertbox/writing-numbers. html>.

Graphics etc

Amazingly, the evidence indicates that users may actually *ignore* graphics (diagrams, illustrations, animated pictures etc) on a website. Research done by the US Poynter Institute indicates that the first time users visit a website, they are twice as likely to look at text, and tend to ignore the images on the site. The users in the Poynter study only looked at the images on their second or third visit to a site.[52] One reason for this could be that website users are ignoring material that they expect to be advertisements. Two studies have found that users ignore advertisements placed at the top of a web page (where advertisement "banners" are usually found) and paid more attention to advertisements placed lower down the page.[53]

On the other hand, researchers have shown that graphics and other visual aids are better than text for getting across simple messages. Text was shown to be more persuasive for complex messages.[54]

This raises the interesting question of how effective as communication are the new, more complex, animated graphics and "interactive" design techniques. These techniques are often described as "youth oriented" or as aiming to reach members of the "MTV Generation" or "Generation X" and their younger siblings. The assumption is that:

> the "TV generation" are developing different ways of reading and processing visual information to preceding generations. Not restricted to reading sequentially and contiguously, the Post-modern and post-Post-modern generations appear to have developed what we might call "quick-grab literacy – the ability to absorb multiple hybrid visual codes and quick bytes of instant information."[55]

---

52   Poynter Institute, 1998, *The Stanford Poynter Project* <http://www. poynterextra.org/et/index-col.htm>.

53   Benway, JP, 1998, "Banner blindness: The irony of attention grabbing on the world wide web", *Proceedings of the Human Factors and Ergonomics Society 42nd Annual Meeting, USA, 1*, 463-467 and WebReference.com, 1997 (quoted in Bernard, M, 2002, *Criteria for optimal web design (designing for usability)* (under the heading "Users may often 'instinctively'…") (cited at note 34)).

54   King, WC, Dent, MM and Miles, EW, 1991, "The persuasive effect of graphics in computer-mediated communication", *Computers in Human Behavior, 7,* 269-279.

55   MacKenzie, M, 1994, "Our changing visual environment: Questions and challenges", *Communication News, 7,* No 4, Communications Research Institute of Australia, Hackett, Australia, pages 11-14 at p 12.

However, there is some evidence to indicate that animated graphics can distract users from the text on the page and may cause them to miss the main points.[56] If the message of the text is important, experts suggest keeping animated graphics to a minimum.

Web conventions

Researchers have shown that users overwhelmingly prefer sites that follow the usual web conventions.[57] Although Michael Bernard points out that there are very few of them, he lists some:

- Follow the standard hyperlink[58] colors: blue for non-visited hyperlinks, purple for visited hyperlinks, and red for active hyperlinks (but if you have a site with a blue background – or any dark color – please choose a color that can clearly be contrasted from the background color. That is, if the choice is to either violate the standard or not be visible, choose visibility!).
- Place a navigational link to the homepage at the upper left corner and bottom of each page.
- Place the site's internal hyperlinks at the bottom of each page (in addition to other places).
- Images and text space should not cause horizontal scrolling on lower resolution screens.
- At the bottom of each page, place the date that the page was updated and the URL address.
- The text should facilitate the scanning of information.
- Use ALT-Tags[59] for graphics, especially for graphics that search as hyperlinks.

Bernard also suggests that web designers follow the convention of underlining hyperlinks when they are text based (for example, <http://

---

56 Benway, JP and Lane, DM, Dec 1998, "Banner blindness: Web searchers often miss 'obvious' links", *Internetworking, 1.3* <http://www.internettg. org/ newsletter/dec98/banner_blindness.html>; Wright, P, Milroy, R and Lickorish, A, 1999, "Static and animated graphics in learning from interactive texts", *European Journal of Psychology of Education*, XIV, 203-224.

57 Bernard, M, 2002, *Criteria for optimal web design (designing for usability)* (under the heading "How can I make sure my site follows general Web conventions?") (cited at note 34); Nielsen, J, *Alertbox*, 1997 <www.useit.com/ alertbox/980322.html>.

58 See note 49.

59 An ALT-Tag is a short text description of (in this case) an image that is visible even if the image fails to load.

www.plainlanguagelaw.com>).[60] Web design expert Jakob Nielsen agrees and, in a 2004 article, he sets out several other guidelines for "visualizing" links, such as the very important "generally avoid color for text unless it's a link". [61]

Readers with special needs

We have already seen that older readers may be more comfortable reading a larger type size. We have seen that cultural differences can also be significant.[62] Much of the research into legibility and readability has taken place in the United States, so it may not apply to readers from other cultures. Readers with disabilities may also have special needs.

Guidelines to help website developers have been published by a group called the World Wide Web Consortium (WC3). This group has member organisations all over the world working together to develop common protocols for the Web. Their Web Accessibility Initiative has developed guidelines, checklists and techniques to help web designers make websites accessible for people with a variety of disabilities.[63] And in Australia, the Human Rights and Equal Opportunity Commission has produced advisory notes on accessibility of web pages.[64] They take into account the WC3 web accessibility guidelines.[65]

For the more general audience, the evidence suggests that most of us are most comfortable reading what we are most used to. For some, that might mean the Times or Times New Roman typefaces we often see in books and our daily newspapers. But that doesn't hold true for everyone. Australian research indicates that Australian readers are

---

60 Bernard, M, 2002, *Criteria for optimal web design (designing for usability)* (under the heading "Make action-objects visible") (cited at note 34).

61 Nielsen, J, "Guidelines for Visualizing Links", *Alertbox*, 10 May 2004 <http://www.useit.com/alertbox/20040510.html>.

62 Page 299 (**Colour and texture**).

63 See <http://www.w3.org/WAI/Resources/#gl> for the guidelines, checklists and techniques and <http://www.w3.org> for information about WC3. One of the guidelines requires the "clearest and simplest language appropriate for a site's content" <http://www.w3.org/TR/WCAG10/> (guideline 14.1).

64 <http://www.hreoc.gov.au/disability_rights/standards/www_3/www_3.html>.

65 See also p 307 (**Best practice guidelines**).

now familiar with sans serif text too.[66] This suggests that we should ask the members of our target audience what they want. And we should seriously consider testing.[67]

Best practice guidelines

Some organisations have developed Best Practice Guidelines for websites. In Australia, the Department of Broadband, Communications and the Digital Economy has produced a guide to website standards.[68] As noted earlier, the US Department of Health and Human Services has a website – usability.gov – devoted to making websites more usable, useful and accessible. And the government of Canada has an Internet Guide website, which gives tips on how to evaluate websites and improve and test their usability.[69]

There are some guidelines particularly directed to lawyers and legal websites. For Australian legal websites the Legal Information Standards Council has developed "Best practice guidelines for Australian legal websites".[70] And in February 2003 the Elawyering Task Force of the American Bar Association approved and published "Best Practice Guidelines for Legal Information Web Site Providers".[71]

The Legal Information Standards Council guidelines refer specifically to the need for information that does not exclude or disadvantage people with a disability (as required by the Disability Discrimination Act 1992 (Cth)).

Summary

Lawyers, courts, judges and other law-related organisations are now commonly communicating with their audiences through the internet and via websites. They need to be aware that websites and documents displayed on the internet should not just be written; they should be

---

66 MacKenzie, M, 1994, "Our changing visual environment: Questions and challenges" (cited at note 55).

67 See Chapter 17.

68 <http://www.e-strategyguide.gov.au/build_a_website/web_standards>.

69 <http://www.tbs-sct.gc.ca/ig-gi/abu-ans/abu-ans-eng.asp>.

70 <http://ljf.itechne.com/ljf/app/&id=80C7F82638D67690CA257169000AB 56A>.

71 <http://www.elawyeringredux.com/2008/12/articles/elawyering-ethical-issues/best-practice-guidelines-for-legal-information-web-site-providers/>.

designed according to recognised web-design principles. Some of the principles to keep in mind are:

General

- Document design principles may apply differently to documents displayed on a computer screen. But the basic principles remain the same.
- Make sure your text is "scannable": use keywords, headings and sub-headings, lists, and one idea per paragraph.
- Start with your conclusion and halve your word count.
- Think like your reader to work out what structure will work best.
- Consider using an electronic publishing specialist to help structure your documents.

Sections, headings, navigation aids, links, summaries

- Break down content into smaller units, with a maximum of five A4 pages for any one section.
- Use one heading per screen, "signposting " techniques, "bridging" words, cross-references and hyperlinks.
- Make sure your headings and labels are helpful to non-expert readers.
- Use summaries at the beginning of each section to help readers select the detail they need.

Writing style and content

- Be brief, to the point, and use informative and concrete words – up-front especially.
- Give readers "actionable" content. Help them achieve their goals quickly and move on.
- Use words that your readers will know and use themselves, so they can find your words when searching.
- Try to anticipate the uses the reader might have for your document, and write accordingly.
- If you want to demonstrate your expertise and experience, do it in thoughtful, well-written articles. Even if long, they will show your strengths better than short, slapdash, blog-type writing.

- Put the most important information in your first two paragraphs. In a menu or list, make the first two words informative.

Format and typography

- Use a flush-left, ragged-right format, and have all menus, headings, paragraphs, bullet points and other lists flush-left too.
- Within limits, typeface choice does not make a significant difference to legibility, but some typefaces (such as **Verdana** and Georgia) have been designed specifically for the screen.
- Don't forget that screen-displayed documents may be printed out to read later.
- Most 10, 12 and 14pt typefaces are probably equally legible on-screen, but some experts recommend using larger type size than you would for paper documents, especially if your readers are older.
- Don't use too many typefaces, and do use them consistently.
- Colour choice is governed by technical, psychological and cultural considerations. Use background colour only for a reason: for example, to group related material together.
- Don't use coloured type for text (except for things like links, where there is a colour convention). Black type on medium gray, darker gray or off-white are the best choices for readability.
- Give readers enough white space in on-screen documents to keep them comfortable, but not so much as to make them scroll excessively.
- Don't fuss too much about line lengths, as long as they are under around 90 characters per line, but again, do not force excessive scrolling. 40-60 characters per line might be good to aim for, depending on layout.
- Don't over-use upper case.
- In general, use numerals (3), not words (three), for numbers.
- Keep animated graphics to a minimum if your text message is important. Text is more persuasive for complex messages.

Best practice

- Follow web conventions and best-practice guidelines.
- Pay attention to any special needs of your readers.

That last point – paying attention to your reader's special needs – suggests not only that we might want to ask them what they want or expect, but also that we might want to find out how they handle what we've written and designed for them. Which brings us to the topic of the next chapter – Testing Your Writing.

In Chapter 17 we consider the idea of "testing" documents, to see if the intended readers *can* actually read them. To the lawyer in a busy private practice, the idea of "testing" his or her legal writing might not sound feasible. But there are various types of testing. So let's keep an open mind about testing, and see what it involves.

Chapter 17
Testing your writing

How can we tell if our readers understand?

If you've reached this chapter by reading the 16 chapters before it, you've been prepared to put in a great deal of effort for plain language writing. If you were a plain language lawyer before you read this book, you know that it takes care and effort to rewrite an old form or precedent in plain language. If you have ever produced complex legal documents (such as mortgages, guarantees, leases, trust deeds, prospectuses or legislation) in plain language, you know the investment of time, intellect and money it can involve.

Can we be sure that this actually makes things easier for our readers? There is evidence that plain language generally improves people's comprehension of legal documents, as we saw in Chapter 3. But how can we tell if that is happening in any specific case? The answer lies in testing.

Do lawyers really need to bother about testing?

In the first edition of this book, there was no information at all on the topic of testing. I had chosen to following my own advice and write for my audience, and I had decided that my audience would include a large percentage of lawyers who were unsure of plain language, or sceptical, or even hostile. I wasn't sure they'd be ready to think about testing documents on potential readers.

In the years since then we've come a long way. Lawyers have begun to see how testing documents can actually be relevant to them, and help them in their daily work.

Lawyers draft all sorts of documents. A great many are short emails or letters addressed to one person. That person may well have no problems at all in understanding exactly what the writer means. I'm not suggesting that we always need to test those single purpose documents. But some of the documents we prepare are more complicated documents that people will consult regularly to check their rights and obligations. And some are public documents of great significance. Lawyers need to know that there are ways of checking whether their documents are likely to do the job they are supposed to do.

Testing legislation

Testing has obvious advantages for legislation, for example. Several legislative drafting offices already test draft laws on readers.

Australia

Both the Australian Corporations Law Simplification Program and the Tax Law Improvement Project used extensive testing. The team working on rewriting the Corporations Law used focus group testing to get feedback on structure of the laws, the texts themselves (some had two rounds of testing) and the new document design. They used testing more to diagnose problems with the structure or the text, than to measure the text's effectiveness. In the tax law rewrite, some of the testing was in the form of "protocol reading". Individuals were carefully observed to see how they handled the text. Sometimes the text tested was not the finished product, but a "prototype". This enabled drafters to explore various drafting approaches to see if they should be pursued.[1]

Also in Australia, the Commonwealth Office of Parliamentary Counsel (OPC) had decided to test two documents a year with user groups.[2] However, events overtook that decision when the Corporations Law Simplification Program and the Tax Law Improvement Project began redrafting two of the most significant pieces of Commonwealth legislation, and systematically testing their drafts. OPC drafters worked on each project and took part in the testing processes.

Since then, legislation drafted by the OPC is tested whenever a client[3] requests it. Usually this is done by means of exposure drafts

---

1   Robinson, V, 2001, *Rewriting Legislation – Australian Federal Experience*, paper presented to a conference in Ottawa, Canada in March 2001, pages 6-7 <www.opc.gov.au/plain/docs.htm>.

2   *Clearer Commonwealth Law: Report of the Inquiry into Legislative Drafting by the Commonwealth*, 1993, Commonwealth of Australia, Canberra, p 102.

3   The government department, instrumentality or other body that needs the drafting done for them.

either aimed at the general public or at a particular interest group. Exposure processes allow interested people to comment in writing, or at focus group meetings (often attended by the drafters). Former First Parliamentary Counsel Hilary Penfold said in 2003 that feedback from exposure drafts relates more often to policy than to drafting matters, but even so the nature of the feedback could show how well people have grasped the subject matter of the drafting, and therefore how well the drafter had communicated the ideas.[4]

Recent examples of public exposures of draft Bills include:

- Various pieces of tax legislation, including the Tax Laws Amendment (Confidentiality of Taxpayer Information) Bill 2009
- Information Commissioner Bill 2009, and the Freedom of Information Amendment (Reform) Bill 2009 (both part of the government's policy to reform the Commonwealth Freedom of Information Act 1982)
- National Consumer Credit Protection Bill 2009
- Carbon Pollution Reduction Scheme Bill 2009 and related legislation
- Corporations Amendment (Improving Accountability on Termination Payments) Bill 2009

Some legislation is "tested" by the Office of Parliamentary Counsel even before it is drafted. In paragraph 47 of the OPC's *Plain English Manual*, under the heading **Consultation**, it says:

> If you use the "plan before you draft" system, the first draft Bill won't be ready until near the end of the project. You might therefore have to have consultations with Departments, etc on the basis of the plan rather than on the basis of the draft Bill. In effect, you have to find alternatives to the standard Office procedures by which the draft Bill is the vehicle for consultation.[5]

More public exposure and testing of Australian legislation is likely in the future. In 2002, the Board of Taxation[6] recommended the use of improved consultation processes to develop tax legislation,

---

4   Telephone interview with M Asprey, 6 May 2003.
5   <http://www.opc.gov.au/about/docs/pem.pdf>.
6   A body that advises the Treasurer on (among other things) the quality and effectiveness of tax legislation and the processes for its development, including the processes of community consultation, and other aspects of tax design.

including "thorough road-testing of draft legislation and related products prior to their implementation".[7] The government accepted this recommendation.[8]

On 16 August 2007 the Treasurer announced improvements to the arrangements for community consultation in developing tax legislation. These changes were in response to the recommendations made by the Board of Taxation in its 2007 Report to the Treasurer, *Improving Australia's Tax Consultation System*. Since 2002, it said, there had been significant improvements in tax consultation arrangements, and they were then (in 2007) consistent with international practice, functioned well, and had community support. Nevertheless, the Report offered 12 recommendations for improvement. The Government endorsed them, and announced that it would work with the community to bring them about. In its **Key Findings** section, the Report recommended consultation with interested parties early in the process:

> Consultation can be conducted in a variety of ways. Whatever the approach, the consultation process should involve early engagement between officials and relevant external stakeholders and/or experts.[9]

Canada

As mentioned in Chapter 4,[10] in 1995 the Canadian government chose a portion of the Explosives Regulations (the Consumer Fireworks Regulations) for a pilot project to rewrite government regulations in plain language. A Department of Justice team ran the project, which demonstrated not only that it was possible to write technical material in plain language, but also the value of extensive user consultation and usability testing.[11]

---

7   Board of Taxation Report *Government Consultation with the Community on the Development of Taxation Legislation*, March 2002, Recommendation 3(iii), p vi <http://www.taxboard.gov.au/content/review.asp>.

8   Treasurer's Press Release, 2 May 2002.

9   <http://www.taxboard.gov.au/content/improving_tax_consultation/index.asp#Report> February 2007, p 1.

10   Page 76.

11   The final report of the plain language pilot project for the Consumer Fireworks Regulations (including a section on Usability Testing) is available online at <http://canada-justice.net/eng/pi/rs/rep-rap/1995/wd95_4-dt95_4/index.html#tphp>. See also the report *Consumer Fireworks Regulations Usability Testing*, Department of Justice, Canada, 1995.

Then in 2000, as part of the plan to rewrite the Employment Insurance Act in plain language, the Canadian government decided to test different versions of some sections of the Act. The testing showed that reading a law and answering questions about it can be a challenging task both for the general public and informed legislation users alike. It also showed that the users did not like certain choices the drafters had made. As a result, the drafters changed their approach. But the researchers found that users appreciated many of the plain language drafting techniques: in particular, improvements in layout and navigational aids. Users reported that they felt less intimidated by the document as a result of these techniques: they inspired user confidence.[12]

New Zealand

In New Zealand in 1998, as part of the project to rewrite the Income Tax Act 1976,[13] researchers tested three versions of a portion of tax legislation (dealing with exempt income). One was the original provision from the 1976 Act, and the others were two (different) simplified versions prepared for the rewrite of that Act. The researchers found that both simplified versions showed higher comprehension rates than the original version, for both professional and non-professional users. Surprisingly, even the tax professionals found the plain language versions quicker to comprehend than the original versions, which they must have been more familiar with. However, professional users did report that they felt uncertain using the new versions. The study also showed that testing in the early stages of drafting a law can give the drafters valuable feedback and insights that they can use while they are still in the process of drafting.[14]

Before the introduction of a new format for New Zealand legislation on 1 January 2002, the Parliamentary Counsel Office undertook testing in the form of an extensive survey of users of legislation including

12   GLPi and Schmolka, V, Aug 2002, Results of Usability Testing Research on Plain Language Draft Sections of the Employment Insurance Act <http:// www.servicecanada.gc.ca/eng/ei/legislation/glpi-english.pdf>.

13   See pages 73-74.

14   McLaren, Prof M, Harrison, Dr J and McAra, E, 1999, *Report on accessibility of new income tax legislation* (unpublished). My thanks to Dr Harrison and Prof McLaren for drawing my attention to this report, and to the Policy Advice Division of the NZ Internal Revenue Department for allowing me to use it.

Members of Parliament, judges, librarians, academics, lawyers, legal publishers and members of the public. Participants received a survey pack with sample formats (in particular, typeface) and were asked to rank the samples in order of preference. The participants' preferences as to typeface were adopted in the new format.

Before 2005 or so, the use of exposure drafts to test different legislative drafting techniques, content and policy was limited in New Zealand.[15] There had been draft exposure bills on insolvency and patents, and the NZ Law Commission had prepared a draft Life Insurance Bill, plus some rule changes had been drafted by the Rules Committee. But the NZ PCO has announced that the use of formal exposure drafts should increase in future, as it has in Australia and the UK. The Attorney-General has encouraged this, so as to get feedback from target audiences and the general public. The PCO predicts this will save time during the select committee stages of Bills.[16]

United Kingdom

The most recent of the three major tax law rewrite projects is the United Kingdom's. The project is administered by HM Revenue and Customs (HMRC), and overseen by two outside committees: a Consultative Committee and a Steering Committee.

The project is "committed to Proceeding with our work on the basis of full consultation". The consultation process involves:

- co-opting specialists inside and outside HM Revenue and Customs to help develop draft clauses
- posting early draft clauses on the internet and inviting comments from anyone interested
- discussing early drafts with the Consultative Committee
- revising drafts in the light of comments received
- publishing the revisions as part of a draft bill for final consultation
- preparing response documents setting out the comments received on drafts, and noting how they were dealt with in the

---

15   Parliamentary Counsel Office, *2005 Annual Report*, p 9, **Exposure drafts** <http://www.pco.parliament.govt.nz/2005-report/>

16   Parliamentary Counsel Office, *2007, Statement of Intent for the period 1 July 2007 to 30 June 2010*, **Changing requirements of instructing departments** p 10 <http://www.pco.parliament.govt.nz/soi2007-2010/>.

Bill before it was introduced into Parliament. This can involve further discussion with the Committees and others.

Interestingly, the consultation process has changed somewhat as the project has gone on. At first, the tendency was to put out large blocks of draft legislation for comment, in formal Exposure Drafts. Now the team prefers to put out smaller parcels of legislation "as and when it is ready". The team have found that those who want to comment on the drafts prefer the smaller parcels, and the team says that process is working well.[17]

Testing other legal documents

If you are a private legal practitioner, testing documents can be relevant to your daily law practice too – perhaps more relevant than you think. For example, some years ago a group of lawyers around Australia worked together to produce industry-standard plain language shopping centre (or "retail") leases. The process of getting a lease that all the interested parties agreed on involved negotiation – and testing. Some of the lawyers who worked on those standard form documents decided to test draft clauses on the building owners, managers, tenants, valuers and others who would be involved in administrative processes like rent review and building maintenance. Input from all these people helped shape better leases that were easier to work with in practice. And what a great marketing exercise! Lawyers were going to their clients, and asking "how can we make this a better document for you?" The result was a better partnership between lawyer and client.

If you are considering putting in the effort to build up your firm's forms and precedents, you might consider involving your regular clients in the process. That way, not only do you build better documents, but you can market your services as well.

Testing makes a better product

Testing does not necessarily have to be formal or time consuming or expensive. At the most basic level, it is really just a part of the writing process: part of the research you need to do to produce a document that is fit for its purpose, and part of the editing you should do to produce the best document you possibly can.

---

17   HM Revenue and Customs, 2009, *Tax Law Rewrite Report and Plans 2009-2010*
      <http://www.hmrc.gov.uk/rewrite/plans2009-10.htm>.

Testing can tell you things about your writing that you would never see yourself. It can show up problems with a document that two lawyers negotiating and haggling would miss no matter how long they argued. It does this because it brings different points of view and different sensibilities to the same document. And it takes the document out of "theory" and into "practice".

Testing can also help you get to know your audience, and that can help your drafting. For example, the Australian Corporations Law Simplification Project team found it helpful to be able to picture their readers:

> A very valuable by-product of document testing sessions is that you get to know your audience personally as it were. The abstract reader becomes a real person across the table trying to make sense of your document. In the tea or coffee break, you discuss that person's professional interests, hobbies, grievances and enthusiasms. When you go back to the office to revise the draft you have a much more vivid and particularised image of the reader. This image is an amalgam of the individuals you have met and got to know in the testing sessions.[18]

Testing takes time, and sometimes money, but it may save time, money and embarrassment in the long run. Consider an important public document like a company's prospectus, for example. It is vital that prospectuses don't mislead or deceive the public. How can you tell whether a prospectus is likely to mislead or deceive? The client will be relying on you as a lawyer to guarantee that. What is your protection?

Testing can give you an indication of the kinds of problems that readers might have with the final version of the prospectus. If you test it on the same class of reader as the prospectus is aimed at, it can give you hard evidence of the reaction of members of that class. It will help you detect potential problems before they arise.

Lawyers are lagging behind the commercial realities on this issue. Manufacturers of all kinds of products, from cars and computers to toys, put them through tough testing programs before release. This ensures that the product does what it is supposed to, is durable and won't explode in the customer's hands. Why should our product – legal documents – be exempt from that kind of treatment?

---

18   Robinson, V, 2001, *Rewriting Legislation – Australian Federal Experience*, p 7, para 24 (cited at note 1).

There is a growing body of learning about what manufacturers call "Usability Testing". Much of that knowledge also applies to testing plain language documents for "usability". Two of the leaders in this field are Dr Janice C Redish and Dr Joseph S Dumas, who have particular expertise in testing legal documents. They have written this about the experience of testing:

> Watching users is both inspiring and humbling. Even after watching hundreds of people participate in usability tests, we are still amazed at the insights they give us about the assumptions we make.[19]

What to test

If there is time, you could test almost everything you write. This might sound like overdoing things, but consider this: one leading Australian law firm has a standing rule that if the secretary or wordprocessing operator who types a document cannot understand the language in it, that person can return that document to the author for revision. That is a first line of testing.

Some lawyers ask a few people around their office for help if they have a particularly difficult drafting problem. This has the advantage of giving you more than one viewpoint and more than one perspective. It is another kind of testing.

Sometimes we may have to fall back on testing our own material on ourselves. This is the most primitive form of testing, more properly called "revising". But even when you revise your own work, you can try to look at it with a different standpoint – a reader's standpoint. To do that requires retiring some distance from the document. Sometimes it is helpful to leave the document overnight to try to get a fresh perspective.

One other easy thing to do on your own is to read your document aloud. Ask yourself: is it easy to read? Does it flow? Does it sound natural? Does it sound logical?

Many lawyers I know have another, informal test they apply to the documents they write or edit for someone else: they ask themselves if a particular relative or acquaintance could understand the document (Uncle Arthur, say, or a neighbour, or a young cousin – specially

---

19   Dumas, JS and Redish, JC, 1999, *A Practical Guide to Usability Testing*, Revised edition, Intellect Books, Exeter, UK, p 32.

selected for this purpose because of they are not experienced in legal matters). Although it is unscientific, this method is at least an attempt to get another perspective.

More and more lawyers are moving to standardise these informal systems by developing checklists, or even formal style guides, for themselves or for their firms. This has been done in legislative drafting offices for many years. It gives standards to "measure" a document against, and so it helps keep documents consistent in style. It also saves the time that can be wasted in different people going over and over the same small points.

No document is in itself too small or too unimportant to test. You can use a small or informal test to match a small or informal document.

Communication is a complex process, and there is so much room for error. We must do what we can to verify the process.

When to test

There is no point in finding out all the things that are wrong with your document once you have dotted all the "i"s and crossed all the "t"s, organised the printing and signed the covering letter. You need to begin testing (or at least test once) fairly early in the drafting process, before your ideas have become fixed and you've gone too far to turn back. If you test early, you'll be more receptive to suggestions, more open to changing strategy, and have more time to incorporate changes. If you test early, you'll find out early if you have any fundamental misunderstandings about how the document works in practice.[20]

If time and money allow, you can test again once you've "fixed" the problems that the first test showed up. You might have fixed the wrong things, or made the problems worse. The only way to know for sure is to test again and compare results.

And if the circumstances are right, you might be able to test again *after* the document has begun to be used. For example, if you have produced a new form, you could test it after it has been introduced. Then you can see exactly how it is actually used in everyday situations, once it has been filled out and has been processed. Then if any problems emerge, you can make changes again.

---

20   See the reference on p 312 to "prototype" testing. See also pages 316-317 on the UK Tax Law rewrite seeking comments on early drafts of clauses, and small parcels of legislation.

How to test: informal methods

So what are our options for testing? I've already suggested 6 informal, but very basic, methods that you might already be using. They are:

- Ask the person who types your work whether they understand it.
- Ask one or more of your other colleagues.
- Revise your own work, but do it after a break, to get a fresh perspective.
- Put yourself in someone else's shoes, and judge your own work as if you were that person.
- Read your document aloud. Is it easy to read? Does it flow? Does it sound natural? Does it sound logical?
- Develop a checklist or style guide to measure your documents against.

Remember, though, that in the writing process your primary aim is to *consider your reader*, and so you are writing primarily for that person. Setting your own criteria for a document, or imagining yourself in some other person's shoes is not the same thing as writing to meet the needs of your actual reader.

There are two other fairly simple methods you might consider using if more formal testing is not possible or appropriate for a particular document.

1. Ask clients for comments

Earlier I mentioned the efforts to produce standard form "retail" leases. Testing in that context can involve a more formal testing procedure,[21] or it can be as simple as matter of circulating a draft document or clause to as many of the interested parties as you wish, and asking for comments – especially comments that will help the document or clause to work *in practice*.

2. Use a computer program

There are several computer programs that check text for grammar and style, and even give you readability statistics.[22] Some come as part of

---

21   See following section **How to test: more formal methods** on p 325.

22   See next section, **Readability formulas**.

wordprocessing software.[23] Some are available on the internet.[24] These programs can be helpful, because they can alert you to things that you hadn't realised about your writing. For example, they can tell you if your sentences are long, or you use too many passives. But there are problems, too. Because they are computer-run, they are inflexible. They apply the same standards (or range of standards) to every document. They don't take into account any special needs of your particular audience. And they won't pick up ambiguities or gaps in your logic. In some programs, it is necessary to eliminate full stops (periods) from abbreviations and the like, because the program will read a full stop as a sentence end and give a better score. So they are "blunt" instruments. But from time to time they can be useful to remind you of your bad writing habits.

Readability formulas

Readability formulas are reasonably easy to use, but the statistics they produce can have serious drawbacks. The Flesch Reading Ease Test, the Flesch-Kincaid Grade Level, the Gunning FOG index, the SMOG formula, the CLEAR analysis formula (still being tested), the Coleman-Liau Grade Level or the Bormuth Grade Level are all examples of tests that use readability formulas. I referred to the Flesch Reading Ease Test in Chapter 4 in the context of the US Plain Language Statutes.[25] These formulas use things like the number of syllables or letters in a word and the number of words or letters in a sentence to determine readability. So a sentence with short, difficult words could receive a better score than a sentence with longer, easier words.

For example, Lewis Carroll's:

Twas brillig, and the slithy toves did gyre and gimble in the wabe; all mimsy were the borogroves, and the mome raths outgrabe.[26]

---

23 The Flesch-Kincaid formula comes with Microsoft Word. Note that (as at my press-time) Microsoft's version does not score above grade 12, which corresponds to the most senior US school grade, although the formula was designed to score up to grade 16/17. Grammatik comes with WordPerfect.

24 For example, Readability Calculations (<www.micropowerandlight.com>), GrammarExpert Plus (<www.wintertree-software.com>), Spellcatcher (www.rainmakerinc.com), Added Bytes Check Text Readability (www.addedbytes.com/readability), SMOG: (www.harrymclaughlin.com/SMOG.htm) and WordsCount (including CLEAR analysis formula) (http://www.wordscount.info/index.html).

25 See p 67.

26 *Through the Looking Glass*, Chapter 1.

receives good score of 70.10 on the Flesch Reading Ease Test – which rates it as slightly easier to read than "standard" writing. It also receives a good Flesch-Kincaid Grade Level – 6.34, which means that that it could be read by a person with 6.34 years of schooling. And so it probably could – but what does the sentence mean?

The basis of these scores is also questionable for another reason: the Flesch tests were first developed for the military in the 1940s in the United States. Critics of the Flesch-Kincaid reading grades point out that the scale is geared to a fifth grade reading level, since a fifth grade education was considered sufficient for military recruits in the 1940s. They say the scale is increasingly unreliable above sixth grade.

There's also the question of what the "grade level" actually means. A text rated at grade six level means that average sixth grade students would find the text a real challenge to their abilities. Therefore a large proportion of sixth graders would not understand much of the text. Some of the other readability formulas were developed for, and tested on, children, so their application to adults is doubtful.

There are other criticisms: Dr Mark Hochhauser lists several of them in a 1999 article, and responds to each of the criticisms as well. Here's his summary of the criticisms:[27]

- The grade levels of readability formulas are not equivalent across all formulas.
- They ignore text structure and organisation.
- They are limited: you can use short sentences and short words and still be obscure.
- They don't consider the reader as an individual with background, culture, motivation and so on.
- Readability formulas encourage dumbing down.

Hochhauser's response comprehensively dismisses the last criticism. The other criticisms reveal the weakness of readability formulas. Nevertheless, readability formulas can have their uses. For example, quoting a poor readability score may convince its author that it needs rewriting.[28] But receiving a good readability score does not prove that a document is readable.

---

27   "Some pros and cons of readability formulas", *Clarity* No 44, Dec 1999, p 27.

28   This point is made in another excellent review of the value of readability formulas: the Plain Language Institute's *Plain Language Notes*, Feb 1993, Vol 1, No 3.

At a symposium held by the US Center for Plain Language in 2007 Rachael Keeler of communication consultants Siegel+Gale, presented a paper illustrating how good intentions can often block the road to clear communication. She said, on the topic of readability formulas:

> For the most part, they are worthless because they do not account for context, audience familiarity with the subject matter or true comprehension. Text run backwards through a readability formula will get the same score as it does run logically. Don't fall into the trap of scoring your document to tout its ease of use.[29]

In 2007, Martin Cutts, of the UK-based Plain Language Commission published a paper on readability formulas, and he summarised it this way:

> Readability tests offer an easy and relatively cheap way of assessing the apparent level of difficulty of a document. Though their simplicity and scientific veneer make them attractive for propaganda, the tests are crude. This paper suggests that discussion groups and one-to-one interviews are better for assessing clarity. Yet these methods are usually feasible only where cost and speed are not important ... [E]ditorial judgment based on experience will usually be the best aid. A readability-test score should be only a minor factor in making that judgment.[30]

For many reasons, readability formulas are unlikely to be an accurate measure of the readability of legal documents by adults in, say Australia in the 21st century. I once applied the Flesch Test to an extremely difficult section of the Australian Income Tax Assessment Act 1936.[31] Although it rated as "fairly difficult", that rating indicated that a high school student could read it.[32] But even experienced tax

29 Center for Plain Language, *Plain Language: Public Policy and Good Business* Symposium, 12 Oct 2007 <http://www.centerforplainlanguage.org/events/symposium_2007.html>.

30 Summary from email to PLAIN forum 8 Feb 2008. Paper: Cutts, M, 2008 *Writing by numbers: Are readability formulas to clarity what karaoke is to song?* <http://www.clearest.co.uk/files/WritingByNumbersKaraoke.pdf>.

31 Section 21A, which deals at great length and in great detail with "non-cash business benefits" received by taxpayers and how they can be deemed to be income for tax purposes. A new Income Tax Assessment Act 1997 rewrote portions of the old 1936 Act, including section 21A. But the 1936 Act remains on the books (partly to cater for the affairs of taxpayers before the 1997 Act came into being, and partly because not all of the 1936 Act has been rewritten). See p 73.

32 Test applied using Microsoft Word 6.0.1 software, grammar check function

advisors have significant problems understanding that particular section. It received a reasonable score because it had many subsections, all separated by semi-colons (which the test counts as the end of a sentence). And it contained short words like "tax" and "cash" and "deem" and "income". But that didn't make it any easier to understand. So you can see that these formulas have their limits as measures of comprehension. Which of course makes it a matter of concern when legislation, such as the US Plain Language statutes, stipulates that one of these formulas must be used to calculate reading age level, and makes that the standard for readability of a document.

How to test: more formal methods

There are other more formal methods of testing. The one to choose depends on several things. What sort of a document is it? How often will it be used? Who will use it? How much time and money is involved in the document? How much time and money is available for testing? And what sort of access do you have to people who are prepared to read legal documents that just *may* be less-than-scintillating?

If you have a project that warrants more than just informal testing, you might need to consider getting expert help. Testing, like document design, is easy to do on a basic level, but to get a professional result you probably need to consult a communications expert.

Here is a brief description of nine testing techniques that the experts use. You might be able to adapt them to your own circumstances. Each method involves assembling a group of people who represent the likely users or reader of your document (a "user group").

The aim here is to try to get a group that represents as closely as possible the type of people who will be reading and using the document. You don't necessarily have to have a huge group – just a representative one. You may prefer to test several smaller groups rather than one large one, to give participants a better chance to contribute.

You may choose to conduct the tests within the environment of your own organisation, or you may prefer a "laboratory" situation. A laboratory can be anything from a room set up with no distractions and a good ability to observe the group at work, to a fully fledged usability lab, with test room and observation room.[33]

---

33   Dumas, JS and Redish, JC, 1999, *A Practical Guide to Usability Testing* (cited at note 19) has a whole chapter (Chapter 15) on the test environment.

Once you have selected the group and the testing environment, you have several options.

1. *Interview*

Give your group sufficient time to read the document you are testing, and then interview them after they have read it. This will tell you if anything has worried or confused your readers. You can also ask them questions about what they might have expected to find in the document, or how they would use it themselves. In an interview, you can adjust the questions you ask, depending on the responses you get to previous questions. You could do the interview individually, or in a group, but if you interview the group you need to make sure that you get a view from the quieter members of the audience. You can also do an interview in conjunction with the other tests I'm describing.

2. *Set a multiple choice questionnaire*

This option is probably easiest on the participants, because they don't have to explain in words their understanding of the document. It is also easy on the questioner, because it does not have to be done individually. But on the other hand, a questionnaire may well reflect the mind-set of the questioner, and it does not allow for discussion or elaboration. The questions might completely miss some aspects of the document that are confusing or ambiguous.

3. *Set some problems*

This option will give you a good idea of whether the document is *usable:* that is, whether people can use the document as they will need to in reality. You probably need to set a range of problems so that you cover as much of the document as you can. But again, the problems you set might miss some of the confusing or ambiguous aspects of the document.

4. *Set a comprehension test*

In a full comprehension test, you could include multiple choice questions and problems like those I've just described, with the idea of anticipating the problems people might face when they are actually using the document. But it is important to get more information from the test than just whether people get the answer right or wrong. You should also ask participants to make a note of how they reached their answer, the sections of the document they consulted to find each answer, and the time each answer took. Remember, people might get the answer eventually, but take more time than they should because they are confused or sidetracked.

5. Check the response time

Another kind of test just asks one or more simple questions about a document, and then times how long it takes the participants to find the answer. This would be suitable for a simple kind of document, where the purposes and uses of the document are pretty clear, and you can phrase your questions accordingly.

6. Ask them to fill in the gaps

In this test, called a "Cloze" test, you test whether the readers understand a section of a document (often a 100-word sample) by giving readers that section, but with a word removed at regular intervals (often every fifth or sixth word) throughout the section. Then you ask readers to fill in the gaps. This test is used to gauge a reader's overall understanding of what they've read. A poor result on a Cloze test tends to show that people do not grasp enough of the context to enable them to have an educated guess at the missing words. It can show that you need to concentrate on giving *more* information – more context – in the document, or outside it. Cloze tests are often preferred to traditional multiple-choice tests for testing reader comprehension.

There is a more recently developed alternative to the Cloze test called the C-Test. Using four to six short texts, you delete the second half of every second word, beginning with the second word of the second sentence. The first and last sentences remain unchanged. The students have to restore the missing parts of the words. Typically there are 100 gaps. The restored words must be 100% correct.[34]

7. Ask them to paraphrase something

This test is usually given to one person at a time. Participants have to read out the document, one sentence at a time, and then paraphrase that sentence in their own words. This not only allows you to hear what errors the participant has made, but also gives

---

34   For more detail, see <http://eca.state.gov/forum/vols/vol31/no1/p35.htm>.

you an idea of why the participant made the errors – which words caused the problem.

8. Ask them to think aloud as they read

This test is similar to the paraphrase test, in that individual participants read the document aloud one sentence at a time. But instead of paraphrasing the sentence, the participants just say what they think about whichever aspects of any word or sentence (or the whole document) they want to comment on. The idea is to understand the thought processes that the reader goes through in trying to understand the document – what words cause them problems, where the information gaps are, what extra information they need when, and so on. Sometimes this can be an uncomfortable process for one person on their own, and some experts suggest that you do the test in pairs, with both people talking about the document as they work through it together.

9. Do a formal usability test

This type of test usually combines elements of the other tests I've just described, but on a one-to-one basis, closely observed by experts. They devise real-life problems and as the participants work through the questions and problems they are encouraged to speak their thoughts out loud. The experts often videotape the sessions so that they can continue to analyse the sessions in more detail later. This visual evidence is said to be very valuable, especially when you need to convince others that there is a problem with a document. Dr Janice Redish has described it this way:

> Seeing readers hunting for information, looking for an index, or going to the table of contents over and over as each section they look at turns out not to have the information they need and hearing them voice their frustration is more powerful than just counting their incorrect answers on a comprehension test.[35]

There are several good reference works that either deal specifically with testing legal documents or describe methods that can easily be adapted to testing legal writing.[36]

---

35   Krongold, S, "Writing Laws: Making them Easier to Understand" (1992) 24 *Ottawa L Rev* 495 at 548.

36   For more detailed information about testing, see Dumas, JS and Redish, JC, 1999, *A Practical Guide to Usability Testing* (cited at note 19). There is a

What to do with the results

Once you have your test results, you have to decide what to do with them. You may agree or not agree with some of the test group's comments. You may agree, but not be able to come up with a good alternative. You may need to do more testing, perhaps with a different range of alternatives or a different group. There are no rules to tell you exactly how to take test results into account. Testing might show you where the problems are in your document, but it will not always give you solutions to those problems. Usability testers recommend that once you have gathered information about your "users", their goals and their tasks, you should set goals for your document. Once you have those goals, you can then work on specific ways to achieve those goals.[37] The idea here is to recognise that you may not be able to satisfy the needs of *all* readers, so it may be helpful to have set some general goals to return to when solutions seem elusive.

There are two further factors to keep in mind when considering what to do about test results. The first is this: the "victims" of a situation or the people with a problem are not always the right people to suggest the solution. They are experienced with the problem and they will help you identify it, but finding the *solution* is up to you.

---

section written by Dr Redish on testing a statute, in Krongold, S, "Writing Laws: Making them Easier to Understand" (1992) 24 *Ottawa L Rev* 495 at 544. See also Goldsmith, P, Reid, G and Sawyer, S, 1993, *Reaching your readers: A fieldtesting guide for community groups*, Legal Services Society of BC, Vancouver and Rubin, J and Chisnell, D 2008, *Handbook of Usability Testing*, 2nd edition, Wiley Publishing Inc, Indianapolis. There is also a chapter on testing in Pringle, J, 2006, *Writing Matters* <http://www.nald.ca/library/ learning/writmatt/cover.htm> and Eagleson, RD, 1990, *Writing in Plain English*, AGPS Press, Commonwealth of Australia, Canberra p 80. Martin Cutts describes his testing of the Clearer Timeshare Act in Cutts, M, 2000, *Lucid Law*, 2nd edition, Plain Language Commission, High Peak, England, pages 22-28. There is some information about testing in Duckworth, M and Mills, G, 1996, *Organising a Plain Language Project*, Federation Press, Sydney, at pages 18-19 and 63. And see the article by Huron, DI, "Testing plain language texts with adult learners", *Clarity*, No 51, May 2004, p 24. There are even videos on the internet demonstrating usability testing. Type "Usability testing" into your search engine. There is a huge amount of information on Youtube and other websites.

37   Dumas, JS and Redish, JC, 1999, *A Practical Guide to Usability Testing*, pages 348-351 (cited at note 19).

The second thing to remember is that in testing we are looking for objectivity about our documents – not justification for our writing style or the decisions we made in our drafting. We must be careful not to taint our test results with enthusiasm for our own ideas.

Testing keeps us honest

I see the role of testing in plain language writing as a way of keeping ourselves honest. We must work hard to simplify our documents, and to eliminate legalese from legal writing. We all need to keep building up our plain language writing skills, and honing them by practice. The process never ends, even for a plain language expert. But we must also keep asking the question: are we considering our reader? Are we doing everything we can to make our writing as clear and plain and readable as we can? Will our readers understand what we have written?

We have good evidence that using plain language writing techniques does make our writing easier to read and does improve reader comprehension. And we now have powerful incentives to make us write in plain language. But much of the time, when we write in plain language we do not actually know for sure whether our efforts are hitting the mark.

Testing allows us to tell, with some objectivity, if what we are doing is working.

Chapter 18
Any questions?

I said at the beginning of this book that the conclusion would be in Chapter 1 with the introduction. And it was. I said in Chapter 1 that this book was about drafting in a new way. Drafting to communicate, rather than just to record. I said that when we draft legal documents we should be able to use some of the same techniques that we use in everyday communication. I wanted to convince you that there is no need to cling to old formulas and archaic language, because new simple language can do the same job just as well.

I should have done that by now, and given you some of the tools you need to begin writing in a new way – unless of course you are already writing in plain language, as many lawyers do, sometimes without realising it.

If I have been successful, there is no need for any more encouragement from me now. But I suspect you might have a few questions still nagging away. Or you might have to answer questions about plain language from other people. So in this, the last chapter of this book, I have tried to anticipate those questions.

Is plain language a new language?

It is not a new language. It is just an attempt to write English (or French or German or whatever else) in a clear and simple style.

Is a plain language document always shorter than a document written in traditional legal style?

Not always. It depends on whether the traditional version contained much unnecessary material. Sometimes a plain language document is longer than the traditional equivalent: for example, if the plain language version needs to have a lot of explanatory material in it. Brevity is *one* of the aims of plain language, but not the only one. We never sacrifice clarity for brevity.

Is it possible to be too brief?

Yes. Sometimes in our eagerness to cut out unnecessary material we cut out necessary material as well. But we must give the reader everything they need to understand what we write.

There are some words and phrases that might not be *strictly neces sary* to convey our meaning, but might assist the reader to understand our meaning more easily. They do serve a useful purpose and don't need to be cut. If we simply aim to reduce the number of words in our document it might be as unreadable as an overlong document. As Horace said:

> I strive to be brief, and I become obscure.[1]

Remember that some words don't necessarily add to meaning, but do add to readability. Again, brevity is *one* aim of plain language writers – but not at the expense of clarity.

Is it possible to oversimplify?

Of course it is. Remember Albert Einstein's warning:

> Everything should be made as simple as possible but not simpler.[2]

There is no need to choose every word to suit the lowest common denominator. That might be offensive to readers of average intelligence. All that is necessary is that you pitch your writing at the appropriate level for your likely audience. Only you can judge that.

Why should we break with the past?

We are not really breaking with the past. Plain language is not a new idea. There have always been plain speakers and writers. What we are doing now is simply recognising the rights of our readers. We have a responsibility to serve the changing needs of our clients and the others who might read our documents. This might involve updating our writing style to suit the requirements of the present (and the future). It might mean that we must be more selective in what we keep from the past, recognising that tradition alone is not enough to justify using difficult or unfamiliar words.

---

1   *Ars Poetica.*
2   Attributed to Albert Einstein by *The Bloomsbury Treasury of Quotations*, 1994 Bloomsbury Publishing plc, London, p 629.

What about the "time-honoured" words?

Just because a word or phrase meant one thing in the past, even the recent past, that is no guarantee that it will mean the same thing at all times in the future, and in all other circumstances. And it does not mean it is the best word or phrase for the purpose. It is the legal principles that matter, not the forms of words. We have a responsibility not just to know and understand the law, but also to write so that we can be understood and acted on, and so that the intention behind the document is clear. "Time-honoured" words may or may not do that. Only you can judge. But there may well be a better, clearer way.

But why should we bother? We've got on well enough until now

Our clients are asking questions. They are demanding a change. Our governments, our legislators and our courts have taken a fresh look at lawyers' language. There are new dimensions of professional liability for the language that lawyers use. Plain language allows us to show our skills as lawyers more dramatically and efficiently. Today clients are prepared to pay for legal services in plain language. Soon they will not pay for legal services *unless* they are in plain language.[3]

How do I justify the cost and time to write in plain language?

Former US Securities and Exchange Commission Chair Christopher Cox was asked this question at a seminar in 2007. Without missing a beat, he replied: "If investors are promised information and they don't get it in a form they can understand, they're being cheated".[4]

As far as I am concerned, the same goes for all clients, and all readers.

But we don't have time to rewrite all our precedents

No one is suggesting that we must start by rewriting all our precedents - although it is a great place to practise, and you certainly learn a lot from the exercise.

---

3   To paraphrase Christopher Balmford (see p 83).
4   Mercer, M, "Plain Language Symposium: a Success by Any Measure", *Simply Plain*, Vol 2, Issue, 2, Oct – Dec 2007, p 2 <http://www.centerforplainlanguage.org/downloads/Simply_Plain_No6_Winter_Vol2_Iss2.pdf>.

The best place to start is with a clean sheet of paper. Next time you write a letter of advice. It is easier to write in plain language if you are starting from scratch. Writing in plain language is not as daunting if you don't have pages of legalese to "translate". The best advice is to start small, and gradually hone your skills.

As their writing skills improve, most people eventually get so enthused about plain language that they can't stand the look of traditional style documents and can't wait to rewrite any documents they are likely to use often.

How do I deal with amending a document that is written in the traditional style? Plain language really stands out next to legalese

That is true. You certainly shouldn't insist on rewriting the whole document to make the styles accord. Apart from the fact that it would take too long – and the client probably wouldn't want to pay for it – it might also seem discourteous to the writer of the document. But there is no need to imitate the traditional style either. Just try to state what you have to state as plainly and simply as possible, making sure that there are no ambiguities created in the process.

And don't be tempted to ridicule the writer's "traditional" style. Your own clear writing style is likely to be a more persuasive advocate for plain language.

I've got rid of the legalese. Is that all there is to plain language?

No. Plain language writing is about more than just the words on the page. It involves looking at the whole process of communication. It considers the needs and abilities of the reader, the purposes of the writing, the way the material is organised and the layout and design of the document. It looks at ways of finding out whether the document is going to do its job. And the definition of "plain language" continues to expand as we learn more about communication and writing. So plain language is not just a matter of "translating" the words on a page. It looks at writing and documents in a much wider context than that.

Should I write differently for email?

No. Email and the internet are simply different media for the writer, and plain language is appropriate for all media of writing. But the immediate, international and informal aspects of email and the internet do have implications for the way we write. We need to be aware that we are writing for a potentially limitless audience, and one that may not be familiar with our conventions of communication. And despite the informal nature of email, we still need to check our writing carefully for typing, spelling and other errors, and use appropriate punctuation, grammar, courtesy and even an appropriate typeface.

How closely should I follow all these plain language guidelines?

That is a difficult question to answer without a context. In fact, most things about plain language are difficult to discuss without a context: without using concrete examples. Most objections to plain language drafting that look sensible enough or plausible enough in theory (such as "we must use the time-honoured words") fall away when put to a practical test.

We need to be flexible in the way we apply plain language guidelines. There are no hard-and-fast rules, other than "consider your reader".[5] If you try to follow the guidelines set out in this book too rigidly, you will probably end up too inhibited to write anything at all. Start gradually, look critically at your writing, try practising one or two of the techniques I've described, and let your talent for plain language writing emerge. It will.

How will I know when I'm writing in plain language?

Just as there are no hard-and-fast rules in plain language writing, there are no standards to measure yourself against to tell you *when* you are writing in plain language. There is no one "orthodox" form of plain language. If you follow the guidelines in this book, or even some of them, your writing will be simplified. It will be easier to read than it was before. It is a gradual process. There is no line with "legalese" on one side and "plain language" on the other.

---

5   See Chapter 5.

What is more, any document that is said to be written in "plain language" (including this book) can probably be improved, simplified further, redesigned, and made easier to read in many different ways. No one has all the answers and all the techniques. It is important to be flexible and listen to criticism carefully, without getting discouraged. It is also important to offer criticism sympathetically.

Remember that just putting in a lot of effort to write in plain language does not guarantee that what you produce will be in plain language. People often "confuse the effort with the outcome".[6] That's one reason why so many documents that are claimed to be in plain language are clearly not.

One way to find out whether there is room for improvement is to consider testing your document, using one of the methods described in Chapter 17.

There is always room for improvement, and any improvement will be gradual. The most important thing is to be alive to the issues and aware of the potential problems with legal writing.

How do I start?

The best way to learn plain language drafting is by practice. Any document at all is suitable to practise on. Start now.

---

6   This useful phrase was used by Dr Mark Hochhauser, in "Some pros and cons of readability formulas", *Clarity* No 44, Dec 1999, p 27.

Thank you

There are many people who have helped me with this book. Some were plain language specialists, and some were not. All were very generous with their time, and very patient with my (often obscure, and always annoyingly persistent) questions.

I want to thank in particular Mark Adler, Christopher Balmford, Peter Bartlett, Professor Peter Butt, Sir Edward Caldwell, Dr Nittaya Campbell, Richard Castle, George Clark, Martin Cutts, David Dapper, David Elliott, Nicole Fernbach, Derrick Fine, Dr Jacqueline Harrison, Philippe Hallée, Professor Joseph Kimble, Phil Knight, Robert Lowe, Professor Margaret McLaren, Mary Montague, Hilary Penfold QC, Millie Patel, Wai-chung Suen, Anne Wagner, and Jon Fuller, Simon Williams and other members of the UK Tax Law Rewrite Project team. Some of you helped with earlier editions, some with this 4th edition, some with all editions. I am grateful to you all.

Again, to all the others who have helped me by spending time on the phone with me, or sending me copies of a report, a judgment, or an article, sincere thanks. *You know who you are.*

And finally, to my husband Lindsay Powers. In countless ways you have made this book, and so much else, possible. Your immense support should really entitle you to billing as co-author of this book. Once again, no plain words can express my gratitude.

Index

A fortiori, 132, 176
A maximum of, 191
A, an, 179-180
Ab initio, 176, 233
Abatement, 220
Abbreviations, 76, 143, 243, 245, 247
Aboriginal people, 91
Above, 137, 179, 233
Abovementioned, 136, 233
Accordingly, 194, 233
According to, 183-184, 235, 238
Accuracy, 31, 34, 42, 92, 248, 297
Active voice, 153-154
Acts Interpretation Act 1901 (Cth), 139, 172, 218-219, 229-230
Acts Interpretation Act 1954 (Qld), 122, 218, 229
Acts Interpretation Act 1915 (SA), 122, 150
"Actual" meaning, 22
Adbooth Pty Ltd v Ryde City Council, 200
Adduce, 233
Adjectival clauses, 124
Adler, M, 104, 120, 143, 210, 337
Adverbial clauses, 124
Advertisements, 304
Adoption Regulations 2008 (Vic), 48
Aetna Life & Casualty, 36, 65
Affidavit, 130
Affix, 220
Aforesaid, 30, 136, 233
Agricultural and Rural Finance Pty Limited v Gardiner, 131
Aitken, JK, 125, 151, 188, 212
Alberta, 41, 71, 82
Alberta Law Reform Institute, 82
Albeit, 233
Al-Kateb v Godwin, 211, 222
All, 179-180, 232, 233

Allege, 233
Allied Irish Bank, 86
ALS Scan, Inc v Digital Service Consultants, Inc, 255
ALT-Tags, 305
Amadio, Commercial Bank of Australia v, 52-54, 193
Amend, 233
Amos v Brisbane City Council, 222
Amounts, 187, 190-191
Amounts of time, 190-191
AMP Insurance, 65
Ancillary, 233
And, 199-205
And/or, 205
Animated pictures, 304-305, 309
Annex, 233
Annexures, 115-117
Annuities, 20
Answers as headings, 272
Anton Piller KG v Manufacturing Processes Ltd, 133
Any, 179-180, 232, 233
Appendixes, 115-117
Appurtenant to, 233
Arabic numbers, 274, 286
Archaic language, 21, 99, 135-137, 182, 184, 186, 187, 228, 331
Arial typeface, 262, 264, 286, 295, 297
Aristotle, 27
Arthur, Sir George, 90
Articles of impeachment, 98
As soon as possible, 188-189, 190, 234, 235
Ascham, Roger, 27
Asia, 45
"Assigned" meaning, 24
Associative patterns, 291
Asterisks, 146-147, 245, 271, 273, 279
At all times, 150, 186

At any time, 151, 184-186, 233
At first blush, 132
At least, 191
At this particular point in time, 184
At this point in time, 136, 233
Audience, 90-96, 99, 101, 103, 232, 243, 250-251, 262, 270, 286, 306-307, 311, 316, 318, 324, 326, 332, 335
Audience, primary, 91-92, 95-96, 99, 103
Audience, secondary, 91-92, 95-96, 99, 101, 103
Australian Bankers' Association, 46
Australian Broadcasting Commission v Australasian Performing Right Assn Ltd, 219
Australian Concise Oxford Dictionary, 23-24
Australian government *Style Manual*, 120, 169, 172, 263, 265, 290-291, 296, 298, 299, 300, 301, 302
Australian Institute of Judicial Administration, 81
Background, 240
Background colour/ texture, 262, 284, 287, 299-300, 305, 309, 337
Background (factual) material, 182-183, 220, 230
Bacon, Lord, 33
"Bad" English/writing, 13, 28, 43, 56, 66, 163, 171
Balmford, C, 39, 58, 59, 63, 77, 83, 84, 333,
Bangoura v Washington Post, 254
Bank of America, 36
Bank of Baroda v Panessar, 189
Bank of Credit and Commerce International SA v Ali, 220
Bank of Ireland, 86
Bank of Nova Scotia, 38, 65
Banking Practice (Australian), Code of, 46
Banking Practice (NZ), Code of, 88
Banking Practice (RSA), Code of, 86-87
Bankruptcy and Insolvency Act 1992 (Canada), 180

Banners, 304
Barristers, 27, 30, 55, 90, 124, 228, 241, 251, 288
Barron's magazine, 252
Barron's Online, 252-253
Bath and Montague's Case, 183
Below, 179, 233
Bentham, Jeremy, 30
Berezovsky v Michaels, 254
Bernard, Michael, 299, 305
Between, 191
Bit-mapping, 295
Black, 230
Black v Breedon, 254
Bleak House, 30-31
Blog, 293, 308
Blomley v Ryan, 52
Boehm v Director of Public Prosecutions, 228
Bold type, 117, 145-147, 259, 260, 273, 279-281, 286
Bona fide, 176, 233
Bond v Hongkong Bank of Australia, 190
Bondi tram, 133
Bonitto v Fuerst Brothers & Co Ltd, 205
Book Antiqua typeface, 264, 251, 275
Bookman Old Style typeface, 249
Bormuth Grade Level, 322
Boxes, 93, 130, 259, 270, 281-282, 291
BP Australia Ltd v Brown, 158
Brevity, 78, 139, 173, 331-332
Bridging words, 291, 308
British Columbia, 57, 69, 82, 209, 230
Browser, 294
Brush typeface, 262
Bullets, 123, 271, 273, 275, 277, 279, 290, 293, 302, 303, 309
Burke, James, 32
Burke v NYP Holdings Inc (c o b New York Post), 254
By virtue of, 184, 233
Calibri typeface, 244-245, 297
California, 6-7
Calisto typeface, 297
Callaway, FH, QC, 216
Cambria typeface, 297

Caminetti v United States, 210

Canada, 37, 38-39, 41, 57, 64, 65-66, 69, 71, 76, 80, 81-82, 84-86, 121, 125, 151, 170, 173, 190, 253-254, 276, 307, 314-315,

Canadian Bankers' Association, 69, 85

Canadian Bar Association, 65, 74

Canadian Institute for the Administration of Justice, 82

Canadian Law Information Council, 74

Canadian Legislative Drafting Conventions, 65-66

Canons of interpretation/ construction, 134, 222, 224-227

Capita Finance Group, 39

Capital letters for definitions, 139, 145

Captions, 291

Carroll, Lewis, 322

Carter, President James, 66, 70

Case, 124-128, 178-179

Case citations, 177

Case references, 177

Case law, 25-26

Castle, Richard, 214, 337

Centre for Microeconomic Policy Analysis, 39, 40, 83

Center for Plain Language (US), 324

Centre for Plain Legal Language, 39, 40, 82, 267, 275

Centred text, 265-266, 302

Chacmol Holdings Pty Ltd v Handberg, 183

Chadha v Dow Jones Company Inc, 254

Chairman, 172-173

Chairperson, 172-173

Chairwoman, 172-173

Chancery, 30

Charles XII, 66

Charts, 105, 270, 282-3, 286

Checklist, 104, 276, 282-283, 298, 306, 320, 321

"Chemist's English", 28

Chemists, 28

Chew v The Queen, 121

Children (Community Service Orders) Act 1987, 48

"Chunks" of information, 111, 118, 290

Churchill, Sir Winston, 164

Citibank, 31, 34-35, 45, 65

Citi Cards, 35

Citigroup Inc, 34-35

Citizens' Summary (EU), 77

Civil Procedure Rules 1998 (UK), 68, 79-80, 133, 176

Civil Procedure Rules 1999 (Qld), Uniform, 51

Civil Procedure Rules 2005 (NSW), Uniform, 51, 133

Civil Procedure Rules (US, Federal), 79, 207, 215

Clapham omnibus, man on the, 132

Clarica, 86

"Clarity" Awards, 84

Clarity (organisation), 84

"Clarity Commitment" (Bank of America), 36

Clark, Helen, 159

Clauses, 118, 120, 123, 124, 127--128, 159-161, 178

"Clause sandwiches", 114-115

CLEAR analysis formula, 322

"Clear English", 14

"Clear and conspicuous", 14

Clearer Commonwealth Law, 4, 94, 312

CLERP, 75, 229

Cleveland Clinic, 37

Clients, 3-4, 8, 10, 21, 34, 45, 47, 53, 57-60, 62, 65, 83, 84, 90, 91-92, 97, 99-101, 104-106, 109-110, 129, 176, 177, 196-197, 214, 317-319, 321, 332-334

"Cloze" Test, 327

Colby Corporation Pty Ltd v Commissioner of Taxation, 221

Code of Banking Practice (Aus), 46

Code of Banking Practice (NZ), 88

Code of Banking Practice (RSA), 86-87

Cody v J H Nelson Pty Limited, 215

Coleman-Liau Grade Level, 322
Collector of Customs v Brian Lawlor, 184
Collins, Dr M, 241, 246, 250, 253, 255
Colour, 259, 271, 275, 283-284, 286, 287, 299-300, 306, 309
Colourful language, 132-133
Columns, 264-265, 266-267, 268, 302
Commas, 121, 122, 124
Commercial Bank of Australia v Amadio, 52-54, 192-193
"Commercial" contracts, 212, 220
"Commonly acceptable" meaning, 24-25
Commonwealth Parliamentary Counsel (Aus), 75, 95, 118, 127, 146, 172, 178, 184, 203-204, 212, 236, 253, 271, 272, 312-313
Communication, 2, 10, 16, 21-24, 34, 58-59, 62, 64, 77, 122, 132-133, 198, 243, 245-246, 287, 320, 331, 335
Communications Research Institute of Australia (CRIA), 261
Companies (Acquisition of Shares) Act 1980, 42, 44
Competitive edge, 45-47
Complaints against solicitors, 58-60
Comprehension test, 326-327
Computer programs (grammar and style checks), 321-322
Computer screen, 9, 145, 262, 286, 287, 288-310
Conclusion, 1-2, 8, 290, 308, 331
Condition, 124-128, 162, 178, 214, 239
Confusing labels, 142-143
Constitution of South Africa, 77, 171, 173, 207-208
Construction, "purposive" approach to, 121, 219-221
Construe, 234
Consumer contracts, 31, 34-35, 38, 64-65, 66, 67, 87-88, 212-213
Consumer credit laws, 5, 47, 50, 87-88, 119, 270, 313
Consumer loan note, 31, 34, 65
Consumer movement, 64

Consumer Protection Act 2008 (RSA), 87-88
Context, 13, 17, 24, 25, 26, 97, 101, 110, 127-128, 135, 147, 152-153, 183, 189, 207-208, 210, 212, 219, 220-221, 224, 232, 237, 250, 257, 324, 327, 335
Contra proferentem, 224, 227
Contracts Review Act 1980, 51
Contrast, 261, 281, 299, 300, 305
Convention on Choice of Court Agreements, 257
Conventions, 23, 65-66, 120, 242, 243, 277, 303, 305, 309, 335
Conveyancing Act 1919 (NSW), 126, 182, 224
Coode's rules, 124-126, 150, 178
Coode, George, 124-126, 150, 178
Corbett, M M (fmr Chief Justice RSA), 31
Coroner Reform Bill (UK), 78
Corporations Act 2001, 38, 50, 94, 139, 145, 157-158, 228-229
Corporations Law, 46, 74-75, 94-95, 145, 158, 170, 229, 312, 313, 318
Corporations Law Simplification Program, 46, 67-75, 94-95, 145, 157, 170, 312, 318
"Correct" meaning, 24
Cost of Borrowing Regulations (Canada), 85
Courier typeface, 264, 295
Court reports, 34
Courtesy, 101-102, 103, 177, 334, 335
Covenant, 20, 210-211
Cover the field, 132
Covering letter and separate memorandum, 110
Credit Act 1984 (NSW), 119
Credit cards, 14, 35-36, 38
Credit laws, 5, 47, 50, 87-88, 119, 270, 313
Crimes Act 1914 (Cth), 47
Crimes Act 1958 (Vic), 230-231
Cross-references, 192, 279, 282-283, 291, 308

Cultural differences, 284, 306, 309
Curial, 234
Curlz typeface, 297
Cutts, M, 66, 146-147, 251, 265, 269, 302, 307, 324, 329, 337
Dangerous Substances (Explosives) Regulation 2004 (ACT), 49
David Grant & Co Pty Limited (Rec Apptd) v Westpac Banking Corporation, 157-158
Day and year first hereinbefore written, the, 136, 234
De facto, 176
Dear sirs, 101, 105, 171, 243
Decimal numbering, 274-278, 286
Decimate, 23-24
Decimating, 24
Declaration of Independence, 30
Decline and Fall of Gobbledygook, 69, 85
Defamation, 252-257
Definitions, 23-24, 75, 137-148, 204, 213, 223, 279, 281
Demise, 131
Demised premises, 17
Demur, 234
Denmark, 64
Denning, Lord, 12-13
Deputy Commissioner of Taxation v Clark, 133, 226
Derive, 234
Design principles, 258-259, 286, 288, 289, 294, 304, 306, 308
Details, 91, 97, 101, 105, 110, 115-117, 138, 141, 144, 160-161, 177, 292, 303, 308
Diagram, 75, 105, 270, 282-283, 286, 304
Dick, Robert, QC, 65, 125, 135, 151, 152, 177, 178, 185, 200
Dickens, Charles, 30-31
Dickerson, Reed, 180
Dictated by, 234
Dictionaries, 17, 23-25, 138-139, 170, 206
Dictionary, 138-139, 144-146
Disability Discrimination Act 1992, 307

Disbursements, 234
Discovery, 79
Discretion, 158, 214, 217-218
Dishonour, 131
Disraeli, Benjamin, 32
Document add-ons, 115-117
Document design, 14, 258-287, 288-310, 334
Document Design Center, Washington DC, 42, 81
Doonan, E, 212
Dot-points, 123, 271, 273, 275, 277, 279, 290, 293, 302, 303, 309
Double negatives, 158-159
Doublets, 99, 134-135
Dousi v Colgate Palmolive Pty Ltd (No 2), 227
Dow Jones & Company Inc v Gutnick, 252-256
Drafting by stealth, 192-193
Driedger, Dr EA, QC, 125, 178
Duckworth & Mills, 39, 40, 329
Duke of Brunswick v Harmer, 254
Duke of Wellington, 27-28
Dumas, J S, 319, 325, 328, 329
Durban Principles, 256
Each, 135, 179-180, 234
Each and every, 135
Eagleson, Dr R, 207, 210, 214, 329
Edward VI, 29
Eg, 176
Egerton, Chancellor, 33
Eggshell skull, 132
Einstein, Albert, 27, 332
Ejusdem generis, 133-134, 211, 224, 226
Elawyering Task Force, 307
Electricity Supply (General) Regulation 2001 (NSW), 48
Elegant variation, 142, 224, 225
Electronic bulletin boards, 242, 252, 255
Electronic document design, 288-310
Electronic mail/ email, 9, 111, 194, 241-257, 288, 302, 311, 335
Elizabeth I, 32

Email, 9, 111, 194, 241-257, 288, 302, 311, 335
Emoticons, 245-247, 249, 250
Emphasis, 18-19, 112, 115, 137, 179-180, 186, 248, 278, 281
Employment Insurance Act (Canada), 76, 315
Endings, tired, 195-196
English, 134-135, 176-177, 197, 331
Entry, 230-231
Equititrust Ltd v Bosiljevac, 241
Equivocating, 196-197
Esher, Lord, 225
Estop, 130-131, 234
Estoppel, 130-131, 183
Estoppel by representation, 183
Et al, 176, 234
Ethics, 57, 59
Ethics, Statement of (Law Society of NSW), 59
European Community, 64, 76
European Union, 76, 77
Every, 135, 179-180, 234
Ex parte, 176
Exclusive service, 20
Execute, 117, 131, 236
Execution clauses, 116, 117
Explanatory memoranda, 223
Executive Memorandum, US, 70
Explanatory notes (UK bills), 68, 78
Explosives Regulations (Canada), 76, 314
Exposure drafts, 312-313, 316-317
Expressio unius est exclusio alterius, 129-130, 133-134, 224
Extraman (NT) Pty Ltd v Blenkinship and Others, 205
Extraneous, 234
Extrinsic material, 223
F-pattern, 293
Facebook, 241, 245, 251
Fairness and justice, 51-53
Fair Trading Acts, 48, 52
Fair Trading (Retirement Villages Code) Regulations 2006 (WA), 49
Fair Work Act 2009 (Cth), 47

Fair Work Act 1994 (SA), 49
Fair Work (General) Regulations (SA), 49
Family Court of Australia, 80
Family Law Act 1975, 47
Federal Aviation Administration (US), 71
Federal Communications Commission (US), 37
Federal Court Rules, US, 78-79, 118, 207, 215
Federal Register (US), 66, 70, 71
Felsenfeld, Carl, 31, 262-263, 265, 280, 287
Fertile octogenarian, 132
Filing fees, 33
Financial Consumer Agency of Canada, 85-86
Finding things, 271, 300
"Fine distinctions", 19
First National City Bank, 31, 65
Fit and proper, 135
Flesch Reading Ease Test, 67, 322-323, 324
Flesch, Rudolph, 67
Flesch-Kincaid Grade Level, 87, 322-323
Flexibility, 13, 125, 138, 141, 163-164, 174-175, 190, 209, 249, 291, 328, 335, 336
Flow chart, 105, 270, 282-283
Focus groups, 35, 41, 58, 73, 75, 312, 313
Foggy writing, 27
Fonts, 244-245, 260-262, 281, 286, 294-297, 298
Food and Drug Administration (US), 71
Footnotes, 10-11, 145-147, 279
Foreman and *foreperson*, 173
Foreword, 1
Formality, 13, 16, 18, 72, 98-100, 103, 125, 155, 171, 241, 243-244, 248-250, 257, 267-268, 279, 296, 321-324, 325- 328, 335

Forms and precedents, 34, 60, 83, 131, 137, 317

Forms, rewriting and redesigning, 34-42, 44, 65, 69-72

Forthwith, 188-189, 235

Fowler, HW & FG, 119, 170

Fraser v NRMA Holdings Ltd, 60-61

Free and clear, 135

Free shares, 61

French, 12, 121, 134, 331

From, 191

From and after, 135

From time to time, 184-186, 235

Full stop, 120, 124, 322

Future, 21, 91-92, 149-153, 165, 184, 187, 205-206, 212, 214, 215-217, 278, 332, 333

Future, in the, 236

Future meaning, 25

Future tense, 17, 149-153, 184, 205-206, 212, 214, 215-217, 239

Futures Industry Act 1986, 42, 44

Gaps, fill in the, 327

Garcia v National Australia Bank Ltd, 55, 193

Gardiner, Agricultural and Rural Finance Pty Limited v, 118

Garner, Bryan, 79, 178-179, 188, 214, 218, 226

Gas Supply (Natural Gas Retail Competition) Regulation 2001 (NSW), 48

Gender, 165-174

Gender-neutral language, 78, 165-174, 229

Generation X, 304

Geneva typeface, 295

George Patterson, 56-57

Georgia typeface, 262, 286, 295, 296, 309

Gibson v ANZ Banking Group (NZ) Limited, 189

Give devise and bequeath, 135, 235

Give consideration to, 161, 235

Goldsbrough v Ford Credit Aust Ltd, 54, 193

Good faith, 131, 233, 240

Goods and chattels, 135

Gopen, George, 28

Gowers, Sir Ernest, 27, 119, 124, 194, 206, 209

Government Cleaning Services v Ellul, 227

Grammar, 2, 120, 149-175, 217, 221, 321-322, 335

Graphics, 270, 286, 298, 304-305, 309

Greig v Stramit Corporation Pty Limited, 158

Guarantees, 5, 47, 50, 53, 54-55, 82, 311

Gunning Fog Index, 322

Gutnick, Joseph, 252-253

Habit, 3, 8, 34, 43, 135, 136, 176-193, 197, 248, 289, 322

Hackneyed phrases, 195-196

Had and received, 135

Hale, Sir Matthew, 32

Halsbury's Laws of England, 188-189, 210-211

Halsbury's Laws of Australia, 188-189, 211

Hanel and Another v O'Neill, 228-229

Harrods v Dow Jones & Co Inc, 254

Harsh contracts, 51

Have and hold, 135

He or she, 166

Headings, 111, 116, 117, 171, 183, 261, 268, 271-273, 279, 281, 283, 285, 286, 290, 291, 292, 293, 308, 309

Headings and points, 105

Health and Human Sciences, Dpt of (US), 71, 301, 307

Hearsay, 130

Helvetica typeface, 295

Hereafter, 136, 186-187, 235

Hereby, 136, 235

Herein, 136, 235

Hereinafter, 136-137, 186-187, 235

Hereto, 235

Heretofore, 136-137, 186-187, 235

Hereunto, 136, 235, 236

Herewith, 136, 235

Highlighting, 271, 279-281, 286, 290, 291

Hillary, Sir Edmund, 159

Ho Song Lu v Minister for Immigration and Multicultural and Indigenous Affairs, 237

Hochhauser, Dr M, 323

Hoffman La Roche Inc, 36

Holmes, Oliver Wendell, 13, 22

Home Owners Warranty Corporation, 36

Home pages, 251, 288, 305

Horace, 332

Horne v Deputy Commissioner of Taxation, 158

Houlahan v Australian & New Zealand Banking Group Ltd, 54-55, 193

Houston v Burns, 121

House of Representatives Committee Reports (Aus), 4, 94

Howsoever, 137, 235

Hughes, Robert, 91

Human Rights and Equal Opportunity Commission, 306

Hutley, Justice, 13

Hyperlinks, 242, 290, 291, 303-305, 308

Hypertext document, 242, 303

ICAC, 72

Ie, 176

If, 177-179

If ... then, 126-128

Illustrations, 304

Image of lawyers, 57-58, 62

Immediately, 188-190

Imperative mood, 153, 205-210, 214, 215

In accordance with, 235

In cases in which, 177

In cases where, 177

In the matter of Opes Prime Stockbroking Limited, 241

Incur, 235

Indicia, 236

In personam, 176, 236

In pursuance of, 184, 236

In the exercise of powers conferred by, 184

In witness whereof, 116, 136, 236

Includes, 138, 140-142, 172, 205, 237

Inclusive, 191, 201

Income Tax Act (NZ), 73-74, 135, 278, 315

Income Tax Acts (UK), 20, 74

Income Tax Assessment Act 1997 (Cth), 73, 76, 138, 144, 146, 270, 277, 282, 324

Indefinite article, 179-180

Indemnify, 60, 130, 236

Indenting, 271, 284-285, 286

Independent Commission Against Corruption (ICAC), 72

Indexes, 271, 285, 286

India, 64

Industrial Relations Act 1999 (Qld), 48

Industrial Relations (Superannuation) Regulations 1997 (WA), 49

Infinitive, splitting, 163

Informality, 98-100, 103, 125, 155, 171, 241, 243-244, 248-250, 257, 267-268, 279, 296, 319-324, 325, 335

Information Design Center, Washington DC, 42, 81

Ingram, Re, 200

Injunction, 130, 133

Inland Revenue (NZ), 74

Insofar as, 236

Instrument, 131, 236

Insurance companies, 36-39, 45-46, 60, 65, 85, 86, 88,

Insurance policies, 37-39, 46, 65, 67, 86, 119

Intagro Projects Pty Ltd v Australia and New Zealand Banking Group Ltd, 229

Interactive design techniques, 304

Interlocutory, 236

Internet, 95, 241-257, 288, 302, 307, 316, 322, 329, 335

Interpretation Act 1897 (NSW), 211

Interpretation Act (Northern Ireland) 1954, 151, 187

Interpretation Act 1987 (NSW), 211

Interpretation Act 1999 (NZ), 151

Interpretation Act 1984 (WA), 150

Interpretation Act (Canada), 151
Interpretation Act [RSBC], 209, 230
Interpretation Acts, 68, 150-151, 211, 223-224, 229-230
Interpretation of Legislation Act 1984 (Vic), 122, 187, 211
Interpretation, legal, 150-153, 183, 200, 219-231
Interrupting sentences, 159-161
Interviews, 324, 326
Introduction, 1, 2, 8, 170, 183, 240, 271, 282, 292, 331
Introductory material, 182-183
Inverted pyramid, 290
Investors Compensation Scheme Ltd v West Bromwich Building Society, 220
Ireland, 35-36, 69, 86, 206, 220
Irish Law Reform Commission, 69
Irish Life, 86
Is required to, 210, 237
Is to, 210
Is to be, 215
Issue, 237
Italics, 145, 147, 259, 260, 281, 286
James, William, 10-11
JC Penney Company Inc, 36
Jefferson, Thomas, 30
Johnson, Samuel, 164
Jointly and severally, 132
Jones v Evans, 230
Judges, attitudes of, 227-231
Judicial Colleges (Aus), 80-81
Judicial Commission (NSW), 80
Judgments, 31, 80-81, 82, 107, 288
Judgment-writing programs, 80-81, 228
Jurors, 44, 58, 92
Justice, fairness and, 51-53
Justice Reform Committee of British Columbia, 69
Justified text, 265-269, 286, 302
Kay v South Eastern Sydney Area Health Service, 121
Keep and maintain, 135
Keep indemnified, 60, 236
Kennan, the Hon J, QC, MLA, 209

Kennedy, Donald, 28
Keywords, 272, 290, 292, 308
Kimble, Prof Joseph, 37, 44, 61-62, 66, 77, 79, 81, 98-99, 195, 207, 213-216, 228, 337
King v Lewis, 254
Kirby, Justice, 222, 227, 256
Kitakufe v Oloya, 254
Klemt, Becky, 6-8
Laboratory (usability testing), 325
Labour Relations Act 1995 (RSA), 77
Landscape format, 265
Laramie, Wyoming, 6-7
Latin, 7, 28, 79, 129, 135, 176-177, 224-226
Law Commission (England and Wales), 254, 256
Law "constantly speaking", 150-153, 185
Law of Property Act 1925 (UK), 182
Law firms, Australian, 45-47, 58, 83, 99, 210
Law Reform Commission of Victoria, 31, 42, 44, 68, 93, 125, 145, 184, 209, 275-276
Law Society (England & Wales), 83, 143, 210
Layout, 14, 37, 75, 78, 82, 83, 105, 232, 258-287, 288-310, 315, 334
Leading, 263, 269, 286
Leases, 17, 67, 106, 107, 116, 119, 311, 317, 321
Legal action, 124-128
Legal and Constitutional Affairs Standing Committee Enquiry, 4, 94
Legal buzzwords, 132
Legal dictionaries, 25, 179, 186, 188, 207, 210, 214, 217, 218, 225, 226
"Legal drafting", 2
Legal fiction, 20
Legal Information Standards Council, 307
Legal Profession Act 2004 (NSW), 48
Legal Profession Act 2004 (Qld), 48
Legal Profession Act 2004 (Vic), 48
Legal Profession Act 2006 (ACT), 49

Legal Profession Act 2007 (Tas), 49
Legal Profession Act 2008 (WA), 49
Legal Profession Act (NT), 49
Legal Services Commissioner (NSW), 59
Legal subject, 124-128
Legal words and phrases books, 25
"Legal writing", 2
Legal Writing Institute, 81
Legalese, 2, 9-10, 15, 29-32, 41-43, 45, 57, 60, 81, 90, 99, 183, 334-335
"Legality, principle of", 222
Legibility, 50, 259-264, 283-284, 286, 294-298, 306, 309
Legislation, organisation of information in, 107
Legislative Counsel Office, Ontario, 170
Legislative Drafting Conventions of Canada, 65-66
Lessee, 17, 142
Lessor, 17, 142
Letters of advice, 106, 107-110
Levicom International Holdings BV and Levicom Investments Curacao NV v Linklaters, 56
Lewis, In re, 205
Lewis v Nortex Pty Ltd, 183,
Line length, 264-265, 268, 269, 286, 301-302, 309
Linguists, 64, 66, 149, 174, 207
Lists, 97, 104-105, 112-113, 115, 123, 134, 200-204, 264, 270, 273-275, 277, 279, 282-283, 286, 290, 291, 302, 308-309
Litigation/law suits, 34-38, 56, 65, 79, 228
Lloyd's Bank plc v Waterhouse, 5
Loan and security documents, 106-107
Local Court Rules (NT), 49
Local Government Act 1989 (Vic), 48
Local Government Act 1993 (NSW), 270, 272, 281
Local Government Act 1999 (SA), 48
Locke, John, 32
Lodge, 237

Long-term Insurance Act 1998 (RSA), 88
Loutchansky v Times Newspapers (Nos 4 & 5), 254
Lovick v Brough, 196, 209, 230
Lower case, 274, 280-281, 302
Mackenzie v Duke of Devonshire, 183
Macquarie Dictionary, 206
Macquarie University, 170
Magic words, 8, 18-21, 134
Magna Carta, 176
Magnuson-Moss Consumer Product Warranty Act, 65
Make a statement, 161, 237
Make an application, 161, 237
Make payment, 161, 237
Make provision, 161, 237
Manifest, 237
Man on the Bondi Tram, 133
Man on the Clapham Omnibus, 132
Man on the Shau Ki Whan Tram, 133
Maradana Mosque (Board of Trustees) v Mahmud, 152
Mareva Compania Naviera SA v International Bulk Carriers SA, 133
Marketing, 47, 105, 110, 194, 317
Martin Inquiry, 46
Mason, Sir Anthony, 31
Material, 237
Maxims, legal, 129, 224-227
Maxwell on the Interpretation of Statutes, 152-153, 226
May, 207, 217-218, 230, 236-237
May not, 156-158, 218, 236
May only, 156-158, 163, 218
McCabe Builders (Dublin) Ltd v Sagamu Developments Ltd, Laragan Developments Ltd and Hanly Group Ltd, 220
McCann v Switzerland Insurance Australia Ltd, 227
McMullin v ICI Australia Operations Pty Ltd, 228
Meaning, "actual", 22
Meaning, "assigned", 24

Meaning, "commonly acceptable", 24, 25
Meaning, "correct", 24
Meaning, future, 25
Meaning, "grammatical", 169, 221-222
Meaning, "natural", 22, 23
Meaning, "ordinary", 24, 25, 222, 231
Meaning, past, 25-26
Meaning, "plain", 201, 220-223
Meaning, present, 25
Meaning, "proper", 22, 24
Meaning, "true", 21-24
Meaning, "well settled", 228
Meanings, 14, 18, 20, 22-25
Means, 138-139, 140-141, 149-150, 237
Means and includes, 140-141, 205, 237
"Mechanics of payment", 189-190
Medical consent forms, 42, 44
Mellinkoff, David, 13, 32, 102, 121, 131, 134-135, 167, 186-187, 188, 205, 210, 225-226
Mens rea, 176, 237
Menus, 302, 309
Merrill Lynch, 37
Metcalfe, Re, 200
"Method statements", 75, 146, 282-283
Michigan Bar Journal, 81
Miranda v Arizona, 133
Mirandise, Mirandize, 133
Misleading or deceptive conduct, 52, 61
Misleading definitions, 141
Mistakes, 212, 214-215, 250, 257
Mister Broadloom Corporation (1968) Ltd v Bank of Montreal, 190
Mitchell v Henry, 230
Mitigate, 237
MKM Capital Pty Limited v Corbo & Poyser, 241
MLC Ltd v O'Neill, 227
Monaco typeface, 295
Moneys, monies, 184, 237
Mort v Lois, 241
Motorola Corporate Finance Department, 36
Ms, 165

MTV Generation, 304
"Multi-layering", 93
Multiple choice questionnaire, 326
Munro v Shackleton, 38-39
Must, 205-215, 217-218, 236-237, 239
Must not, 218, 236, 237
Mutatis mutandis, 176, 237
Mylward v Weldon, 33
Myriad Pro typeface, 264
MySpace, 251
Nanaimo (City) v Rascal Trucking Ltd, 121
National Australia Bank v Nobile and Nobile, 54, 193
National Consumer Commission (RSA), 88
National Consumer Council (UK), 66
National Consumer Credit Reform legislation (Aus), 119, 270
National Credit Act 2005 (RSA), 87-88
National Credit Code (Aus), 47, 50
National Institutes of Health (US), 71
"Natural" meaning, 22-23
Navigation aids and signposting, 75, 271, 281-283, 291, 305, 308, 315
Negatives, 156-159, 174, 191, 218
Netiquette, 246
Neutral words, 169
NewCenturySchoolbook typeface, 264
New South Wales Parliamentary Counsel, 96, 118, 172, 210, 275, 282
Newtronics Pty Limited (recs and mgrs apptd) v Gjergja and Anor, 158
New York State, 67
New Zealand, 64, 68, 73-74, 80, 88-89, 146, 159, 165, 171, 189, 190, 315-316
New Zealand Bankers' Association, 88
New Zealand Law Commission, 68, 73, 316
New Zealand Parliamentary Counsel Office, 173, 315-316
Nielsen, Jakob, 289-290, 293, 302, 303, 306
Nixon, Richard, 1, 66, 70
NLRB v Federbush Co, 223
Nominalisation, 161

Non est factum, 5
Northern Ireland, 151, 187, 209
Norwich Group, 39
Noscitur a sociis, 225
Not less than, 191, 237
Not more than, 191, 237
Nova Scotia, Bank of, 38, 65
Now, 184, 187, 233, 235, 237
NRMA Insurance Limited, 37-39, 45, 46, 65
NRMA (motorists' organisation), 60-61
Nugatory, 132
Null void and of no effect, 135, 238
Numbering systems, 73, 258, 274-278, 286
Numbering, 116, 271, 273-278, 286
Numerals, 243, 303, 309
Numerals, Roman, 114, 274
NZI Insurance, 65
Obama, Barack, 1
Obiter dictum, 176, 238
Obligation, 201, 205-207, 209-210, 212-215, 217-218
Officialese, 29
Officials, 27-29
On all fours with, 132
On demand, 189-190
Once only definitions, 141
One, 168
Onus, 238
Ontario, 170, 210, 254
Openings, tired, 194-195
Operative part of document, 94, 182-183
Opes Prime Stockbroking Limited, In the matter of, 241
Oppressive contracts, 51
Or, 199-205
Oral judgments, 81
Oral pleadings, 32
Oral traditions, 3, 32
"Ordinary" meaning, 24, 25, 222, 231
Organisation, 14, 82, 105, 106, 111, 192, 295, 323
Orwell, George, 28, 43, 164-165, 174, 197

Otiose, 132
Pacific Carriers Ltd v BNP Paribas, 220
Painter, Judge Mark P, 31-32
Palatino Linotype typeface, 264
Paperless office, 251
Paragraphs, 111-115, 118, 127-128, 202-203, 269, 272, 274-275, 290, 293, 308, 309
Paraphrasing, 327-328
Pari passu, 238
Parliamentary Counsel, 65, 69, 78, 95, 96, 118, 127-128, 146, 172, 173, 178, 184, 203, 209, 210, 212, 215, 236, 272, 276, 282, 312-313, 315
Pascal, Blaise, 43
Passive verbs, 28
Passive voice, 72, 153-154, 174, 322
Past/past tense, 25-26, 152, 185, 187, 332-333
Past, in the, 236
Past meaning, 25-26
Patronising, 100
Payments in gross, 60
Penalties, 21
Pepper v Attorney-General, 227
Per capita, 176
Per cent, 176
Per stirpes, 176, 238
Perception and preference, 244-245, 296-297
Period, 120, 322
Permission, 199-201, 206, 213, 217-218
Permit/permitted to, 25, 236-237
Peruse, 238
Petelin v Cullen, 5
Pfizer Inc, 36
Piesse, 125, 151-152, 185, 188, 212
Pixels, 289, 295, 299
PLAIN (Plain Language Action & Information Network), 70
PLAIN (Plain Language Association InterNational), 72, 84-85
"Plain English" and "plain language", 5, 12, 14, 34, 37, 47, 65, 78, 84, 87, 88, 227, 228, 229, 334, 335, 336
Plain English and the Law, 68, 93

Plain English Awards (NZ), 88
Plain English Campaign (UK), 66, 77
Plain English Foundation (Sydney), 72, 83, 155
Plain English Handbook (SEC), 71
Plain English Manual (Australian OPC), 118, 128, 146, 178, 184, 203-204, 212, 236, 270, 272, 313
Plain English Week (NZ), 88
Plain Language Centre (Toronto), 81-82
Plain Language Commission, 66, 324
"Plain Language column", Michigan Bar Journal, 81
Plain language or plain English committees, groups, sections, 81-85
Plain Language Institute (Vancouver), 82, 173
Plain language laws (US), 34, 65, 66-67, 322
Plaintiff, 79, 142
Planning, 43, 104-106, 111, 232, 313
Pleadings, 32, 33, 51, 79
Plural, 168
PMT Partners Pty Ltd v Australian National Parks and Wildlife Service, 134
Points (type size), 262-264, 265, 269, 297-298, 286
Poisons Regulations 1965 (WA), 49
Police codes, 28
Politicians, 27, 57, 65, 67
Pomposity, 13, 53, 98, 101, 102-103
Portrait format, 265
Poultry Act 1968 (NZ), 141
PowerPoint, 264, 270
Practising Law Institute (US), 210
Preamble, 33
Precedents, 3, 25, 30, 31, 34, 60, 83, 131, 137, 333-334
Precocious toddler, 132
Precision, 15, 62, 188, 190
Preface, 1
Premises, 16-17, 136, 238
Prenn v Simmonds, 220
Present meaning, 25

Present tense, 149-153, 185, 206, 208, 212, 215-217, 239
Presents, these, 113-114, 136, 239
Prideaux v Director of Public Prosecutions (Vic), 230
"Principle of legality", 222
Printing, 32, 259, 283
Prior written authorisation, 16-17
Product Disclosure Statements, 14, 35, 38, 41, 50, 71, 85
Professional approach, 99, 100-101, 103
Project Blue Sky Inc v Australian Broadcasting Authority, 221
Prologue, 1
Promise, language of, 216
Promissory Note, 34
Pronouns, 28, 166-171, 180-181, 239
Proofreading, 249
"Proper" meaning, 22, 24
Prospectus, 60-61, 70, 91, 311, 318
Propound, 238
Proscribe, 238
Provided that, 161-162, 238
Provisos, 161-163, 175, 192
Punctuation, 118, 119, 120-123, 204, 223, 248, 250, 335
Purpose, 15, 92, 96-97, 103, 105, 106, 110, 213, 219-221, 250, 259, 262, 272, 284, 286, 287, 289, 300, 311, 317, 327, 334
"Purposive" approach to construction, 121, 219-221
Pursuant to, 183-184, 238
Quantum, 238
Quantum meruit, 176
Questionnaire, multiple choice, 326
Questions as headings, 271-272
Quid pro quo, 176
Quirk, Randolph, 22-23, 122, 163-164
R v SA, 228
R v Secretary of State for Home Department; Ex parte Simms, 222
Ragged text, 265-268, 286, 302, 309
Ratio decidendi, 238
Rava v Logan Wines Pty Limited, 227
Re, 176, 238

Readability, 35, 53, 62, 67, 72, 232, 248, 259, 265, 267, 269, 286, 294, 295, 299, 300, 306, 309, 332

Readability formulas, 67, 72, 321-325

Reader's Guide, 75

Reading speed, 41-43, 294, 297, 300, 301

Real Estate Institute of New Zealand (REINZ), 88

"Reasonable construction" rule, 224

Reasonable time, 188-190

Recitals, 33, 182-183, 240

Rectify, 238

Redish, Dr JC, 263, 265, 266, 281, 302, 319, 325, 328

Related material, 110-111, 284, 300, 309

Relative clauses, 124

Remise release and quitclaim, 135, 238

Remit, 238

Render, 238

Renton Committee, 67

Renton Report, 67

Requisite, 239

Res ipsa loquitur, 176, 239

Residential leases, 50, 67

Response time, 327

Residential Tenancies Act 1994 (Qld), 50

Rest residue and remainder, 135, 239

Retirement Villages Act (NT), 49

Retirement Villages Regulations 2006 (SA), 49

Revell v Lidov, 255-256

Right and wrong, 18-19

Right words, choosing the, 19, 21, 197-198

Robinson, Dr S, 25, 152

Rogers, Will, 30

Roman, ancient, 176, 260, 287

Ronald Elwyn Lister Ltd v Dunlop Canada Ltd, 190

Roosevelt, Franklin D, 29

Rosenberg, Scott, 251

Royal Botanic Gardens and Domain Trust v South Sydney Council, 222

Royal Insurance Company (Canada), 37, 65

Rudeness, 101, 103

Rugby rulebook (NZ), 89

Rumsfeld, Donald, 1

Ryledar Pty Limited v Euphoric Pty Limited, 220

SA, R v, 228

Said, the, 180-181, 239

Saffron Sun Pty Ltd v Perma-Fit Finance Pty Ltd (In Liq) and Others, 229

Salon.com, 251

Salutations, 171-174

Same, the, 180-181, 239

Sans serif typeface, 260-262, 281, 286, 295, 296, 297-298, 307

Sapir, Edward, 174

Satisfaction, 131

Saunders (Executrix in the Estate of Rose Maude Gallie) v Anglia Building Society, 5

Save and except, 135, 239

Save harmless, 60, 236

Savings (money), 34-37, 39-41, 45, 62

Savings (time), 36-37, 39-41, 41-43, 45, 62, 242, 248, 278, 316, 318, 320

Scannable text, 290, 308

Scanning, 285, 289-290, 292, 302, 305, 308

Scapira v Ahronson, 254

Schedules, 115-117, 192

Scheer, R, 298

Schoenfeld, Robert, 28

Science (journal), 28

Scientists, 24, 27-28

Scrolling, 289, 291, 300, 301, 305, 309

Secretary, Dept of Social Security v Pellone, 227

Secret language, 132

Secured Property, 137

Securities and Exchange Commission/ SEC, (US), 41, 70-71, 158, 333

Sentence length, 55, 118-120, 124, 250, 322-323, 325

Sentence structure, 14, 21, 105, 115, 117-118, 124-128, 159-161, 259

Sentencing Act 1991 (Vic), 48

Sentry Insurance, 36, 65

Serif typeface, 260-262, 281, 286, 294, 295, 296, 297-298

Shall, 16-17, 79, 149-150, 153, 205-218, 230, 239

Shall not, 218

Shau Ki Whan tram, 133

Shaw, Lord, 121

Shell Oil Company, 36

Shepherds Producers Co-op Ltd (in liq) v Lamont, 200

Short-term Insurance Act 1998 (RSA), 88

Short-term memory, 127

"Shredding", 114-115

Signals, 123, 139, 145, 245, 268, 271, 279, 286

Signposting techniques and navigation aids, 75, 271, 281-283, 286, 291, 308, 315

Simon Graduate School of Business Administration Inc v Minister Administering National Parks and Wildlife Act 1974 (NSW), 227

"Simple" English/ language, 36, 37, 61, 65

Simplicity, 12, 15, 27, 28, 78, 102, 103, 278, 332

Sincerity, 101, 136, 196

"Single publication" rule, 254-255

Singular use of *they*, 169-171

Sinochem International Oil (London) Co Ltd v Mobil Sales And Supply Corporation & Anor, 227

Skimming, 97, 269, 289-290, 292

Slang, 243

Small Business Guide, 94-95

Small print, 54, 258

SMOG formula, 322

SMS (Text messages), 241, 243

Snail in the ginger beer bottle, 133

Social Security Act 1991, 75

Social Security Administration (US), 71

Socpen Trustees v Wood Nash & Winters, 56

Solicitors' Code of Conduct 2007 (UK), 84

Solicitors Regulation Authority (UK), 84

Sounding in, 239

South Africa, 31, 64, 77-78, 86-88, 171, 173-174, 197, 207-208, 256

Southern California Gas Company, 36

Space between characters, 259, 296

Special needs readers, 102, 306-307, 309-310

Specialists, 15, 129, 290, 316

Spigelman, CJ, 221, 222, 226

Spell checking software, 248

Spelling and typing errors, 248-249

Spence, George, 33

St Paul Fire and Marine Insurance Company, 36, 65

Star v National Australia Bank Ltd, 158

Starting point, 186, 187-188, 189

Stealth, drafting by, 192-193

Stream of consciousness, 112, 118

Strobe, 299

Stroud's Judicial Dictionary, 186

Structure, 21, 104-128, 149-179, 232, 290-291, 308, 323

Structure, sentence, 14, 21, 105, 115, 117-118, 124-128, 159-161, 259

Style Manual, 120, 169, 172, 263, 265, 290-291, 296, 298, 299, 300, 301, 302

Style Subcommittee, US government, 78-79, 207

Sub-clauses, 120, 124

Sub-headings, 273, 290, 308

Subjunctive mood, 155

Submit, 239

Subordinate clauses, 124

Subordinate Legislation Act 1989 (NSW), 48, 172

Subordinate Legislation Act 1992 (Tas), 49

Sub-paragraphs, 112-115, 274

Subpoena, 79, 130, 176

Sub-sections, 120, 121

Sub-sub-paragraphs, 113, 274-275
Such, 180-182, 239
Suffice, will, 240
Sui generis, 176, 239
Sui juris, 176, 239
Sullivan law, 67
Summarising, 117, 272, 292, 308
Supreme Court Act 1958 (Vic), 228
Supreme Court of Queensland, rules
    of, 50-51
Swan, Judith, 28
Sweden, 64, 66, 77
Swift, Jonathan, 29
Sydney University, 40, 82, 170
Symbols, 18, 23, 123, 145, 146, 147, 176,
    245-248, 249, 259, 271, 273, 279, 286
Synonyms, 18, 134-135, 178, 217, 218
Table of contents, 1, 271, 285, 286, 328
Tables, 75, 146, 259, 265, 270-271, 282,
    283, 285, 286
Tabs, 113, 278
Target Stores, 36
Tax laws (Aus), 46, 73, 75-76, 144, 146,
    276, 277-278, 282-283, 312-314, 324
Tax laws (NZ), 42, 68, 73-74, 146, 278,
    315-316
Tax laws (UK), 68, 70, 74, 208, 316-317,
    337
Tax Law Improvement Project, 73, 144,
    146, 276, 277, 282, 283, 312
Taxpayers' Charter (ATO), 72
Technical terms, 15, 61, 87, 92, 129-130,
    136, 139, 211, 314
Telecom Decision CRTC 2007-75, 121
Telecom Decision CRTC 2008-62, 121
Telecommunications (Interception and
    Access) Act 1979 (Cth), 47
Tense, future, 17, 149-153, 184, 205-206,
    212, 214, 215-217, 239
Tense, present, 149-153, 185, 206, 208,
    212, 215-217, 239
Terms of art, 130-132
Testament, 239, 240
Testimonium, 116, 117
"Testing" documents, 14, 42, 44, 310,
    311-330, 336

"Testing" legislation, 42, 75, 312-317
Text messages (SMS), 241, 243
Texture, 299-300
"Theme statements", 282
Therapeutic Goods Regulations 1990
    (Cth), 47
They, singular use of, 169-171
 "Think aloud" test, 328
Thornton, GC, 179, 181, 210, 217
Three-letter acronyms (TLAs), 247
Thurber, James, 164
Time, 184-186
"Time-honoured" language, 8, 17, 189,
    333, 335
Times typeface, 306
Time savings, 36-37, 39-41, 41-43, 45,
    62, 242, 248, 278, 316, 318, 320
Times New Roman typeface, 264, 295,
    306
Tired endings, 195-196
Tired openings, 194-195
TLAs, 247
Toll (FGCT) Pty Ltd v Alphapharm
    Pty Limited, 220
Tone, 13, 72, 98-100, 103, 232, 244, 245,
    246, 249, 250
Tophams Ltd v Earl of Sefton, 25
Too many definitions, 143-144
Towne v Eisner, 22
Trade Practices Act 1974 (Cth), 50-52,
    61
Trade Practices Commission reports,
    46
"Tried and true" precedents, 34
Triplets, 134-135
"True" meaning, 21-24
 "$2.1m comma case" (Canada), 121
Type size, 261, 262-264, 265, 269, 286,
    295, 296, 297-298, 302, 306, 309
Type style, 260
Typeface, 58, 244-245, 257, 258, 259,
    260-265, 269, 281, 286, 290, 294-298,
    306, 309, 316, 335
Typesetting algorithms, 267
Typography, 68, 78, 259-260, 267, 268,
    269, 281, 294, 295, 296, 309

UAW and Massey Ferguson Industries, Re, 210

Uberrimae fidei, 176, 240

UK Civil Procedure Rules 1998, 68, 79-80, 133, 176,

UK Office of Parliamentary Counsel, 78, 173, 209, 215

Uncommon words, 17, 129

Unconscionable contracts, 51-53

Under, 183-184, 233, 238

Underlining, 147, 279-281, 286, 303, 305

Undermentioned, 240

Undersigned, the, 240

Understating, 196-197

Undue, 240

Unenforceability, 5, 20, 54, 56, 62

Unfair or unjust contracts, 50, 51

Unfair practices, 51

"Unfair terms", 50, 87

Unforeseen circumstances, 22

Uniform Civil Procedure Rules 2005 (NSW), 51, 133

United Kingdom, 20, 39, 56, 64, 66, 67-68, 69-70, 74, 78, 84, 173, 189, 190, 208, 220, 316-317

United States, 6, 34, 45, 56, 64, 65, 70, 78, 81, 98, 121, 133, 169, 210, 223, 225, 254-256, 306, 323

United States Institute on Aging, 298

United States Library of Medicine, 298

United States National Bank of Oregon v Independent Insurance Agents of America, Inc, 223

United States Poynter Institute, 304

Unity of thought, 119, 124

University of Sydney, 40, 82, 170

Unjust or unfair contracts, 50, 51

Unto, 136, 240

Upon, 136, 240

Upper case, 248, 258, 274, 279-281, 286, 302-303, 309

URL, 305

US Executive Memorandum, 70

US Federal Court Rules, 78-79, 118, 207-208, 215

"Usability" testing, 307, 311-330

Useless definitions, 142

"User-friendly English", 14

Verba accipienda sunt secundum subjectam materiam, 225

Verba chartarum fortius accipiuntur contra proferentum, 224

Verba cum effectu accipienda sunt, 224, 225

Verba generalia restringuntur ad habilitatem rei vel aptitudinem, personae, 225

Verba intentioni, non e contra, debent inservire, 224

Verba ita sunt intelligenda ut re magis valeat quam pereat, 224

Verba relata hoc maxime operantur per referantiam ut in eis inesse, videntur, 225

Verbosity, 27, 30

Verbs into nouns, 161

Verdana typeface, 262, 286, 295, 296, 309

Versus, 176

Veteran's Benefits Administration (US), 41, 71

Victorian Attorney General, 39, 178, 209

Victoria (state), 48, 52, 172, 187, 252-253

Victorian Law Reform Commission, 31, 42, 44, 68, 93, 118, 125, 145, 184, 209, 275-276

Visual aids, 304

Visual presentation, 270

Vocabulary, 12, 98, 213, 232-240, 250, 259

WACB v Minister for Immigration and Multicultural and Indigenous Affairs, 222

Waiver, 130-131

Waldron v Royal Bank of Canada, 190

Wales, 69, 79, 83-84, 133, 176, 209

Wall Street Journal, 8, 252

Watt v State Bank of New South Wales, 55

Warranty, 130, 216
Web-based legal research, 288
Web conventions, 305-306, 309
Websites, 70, 72, 84, 95, 241, 242, 243, 251, 283, 288-289, 291, 292, 296, 297, 298, 299-301, 303, 304, 306-307
Wellesley, Arthur, 27
Wellington, Duke of, 27
Westminster Hall, 33
Whatsoever, 137, 240
When, 177-179, 238, 240
Where, 177-179, 240
Whereas, 69, 182-183, 240
Wheresoever, 137, 240
Wheildon, Colin, 260-261, 263, 265-266
Whilever, 240
White, 29, 230
White background, 284, 287, 299, 309,
White space, 111, 114, 267-270, 280, 286, 300-301, 309
Whorf, Benjamin Lee, 174
Whosoever, 137, 240
Will (future), 206, 216-217, 239
Will and testament, 135, 237, 240
Will-Harris, Daniel, 298
Williams, Glanville, 19-20, 24, 174, 197

Withholding tax, 130
Witnesseth, 136, 238
Witness whereof, in, 116, 136, 236
Woolf, Lord Chief Justice, 68, 79
Word clusters, 136
Word strings, 133-134
Work Health Court Rules (NT), 49, 276
Workplace Injury Management and Workers Compensation Act 1998 (NSW), 48
World Wide Web, 251-253, 306
Writ, 79
Writemark (NZ), 88
Writer, the, 194
Writing style, 29, 81, 96, 139, 244, 292-293, 308-309, 330, 332. 334
Writing for the computer screen, 274-275, 293
Written pleadings, 32, 33, 51, 78
Wydick, R, 121, 122
X-height, 261, 263
Yarmouth v France, 225
You, 13, 168, 169, 206
Young Offenders Act 1994 (WA), 49
Young v New Haven Advocate et al, 255
Zar, Jerrold H, 249
Zinsser, William, 3, 12, 29, 120, 164, 244, 257

Uniform Evidence Law

Text and Essential Cases

2nd edn

John Anderson & Peter Bayne

John Anderson builds on the work of Peter Bayne in the 1st edition, continuing his style of integrated discussion of the uniform Evidence Acts with evidentiary principles to achieve a seamless analysis of the law.

Key cases illustrating both judicial interpretations of the uniform Evidence Acts and judicial statements of evidentiary principles are extracted and clearly explained by the authors. The significant legislative amendments to the uniform Evidence Acts resulting from the Australian Law Reform Commission's Uniform Evidence Law Report of December 2005 are incorporated, ensuring best coverage of the law in the uniform Evidence Act jurisdictions.

The book is also an essential tool for understanding the practical operation of evidence law in the various litigation contexts in which it arises.

Praise for the first edition

> This is a good book. … It is always a pleasure to read texts such as Peter Bayne's where one can understand the point in a paragraph without multiple re-readings…Quite clearly, if you reside in uniform evidence law jurisdictions, this text is an excellent one… I would highly recommend this text …
>
> *Ethos*

> This is a first rate book…I can only echo the sentiments of Justice Carolyn Simpson who said in the foreword, *"I commend Peter Bayne for this worthwhile attempt to refine the principles under which we now must act, and look forward personally to benefiting, in a practical way, from his efforts in this regard."*
>
> *Tasmanian Law Society Newsletter*

2009 • ISBN 978 1 86287 745 0 • paperback • 717 pp • $85

Understanding Ethics

Noel Preston AM

Preston provides a superb introduction to moral reasoning in
world where old certainties have vanished. His comprehensiv
coverage of contemporary modes of ethical reasoning, written i
an elegant, accessible style, makes a marvellous text.

Professor Sandra Berns

- The Planet and the Environment
- Professional Life and Workplaces
- Life, Love and Sexuality
- War, Terrorism and Violence

Dr Noel Preston AM has combined an academic career with an acti
ist's life. He has been a prominent grass roots campaigner and socia
justice commentator in Queensland from the Bjelke-Petersen year
Previously an Associate Professor at QUT and director of Unitingcar
Queensland Centre for Social Justice, he is currently an adjunc
Professor at Griffith University.

2007 • ISBN 978 1 86287 662 0 • paperback • 256 pages • $39.95

ALSO AVAILABLE FROM THE FEDERATION PRESS

Discrimination Law and Practice
3rd edition
Chris Ronalds

This is the 3rd edition of the seminal textbook on the practical application of Australian discrimination law. Its concise account marries clarity with depth and is suitable for all involved in this branch of the law – lawyers, business people, human resources and industrial relations staff, advocates and students.

Discrimination Law and Practice has been thoroughly updated to reflect developments in the key areas of employment, education, harassment and victimisation. This edition focuses in particular on:

- the impact of changes in the federal arena;
- trends in remedies, including the level of monetary damages;
- the meaning of "direct" and "indirect" discrimination following the High Court decisions in *Purvis v New South Wales* and *New South Wales v Amery*;
- the intersection between discrimination law and industrial law; and
- the use of discrimination law principles in unfair dismissal cases.

Praise for previous editions

> … an excellent guide to discrimination law. It is well researched, skilfully compiled and easy to follow. I strongly recommend it to lawyers and non-lawyers alike.
>
> *Law Society Journal of NSW*

> [I]ts concise approach and clear layout makes it easy to browse and locate relevant interest areas.
>
> *Human Resources*

> Arguably the best available starting point for an understanding of the basic concepts.
>
> *Public Administration Today*

> … an indispensable handbook for practitioners …Topic by topic the author examines the law clearly and concisely…
>
> *Victorian Bar News*

2008 • ISBN 978 1 86287 670 5 • paperback • 288 pages • $59.95

Administrative Law

Context and Critique
2nd edition

Michael Head

Dr Head provides a clear and succinct statement of administrative law. He explains the legislation, the rules and the principles and includes pithy and critical summaries of the main cases. His commentary goes further and puts this detailed legal analysis into the political, social and judicial context in which administrative law operates.

Reviews of 1st edition:

A very useful guide that provides an overview of this difficult area of law as a primary guide for the student. Practitioners will also find [this book] an invaluable first point of reference. The book is written in a clear and concise style [which] allows the reader to quickly establish the relevant principles ... The book achieves its purpose of making administrative law understandable, accessible and interesting. ... For those of us who work in this area of law, Michael Head's book is an essential addition to the library.

Victorian Bar News

Head's concise text ... gives an up-to-date, honest, pithy and accurate account of administrative law in Australia today. ... Nine chapters explain in thorough yet comprehensible detail the various areas of judicial review available to parties aggrieved by an administrative decision.

Qld Lawyer

2008 • ISBN 978 1 86287 690 3 • paperback • 336 pages • $59.95

Mental Capacity

Powers of Attorney and Advance Health Directives

Berna Collier, Chris Coyne and Karen Sullivan

When is a person in a fit state to execute an enduring power of attorney or an advance health directive? The complex mix of medical, legal and ethical issues continue to provide difficult, practical issues for individuals, their professional advisers, their families, and the courts and tribunals. This cross-disciplinary book analyses the law and the medical and psychological perspectives and includes case studies to highlight problems and suggest ways of resolution.

Mental Capacity:

- Provides an overview of the framework of law within Australia
- Focuses on the law as it currently stands in relation to assessing mental capacity, including a consideration of the interaction between legal and medical standards
- Analyses the importance and difficulties of defining and judging capacity in the medical context
- Examines best practice in relation to health-based competency assessments
- Looks at the role of the neuropsychologist in determining the extent and characteristics of cognitive impairment

**2005 • ISBN 978 186 287 426 8 • hardback • 192 pages
rrp $60.00 Direct Price $55.00**

The Law of Real Estate Mortgages in Australia

3rd edition

WD Duncan and WM Dixon

The book is extremely user-friendly. ... The authors' analysis demon strates the complexity of the law of mortgages, yet they successfully manage to explain the law, minus the complexities via their use o simple and understandable English and a minimum of legal jargon.

The publication goes beyond the basics; the authors recognise legisla tive and common law defects and gaps, discussing difficulties caused by varying judicial interpretations and then providing solid practica advice or suggestions to overcome such problems, as well as insigh into the nature and possibilities of future legal developments, based on current trends. ...

a welcome addition to the circle of great legal academic works.

The Queensland Lawyer

The Law of Real Property Mortgages will no doubt be appreciated a: a standard text in this area...

Australian Law Librarian

This book provides value in offering a presentation of the law relating to real property mortgages in Australia, organised in a systematic and accessible manner. Relationships between legal principles are clearly stated. There is a logical progression in the discussion through topics. Practitioners will appreciate the succinc statements of the law, together with supporting references.

Proctor

[A] welcome contribution to this area of law

Law Institute Journal (Victoria)

2007 • ISBN 978 1 86287 648 4 • paperback • 397 pages • $85